RACE *and the* Making *of*
the MORMON PEOPLE

RACE *and the* Making *of th*

MAX PERRY MUELLER

Mormon People

THE UNIVERSITY OF NORTH CAROLINA PRESS   Chapel Hill

Set in Utopia by Tseng Information Systems, Inc.
Manufactured in the United States of America

The University of North Carolina Press has been a
member of the Green Press Initiative since 2003.

Cover illustration: portrait of Jane Manning James by Parry Merkley,
courtesy of the Church of Jesus Christ of Latter-day Saints; classic arch
with Corinthian column by archideaphoto, iStockphoto.com.

Library of Congress Cataloging-in-Publication Data
Names: Mueller, Max Perry, author.
Title: Race and the making of the Mormon people / Max Perry Mueller.
Description: Chapel Hill : The University of North Carolina Press, [2017] |
Includes bibliographical references and index.
Identifiers: LCCN 2017005572| ISBN 9781469633756 (cloth : alk. paper) |
ISBN 9781469636160 (pbk : alk. paper) | ISBN 9781469633763 (ebook)
Subjects: LCSH: Church of Jesus Christ of Latter-day Saints—History. |
Mormon Church—History. | Book of Mormon. | Race—Religious aspects—
Mormon Church. | Race relations—Religious aspects—Mormon Church. |
Mormon Church—Membership. | Mormons—West (U.S.)
Classification: LCC BX8611 .M77 2017 | DDC 289.3089—dc23
LC record available at https://lccn.loc.gov/2017005572

This book is dedicated to the memory of

JASON RAIZE ROTHENBERG (1975–2004)

CONTENTS

FIGURES

ACKNOWLEDGMENTS

On our honeymoon in 2009, I dragged my wife, Anna, to This Is the Place Heritage Park. Located in Emigration Canyon overlooking Salt Lake City, the park is a sprawling living history complex and replication of a nineteenth-century Mormon pioneer village. It marks the site where on July 24, 1847, Brigham Young, suffering from the flu, rose from his sickbed in the back of Wilford Woodruff's wagon to get his first look at Utah's Great Basin. "This is the place," Woodruff recalled the prophet declaring, where the Mormons would end their Exodus and build their Zion.

I begin these acknowledgments where I will end them—thanking my wife, and in this case begging her forgiveness for turning our honeymoon into a research trip. But our afternoon at This Is the Place was fruitful, at least for my own scholarship. In the bookshop, I came across Kate B. Carter's *Story of the Negro Pioneer* (1965), which contains a collection of first- and secondhand stories about the small group of black Latter-day Saints as well as the stories of black slaves of white Saints who settled in Utah in the 1840s and 1850s. I flipped through the compilation and eventually came across Jane E. Manning James's autobiography. Entranced, I read James's telling—or at least, as I discuss in this book, her telling as recorded by her white scribe—of her conversion to Mormonism in the 1840s, her trek from her home in Connecticut to gather with the Saints in Joseph Smith's Nauvoo, Illinois, and her experiences as a Mormon pioneer and matriarch of Utah's first and most prominent black Mormon family. In that bookshop, I decided that this story of a black Mormon woman who joined a church in her youth that welcomed her with, relatively speaking, open arms and that, by the time she died, was much more ambivalent about her place among the Saints, was the story that I wanted to tell in my first book.

When I began to dig deeper into this history, I found that there was more to James's story than simply the origins of the Church of Jesus Christ of Latter-day Saints' antiblack theology and practice. There is much more to the history of race and Mormonism than declension from racially inclusive roots to the racial particularism with which the church was long associated. But I have the next seven chapters to tell that story, so I'll stick to the task at hand here and acknowledge the people and institutions that have helped me tell it!

First, let me express my great appreciation for my mentors. I was fortunate to have David Hempton as a teacher and mentor, since I began my graduate work at Harvard University. As I transitioned from student to mentor, I have aimed to be the kind of generous but critical, in both senses of the word, reader and commenter of my own students' scholarship, as well as the kind of consummate cheerleader of my students that he has been for me. The same can be said of Laurel Thatcher Ulrich. Even though (or because) she is one of the celebrated historians working today, Laurel models for her students unbounded excitement and curiosity for the stories she tells and the unending work ethic to tell them succinctly, ethically, and beautifully. Marla Frederick has offered great feedback on early and late versions of this book. Her own scholarship and approach to teaching serve as an aspirational model for my own. David Holland has offered me the kind of invaluable mentoring—scholarly, professional, and otherwise—for which he will surely earn the appreciation of a generation of Harvard students. I began my first scholarly work on race and Mormonism in R. Marie Griffith's "Lived Religion" class. I'm so grateful for her support as well as for the opportunity to help her and Tiffany Stanley launch the journal *Religion & Politics* at the John C. Danforth Center on Religion and Politics at Washington University in Saint Louis. Tiffany is a writer's editor, and that's the highest praise I can give. This book is also in part the scholarly progeny of a long parti- and matrilineage of the North American Religion Colloquium (NARC), which David Hall ran with his famous grace and wisdom for much of my time at Harvard. My gratitude to my peers, especially Brett Grainger, Kip Richardson, Ryan Tobler, Elizabeth Jemison, Eva Payne, David Smith, Matthew Cressler, Dana Logan, and mentors Ann Braude, Leigh Schmidt, and John Stauffer, in this storied community.

As is the case with the Latter-day Saints I study here, the importance of lineages is very real. A beloved and respected NARC alumnus Michael McNally was my undergraduate advisor at Carleton College. At Carleton, I realized that I wanted to do what Michael does so well for the rest of my life. My deepest gratitude to the Carleton College religion department for caring for the intellectual and personal well-being of its students. Special thanks to Louis Newman and Roger Jackson. My thanks to my (all-too brief) colleagues at Mount Holyoke College, especially to Michael Penn and Jane Crosthwaite. My deep gratitude to the Center for Humanistic Inquiry (CHI) at Amherst College, where I spent a year as the CHI's inaugural Robert E. Keiter 1957 postdoctoral fellow—invaluable time that allowed me to revise this book. My thanks to Amherst's religion department for the chance to teach its wonderful students. I'm honored now, and hope to be for years to come, to call the Department of Classics and Religious Studies at the University of Nebraska–Lincoln my home. Thanks especially to the polymath Sarah Murray for updating my Utah territorial map.

This study is fundamentally about the historical archive as a site where history is not just preserved but made. As such, I owe much to the archivists at the LDS Church History Library and Archives (CHL) who made me feel at home among the miles of stories that the Latter-day Saints recorded on paper, tintypes, microfilm, and hard drives. In particular, thanks to Bill Slaughter, Michael Landon, and Brittany Chapman for fielding questions large and small. Many thanks to my fellow CHL patrons; Ardis Parshall first told me of "Walker's Writing"; Connell O'Donovan and Amanda Hendrix-Komoto were intellectual companions during many hours in the archives. Thanks to the juvenileinstructor.org crew, especially Matt Bowman, Chris Jones, Jonathan Stapley, and Ben Park; each has helped this "Gentile" navigate the intellectual and cultural world of the Saints. Thanks also to Grant Hardy, who critiqued my Book of Mormon chapter. My great thanks to the Genesis Group, the storied community of black Latter-day Saints in Utah and their allies, especially to the Genesis Group cofounder Darius Gray and his longtime writing partner Margaret Young, as well as to Don and Jerri Harwell, Tamu Smith, and Keith Hamilton. My great thanks to Louis Duffy, Jane Manning James's great-great-grandson, for helping me to secure a copy of James's first patriarchal blessing. Also many thanks to Jane Hafen, Brenden Rensink, John Turner, and Ann Braude, who read the Wakara chapters at various stages. Thanks also to Patrick Mason, Kathleen Flake, Terryl Givens, Newell Bringhurst, and Armand Mauss. And great thanks to Spencer Fluhman for his generous mentorship.

Many fellowships supported my research and writing. These include the John L. Loeb Fellowship at Harvard, two Warren Center fellowships, and a Harvard GSAS summer predissertation fellowship. The University of Utah's Tanner Humanities Center Mormon Studies Fellowship allowed me to spend a full year in Utah; thanks to the center's director, Bob Goldberg, as well as to Colleen McDannell and W. Paul Reeve for making me feel at home in Salt Lake. A University of Nebraska–Lincoln ENHANCE CAS grant provided funds to support the final production of this book. Parts of chapter 4 and the epilogue come from my article "Playing Jane: Re-Presenting Black Mormon Memory through Reenacting the Black Mormon Past," *Journal of Africana Religions* 1, no. 4 (2013): 513–61, which is reproduced here by permission of Pennsylvania State University Press. Special thanks to Parry Merkley for the use of his painting of Jane Manning James for the cover of this book.

Thanks, of course, to my family for a lifetime of support. Thanks to my mom and pop, my stepparents, my aunts, and my grandparents for telling me to do what I love best and who supported me so I could do just that. I recognize that aspiring to become a professional thinker is a luxury created by the hard work of my family. I hope that I have done work that honors their sacrifices. Last (as I did first), let me thank my wife, Anna. In 2006, Anna accepted my proposal of marriage and came with me to Boston so that I could begin my graduate work. She graciously let me spend summers as well as the school year of 2011–12 in Utah. She does not always understand my obsession with American religious history. Nevertheless, she has patiently listened while I share my enthusiasm with her and with unsuspecting guests at our many dinner parties, nudging me ever so gently when I go on too long! Now more than a decade after we started our lives together, I type these words with our daughter, Sophie Aya Mueller, asleep on my chest.

RACE *and the* Making *of*
the MORMON PEOPLE

Fig. P.1. Portrait of Joseph Smith Jr., 1843.
(W. B. Carson, photographer; Library of Congress)

PROLOGUE
Visions

Joseph Smith's Visions

Joseph Smith Jr. was seventeen years old in 1823 when the Angel Moroni first appeared to him in the bedroom that he shared with his five brothers in their western New York log home. The tall, flaxen-haired, blue-eyed, semiliterate farm boy had just finished his nightly prayers. Suddenly a personage "glorious beyond description" appeared before him, Smith recalled years later. Moroni, the historian-prophet and last member of a white-skinned race of pre-Columbian Native Americans resurrected as an angel, hovered above the floorboards. Moroni's gleaming white robes emitted such bright light that the dark room seemed to be filled with noonday sun.[1]

In 1830, at the age of twenty-four, Joseph Smith established a religious movement that, by the time an anti-Mormon mob assassinated him in 1844, had become an international community with tens of thousands of members (fig. P.1). By the end of the twentieth century that number would surpass ten million. But on the evening before his first vision of Moroni, Smith felt completely alone, unsettled, and unworthy. As he recalled in his "History of Joseph Smith," throughout his teenage years, Smith had made a study of his life. And he found that his life was divided between seeking spiritual and earthly fulfillment. He strove to do good. He helped provide for his family—a set of downwardly mobile Yankee New Englanders turned perpetual debtors—by working their rented farmland in western New York. Desperate for income, for a time Joseph Jr. even joined his father and namesake in money digging. The two Josephs used divining rods and seer stones in hopes of locating buried treasure. Upstate folklore held that centuries before, Spanish conquistadors had hidden gold and silver in caches throughout the American countryside.[2]

Smith strove to follow the dictates of God. But he was prone to the "weaknesses of youth."[3] As Smith saw it, a major part of the problem was that the world was divided over the question of religion. In particular, Smith was in a state of "darkness and confusion" over the question of which church could best help him live righteously. Around the age of fourteen, Smith made his first direct appeal to God for wisdom. And God, along with his Son, directly appeared to him. During this first vision, the Son told Smith that the extant "sects"—the Methodists, Presbyterians, and Baptists that proliferated in his corner of Upstate New York and made noisy claims to a singular Christian truth—"were all wrong."[4] A purer gospel truth would soon be restored. And this restoration would not only help Smith make his own divided life whole. It would also serve as a new vision of the restoration of Christ's church as well as a reunification of God's covenantal people.

Smith followed the Heavenly Father and Son's admonition not to join a church. Yet Smith had to wait several more years in darkness before he received the lens—in the form of a new scripture written on ancient golden plates—that would illuminate this restorative vision. Thus in 1823, he once again called on God. And God sent Moroni to the soon-to-be prophet. It took Moroni another four years to disabuse Smith of the notion that the treasure's true worth was not in the quantity of the precious metals but instead in the quality of the precious words engraved on them. But on the night of September 22, 1827, atop a hill near the Smith family's farmstead in Palmyra, Moroni finally entrusted Smith with the plates. In fits and starts, Smith translated the plates' "Egyptian" characters into English. The new translation revealed a radical new way of seeing the past and future, and a particularly American-centric way at that.[5]

And yet Smith also found in this new gospel, which he published in March 1830 as the Book of Mormon, echoes of a very old story of a family torn apart by sin. Like most of his contemporaries, Smith accepted as fact that human history began with the Bible's account of Adam, Eve, and their children (and then human history began again after the flood with Noah, his wife, and their children). And he accepted as fact that history's first families splintered from their original unity after one branch of the family sinned against the others. According to the standard early nineteenth-century interpretation of the Bible, so that the sinners' perfidy would be remembered down through the ages, their descendants were cursed with dark skin. These divinely sanctioned curses led to the formation of separate and unequal human races.[6] These races eventually worshipped different gods, spoke diverse languages, warred against and enslaved one another. The Book of Mormon contained a New World version of this old-as-Adam story. Out of fratricidal jealousy, a family of Israelites exiled in America split into distinct factions: Moroni's long-extinct Nephites and their more savage, dark-skinned kin, the Lamanites, a remnant of which became America's Indians. But unlike the Old World gospel, the Book of Mormon taught that racial fault lines were not real or necessarily permanent. That is, they were not of God's design but the result of human failing.

Over the next decade and a half, Smith would receive more divine revelations about how to restore the human family to its original unity and expand the human family exponentially for time and eternity. God would reveal how, in baptismal waters, the living could invite the dead to join the new Mormon covenant, and how Mormon men could be married to more than one wife, multiplying the membership of the covenant on earth and in the heavenly kingdoms to come. However, the method for solving racial schisms within the prophesied covenantal people of history's last days was included in the Book of Mormon itself. Smith and his followers were mandated to return the Book of Mormon to the descendants of its original owners: the so-called American Indians. And white Mormons were called to create new spiritual and familial—perhaps even matrimonial—covenants with their would-be Indian brethren so that the Indians, too, could become once again "a white and a delightsome people" (2 Nephi 30:6).[7]

Arapeen's Visions

Twenty-five years later, at the Mormon settlement in Sanpete Valley—one hundred miles south of Salt Lake City—a Ute Indian chief named Arapeen sought out Mormon leaders.[8] He wanted to recount to them his own set of visions. Arapeen, who had been baptized and ordained a Mormon elder a few years before, asked his white brethren to write down his visions so that they could be sent north to Joseph Smith's successor, Brigham Young, in Salt Lake, the capital of the Mormons' Zion in the Intermountain West, which the Mormons established in 1847 following the assassination of Joseph and his brother Hyrum in Illinois in 1844.

Like Joseph Smith's visions of Moroni, the Heavenly Father, and the Son, Arapeen's visions were didactic. Arapeen explained that two separate personages appeared to him. Each carried messages of admonition for both "white" and "red" Mormons alike. First, Arapeen explained that "Walker" (Wakara), the recently deceased leader of the once powerful Utes, whom the Mormons were systematically displacing from Utah's most fertile lands, had appeared to him (fig. P.2). Like his brother Arapeen, Wakara—remembered as a kind of a cosmopolitan, polyglot Indian who dressed "in European fashion" while adding his "own gaudy Indian trimmings"—had been baptized and ordained a Mormon elder. As part of his ordination, Wakara asked the Mormon leadership to give him a white wife. The request was not granted.[9] But soon after joining the church, in the mid-1850s Wakara waged war against his Mormon brethren in an attempt to protect his people's hunting and fishing grounds. He also wanted to protect the Utes' lucrative trade in Indian slaves, a trade that the Mormons abhorred. Brigham Young even instructed Mormons to buy enslaved Indians in order to free them and raise them in Mormon homes as they would their own chil-

Fig. P.2. Portrait of Wakara (left) and Arapeen, 1854. (Photographic print of engraving based on W. W. Major's painting of Wakara [1854]; courtesy of the Church Archives, the Church of Jesus Christ of Latter-day Saints)

dren so that they could become good Mormon brothers, sisters, and perhaps even wives. (In practice, however, these "freed" Indians often joined Mormon households not as beloved family members but instead as indentured servants, working off the cost that their putative Mormon parents or husbands incurred to liberate them from their Indian captors.) In Arapeen's vision, Wakara told Arapeen that as the Utes' new leader he was now charged with "cultivat[ing] good peace" between the Mormons and the Utes. Arapeen pledged to do his part. He would "put a ball and chain" on any Indian who continued to steal Mormon cattle or horses.[10]

Arapeen explained that the Lord had also appeared to him. And the Lord told him to admonish the whites to do their part to secure peace. In the early 1830s, the earliest Mormons believed that their principal responsibility was to bring the newly restored gospel contained in the Book of Mormon to the Indian remnant of a lost branch of Israel in America. Together with these Lamanites, the white Mormons would build up a New Jerusalem in the New World—a millennial city where the elect would gather to prepare for Christ's return. And while they waited, inside this city's sacred temples, white and red Latter-day Saints would perform covenantal rituals of baptism and marriage that would seal them together into eternal families. The early missions to the Lamanites mostly failed. Mormon missionaries had much more success converting white Americans and Europeans. By the mid-1850s, the hoped-for mass Indian conversion was waning. Instead, the Mormons focused on making white converts, many gathering to Utah from the British Isles and Scandinavia, into respectable Mormon pioneers—teaching them to farm and ranch the rocky soil of the Great Basin; to read, write, and pray in English; and to fend off marauding Indians.

Arapeen explained, "in the lords talk and not mine," that the white Saints had been wrong to abandon their red brethren in favor of the white immigrants. The Lord told the Ute chief that it was the Europeans, and not the Indians, who were out of place in Utah. "[The] danes," Arapeen explained, "do not understand the mormon nor Indian talk and ways." The Lord also chastised the Mormons for converting land divinely dedicated for communal use into private ownership. "The timber, and the water and horses all was the lords and did not belong to the indians nor the Mormons." If the white Mormons and Indians shared these lands and united so that "all people was good and at peace"—which was the hope, after all, of the earliest Mormons—then the Lord "would live on the earth and not go back." But if the white Mormons "throwed away the lords words" and continued to abuse the Indians, Arapeen prophesied that they would be cut off from the Lord, who would no longer "go to their meetings."[11]

Jane Manning James's Visions

A half a century later in Salt Lake City, an elderly and widowed African American Mormon named Jane Manning James explained how, like Joseph Smith and Arapeen, she, too, had experienced visions. But her visions were not of resurrected angels, recently deceased Indian chiefs, or members of the Godhead. She had a vision of Joseph Smith himself. Even before she saw him in person in the Smiths' Nauvoo Mansion House in 1843, James "knew it was Brother Joseph because I had seen him in a dream," she told fellow Mormons in Salt Lake.[12] And James explained that, in turn, Joseph Smith viewed her as the embodiment of faith. After all, even before she became a member of the first pioneer class of 1847 to make the arduous trek to Utah, James and nine family members overcame frostbite, illness, and penury—not to mention persecution from within and outside the Mormon community—to make a thousand-mile trek from their home in Connecticut to join the Saints in Nauvoo, Illinois (fig. P.3). When the road-

Fig. P.3. Jane Manning James (far left and inset) and other pioneers of 1847 (1905). (Charles R. Savage, photographer; courtesy of L. Tom Perry Special Collections, Harold B. Lee Library, Brigham Young University, Provo, Utah)

weary black converts arrived on his doorstep, the prophet was so impressed by James's dedication to the gospel that he and his wife Emma not only housed the young black convert in his home and gave her a job as a servant. They even offered to adopt her into their family, a family that, Joseph Smith taught, would endure for eternity.[13]

In the 1830s, Joseph Smith Jr. explained that he composed his "History" to respond to critics who had labeled him a charlatan and a blasphemer for claiming that God was still speaking, and speaking to him in particular.[14] Likewise in the mid-1850s, Arapeen wanted his visions preserved in the written record of early Mormon history to show that the Indians were more than godless heathens. The Lord spoke to Indian prophets as well as white ones. Though she did so less overtly, in turn-of-the-century Utah, during church and community meetings, in private correspondence with church leaders, and most importantly in her autobiography, Jane Manning James also challenged how others viewed her, including Joseph Smith Jr.'s nephew and namesake, then church president Joseph F. Smith. This Joseph Smith's views on the place of people of African descent in the Mormon community differed from his uncle's. He asserted that because James was born into a cursed race, she was not eligible to participate in the temple ceremonies required to reach the highest levels of heaven. Joseph F. Smith did recognize her as a member of Joseph Smith Jr.'s eternal household. But he labeled her the family's eternal servant, not the first Mormon prophet's adopted daughter. To be sure, James accepted the notion that, as a black woman, she carried the sin of her biblical forefathers on her skin and in her veins. As such, James recognized that marriage as a plural wife to a white priesthood holder—a common practice for widows in Mormon Utah—was out of the question for fear of tainting the pure bloodlines of God's chosen people. (As the mother of a "half-breed" son—the result of a relationship with a white preacher during her pre-Mormon days—the fear of racial "amalgamation," of which the Mormons' antipolygamy detractors already accused them, was not theoretical in her case.) Yet James also pointed to other Mormon scriptures that contain visions for a restored human family open to all who lived in accord with the restored gospel. As a faithful Mormon, "Is there no blessing for me[?]" she asked.[15]

The late nineteenth-century church prophets refused to answer this question, or at least not in a way that James found satisfactory. So, like her beloved Joseph Smith Jr., in her autobiography James made a study of her life. And she demonstrated that this life was a thoroughly Mormon one—a life worthy of the Mormon blessings she sought. She was a baptized member of the church. She had received the gift of the Holy Ghost. She was an eyewitness to the early, secretive days of polygamy. She was an intrepid pioneer to Utah and a matriarch of a large Mormon family. But she wanted more, and believed that she deserved more. In particular, she wanted to be sealed for eternity to Joseph Smith Jr. as the prophet's daughter in the temple in Salt Lake City. By telling her story, James hoped that the current church prophets would accept her as had their predecessor: not as a black woman but as a Mormon woman, a sister in the gospel. Through her dedication to the church and its leaders, James had demonstrated that she had shed the cursed legacy of her race. James was so thoroughly Mormon that, as she explained to a white Mormon friend a few years before her death in 1908, "I am white with the exception of the color of my skin."[16]

INTRODUCTION

Race on the Page, Race on the Body

This is a study of race and how Americans write about it. In America, writing about race with ink and paper has shaped the race that people see on the flesh and bone bodies of others and of themselves. Words that describe degrees of distinction—shade of skin, curl of hair, shape of lips and eyes—get read onto bodies as distinctions of kind. That is, in American history, writing about race has done the cultural work of defining racial sameness as well as racial difference. Yet in America, writing about race does not end with racial description and classification. Race requires narration—the writing of origin narratives describing how different races came to be.

This book examines how American race histories have often been American religious histories, too. In particular, this book traces the critical role that religion played in the formation of the three original American races: "black," "white," and "red." The early history of the Church of Jesus Christ of Latter-day Saints serves as a case study of how Americans of Native, African, and European descent became distinct races, with distinct histories and distinct racial characteristics, occupying distinct rungs on the racial hierarchy. Yet early Mormonism is also a case unto itself. Mormonism presented its believers with a radical new worldview that understood all schisms within the human family—religious, political, and racial—as anathemas to God's design. Based on this new worldview, the Mormon people challenged as well as reaffirmed the essentialist nature of the racialized American peoples. In this book, I argue that for the early Mormons, the construction and deconstruction of what it meant to be, to act, and to look black, white, and red were as much literary projects as they were literal ones. How Mormons wrote about race affected how they sought to make their converts into respectable Mormons—industrious, pious, obedient, and, as we will see, metaphorically and sometimes even literally white. How Mormons wrote about race also affected how they sought to shape and shade the image of those people who rejected their new gospel. Mormons often described these enemies of the faith as red or black—signifying impiety, apostasy, heathenism, and savagery—including those enemies of Mormonism whom other Americans saw as white.

What do I mean by claiming that, for scholarship on religion and race in American history, early Mormonism can serve as a case study *and* a particular case unto itself? Among a certain set of historians, sociologists, and literary critics, it has become axiomatic to call Mormonism "the American religion." This is true not only because Mormonism is the largest and most prominent religion born on American soil. It is also true because the faith is seen to embody many of the paradoxes at the heart of contemporary American culture.[1] The church is hierarchical and democratic, corporatist and populist, Arminian and covenantal, racially universalistic and racially particularistic. Likewise, throughout the twentieth century, the Mormons had great success in integrating themselves into the American cultural and political conservative mainstream. With important exceptions, Mormons are known to be reliably Republican, pro-life, and anti–gay marriage. Mormons are recognized for their business acumen. The armed services as well as the FBI and CIA heavily recruit at church-run universities because Mormons are seen to epitomize patriotism, high personal and familial moral standards, and respect for authority. In his first Sherlock Holmes novel, *A Study in Scarlet*, published in 1888, Sir Arthur Conan Doyle depicted Mormon men as lascivious, violent, and secretive, more akin to despotic Oriental sultans than champions of American democracy. A century later, from Tom Clancy spy thrillers and *South Park* episodes to Tony Award–winning Broadway musicals and touring tabernacle choirs, as Terryl Givens has noted, in American popular culture, the Mormon man has become a "shorthand" for the "clean-cut, patriotic guy-next-door."[2] Not to mention that this Mormon guy-next-door is also white and often rich.

The Mormon as a stand-in for the American is a recent phenomenon, and a not fully realized one. As J. B. Haws has argued, though Mormon *individuals* have gained increasing favorability in American culture, this change has "yet to dispel deep-seated suspicion and serious scrutiny of the church—*the institution*—in the minds of a surprisingly sizable segment of the U.S. population."[3] As such in the twentieth and twenty-first centuries, despite its fervent professions of a shared faith in God and country, the long memory of the church's contentious relationship with much of the rest of America during the nineteenth century keeps the church marginalized, if not often maligned, in the American imagination. This is the legacy of the church's once unorthodox marital theologies and practices; its beliefs in an open canon; its history of political antagonism with and persecution by the U.S. government; its geographic isolation in the Intermountain West; and, of critical importance for this study, its unique views of Native Americans as well as its antiblack theologies and policies. Only in 1978 did the church end its more than century-long ban on black men from holding the Mormon lay priesthood and end the ban on black Mormon men and women from entering the temple, where the most sacred rituals of the faith take place. And only in 2013 did the church officially distance itself from the theological basis for such exclusions, which had been articulated for more than a century at the highest levels of the church's hierarchy. Mormon prophets from Brigham Young, who assumed leadership of the church after Joseph Smith Jr.'s assassination in 1844, to Joseph Smith's grandnephew Joseph Fielding Smith, who served as church president in the early 1970s, asserted in speeches and widely read theological treatises that because they were members of a divinely cursed race, people of African descent were spiritually unworthy to be full members of the church.[4]

The present image of contemporary Mormonism frames the present image of Mormonism's past. That Mormonism is still viewed at some remove from the center of American culture has long led many scholars of U.S. history to assume that Mormon history exists apart from the main narrative arc of this history.[5] This perception holds true for the main focus of this study: that Mormons—themselves long considered a "problem" people—did not participate in the great debates over the most intractable and divisive "problems" in nineteenth-century America, the "Negro" and "Indian" problems; that, as members of an insular new religious movement living what they believed were history's latter days, the Mormons concerned themselves with Christ's imminent return from heaven, not with the immediate, earthbound racial strife of antebellum America; that as a western frontier people, the Mormons did not partake in the politics playing out on the north-south crease that divided America geographically and politically into one half free and the other half slave.

Yet early Mormons did in fact have a lot to say or, more precisely, a lot to write about race. They contributed to the theological and political debates about slavery and about the place of free blacks in the American Republic. In the 1830s, Joseph Smith penned defenses of slavery that sounded like any number of proslavery southern tracts. In the 1840s, he reversed his view and argued that holding blacks in bondage was an affront to the founding principles of the Republic. Brigham Young legalized "African" slavery in Utah, but in ways that he believed would prevent the abuses of southern Slave Power as well as to prevent "miscegenation." What's more, early Mormon historical writings—including Mormonism's foundational text, the Book of Mormon and Joseph Smith's revelations—spoke directly to the fate of America's Native peoples. In many ways, early Mormon history was defined by the belief that white Mormon converts were divinely called to convert, civilize, and create covenants—religious as well as matrimonial—with Native Americans and to create a New Jerusalem where Latter-day Saints would await Christ's second coming. In Utah, Brigham Young encouraged the faithful to buy Indian slaves from evil Indian slave traders like the Ute chiefs Wakara and Arapeen and raise them in their homes. The Mormon missionary successes in Britain and Scandinavia, which led to mass European emigration to the Mormons' Zion in Utah, as well as their conflicts with other white Americans, meant that the Mormons also participated in defining "whiteness" as both a distinct and distinctly American racial category. And yet, I assert here, the Mormons also created a new, distinctly white Mormon race to which even other white Americans did not belong.

Others have made similar arguments regarding the Mormon relationship with (and challenge to) the predominant history of race in America. Previous works, however, have foregrounded the racialized experiences of "white" Mormons. Such studies focused on how Mormons of European descent were racialized by non-Mormon political and religious elites, mostly owing to the supposedly racial denigrating effects of polygamy, and how these white Mormons asserted their superior whiteness often by targeting nonwhites for race-based political and religious exclusion, persecution, or bodily harm. Like other "ethnic" white Americans (such as Germans, Jews, Irish, and Italians) whom Matthew Frye Jacobson has described as belonging to categories of "variegated whiteness" in the eyes of Anglo-Saxon Protestant elites, white Mormons demonstrated their whiteness over and against black Americans and other nonwhite racial minorities in minstrelsy troupes, newspaper editorials, church sermons, and occasionally lynch mobs.[6] This book is the first major study of race and Mormonism that foregrounds the experiences of nonwhite Mormons, especially early church members of African and Native American descent. My goal is to demonstrate how these nonwhite Mormons resisted, acquiesced, and sometimes embraced the racialized theologies of Mormonism (including those arising from the Book of Mormon and other Mormon scriptures) to argue for their inclusion within the sacred Mormon community and the sacred Mormon historical narrative. These nonwhite Mormons' experiences were not peripheral to this history. Instead, they were central to the shaping of church policies and theologies on race from the founding of the church in 1830 to today. My decision to emphasize such experiences is both intellectual and ethical—to demonstrate how doubly and sometimes triply marginalized Mormons (such as Jane Manning James, who was black, Mormon, and female) were (among) the leading actors in the historical narrative that most affected them.

To accomplish these goals, this book analyzes together two seemingly contradictory theses—a case study and a case unto itself—about the Mormon people and their relationship with the rest of the nation. First, the case study: the history of Mormonism and race is representative of the history of religion and race in America. Among theorists of race, the adage that race is a social construct which, as sociologist Angela James writes, is also a "social fact . . . [that] appears in social life as ubiquitous, omnipresent, and real," has become well understood, if not well worn.[7] Less so are historical studies of the theological mechanics of such construction projects. In what follows I undertake such a study by examining how the Mormons shaped—on both the written page and flesh and bone bodies—the black, red, and white American races. Like their early modern predecessors, the earliest Mormons understood race to indicate descent from an original, common forefather, most often a biblical one. And they wrote about the races as such. Yet when Mormonism was founded in 1830, the idea of race in the United States increasingly took on its modern meaning, which deemphasized race as (biblical) descent and emphasized race as (secular) biology. Observable physical features reflected innate intellectual and moral capacities. Race description became race prescription. Bodies labeled as "red" were by definition home to savagery and heathenism; bodies labeled as "black" were by definition sites of labor, violence, sexual desire, and sexual panic; "white" bodies housed civilization, politics, and Christianity.

In many ways, the Mormons accepted and reinforced these standard American racial classifications and the standard cultural ideas that they signified. And yet the earliest Mormons also believed themselves to be divinely called to challenge the idea that race was a real and permanent category of human division. As such they challenged what we might call the "secularization of race." They argued that faith more than paternity shaped both an individual and even a people's racial identity. Race was not the result of biological evolution. Instead race developed from human history, when a people demonstrated—or failed to demonstrate—their ability to abide by God's law.

Second, Mormonism is also a particular case unto itself. Ironically, what we might think of as their proto-postmodern view of race as a historical construct led the early Latter-day Saints to interpret and write about their historical experience in racial and increasingly racially exclusive terms. As literary critic Harold Bloom has argued, perhaps unique in American history, "the Mormons, like the Jews before them are a religion that became a people."[8] In 1855, Brigham Young's older brother Joseph Young also said as much. Because of their particular theologies and practices, their particular historical experiences of religious persecution, and their particular views about the destinies of the races in history's last dispensation, Young declared, "I am aware that we are a peculiar people."[9] In this book, I expand on three generations of scholars of Mormonism who have traced how Mormons became such a peculiar and distinct people, even an "ethnic minority."[10] However, whereas previous studies on Mormonism's ethnic peculiarity have tended to focus on Mormon racial construction from the outside *in*—in other words, how nineteenth-century Mormons were racialized by outsiders and subsequently how the Mormons responded by whitening themselves and darkening others—this project starts from the inside and moves *out*. I argue that the Mormon project of racial purification and reunification was sui generis to the faith. Even before the founding of the church itself, the divine mandate to solve humanity's race problem was present in the minds of the founders and in the church's foundational text, the Book of Mormon.

"Race" Spelled with Three Letters

Analyzing these two theses together—Mormons as representative *and* Mormons as particular—leads to my third and perhaps most important thesis: that if the first construction site of the races in American history was on paper, this paper was religious in nature. After all, early Americans were a people of the book: the Bible. And in the historical narrations of the Bible, early Americans found that the origin of what separated humans *first* from God and *second* from each other was sin. As such, before elaborating on the historical and theoretical arguments I make in this book, I need to flesh out the precedents in early America of the interplay between the projects of narrating race and the projects of racializing bodies.

During the early Republic race evolved to become a hierarchical and immutable category of human division. As race took on its modern form, narratives of racial origins were increasingly written as secular and scientific histories. These histories pointed less to ancient biblical forefathers and more to geographical fatherlands. In other words, instead of the long-accepted idea that descendants of Noah's sons populated the known world—Europeans from Japheth, Africans from Ham, and Asians from Shem—Europeans were understood to come from Europe, Africans from Africa, and Asians from Asia. On these continents, distinct races developed, whose observable physical features supposedly reflected their relative and classifiable intellectual and moral capacities.[11] In 1830, the year that the Book of Mormon was published, the founder of the University of Louisville's School of Medicine, Dr. Charles Caldwell, released a polygenesis treatise in which he argued that the book of Genesis contained the origin story of only the Caucasian race. Caldwell claimed that the roots of racial differences were found not in the biblical archive but instead in the biological one—for example, locating the "Caucasian's" superior intellect to that of the "African" through comparisons of the relative volumes of the two races' crania.[12]

This book studies the historical period during which race was undergoing the process of secularization that Caldwell's (pseudo)scientific work embodies. When Mormonism was founded, biblical histories of racial origins were most often understood not as allegory but instead as an accurate accounting of ancient history. And these histories carried the imprimatur of divine inspiration and infallibility, which no secular history could enjoy. For the Mormons and their race-writing predecessors, biblical figures such as Adam and his sons, Cain and Abel, Noah and his sons, along with Abraham, Isaac, Jacob, and Joseph, were not characters in some morality play. They were historical figures of the past whose legacies affect the present.

The first English colonists in New England and Virginia portrayed their initial errand into the American wilderness as, at least in part, a mission to redeem the Indians from their heathenism and restore them to the universal human family. The Indians were wrong when they spoke about their own genesis, springing up like the other American flora and fauna, as Roger Williams reported the Indians' version of their origin story, "like the trees of the Wildernesse."[13] Williams and other English colonists sympathetic to the Indians asserted that the Indians belonged to a global and ancient human race. They, like the English, were all issued from the same dust into which God had breathed life. Indians were not naturally savage. They were savage because their environment was. The cure for savagery was to fell the woods and erect English-style homes, farms, and meetinghouses where the Indian's heathenism would be worked and worshiped out of him; where the Indian would be baptized and catechized and given a Christian name; where he would learn to dress, to farm, to read, to write, and to pray like an Englishman, until he became one.[14]

Religion was thus seen as a tool to tame not only the wild Indian's body and mind but also the wilds of the New World. After all, as historian and missionary to the Indians Daniel Gookin explained, civilized Christian communities—the kind that he attempted to establish for the Indian converts who lived in the "Praying Towns" for which he served as superintendent in Massachusetts in the 1670s—begot Englishmen. America's natural environment begot Indians, "brutish barbarians." Their hair, "black and harsh, not curling; their eyes, black and dull," reflected the lack of "means of cultivating and civilizing" their inner lives, from which the fair-haired, gray-eyed Englishmen had long benefited. In examining the state of uncivilized Indians, Gookin suggested, there but by the grace of God go the English—that "we may see, as in a mirror [ourselves] . . . the woeful, miserable, and deplorable estate, that sin hath reduced mankind unto naturally."[15]

Yet, at least according to many early American historians of English-Native relations, the difference between the English and the Indian did in fact prove to be innate, not environmental. The Indians' outward expressions of savagery in the face of the English's benevolent efforts to cultivate in their human brethren a Christian spirit—demonstrated by refusing baptismal waters and by waging war against English bodies and English infrastructure—pointed to a heathenism passed down through the generations.[16] The English colonial settler historians presented themselves as merely taking down dictation. They transcribed the Indians' bloody deeds into words. However, the English and later the Americans narrated the conflicts between Indians and Anglo-Americans not as clashes of cultures but as wars of races. Against the cruelty and savagery of the red, heathen Indian, white Americans drew themselves on the page as a Christian people of virtue, piety, and mercy.[17] "The waves of population and civilization are rolling to the westward," proclaimed Andrew Jackson in his annual address to Congress in December 1830, in which he celebrated the passage of his Indian removal program. The American nation was expanding, "filled with the blessings of liberty, civilization and religion," of which the "red men" by dint of their inborn anticivilization characters could not be a part.[18]

If the Indian race did not originate from the American environment, early American historians had to look elsewhere, and much earlier in history. Two centuries before Jackson announced the "happy consummation" of his efforts to clear the American landscape of its native "savages," some of the backers of John Winthrop's efforts to create a church of visible saints in New England read the red race's origins into the origins of the races recorded in the Bible. Church of England clergyman John White, who helped the Massachusetts Bay Colony secure its royal charter, noted that some settler colonists believed that they need not concern themselves with efforts to include the "Natives" of America in their new covenantal community because they were descendants of Ham. Ham's sin against his father, Noah, resulted in Noah cursing Ham's posterity with dark skin and separating them from his worthier offspring until (all but) the end of time. But this was a minority opinion, the result of speculation about how the Indians in America related to the postdiluvian scattering of Noah's progeny, history's second "first family" that survived the flood on Noah's ark.[19]

The racial origin of the first Africans brought to America as slaves was no such mystery. The long-held consensus was that Africans' black skin was the outward expression of the curse placed on their forefathers Ham and Cain. Blackness served as a reminder of the two biblical antiheroes' sin of violence and betrayal against their family members. For much of seventeenth- and eighteenth-century American history, Noah's curse on Ham's son Canaan—that "a servant of servants shall he be unto his brethren" (Genesis 9:25)—justified the enslavement of Africans as well as their exclusion from Christian rites like baptism, communion, and marriage. The equality of all believers inherent in Christian theology was incompatible with the idea that one part of the Christian family could own another.[20]

As such, for a time in early American history, the story of the black race's original sin made the "black" racial identity synonymous with "slave" and antithetical to "Christian." However, for many proslavery advocates, starting in the Revolutionary Era and continuing through the Civil War, black, slave, and Christian became mutually constitutive and mutually constructed. The history of Noah's curse had separated Ham's sons and daughters—exiled to the African continent—not only from Noah's more favored descendants but also from the light of the gospel. The founding father of the Southern Presbyterian Church, Benjamin M. Palmer, wrote in 1858 that in Africa "under a glowing sky, nature harmonize[d] with their brutal and savage disposition." Through God's providence, God had given the American people a "historic mission." To Palmer and other defenders of slavery, the race histories that began with the scattering of Noah's progeny culminated in America, where a new white "race" was formed out of Japheth's offspring—a "confluence of all the tribes and tongues of Europe." In America, with God's blessing, the institution of slavery established the proper and mutually beneficial relationship between this new white race and Ham's black race, whose dark skin marked them as slaves in perpetuity.[21] Slavery has always existed in human history, another Presbyterian minister, George D. Armstrong, wrote in 1857. But "Christian slavery" in America divests the institution "of its incidental evils" because the Christian "Church labor[s] to make good masters and good slaves, just as she labors to make good husbands, good wives, good parents, good children, good rulers, good subjects."[22]

"The Restoration of All Things"

When Joseph Smith Jr. gathered some sixty followers on a farmstead in western New York State on April 6, 1830, to found what he then called the "Church of Christ," the first prophet of the Latter-day Saints did not establish his new religious movement with the explicit purpose of resolving the original sin of race. Nor did Smith claim that his divine mandate was to solve what other leading Americans described as the original sins of the American nation—slavery and Indian removal.[23] Instead, Smith described his mission as transcending the politics of the day. Smith was called by God to restore Christ's true church, which had been corrupted during the two millennia since Christ's first earthly mission. And he was called by God to gather together a restored chosen people, build a New Jerusalem, and await Christ's ultimate return.

Yet by definition, what Joseph Smith described in an August 1830 revelation as the "restoration of all things" involved this-worldly politics.[24] Before New Jerusalem would be ready to receive the returned Christ, Mormon converts had to be unified into one covenantal people, which included the restoration of the races. To be sure, the early Latter-day Saints recognized that much of antebellum law, politics, and culture were designed around the belief that the races were separated by divine design and nature's biology and should be kept as such. However, they found a different vision for the fate of the races in their foundational text, the Book of Mormon. They believed that this New World gospel restored "plain and precious things" that had been lost through the millennia from the Old World biblical canon. One of the most precious of these lost-and-restored gospel messages was that paternity did not, in fact, determine destiny. The Book of Mormon teaches that Christ's atoning sacrifice provides the "infinite" potential for "all mankind"—even those men and women who carry the curses of their forefathers on their skin—to become full members of the restored Church of Christ.[25] And the earliest Latter-day Saints attempted to build up the New Jerusalem as well as to shape the people whom they expected to inhabit it around this audacious vision.

This book traces how the early Mormons attempted to enact their vision of restorative racial universalism. This book also traces the external and internal forces that led to the failure of these efforts to create a (relatively) racially inclusive people and instead resulted in creating a Mormon people whose racial particularism—in particular, whose whiteness—became a hallmark feature of their identity well into the second half of the twentieth century. To enter into this history requires a reorientation of the standard understanding of the relation between race and scripture in the nineteenth century. It also requires a redefinition of what we mean by both "race" and "scripture."

In antebellum America, defenders of slavery were not the only people to turn to the Bible to justify divisions between whites and blacks. Many slaves and free African Americans challenged proslavery readings of Genesis, which held that by dint of their descent from Canaan, they were to be "servants of servants." Instead, they invoked the story of Exodus, in which they saw themselves as America's oppressed but chosen people. Some twenty-five miles west of Palmyra, New York, where Joseph Smith would publish the Book of Mormon three years later, on July 5, 1827, a former slave named Austin Steward gave the Emancipation Day speech in the abolitionist stronghold of Rochester. "Slavery has been your curse, but it shall become your rejoicing," Steward told the slaves made officially free that day in New York. "Like the people of God in Egypt, you have been afflicted; but like them too, you have been redeemed."[26] Prominent Native American Christians also turned to the Bible to challenge their maltreatment. In 1829, the Methodist minister and Pequot activist William Apess wrote that since he could not find the "opprobrious epithet" of "Indian" in the Bible, he concluded that "whites" had imported the word "for the special purpose of degrading" the true "Natives" of America. He even claimed that, unlike Americans of European descent, these Natives "are the only people who retain the original complexion of our father Adam."[27]

Scholars of race and religion have often claimed that such interpretations on all sides of the American "race problem" are historically contingent. Americans wrote race into scripture in response to historical experience, when scripture actually has little to say on the subject.[28] And yet, I argue that the history of race and religion in America is incomplete if interpretations of scripture are understood as mostly reactions to, rather than shapers of, history. History makes theology. But theology makes history, too. This book inverts the usual focus on how Americans' views on race influenced scriptural interpretation. Instead, I pose the question: What would a history of race and religion in America look like if we were to examine how scriptures have created theological lenses through which Americans have viewed various racial and ethnic populations of Americans?[29]

Early Mormon history is uniquely suited for such an inversion of the dominant understanding of the relation between history and scriptural interpretation. To find divine direction on the issues of race, most antebellum Christians had to read between the lines of a closed canon written millennia removed from the religious and racial worlds of the early Republic. Compared to other Christian "sectarians" with whom they competed for members, the Mormons claimed to have a clearer view onto the truth about race. After all, the Mormons had access to more accurate race writings. They had a restored gospel, a reopened sacred canon, and reappointed divine prophets who could provide answers to the race questions of the day. For the first few years of Mormon history, the most influential Mormon race writing was the Book of Mormon itself. The book taught its earliest believers that race was not real. That is, race was not a permanent part of God's vision for humanity. Race entered into history as the result of sin. Thus, solving the race problem involved removing the racial distinctions that marked off certain members of the human family from others.[30] And the Book of Mormon mandated its earliest believers—those white Americans to whom the book would first be restored—to become missionaries. They were charged with spreading Christ's gospel of (potential) racial reunification to "all nations, kindreds, tongues, and people, to bring about the restoration of his people upon the earth."[31]

The contention that early Mormons read the Book of Mormon much at all, let alone with such a specific focus, is not widely held. Many scholars have argued that, in the first few years of Mormon history, the book's import was not its actual text but instead its mere existence. Such scholars argue that for its earliest adopters, the Book of Mormon was an eschatological "sign." Its coming forth—out of the ancient American past and into the early nineteenth-century American present—signaled the beginning of the latter days.[32] And yet my contention that the Book of Mormon's actual text played an essential role in the development of a uniquely Mormon racial theology and missionary project is not an act of speculation. Intertextual readings of early Mormon publications, including Mormon newspapers that often printed carefully curated excerpts of the Book of Mormon (see chapters 2 and 3), provide insights into how early church leaders hoped the church's membership would understand the faith's foundational text in relation to Joseph Smith's day-to-day revelations and in relation to the developing canon of other translations. For the early Latter-day Saints, this expanding network of interconnected sacred scriptures created a corrective racialized lens. The Book of Mormon did not replace the Bible as the urtext of Christianity, but instead it clarified its universalistic message.[33]

To be sure, like other antebellum Americans, early Mormons read race on *and onto* the bodies of "black" and "red" Americans. Africans and Indians' dark skins told the history of their ancestors' sins. And early Mormons wrote about what they saw. Like other white Americans, they deployed words like "savage" and "slave," "wicked" and "cursed" to discursively mark off African and Native Americans from more civilized, white Euro-Americans in their ever-expanding archive of public as well as personal writings. Yet in the beginning of the Mormon dispensation, leading Latter-day Saints read and then wrote about race on the page in hopes of erasing it from skin. The earliest Mormons described the race problem as a holistic problem with a holistic solution: based on the Book of Mormon's racial hermeneutic, for early Mormons, "whiteness"—both as a signifier and even as a phenotype—was an aspirational racial identity that nonwhites could achieve through conversion to Mormonism (chapter 1). They hoped to fold red and, in a more limited manner, black Americans into a white—as in *raceless*—Mormon people (chapters 2 and 4). This racial restoration would involve a metaphorical and literal whitening of nonwhites. Starting with the first Mormon mission to Native Americans in 1831, the Mormons were told that the Lord charged them with educating heathenism out of the Indian. The vision for remaking Indians into Mormons would also take place in the Mormon home, even in the Mormon matrimonial bed. By the early 1850s, if not well before, the Mormon leadership encouraged some Mormon missionaries to take Indian women as plural wives. "So that in many generations would not pass," Brigham Young taught the Mormon settlers in southern Utah in 1851, the Native children whom the Mormons bought into freedom from evil Indian slave traders and taught to read and write, to plant and plow, and to raise their own Mormon children, would also "become a white and delightsome people" (chapters 5 and 6).[34]

However, what I describe as the Book of Mormon's "white universalism" proved too ambitious to be tolerated in antebellum America. This was especially true for a new religious movement already viewed as a blasphemous affront to the core doctrines of Christianity, especially the idea of a closed canon. In response to anti-Mormon violence and persecution, which was often associated with accusations that the Latter-day Saints were disrupting the racial hierarchies of the American Republic by "meddling"—including "miscegenating"—with Indians and blacks, the Mormons quickly adapted. They became mainstream and eventually extreme in their views on race. In particular, they became extreme in their views on the inherent supremacy of the white race and the innate and all but eternal inferiority of the black race, though they did maintain hope for mass Indian conversion until at least the 1880s (chapters 4, 5, and 6).[35] When their East Coast critics purposefully conflated Mormon polygamy with another supposed unholy sexual union—mixed-race marriages—Mormon leaders became some of the nation's fiercest opponents of race "amalgamation" and fiercest defenders of white racial purity.[36] Likewise, how the Mormons read their own scriptures changed. They began reading more into the racially exclusionary passages of their expanding canon and less into the inclusive message that the earliest leaders emphasized (chapter 3). By the end of the nineteenth century, the whiteness that had been made universal in the early church became the exclusive purview of whites. And instead of leading to racial denigration, as polygamy's opponents argued was its effect, Mormons claimed that because it brought together the once lost but now rediscovered most divinely favored bloodlines, plural marriage produced a purer breed of white than monogamous American couplings (chapter 3).

Despite my description here of the history of race and Mormonism as a downward trend away from racially inclusive originalism to racial particularism, this is not a history of declension. Instead, it is a history of race as a category that unites as well as divides. I argue that the church's evolving views on race arose out of the dialectal tension between the two central and seemingly paradoxical elements of the Mormon people's identity: a missionary people divinely called to teach the gospel to everyone everywhere and a racially particularistic people who believe that God has, at times, favored certain racial groups over others. Recognizing the important role that this dialectic has played in the formulation of the church's theologies and policies opens up this particular discussion of race in Mormonism, as well as the discussion of race in American religious history writ large, to a more interesting and more important set of queries than the reductionistic question of whether Mormonism is, or has been, fundamentally racist.

These arguments occupy the center of this book's historical analysis. Yet here I also raise another set of related historiographical questions. I ask, in nineteenth-century America how did racial identities affect who gets to write history? By this I mean, first, who decides whose voices get included in the Mormon people's archive—which I conceptualize as written texts, namely public, official church records, printed material including newspapers and sermons, sacred revelations, and translations, private materials including diaries, memoirs, and family correspondence, as well as oral histories and folklore, which together compose the Mormon people's collective memory? Second, who has the ability and the authority to literally put pen to paper? That is, who has access to the type of literacy and literary resources to create narratives of the Mormon people, narratives that explain who the Mormon people are as well as who they are not? Third, for those excluded from these historical narratives, how do they write about (and sometimes write against) their exclusion? In particular, how do they write themselves into the written archive even while often adhering to the assumption that the enterprise of historical narration itself signifies whiteness (chapters 4 and 6)? Last, how does the writing of race in the paper body of an archive affect how race is written onto living and breathing human bodies? How does the act of ascribing racial characteristics—white as civilized, black as cursed, and red as savage—affect the relationships among these different *literarily* racialized peoples (chapter 6)?[37]

How to Read the Book of Mormon

Answering these questions involves the study of how Mormons wrote about race. Such a study is incomplete without an examination of the text that marked the beginning of the Mormon dispensation and introduced its earliest readers to a new way of seeing the world and the people who inhabit it: the Book of Mormon.

Many historians have written about the Book of Mormon. Few have read it. Or perhaps more fairly, few historians have carefully analyzed its content. This has been the case for two main reasons. First, historians have often focused on Joseph Smith's fantastic claims about how the Book of Mormon came to be—that in 1820s Upstate New York, Smith, with the help of an angel, uncovered a cache of ancient gold plates; that on these plates was inscribed a new American gospel and a history of a great American pre-Columbian civilization; and that Smith translated this gospel and history from Egyptian into English. Since the plates are not extant—they were supposedly taken back to heaven after the translation was complete—and since there is no archaeological evidence that matches the pre-Columbian civilization that the Book of Mormon describes, many historians find the Book of Mormon origin claims suspect, if not "scandalous."[38] Second, there is the form of the text itself. For the uninitiated—those who have not grown up Mormon—the Book of Mormon is difficult to comprehend, let alone appreciate. This was Mark Twain's experience: in *Roughing It* (1872), he famously mocked its prose as so clunky as to be sleep inducing, "chloroform in print."[39] Such anti–Book of Mormon animus dies hard. In *The American Religion* (1992), Harold Bloom carried on the then century-old tradition of Book of Mormon illiteracy. In lieu of a close reading of the text, which, he wrote, the book "scarcely sustains," Bloom concluded that summaries of the Book of Mormon would suffice.[40]

For the scholarship of American religion, there is a cost associated with this deliberate Book of Mormon illiteracy. The publication of the Book of Mormon in 1830 helped spawn a global religious movement with today more than fifteen million members spread across six continents. With some 150 million copies—translated in more than a hundred languages—printed, sold, and given away, the Book of Mormon is third only to the Bible and the Qur'an as the world's most reproduced religious text. For the Latter-day Saints, the histories and prophecies contained within the Book of Mormon create an "interpretive community," to borrow from Stanley Fish, a communal mode of reading human experience through this communal lens.[41] For scholars hoping to gain entrée into this unique Mormon mode of reading history, summaries of the book do not, in fact, suffice.[42] Book of Mormon illiteracy directly affects the major contribution of this project: the proper contextualization of early Mormon understandings of racial identities as they relate to religious and political identities in the early Republic. As such, Book of Mormon literacy is a prerequisite for understanding how early Mormons' views on race both reflected and departed from the predominant antebellum conception of race as biblically and biologically predetermined and immutable to change.

Still, there remains the question of how to become Book of Mormon literate. Readers of the Book of Mormon often start from one of two "sectarian" perspectives. As Grant Hardy has explained, most non-Mormons find it "preposterous" that otherwise educated people could read the Book of Mormon as history. By contrast, for Mormons who have grown up reading it, "the complexity and beauty of the book . . . would seem to make it impossible for thoughtful, open minded people to doubt."[43] Mormon scholars like Hardy have charted another path into a critical reading of the Book of Mormon—one that I largely follow here—that brackets "at least temporarily, questions of historicity" and focuses on the text itself in favor of "a detailed examination of what the Book of Mormon is and how it operates."[44] However, even while circumventing the "temporarily" bracketed questions of historicity, I do not think we can nor should we remove the Book of Mormon from its early nineteenth-century origins. By approaching it *as a text* and *as a historical phenomenon*, the Book of Mormon can be read from the perspective of its early believers—from what I call a "hermeneutic of restoration." They understood the Book of Mormon to be the scriptural "keystone," to borrow consciously from Joseph Smith, that binds together a complicated web of scriptural intertextuality, with connections to the archives not only of the sacred past (for example, the Hebrew and Christian Bibles) but also of the sacred future (for example, church records, newspapers, memoirs, and personal correspondence, along with other Mormon translations and revelations).[45]

How to Read and Write about Race

How we read the Book of Mormon affects how we read and write about race in early Mormon history. When it was published in 1830, I argue that the Book of Mormon's first adopters challenged the notion that race is immutable. Yet race was more than a race problem. As Evelyn Brooks Higginbotham has famously put it, in the nineteenth century, race became "a 'global sign,' a 'metalanguage,'" which subsumed all other identities—religious, class, political, gender—into a binary of black and white.[46] I argue that, during the first half century of their church's history, the Latter-day Saints both constructed and contested the notion of black and white as such totalizing categories.

Michel Foucault provides a helpful theoretical framework for describing how the Latter-day Saints did so. In *The Order of Things* (1970), a philosophical-archaeological exploration of the classical human impulse to "name and order," Foucault writes about the relation between "nomenclature" and "taxonomy." Foucault observes that the epistemological naming of the self (or selves) occurs when the self encounters the other. This encounter also creates classifications of selves into orders of family, genus, and species.[47] The early Latter-day Saints did not conceptualize humanity's diversity in terms of the classic Linnaean taxonomy on which race scientists like Charles Caldwell relied to delineate the tropes of racial hierarchies—the anatomical structure of the African's brain, for example, demonstrates that he occupies "a station between" apes and Caucasians.[48] Instead the Latter-day Saints thought about all branches of the human family as sharing paternity in the first man, Adam. From this common Adamic ancestor and then, after the flood, from humanity's second progenitor, Noah, spun out a complicated web of patrilineages. The Book of Mormon—the plates of which were the result of Joseph Smith's own archaeological and revelatory diggings on the Hill Cumorah—promises that during the restoration, Noah's descendants through Shem and Shem's descendants through Abraham, Isaac, Jacob, and Joseph, along with Japheth's "Gentile" progeny, shall gather together in the New World and "build a city, which shall be called the New Jerusalem."[49] The descendants of Ham, it is important to note, are absent from the Book of Mormon's millennial vision. And yet, as I will show, during the first two decades of the church's existence, a few people of African descent nevertheless do get included in the racial restoration project of Joseph Smith's church.

Foucault's archaeology is metaphorical. Smith's archaeology is historical and/or mythical. Yet Foucault's archaeological discoveries still help us to understand Smith's; his findings yielded a new way of seeing or, more aptly, reading the American continent (and beyond) and the people who inhabit it. I argue that one of the early Saints' main theological tasks was to "name and order" the various divisions of the human family. They did so according to specific lineages, which, I will show, were theological categories related to, but not the same as, antebellum categories of race. To be able to restore them to the knowledge of their true selves and to the true knowledge of a universal Adamic (and Noahide) kinship, the divisions of human lineages had to be named (for example, the sons and daughters of Shem, Japheth, and Ham) and ordered according to the hierarchy of these lineages, with descendants of Shem at the top and those of Ham at the bottom. Once named and ordered, these lineages could be marketed according to their spiritual and intellectual characteristics and needs, determined both by the lineage into which they were born and by the civilizations in which they were reared (chapter 2). But until the reunion of these unequal lineages occurs, whiteness and blackness remain powerful signifiers—marking off the Christian from the heathen, the civilized from the savage, the citizen from the slave, and the literate from the illiterate.

Let me pause briefly to reflect on this last distinction between white and dark-skinned people—literacy. It is the most consequential distinction in this study, which examines how the historical archive becomes a racialized space. It is the historian's errand to return to the written archive, again and again, and to rediscover records that went unnoticed or were even repressed in previous iterations of historical narration. When this occurs, historiography—creating new narratives of the "same" history—becomes self-correcting.[50]

Yet the written archive has a race problem. To access the archive, one must pass a literacy test.[51] This means that the writing of history is often segregated. This segregation empowers literate whites to write race into history. Seventeenth-century Anglo-American colonists and nineteenth-century slave owners enjoyed what Jill Lepore has called a "literal advantage" over the Native Americans they tried to convert, displace, or kill and over the slaves they tried to keep in bondage. And this literal advantage was circular: illiterate nonwhites could not respond in writing to the writers who labeled them as less than human—ahistorical savages or unredeemable slaves.[52] The construction of race—the race of a white, writerly self and the race of a nonwhite, nonwriterly other—is an act of writing in general and an act of writing history in particular.[53]

Of course, nonwhites write, too. They put pen to paper to archive their own histories. And often, they do so to challenge how they have been written about in (or written out of) history. And yet, in the history of early Mormonism, the existence of the nonwhite writer is a rarity. The writerly Jane Manning James (prologue and chapter 4) and the writerly Chief Wakara (chapters 5 and 6) cannot escape the racialization of their own writings. Even when black and Native Americans produce writing, white writers are almost always called on to authenticate these writings. This authentication process often leads to editing—solicited or not—of the nonwhite writer's written words, which in turn can alter and diminish the subjectivity of the nonwhite writer's writerly self.

Reading and Writing Race in Mormon History

Using the evolution of Mormon racial theologies and practices as a point of entry, this book grapples with the hermeneutics *and* historiography of the American "race problems." Its chapters flow (more or less) chronologically from the publication of the Book of Mormon in 1830 to the death of Jane Manning James in 1908. The chapters also follow the Mormons along what we might call the long Mormon trail—moving westward from New York to Ohio and Missouri, then to Illinois, and finally to Utah's Great Basin, with brief excursions into the mission fields of Europe, the Near East, and the Pacific Islands. In chapter 1, I investigate the Book of Mormon's relevance to three of this project's most important and interconnected subjects: race, literacy, and the writing of history. First, in terms of race, I elaborate on what I call the Book of Mormon's "white universalism." Within Mormonism's foundational text there are both universalistic and exclusivist racial impulses, which together inform the racial theology and history that comes after its publication in 1830. The Book of Mormon teaches that Christ's death and resurrection opened up the covenant, which once belonged exclusively to the Lord's chosen people, to not only "Jew and Gentile." Instead, "he inviteth them all to come unto him," exclaims the Book of Mormon's most universalistic passage (2 Nephi 26:33), "black and white, bond and free, male and female." He even "remembereth the heathen; and all are alike unto God."[54] Yet the heathen and the black Mormon will not remain so for long. Covenanting with the righteous leads to the cultural and perhaps even literal whitening of converts who carry the curses of their forefathers on their skin and in their blood.

Second, this whiteness also signifies literacy. The Book of Mormon teaches that the act of reading written records left by a people's forefathers, as well as the act of adding to this people's archive, is how God's chosen people remember their heavenly father's commandments and covenants "from generation to generation."[55] To read, to write—in other words, to be historical—is to be fully human. That only the Nephites directly add to the archive of what would become the Book of Mormon substantiates the power of literacy to define whiteness as the universalized category of humanity.

The connection between whiteness and literacy leads to the third racialized subject that I analyze in the Book of Mormon: to control what gets written and, thus, what gets remembered in this ancient American Christianity.

The Nephite prophets and historians who write the Book of Mormon enjoy what I call a "narrator's prerogative." By this I mean that they draw from an archive of written records to create an abridged, synthesized, and intertextual narrative. This narrative is a devotional history. The narrators intend to guide future readers to accept the gospel contained within the Book of Mormon, to restore God's true church, and to build up New Jerusalem. To do so, these historians consciously include some historical actors and historical events and leave out others—in particular racial others.

The Book of Mormon is thus the first installment of the "Mormon archive." As such, I argue that it shaped not only how early Latter-day Saints viewed the racialized people whom they encountered. It also shaped how they wrote about them as objects of missionary work, colonization, displacement, exclusion, and violence. And yet, I argue that the Book of Mormon also contains a warning of the pitfalls of the (white) narrator's prerogative—the cost associated with ignoring dark-skinned voices in the narration of ancient and latter-day Mormon history. Ironically, the Book of Mormon itself draws our attention to the need to include histories of the marginalized in Mormon record keeping. These histories often provide correction, even revision, to the dominant white historical narrative.

In chapters 2 and 3, I focus on how the Book of Mormon's radical new racial hermeneutic was interpreted and applied during Joseph Smith's tenure as church president and prophet (1830–44). In chapter 2, I examine the Mormons' first formal marketing efforts—a mission to the Lamanites—to a community of Delaware Indians in exile, living twenty-five miles west of where the Saints attempted to build their New Jerusalem in Jackson County, Missouri. The mission produced not one single Native American convert. Yet how the missionaries wrote about this first mission reveals much about how the archive of Mormon history became a space where the boundaries of Mormon racial identity are constructed and contested. Next, I examine early Mormon efforts to market the Book of Mormon to the Gentiles, whose status as literate whites meant that they were, practically speaking, better prepared to receive the gospel than illiterate Indians. As such, the Latter-day Saints marketed the Book of Mormon to the Gentiles using more efficient and "civilized" means—the written word printed in the Mormons' newspapers and printed on their presses. I also introduce the complicated place that African Americans occupied in early Mormon history. The Book of Mormon does not include the supposed descendants of Cain and Ham in its vision for a New Jerusalem in America. Nevertheless, motivated by the same ideals of the restoration of the original, white human family, the

Saints engaged in a limited marketing campaign to America's "Free People of Color," as they called them in the Saints' first newspaper, the *Evening and the Morning Star.*

In chapter 3, I describe the inward reorientation—the formation of what I call a "contracted covenant"—in which the Mormons engaged after they were expelled from Jackson County in 1833. To articulate what I mean by a contracted covenant, let me explain how I understand the difference between a covenantal "community" and a covenantal "family." Acceptance of the normative claims of the Book of Mormon created a covenantal interpretive community based on a shared belief that the Book of Mormon was a more complete gospel of Christ. Acceptance of the Book of Mormon also led to the creation of a physical, geographical community. In the first years of Mormon history, this community was to be centered at the "City of Zion" near Independence, Missouri.[56] Yet after the trials of the first three years of the church's existence, when accusations that they were meddling with both Indians and blacks helped to justify their forced removal from Jackson County, the covenantal community *contracted.* Turning inward, the Saints discovered that until they could secure a permanent place to build New Jerusalem, the most important building blocks of Zion would not be edifices (save for one, the temple) but would instead be the family of Joseph Smith itself, as well as other Mormon converts in whom ran the blood of the original covenantal family, the descendants of the biblical patriarchs Abraham, Jacob, Joseph, and especially Ephraim, the most favored of the lost tribes of Israel. The Saints bound together these forgotten-and-now-remembered bloodlines through the rituals of baptism for the living and the dead, through the ordination of the priesthood of all (male) believers, and through marriages—including plural marriage. In doing so, the Saints believed that they were restoring the ancient covenantal family during the latter days before the end of history and preparing to expand this family exponentially for the eternity to come.

In chapter 4, I examine the period during which the Latter-day Saints built "the City of Joseph" in Nauvoo, Illinois. During this time, in a limited manner the Saints attempted to create a Zion that included people of African descent. Both contemporaneous and retrospective archival records from this period portray Joseph Smith Jr. as a prophet who welcomed blacks as (all but) full members of the Mormon covenantal community. Yet Joseph Smith and other Smith family members were far from colorblind. In fact, the Smiths' willingness to accept black Mormons like Jane Manning James was predicated on the black Saints' ability to overcome the legacy of spiritual inferiority of the cursed lineages into which they were born. If they remained faithful to the gospel, then their cursed bloodlines would be purified. This inward change meant that these black Saints could become equal to their white brethren and (eventually) white themselves. However, fear that their (still) tainted bloodlines would contaminate the pure blood of their white brethren meant that the black Saints could not covenant spiritually as well as matrimonially as did their white and even red brethren.

In chapters 5 and 6, I focus on the building up of Zion's infrastructure in Utah during Brigham Young's tenure as leader of the church (1844–77). This infrastructure comprised Zion's built environment. It also comprised Zion's people, who were also under construction. The principal sites of this people building included the flesh and bone bodies of Utah's Native populations, Utah's small African American community, and the European converts gathering to Utah. In chapter 5, I argue that the Mormons set out to build a Lamanite people by employing the tools of civilization, including farms, clothes, grains, schoolhouses, and the (plural) marriage bed. They sought to free the Indians from their savage natures, which would allow them to fulfill their predetermined destiny to covenant with their white brethren. For those Indians who were physically constrained—especially the women and children enslaved by Indian slavers like Wakara and Arapeen—the Saints would buy them in order to free them. As the white Mormons' pupils, servants, adopted children, and plural wives, these freed Indian slaves would learn to choose the right and to become their Lamanite selves.

In chapter 6, I argue that people building in Zion was literary as well as literal. Essential to the construction of the Lamanite was also the construction of the Indian, a character of violence and depravity against which the civilized Lamanite could be drawn. As the Mormon archive grew full of elegiac celebrations of the poor Indian slave—almost always an Indian slave girl—whom the Saints claimed to have purchased into freedom and self-knowledge, Mormons also wrote about the refusal of the Indian—almost always a male Indian slaver—to accept his lessons, an act of defiance that was deemed a demonstration not of human agency but instead of savagery. Through their performances of violence against Mormons and against the Mormons' Lamanites, these Indians proved that they were in fact Indians. And they were made to be so on paper.

I conclude this book with a survey of the history of Mormonism and race after Brigham Young's death in 1877 to the present. For more than a century, the church worked to fortify the racial boundaries around the Mormon identity that Brigham Young erected during his tenure as president and prophet. And yet, pressures from inside as well as outside the church continually contested these boundaries. I also meditate on how and why the church has recently renewed its universalism, and done so in relation to a rereading of the Book of Mormon. Yet this contemporary Mormon universalism is a new universalism. It is cast explicitly in a different shade than the white universalism that was proposed, and in some ways practiced, by the church that Joseph Smith founded in 1830.

1   THE BOOK OF MORMON
A (White) Universal Gospel

For Joseph Smith Jr. and his earliest followers, the Book of Mormon was more than a book. It was an Indian treasure of ancient golden plates unearthed from a hill called Cumorah located just south of an Upstate New York canal town. It was the last material remnant of a once great pre-Columbian American civilization. It was a history of the origins of America's native inhabitants. It was a record of Christ's first mission to the New World as well as a prophetic account of Christ's imminent return (fig. 1.1).

And yet for those who accepted the Book of Mormon and Joseph Smith's claims about where the plates came from and how he translated their ancient reformed Egyptian characters into nineteenth-century English script, perhaps what mattered most was what the Book of Mormon directs its readers to do. The Book of Mormon addresses itself implicitly, and sometimes explicitly, to modern America's ruling racial population.[1] It commands the Gentiles of America—understood initially to be white Anglo-Americans—to restore Christ's true church, the covenants of which had been lost when the "abominable church" fell away from the purity of the original gospel.[2] It commands the Gentiles to bring forth the Book of Mormon to the Indians. After all, Native Americans were actually a remnant of an exiled family of ancient Israelites now in a depraved state and oblivious to their true Abrahamic lineage. It commands the Gentiles to gather these Indians together into one civilized people. It commands the Gentiles to covenant with Indians so that the Gentiles, too, can be numbered among Abraham's seed. It commands the Gentiles to join with their new brethren in America and build a New Jerusalem, the capital city of Christ's coming thousand-year reign.[3]

To be sure, the Book of Mormon was not the only early nineteenth-century project that aimed to reconceive America's past as something approaching sacred. Half a century removed from the founding of the Republic, Americans were, as historian Jan Shipps has written, "busily engaged in the manufacture of instant heritage, substituting inspiration for antiquity with regard to the Constitution and producing a veritable hagiography of popular biography," in particular by making secular saints out of

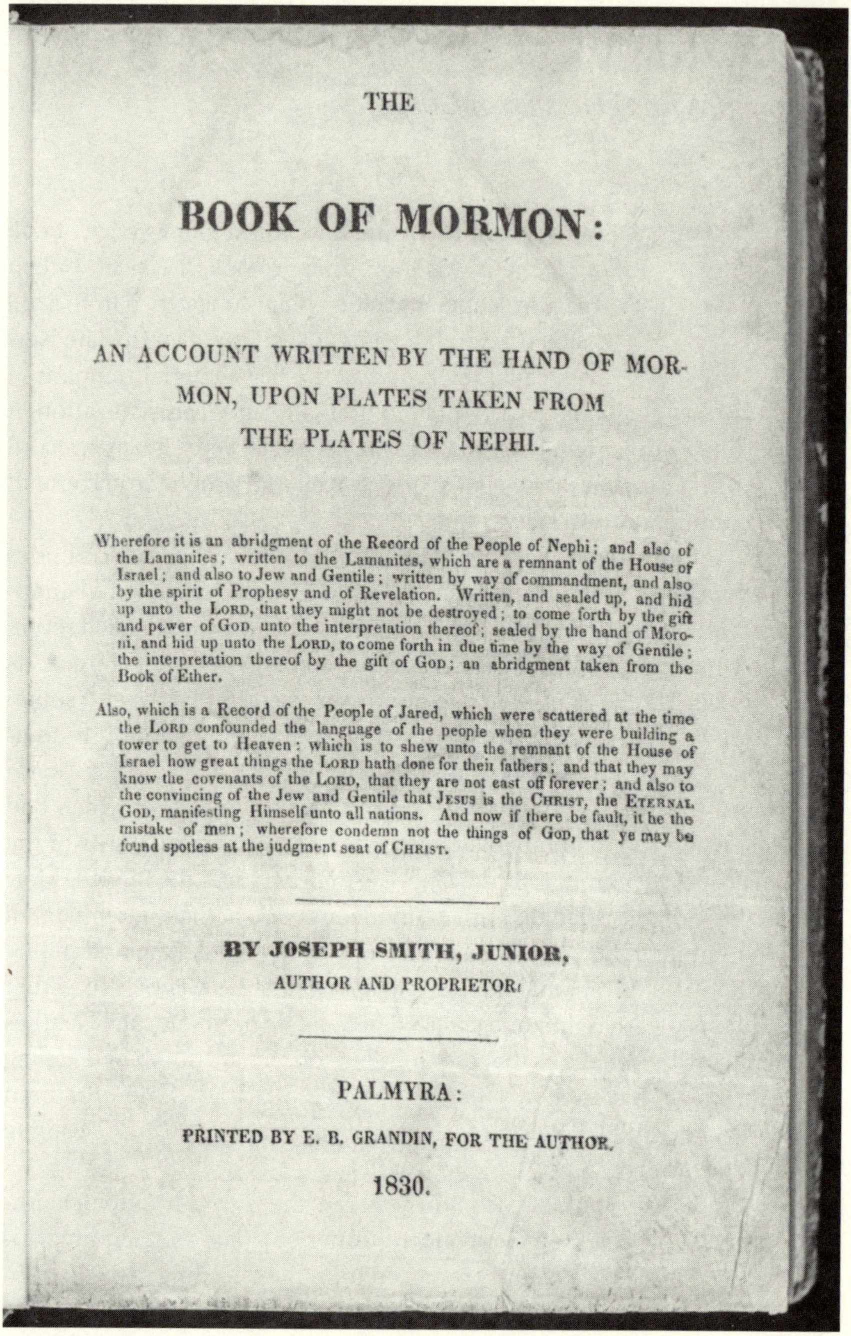

THE

BOOK OF MORMON:

AN ACCOUNT WRITTEN BY THE HAND OF MOR-MON, UPON PLATES TAKEN FROM THE PLATES OF NEPHI.

Wherefore it is an abridgment of the Record of the People of Nephi; and also of the Lamanites; written to the Lamanites, which are a remnant of the House of Israel; and also to Jew and Gentile; written by way of commandment, and also by the spirit of Prophesy and of Revelation. Written, and sealed up, and hid up unto the LORD, that they might not be destroyed; to come forth by the gift and power of GOD unto the interpretation thereof; sealed by the hand of Moro-ni, and hid up unto the LORD, to come forth in due time by the way of Gentile; the interpretation thereof by the gift of GOD; an abridgment taken from the Book of Ether.

Also, which is a Record of the People of Jared, which were scattered at the time the LORD confounded the language of the people when they were building a tower to get to Heaven: which is to shew unto the remnant of the House of Israel how great things the LORD hath done for their fathers; and that they may know the covenants of the LORD, that they are not cast off forever; and also to the convincing of the Jew and Gentile that JESUS is the CHRIST, the ETERNAL GOD, manifesting Himself unto all nations. And now if there be fault, it be the mistake of men; wherefore condemn not the things of GOD, that ye may be found spotless at the judgment seat of CHRIST.

BY JOSEPH SMITH, JUNIOR,

AUTHOR AND PROPRIETOR.

PALMYRA:

PRINTED BY E. B. GRANDIN, FOR THE AUTHOR.

1830.

Fig. 1.1. Title page of the Book of Mormon, 1830. (Courtesy of the Church Archives, the Church of Jesus Christ of Latter-day Saints)

the nation's founding fathers.[4] In this sense, the Book of Mormon's American focus is not surprising. Its prophetic description of the American Revolution as the fulfillment of divine will and the American continent as the "choice land above all other lands" can be read as overtly nationalistic.[5]

Yet the Book of Mormon's claims of America as the Promised Land present themselves as much more ancient and much more audacious than those of America's incipient civil religion. To the antebellum United States, and soon to many other nations around the world, when the Book of Mormon went on sale in E. B. Grandin's print shop in Palmyra, New York, on March 6, 1830, the text introduced a radical new reading of the nation's past. Not only did the new gospel include America as a historical site of early Christianity, but it moved the center of Christian history away from the Old World and onto the New.[6] The Book of Mormon also introduced a new reading of the role that America, and the people who inhabit it, would play in the coming millennium.

The Book of Mormon thus had a past and a future that its first readers had to contend with. And this past and future influenced the evolution of Mormon conceptions of race during the movement's first century. The Book of Mormon's past included the two main populations that dominate the Book of Mormon's pre-Columbian historical narration: the God-fearing, civilized, and white-skinned Nephites and their unbelieving, cursed, and dark-skinned cousins, the Lamanites. These two often-belligerent communities descended from one family of Israelites—Lehi, his wife, Sariah, and their children, who, the Book of Mormon claims, fled to America six centuries before Jesus's birth. The Book of Mormon's future included the Lamanites, or more specifically, their "Indian" descendants. This future did not include the Nephites, whom at the end of the Book of Mormon's history, the Lamanites slaughtered down to the last man. This future also included the Gentiles—the Book of Mormon's first modern-day recipients who were called to restore the "fulness [sic] of the gospel" in human history's latter days.[7]

And yet, the Book of Mormon had a particular present, too. That is, Mormonism's foundational scripture both reflected and departed from the antebellum intellectual and theological world from which it emerged. This is particularly important in relation to how, in the nineteenth century, theology shaped categories of racial difference and created taxonomies and hierarchies of white, black, and red Americans. As such, any discussion of Mormonism and race must begin with a study of the Book of Mormon and how the scripture shaped the interrelated themes of race, literacy, and the racialization of the writing of history in early Mormonism.

First, however, it is critical to state plainly that the Book of Mormon's pre-Columbian American history contains neither "black" Africans nor "white" Europeans. Yet because Americans have long viewed race as a black-white binary, readers of the Book of Mormon have often understood the Nephites to signify white Europeans, while Lamanites have served as stand-ins for dark-skinned people of African descent.[8] In the end of the Book of Mormon's narrative, the Nephites are slaughtered by the Lamanites, who, the Book of Mormon claims, would become the Native Americans, "a dark, and loathsome, and a filthy people." They would be scattered to the four corners of the continent and spend the next millennium living as savage heathens.[9] Yet even with such anti-Lamanite/Indian rhetoric, the Book of Mormon never describes the Lamanites or their supposed Indian descendants as "red" skinned. One might expect such language from a book purporting to contain the true origin story of America's Native peoples and published the same year President Andrew Jackson celebrated the culmination of removing the "red men" east of the Mississippi to "make room" for the westward march of "whites."[10] What's more, even the terms "black" or "blackness" are applied explicitly to skin color only twice in the Book of Mormon (2 Nephi 5:21, 26:33).

To be sure, the Book of Mormon's racial hermeneutic equates whiteness with righteousness, civilization, and Christianity. It defines blackness as heathenism, apostasy, and savagery. Yet this American scripture's racialism is more complicated and more interesting than readings that attempt to map the nation's typical racial binary onto it. Doing so flattens this multivalent text to one single note of white supremacy. In the Book of Mormon, the differences between black and white—between Lamanite and Nephite—are *first* interior in nature and *second* projected as outward appearance. As such, the study of race in the Book of Mormon is not the study of static phenotype. It is the study of dynamic narratology. It is less about skin and more about stories—stories about how racial differences came to be in the past and how such racial differences can be overcome in the future.

For its earliest adopters, the Book of Mormon presented a theology of what I call "white universalism." The text's universalistic missionary mandate to take the restored gospel to "all nations, kindreds, tongues, and people" provided the opportunity for all humankind to participate in the restoration of Christ's one true church in the last days before his ultimate return.[11] Even America's much-maligned Native people—the descendants of the Book of Mormon antihero, Laman, whose dark skin marked them off from the rest of humanity—could be, and perhaps inevitably would be, restored to the original, white human family. (And by implication, the supposed descendants of the Bible's perfidious Cain and Ham were also included in this potential restoration.) Yet within the Book of Mormon, white universalism proves to be less universal than it portends. Ironically, the failure of this white universalism is rooted in the limitations of whiteness as a universal racial category, a reality of which the Book of Mormon itself seems to be aware.

An American Gospel

In A.D. 384, Mormon is old and tired. The last of the Nephite military generals finds himself in the land of Cumorah. There, once again, he is preparing to fight his bloodthirsty enemies and distant kin, the Lamanites.[12] The seventy-four-year-old Mormon has spent a half century in continuous warfare with the Lamanites. These conflicts have reduced the once great Nephite people—rulers of civilizations that rivaled the great cities of the Mediterranean antiquity—to refugees, fleeing from savage Lamanite hordes bent on their annihilation.[13]

Vastly outnumbered, Mormon knows that the Nephites would make their last stand at Cumorah. Yet before this decisive battle, instead of sharpening his sword, Mormon sits down to write a history of both the Nephite and Lamanite peoples.[14] For the good of future generations, Mormon composes this millennium-long saga of faith found, faith lost, and faith found again. He etches these faith-promoting histories on golden plates, which his son, Moroni, later buries atop the Hill Cumorah. More than fifteen hundred years later these plates would be unearthed, translated from the reformed Egyptian in which Mormon writes the history, and then mass-produced as a book that would bear his name.[15]

To compose his history, Mormon has a lot of material to work with. For hundreds of years, Mormon's Nephite ancestors collected a vast archive of epistles, sermons, histories both sacred and secular, prophecies, poems, and apocalypses. These records were engraved on what were collectively called the "plates of Nephi," named after their original author. With each passing generation, a divinely appointed Nephite was chosen to safeguard the plates and continue to add to them so that generations to follow could remember God's providential hand in the Nephites' unfolding history.[16] Centuries later, before his own death, Mormon entrusts the plates to his son, Moroni, the last Nephite to survive the genocide of his people. Yet it is Mormon who takes on the task of sifting through this large archive. From this archival collection, he creates a carefully edited, purpose-driven narrative: to convince future readers that, for the sake of their salvation, they should accept this particularly American gospel.[17]

Mormon begins by borrowing directly from the history left by Nephi.[18] The favored son of Lehi and Sariah, members of the Israelite tribe of Manasseh, Nephi left a record of his family's exodus from Israel. Around 600 B.C., Nephi explains, his family journeyed by boat across the sea to the New World, which he never explicitly calls "America." Instead, echoing the first generations of Anglo-American settlers, Nephi calls the continent both a "wilderness" and the "promised land."[19] Also like the English Puritans, this exodus is done under duress but guided by providence. God prompts the faithful Lehi to take his wife and children out of Israel to avoid the persecution of faithless Jews and before the Babylonians destroy Jerusalem.[20]

Within the first generation after their arrival in the New World, Lehi's family splits into two rival factions. Lehi's elder sons Laman and Lemuel become jealous that God chose their younger brother Nephi to lead this new Israelite American people. Together, Laman and Lemuel conspire to kill Nephi. But God foils the plot. He warns Nephi to flee deeper into the American wilderness with his family and the families of his brothers who remain loyal to him. This new "people of Nephi" become successful farmers and ranchers. With seeds brought from Jerusalem, they plant fields and raise "flocks, and herds, and animals of every kind." They also erect cities and construct temples, the first built to resemble Solomon's Temple. At the same time, like their supposed Indian descendants, the Lamanites become nomadic hunters, "an idle people, full of mischief and subtlety." For their failure to recognize God's appointed prophet on earth, God curses them. Whereas the Nephites are "white, and exceedingly fair and delightsome," the Lord's curse causes "a skin of blackness to come upon" the Lamanites.[21]

This establishes the cultural divisions—often, though not exclusively, manifested as racial divisions—that dominate the Book of Mormon narrative. For most of the next six centuries, Mormon describes a cyclical pattern similar to that of the Nephites' Hebraic ancestors. As the Nephites strive to uphold the Abrahamic covenant and live by Mosaic law, their increasing prosperity and power lead to periods of class divisions and spiritual degeneracy, followed by cycles of repentance and the rebuilding of godly kingdoms. As for the Lamanites, they are most often portrayed as a wicked, idolatrous people who constantly war against their more faithful kin.

Because it is a "gospel of Christ," the central event of the Book of Mormon is Christ's mission to America. During his three-day sojourn in the New World, Christ is very busy. He teaches the Nephites his gospel message—of repentance from sin, of obedience to the Heavenly Father's will, and of faith in his atoning sacrifice. He preaches the Sermon on the Mount. He speaks the Beatitudes. He teaches the Lord's Prayer. He ordains his twelve American disciples and teaches them how to ordain other priests and teachers. These twelve disciples then establish a Christian church in America.[22] Christ also proclaims that the gospel he leaves behind in the Americas contains essential gospel teachings that are not contained in the Bible. To be sure, faithful apostles of Christ originally wrote the "fulness of the gospel" into the Old World's Bible. Yet in the centuries to come, this Bible will be passed from one inept or unfaithful translator to the next. Along the way, it will be stripped of its "most plain and precious parts." Christ explains that he has come to deliver to the Nephites that which is essential for salvation but will be lost in the Old World Bible.[23] Christ therefore instructs his Nephite disciples to make an archive of his New World mission, to write "these things which ye have seen and heard" so that they may be preserved in their purest form.[24] In doing so, the New World, not the Old, becomes the more reliable repository of the true Christian past and future. This purer gospel will be "hid up," only "to come forth unto the Gentiles" centuries later.[25]

During his time in the New World, the resurrected Christ ministers directly to the Nephites. Yet his message of universal salvation also leads to the conversion of large numbers of Lamanites. For two hundred years after Christ's ascension into heaven, the Lamanites and Nephites live together as Christians. They are so unified in their faith that all racial and cultural differences disappear.[26] Yet, the final chapter of the saga that Mormon narrates does not end with peace and piety. "In the two hundred and thirty first year," Mormon writes, "a great division among the people [occurs]," in which Lehi's progeny return to their respective original roles. Whereas many Nephites remain "true believers in Christ," the cursed Lamanites "wilfully rebel against the gospel of Christ." The once-again-wicked Lamanites teach their children not only to hate New World Christianity but also, once again, to hate their Nephite kin.[27]

Finally, in a reversal of the fate of their supposed Indian descendants at the hands of the Anglo-Americans a millennium later, the Lamanites engage in a campaign of Nephite genocide. During this reign of terror, the Lamanites reveal what is perhaps their inborn hatred for civilized Christianity. They not only slaughter the Nephite warriors but also sacrifice them "unto idol gods." The Lamanites make special targets of the Nephites who refuse to "deny the Christ."[28] As such, the Lamanites show that they intend not only to lay waste to the bodies of the Nephites but also to eradicate the hallmarks of Nephite civilization. They destroy the New World Christian church and burn down Nephite towns and cities.[29] Mormon even worries that the very plates that he has been charged with protecting at the cost of his life "[might] fall into the hands of the Lamanites (for the Lamanites would destroy them)."[30]

After the Lamanites hunt down Mormon and a handful of Nephite survivors, it falls to the last surviving Nephite, Mormon's son, Moroni, to narrate the end of "the sad tale of the destruction of my people." Yet, like his father, Moroni writes that his purpose in recording this history is not to curse the Lamanites. Instead, Moroni remains hopeful that "my brethren, the Lamanites in some future day" will read these sacred records. And when they do, Moroni hopes that they will accept the invitation contained within them to accept Christ's offer of salvation.[31]

Restoration and Whiteness

That Moroni's exhortation is addressed to the Lamanites is important. The Nephites do not keep this sacred record for their own posterity. They have none. After Moroni's death in A.D. 421, the Nephite people become extinct. And yet the fact that Moroni names his future Lamanite readers "my brethren" suggests that, although the differences between Lamanite and Nephite prove to be far-reaching for the history of pre-Columbian American Christianity, these differences are, in the long term, superficial. They are literally and figuratively only skin deep. Moroni and Mormon write the Book of Mormon so that in the last days before Christ's ultimate return, their brethren, the Lamanites can read it, repent, and be restored to God. Returning to the faith of their fathers will also restore them to the original, white human family. The curses that once marked them off as inferior will be removed.

Still the question remains, how does this restoration come about? The Book of Mormon teaches that the Lamanites do not restore themselves. In fact, Mormon foresees that, in the interlude between the end of the Book of Mormon history and the text's modern-day restoration, the surviving "seed" of the Lamanites "scatter" throughout the Promised Land. They divide further into tribes who war with one another. In short, they become American Indians: "a dark, a filthy, a loathsome people, beyond the description of . . . even that which hath been among the Lamanites."[32]

For the first few centuries after their own exodus to the New World, the Anglo-American Gentiles will add to the suffering and depravity of the Indians. Both Nephi and Mormon foresee this. They prophesy that the Gentiles will scatter the Indians farther afield from "the land of [the Lamanites'] inheritance."[33] Not coincidentally, the Book of Mormon was published in 1830, the same year the U.S. government approved President Jackson's

Indian Removal Act, forcing many Native Americans from their ancestral homelands. And yet the Gentiles—or at least those Gentiles willing to believe—play a central role in the restoration of the Lamanites to the faith of their forefathers. To be sure, the Book of Mormon reflects the standard antebellum view that the Indians are, by nature, belligerent savages. Yet the Book of Mormon also teaches that the believing Gentiles—who will be the first to read the Book of Mormon, understand its great worth, and, based on its mandates, restore Christ's true church in America—will also look beyond the Indians' current depraved state. In his prophecies, Nephi foretells of a time when the Gentiles who accept the Book of Mormon will also accept the Lord's commandment not to see the Indians simply as a hindrance to the providential westward expansion of the United States' territory, as did many white American political and religious leaders.[34]

During the last days before Christ's return, these believing Gentiles will restore the Indians to the knowledge of their true Israelite identity. These Gentiles will "gather" and unite the various Indian tribes into one people and care for them as "children."[35] Through this paternal care the Indians will become civilized Christians, capable of joining with their white Gentile brethren to form one covenant people. At that time, not only will "the scales of darkness . . . begin to fall from their eyes." Nephi also foresees that "many generations shall not pass away among them" before the Lamanites, too, become "a white and a delightsome people."[36] According to Nephi, when Christ makes his final return to earth at the end of history, he will find his church restored. And its membership rolls will be filled with a people unified under one Christian covenant. The racial assimilation will be so complete that perhaps even Christ will not be able to differentiate Gentile from Lamanite.

As such, the Book of Mormon's past matches its prophesied future. The lessons of religious and racial reconciliation in America's pre-Columbian Christian history correspond with the white universalism prophesied for the millennium to come. Racial divisions are not permanent, or at least they need not be. The racial and cultural differences between Gentiles and Indians, as they had been between Nephites and Lamanites, will prove to be "temporal" and temporary.[37]

Race, Lineage, and the Legacy of the "Second Fall"

The New and Old World gospels agree that all men and women are heirs to Adam and Eve's fall, resulting from the first human family's sin against God.[38] Likewise, paralleling the centuries-old belief that dark-skinned Africans descend from the Bible's Cain and Ham, whose curses resulted from what antebellum racial theorists called "a second fall" brought about by sins against their family members, the Book of Mormon also describes sins against the family, which also result in a curse. The physical manifestation of this curse is dark skin.[39]

In its assertion of monogenesis human origins and in its assumption that dark skin results from twice-fallen ancestors, the Book of Mormon was standard fare in the antebellum United States. In this sense, the Book of Mormon bears the markings of its nineteenth-century "translator," including the linguistic and cultural assumptions about the hierarchies of the races and the taxonomies of these races' ancient origins. Joseph Smith and many of his early followers accepted the notion that the supposed white descendants of Noah's sons and daughters Japheth and Shem were culturally, intellectually, and spiritually superior to the black sons and daughters of Ham.[40] The Book of Mormon does not directly comment on the curse of Ham. Yet its own hermeneutic of race reflects this equivalency of whiteness with humanity—or at least with humanity as it is fully realized—and accursedness with apostasy and depravity.

The first Nephi writes that the Lamanites' curses of "blackness" result from their "iniquity." The first such iniquitous act is Laman's Cainlike attempt to kill Nephi, which stems from Laman's envious rejection of God's choice to name Nephi as the prophetic and political successor to their father.[41] In response, God causes "a skin of blackness to come upon [the Lamanites]." Echoing nineteenth-century social and legal taboos against miscegenation, the Lord hopes that such a demarcation will prevent confusion—and mating—between the righteous and wicked. Black skin is intended to make the Lamanites less "enticing" to Nephi's "white, and exceedingly fair and delightsome" descendants. The Lord goes so far as to warn the Nephites that any progeny produced "of him that mixeth with their [the Lamanites'] seed . . . shall be cursed with the same cursing."[42]

This curse divides Lehi's family into distinct racial and cultural lineages. However, the Book of Mormon presents its own set of assumptions about the origin and destiny of race as a category of human division. And these assumptions helped define early Mormons' hermeneutic of restoration. The Book of Mormon diverges from many nineteenth-century biblically and, increasingly, biologically based racial theories that presented race as an immutable category of human division. Mormonism's foundational text teaches that race is not destiny. When Christ came to America, his church established peace and prosperity for all. The universal gospel created a just, equitable, and unified American Christian society. There were no "rich and poor, bond and free, but they were all made free, and partakers of the heavenly gift." Economic and spiritual parity led to the end of racial distinctions. For two centuries after Christ's New World mission, differences between black and white disappeared altogether. There were no more "Lamanites, nor any manner of Ites; but there were one, the children of Christ." Lamanites and Nephites unified to create one raceless (white) Christian people.[43]

Yet the Book of Mormon is not fully committed to its own faith in the potential of religious and racial restoration of all of Adam's progeny. The return of the Lamanites at the end of the Book of Mormon points to another critical, perhaps even defining feature of the Mormon hermeneutic of race. The sins against the family that Cain, Ham, and Laman commit create "lineages," which the early Latter-day Saints would come to understand as having distinct origins as well as distinct destinies. And although the Book of Mormon teaches that these curses can be removed, that the Lamanite Christians could not abide Christ's gospel message through the generations suggests that the legacy of the curse placed on the first generation of Lehi's rebellious children—which created the divide between the Lamanite and Nephite lineages—was not eradicated. Some two hundred years after Christ's departure, the Lamanites return to their original depravity. Just as they "were taught to hate the children of Nephi from the beginning" of the Book of Mormon's history, Mormon writes that at the end of this saga, these reconstituted Lamanites again "were taught to hate the children of God."[44]

Inchoate in the Book of Mormon, this idea of all but eternal lineages developed gradually during the first decades of Mormon history, and it did so in response to historical contingencies. Such contingencies included failed Lamanite missions, great success among certain white "Gentile" populations, and ever-increasing persecution from other populations of Gentiles who accused the Mormons of disrupting racial hierarchies by marketing their faith to Native Americans and some African Americans. However, for the most part the Book of Mormon presents an expansive view of the possibility for the redemption of all humankind, including the restoration of the racially marginalized to full covenant with the rest of the white human family. The Book of Mormon understands whiteness to be the original and universal racial category.[45] At least compared to their perfidious offspring, Adam was white, Noah was white, and Lehi was white. Their sons—Cain, Ham, and Laman—sinned against their families, the punishment for which was a curse of blackness on their progeny. Yet the Book of Mormon provides a vision for the religious and racial restoration of this fractured human family. When dark-skinned people accept Christ's offer of salvation, their curse is removed. As such, within the Book of Mormon's hermeneutic of restoration whiteness becomes an aspirational identity, which even those cursed with blackness can achieve.

Whiteness and Literacy

Whiteness signifies humanity in a state of accord with both the commandments of God and the cultural norms of man. As such whiteness is the racial category that is, ironically, empty of race. And yet whiteness— as much as blackness—is pregnant with meaning. In the Book of Mormon, blackness signifies cursed, idolatrous nomads who hunt beasts of prey, steal cattle and crops from more civilized peoples, and wage war against them. Whiteness signifies pious farmers and ranchers who build cities and temples and erect walls to keep dark-skinned marauders out.[46]

Perhaps most consequently, whiteness also signifies literacy: the ability to read and remember the history of a people's forefathers as well as to write new histories and add to an ever-growing communal archive.[47] Literacy is also fundamental to religious and racial restoration. At least according to the Book of Mormon's Nephite narrators, the Lamanites cannot or do not keep a record of their own.[48] Thus they forget America's ancient Christian past. They display their antipathy toward this past by destroying all traces of this ancient American Christian civilization.

All traces but one. Buried atop the Hill Cumorah, the Plates of Nephi survived as a forgotten testament to the rise and fall of the various branches of Lehi's offspring. Because of the Nephites' ability to leave a written record of their history and prophecies, this testament did not stay forgotten. Instead Joseph Smith, with the aid of the Angel Moroni, unearthed the plates, translated, and published them as the Book of Mormon. Though they are all long dead, because white-skinned Nephites were literate, their voices can be heard in the latter days. Because they were literate, white-skinned Gentile believers read these voices in a text that they believed restored the plain and precious essentials to the Christian gospel.[49] The Book of Mormon thus becomes the "fulness" of this gospel. It contains the knowledge capable of ending belligerent religious and racial divisions within the human family and restoring this family to its original raceless, white form. Literacy thus unlocks the door to this restored Christian gospel. And what follows naturally from acceptance of it is whiteness.

In a sense, Christ's New World mission is itself a literacy promotion campaign. When Christ gives the Nephites the essentials of the gospel he also commands them to "write the things which I have told you."[50] He wants to make sure that this gospel is remembered so that in the latter days it can be restored to the world in an accurate form. Christ even describes himself as imprinted with the universal offer of salvation from the Lord to humanity. Christ is the logos, the word made flesh. "I bear record," Christ proclaims, "that the Father commandeth all men, everywhere, to repent and believe in me." As the bearer of the record, Christ's mission is to guarantee that he *as text* is preserved in the New World gospel for the sake of "future generations."[51]

Christ also proclaims that the Lord will give to his people "a sign" to mark the beginning of the latter days. But this sign—the Book of Mormon—will come first to the American Gentiles because they are literate and the Indians are not. The Gentiles will read it, repent, and be baptized into Christ's true church, which they will restore in America. Then they will return the book to the Indians. And together, Indian and Gentile—the former of who will reclaim their place in the covenant and the latter of whose faith will allow them to be "numbered among" the restored covenantal people—will build New Jerusalem in America. And from inside this righteous city, they will await Christ's return.[52]

The Narrator's Prerogative

At the end of the Book of Mormon, Mormon and Moroni's description of the Lamanites' increasingly "dark" and "loathsome" state puts the Nephites' whiteness into greater relief. The last two of the book's narrators present themselves as literate, forgiving, forward-thinking Christians. Even though the Lamanites seek to kill them, they write for the sake of the descendants of their illiterate, depraved Lamanite "brethren."[53]

From Moroni's perspective, it is the Nephites' responsibility to write for the Lamanites. Part of Laman's initial rebellion against Nephi is to refuse to "hearken unto . . . [the] words" of God's appointed prophet. The cost of this perfidy is not only to be racially marked off from the rest of Lehi's family. The Lamanites are also "cut off from the presence of the Lord." This means that for the most part, the Lamanites are made deaf to God's commandments. They must rely on the Nephites to record the knowledge that passes between heaven and earth. This also means that the Lamanites are made functionally dumb. The Lamanites are unable to speak, or at least unable to speak so that what they say is remembered. They cannot directly add their own voices and stories to the records that would become the Book of Mormon. The result is that the Nephite record keepers have control over what gets recorded on the Plates of Nephi and, as such, how the Book of Mormon story gets told.[54]

Moroni, Mormon, and Nephi do not hide their enjoyment of what we might call a "narrator's prerogative."[55] They state directly that the Book of Mormon is an "abridgment" of all that they have seen and all that they and their fathers and their fathers' fathers have written.[56] According to the book's narrators, the fact that the Book of Mormon is not comprehensive—that it includes almost exclusively the voices and stories of the Nephites—is not due to some racial or ethnic antipathy. Nor is it in the service of brevity. The "abridgment" Smith published in 1830 was almost six hundred pages long. Instead, God's divinely appointed historians narrate with a purpose: to create a faith-promoting history intended to guide future readers toward the acceptance of the sacred words of God made manifest in the personage of Christ and made definitive in the Book of Mormon.

How these narrators choose to write this history reveals the message that they intend their readers to take away. For example, Mormon does not lay complete blame for the annihilation of the Nephites at the feet of the Lamanites. After all, it is in the Lamanites' nature, passed down from their progenitor Laman, to reject God and to hate their more righteous kin. Instead, after two hundred years of peace and equality, the Nephites, too, revert back to their old ways. Their increased wealth leads them to divide themselves "into classes . . . and began to deny the true church of Christ."[57]

More still, Mormon writes that the Nephites' degeneration continues to the point where the distinctions between "Nephite" and "Lamanite" collapse. "Many of our brethren have deserted over unto the Lamanites," writes Mormon.[58] Save for Mormon's closest kin—the direct descendants of the original Nephi and the keepers of the Nephite records—at the end of the Book of Mormon narrative, the boundary lines between the Lamanites and many Nephites blur to the point of nonrecognition.[59] A belief that is perpetuated throughout early Mormon history, the Book of Mormon teaches that because race is mutable both racial progress *and* declension is possible. If those normally considered "white" reject the gospel, then they, too, can be cursed and lose their claim to whiteness.

The Nephites' disloyalty to their own kin leads to their degeneracy into Lamaniteness. The shock of this declension is so profound that it renders Mormon speechless and unable to record what he has seen: "Yea, tongue cannot tell, neither can it be written."[60] Here Mormon excludes certain parts of what he has witnessed before these events become recorded in order to spare future readers from the "great sorrow because of the wickedness of [the Lamanites and the Nephites]."[61] Mormon does not wish to create a complete representation of a millennium's worth of history. His prerogative is to forget much of the past in service of the future.

Mormon believes that, in the end, all this forgetting will be palliative. This abridged and redacted history will be unearthed when the Gentiles rule America. Then it will be translated, typeset, and printed as a book. These Gentiles will bring this book to the Lamanites. In learning about its content, perhaps even learning to read it themselves, the Lamanites' Indian descendants will rediscover who they really are. They will reconcile with the Lord and build up a New Jerusalem with believing Gentiles. But according to Mormon, such a future can occur only if much of the past is forgotten, especially the savage crimes that the Lamanites themselves committed.[62] The import of the Book of Mormon is not that it is a complete, unbiased record. Instead, the narrators intend that the Book of Mormon serve as a usable past to aid the earliest leaders of the Mormon dispensation in accomplishing their restorationist project.[63]

The Book of Mormon's purpose thus is to help the Lamanites restore themselves to the covenants of their Israelite forefathers. And if the Book of Mormon pattern holds true, these restored Lamanites will unify with the white-skinned Gentiles who bring the book to them in the latter days of history. Together they will become one people, "the children of Christ." Like the converted Lamanites reconciling with the Nephites during the two centuries after Christ's first visit to the New World, in the days before Christ's ultimate return, all "manner of Ites" will disappear as whiteness becomes universal among the Latter-day Saints.[64]

Silent Voices Speak Volumes

This American gospel, which Nephi, Mormon, Moroni, and Joseph Smith Jr. created together, is filled with lessons. There are explicit lessons about forgetting and remembering the Lord's commandments. There are explicit lessons about how to restore Christ's true church and how to create a community of Saints who will gather as one people to await the second coming of Christ. There are also more implicit lessons about race as a mutable category of human division—a schism in the human family created by sin but surmountable through faith in a gospel made universally available to all by Christ's atoning sacrifice.

Still, there are other even more implicit lessons that have implications for how early Mormons came to read and write about race. The segregation of the Book of Mormon's historical record as the domain of white, literate members of Lehi's family presents itself as the natural result of dark-skinned Lamanite illiteracy. And it is just as natural that the white-skinned narrators value the racialized voices and stories of some over others. After all, if the guardians of the Plates of Nephi are also God's chosen prophets and historians, then their prerogative on the history of pre-Columbian American Christianity naturally carries the imprimatur of divine authority.

Yet even if they are divinely called, prophets of God are still human. Moroni prophesizes that, because of "our weakness in writing," many Gentiles who first hear of the Book of Mormon more than a millennium later "will mock" it. On the title page, Mormon writes, "If there be a fault [in the book], it be the mistake of men."[65] Yet specifically, the fact that Lamanite voices are all but silent in the Book of Mormon raises critical questions about these Nephite historians' reliability as narrators.[66] Comprehensiveness, even accuracy, is not their main motivation. Promoting faith is. But undergirding this motivation is the unexamined assumption that white, male storytellers tell the most useful stories. This assumption moves backward and forward in Mormon history and in *the writing* of Mormon history—backward through the Book of Mormon itself and forward through the recording of Mormon history that begins with the publication of the Book of Mormon, the "sign" of the advent of the Mormon dispensation.[67]

The dearth of diversity of racial perspectives in the Book of Mormon, not to mention the perspectives of women, who are even more absent than the Lamanites, means that the Book of Mormon as a restorative lens has distinct blind spots. Yet pointing out these blind spots is not the same as deconstructing the entire Mormon historical project. To the contrary, on the rare occasion when the voices of nonwhite and female Mormons are included in the narrative, they often substantiate the theological and cultural foundations of Mormonism, including the connections among whiteness, literacy, and the innate authority of white Mormon men.[68]

The Lamanite and the Indian

This observation, of course, raises another set of historical problems that require examination and critique. Ironically, the start of such a project can take its cues from the Book of Mormon itself. In its complex, even contradictory representation of (certain) Lamanites and their supposed Indian descendants, the Book of Mormon highlights the dangers that the exclusion of marginalized voices and histories from the Mormon archive presents to the accurate recording of sacred history, even the accurate recording of the gospel of Christ itself.

More often than not, in the Book of Mormon the Lamanite is a foil. For the book's narrators, he is a dark-skinned set piece against which the civilized, white-skinned Nephite can be drawn. Instead of building cities, cultivating crops, and erecting temples like their more righteous cousins the Nephites, the Lamanites are so savage that they even drink the blood of the "beasts of prey" that they hunt in the wilds of America. They are naked, "save it were skin, which girded about their loins." Their own skin is "dark," a mark they carry as a reminder of their forefathers' "transgression and rebellion against their [Nephite] brethren."[69] Most importantly, even after Christ's intervention and their assimilation with the Nephites, the Lamanites prove to be unrepentant enemies of civilization and Christianity. They attack and destroy Nephite cities and sacrifice Nephite women and children to idols. They even try to destroy the Nephite records, the archive from which the Book of Mormon would be written.[70]

When it was published in 1830, the Book of Mormon's downwardly trending Indian was certainly nothing new to early American history or literature. As they marked the United States' ascent from a backwater set of disorganized colonies ruled by tyrannical absentee monarchs to the world's first modern republic with ambitions for empire, Anglo-American writers did so against a backdrop of further deterioration—and disappearance—of America's indigenous peoples.[71]

The English colonists' original promise was that they would bring uplift to the Indian in the form of fencerows, schoolhouses, and congregations. The Puritan John Eliot believed that the Indian who lived in English villages, raised English animals, wore English clothes, and read the English Bible would also confess his sins and submit himself to the waters of baptism. The "heathen" would all but disappear, and the "praying Indian," perhaps even the red Englishman, would emerge.[72] But many Anglo-Americans wrote that Indian violence against their settlements was irrefutable proof that the Indian was an unrepentant enemy of the propagation of religion and the progress of civilization. Historians of King Philip's War, for example, often highlighted the Indians' disdain for symbols of English Christianity. In his *A Narrative of the Troubles with the Indians* (1677), William Hubbard describes a scene in which colonial soldiers came on burned-out English houses. There they also found "a Bible newly torn, and the Leaves scattered about by the Enemy in Hatred."[73] Such accounts of Indian assaults against representations of English society parallel the Book of Mormon's descriptions of the Lamanites' near total success at razing all remnants of the Nephite civilization from the American continent. Mormon buries the Plates of Nephi on the Hill Cumorah to spare them the fate that would befall the Puritans' Bible.

When the English colonists became Americans in the late eighteenth century, many believed that their hard-won liberty was still under threat. But the main front of the war had shifted to the west, where the former Indian allies of the English continued to attack American frontier settlements.[74] Two years before the Book of Mormon was published, James Fenimore Cooper declared that the "noble savage," whom he so famously championed in his *Leatherstocking Tales*, was all but extinct. "As a rule, the red man disappears," Cooper wrote in *Notions of the Americans* (1828), "before the superior moral and physical influence of the white." The Indians were either forced westward, "deeper into the forest . . . [or] they become victims to the abuses of civilization, without ever attaining any of its moral elevation." Those few Indians who remained in Cooper's (and Joseph Smith's) Upstate New York were "all alike, a stunted, dirty and degraded race."[75]

However, in his *Address to the Whites*, delivered in Philadelphia's First Presbyterian Church in 1826, the Cherokee activist Elias Boudinot challenged the racial category of the "Indian" as a misrepresentation of certain Native people's success at raising themselves to the level of white Americans. "To those who are unacquainted with the manners, habits, and improvements of the Aborigines of this country, the term Indian is pregnant with ideas the most repelling and degrading." As such it should not be applied to such elevated "nations" like his own. After all, Boudinot argued that his Cherokee Nation, a people of letters, Christianity, and laws, had become more white—that is, more civilized—than "Indian."[76]

Yet the Book of Mormon's Lamanite is not quite Boudinot's Cherokee, nor is he simply Cooper's Indian. Instead, the Lamanite identity is a paradox. The Lamanite both affirms and transcends the commonplace antebellum descriptions of Native Americans as an unredeemable race of red men, destined to be either isolated from the white man's civilization or exterminated. The Lamanites are depraved apostates. Yet they are also the "remnant" of a great Israelite people. The Lamanites are illiterate and ahistorical, "confounded" as to their own identity because they "harden their hearts" against the words of the Lord. Yet they are also heirs to an uncorrupted record of a long-lost gospel of Christ, and heirs to the covenant of history's "last day."[77]

Even within the Book of Mormon's historical narrative, the Lamanite racial identity is far from immutable. In the decades before Christ's arrival in the New World, the Lamanites' hard hearts soften toward the gospel, and the "more part" of the Lamanites becomes "a righteous people." In fact Lamanite virtue grows to the point that the spiritual hierarchy signified by the Book of Mormon's standard racialized categories is reversed. The Lamanites' "righteousness did exceed that of the Nephites, because of their firmness, and their steadfastness in the faith," writes Mormon. At the same time the Nephites "become hardened, and impenitent, and grossly wicked, insomuch that they did reject the word of God."[78]

"Samuel, the Lamanite"

And yet as the spiritual hierarchy gets inverted, do the Book of Mormon's typical racialized signifiers also change? In other words, do Lamanites become white and Nephites become black? An examination of the case of "Samuel, the Lamanite," a member of the righteous community of Lamanites that emerges in the decades before Christ's arrival in the New World, can help flesh out answers to this question. Paradoxically, in the Book of Mormon it is not a Nephite but Samuel who prophesizes most accurately about the coming of Christ and the meaning of his earthly mission, death, and resurrection.[79] It is also Samuel who most forcefully describes the source of the fault lines within the human family—the results of jealousy, greed, and pride, which most often manifest themselves as distinct racialized categories. Yet Samuel's case demonstrates that these categories do not always remain moored to their original equivalencies of Nephite to righteous and Lamanite to wicked. It is perhaps telling that Samuel does not write down his own prophecies. A white Nephite scribe does. This fact raises another set of questions about race, literacy, and the recording of history: What gets lost in this translation from oral to written? What gets remembered? And what falls into oblivion due to forgetfulness and due to the narrator's prerogative?

During his visit to America (around A.D. 34), the resurrected Christ examines the Nephites' sacred texts. And he finds them wanting. A significant lacuna exists in what was destined to become the Book of Mormon. Christ tells Nephi$_3$, one of Christ's New World disciples (and a direct descendant of the first Nephi, the progenitor of the Nephite people), to "bring forth the record which ye have kept."[80] Jesus Christ takes one look at the record and demands, where are the prophecies of "my servant, Samuel the Lamanite"? In a mocking tone, Christ's asks Nephi$_3$, "Were it not so" that Christ commanded Samuel to "testify" to the Nephites that Christ's atoning sacrifice is available not only to all people *everywhere* but also to all people in every *time*? In other words, Samuel prophesized that the faithful born before Jesus would not be left behind during history's final act simply because of their ill-timed birth. On the last of the latter days, their "graves shall be opened." And they, too, shall rise to the heavens with their fellow Saints.[81]

On behalf of Samuel, Christ rebukes the Nephites for not having "written this thing"—Samuel's prophecy—into the people's sacred archive. Christ's disciples respond to his upbraiding by telling him, "Yea, Lord, Samuel did prophesy according to thy words, and they were all fulfilled." The keeper of the records, Nephi₃, also acknowledges that because Christ reminded him, "Nephi remembered that this thing had not been written." Nephi₃ follows Christ's commandment to give proper place to Samuel's prophetic voice in the Nephite archive. Once it is written down and archived, Samuel's oral prophecy moves instantaneously from oblivion to the level of scriptures to be read and studied for eternity.[82] By ceding the authorial control of the Book of Mormon history to Samuel, Nephi₃ and Mormon also briefly cede control regarding one of the Book of Mormon's most important gospel messages—the power of Christ's universally available atoning sacrifice to overcome even the dictates of time—to a Lamanite. This lacuna is filled. This holy book is made whole. Samuel's prophecies become the center of the Book of Mormon, or at least the center in terms of the Book of Mormon's hermeneutic of race.[83]

"Because I Am a Lamanite"

Samuel's prophecies, now rightfully placed in the Book of Mormon's chronology, allow for a radical new reading of the normal Book of Mormon's racial hierarchy. Christ's intervention here invites readers to perform an intratextual hermeneutic. The reader pages back in the Book of Mormon and moves back in the chronological order of the Book of Mormon narration: from Christ's visit to the New World in A.D. 34 (3 Nephi) to Samuel's prophecies now inserted in the Nephite archive at around 6 B.C. (Helaman 13-16).[84] Here the reader finds Samuel, the Lamanite climbing atop the walls of Zarahemla, the Nephites' capital city. Once the seat of a great and faithful Nephite people, Zarahemla is now filled more with "wickedness and abominations" than with God's law. Samuel takes this high perch because the citizens of Zarahemla "would not suffer that he should enter the city."[85] Samuel is turned away because Zarahemla is a segregated city. Yet, as Samuel's prophecies indicate, perhaps Zarahemla is segregated based on degrees of righteousness as much as it is on shades of skin color. After all, the Lamanites have their own country, where "the more part of them," Mormon explains, "do observe to keep [the Lord's] commandments, and his statutes, and his judgments according to the law of Moses."[86]

Samuel's ascent atop the walls of Zarahemla signifies the culmination of the inversion of the Book of Mormon's normal racial hierarchies. Six centuries before his mission to Zarahemla, the fallout from Samuel's ancestor Laman's conspiracy to kill his brother Nephi establishes two distinct racialized lineages. The Nephites become the white-skinned keepers of the Abrahamic covenant while the Lamanites become cursed, dark-skinned, illiterate apostates. Yet in the half century before Christ comes to the New World, conversion among many Lamanites makes them "righteous," while the Nephites become wicked because they rejected "the word of God."[87] The signifying link between whiteness and righteousness created by the first Nephi's faithfulness, especially in stark contrast to the first Laman's wickedness, proves to be far from fixed.

From atop Zarahemla's walls, Samuel declares to the Nephites below that he has been sent on the Lord's errand. He brings to them the Lord's words, "which he doth put into my heart."[88] Through Samuel, the Lord warns the Nephites that Zarahemla will soon become "ripe for destruction." He prophesizes that at the moment of Jesus's crucifixion in the Old World, the New World's iniquitous cities will be leveled in a conflagration of fire.[89] God's wrath will come, Samuel explains, because the Nephites have made idols out of their riches. With the Lord absent from their city, "envyings, strifes, malice, persecutions, and murders, and all manner of iniquities" take root in Zarahemla. And for this, Samuel exclaims, the Lord curses the Nephites. Out of pride and greed, Laman sinned against God and his brethren. This "second fall" resulted in a curse manifested in dark skin. Likewise, out of pride and greed, the wicked Nephites turn against God and against their brethren—perpetrating acts of violence and economic inequality—for which they, too, are cursed, though the Book of Mormon does not specify a change in skin color.[90]

The majority of the Nephites of Zarahemla do not take kindly to a Lamanite calling them a "wicked . . . and perverse generation." Samuel recognizes the irony of God's messenger coming in what is typically understood as an accursed form: "And now, because *I am a Lamanite*, and have spoken unto you the words which the Lord hath commanded me, and because it was hard against you, ye are angry with me and do seek to destroy me, and have cast me out from among you."[91] Some Nephites do repent. Yet most fail to heed Samuel's warnings. Instead they hurl stones and shoot arrows at Samuel, though he remains unscathed atop the city's wall.[92] The Nephites' ethnocentrism, perhaps even racial antipathy, means that they reject the Lamanite messenger and the message that salvation will come through belief in Christ.

Can a Lamanite Prophet Be White?

The Nephites might have been God's chosen people in the past. But God's favor has, at least in Samuel's lifetime, passed to the Lamanites. This change in status raises the question of the racial identity of the two branches of Lehi's family. To put it plainly, does this inversion of the normal spiritual hierarchy lead to a change in skin color? Do the faithful Lamanites become "white and delightsome"? Likewise, do the cursed Nephites have "a skin of blackness [come] upon them"?

In the prelude to Samuel's prophecies, the Book of Mormon makes it clear that in the generations before Jesus's birth, Samuel and most of his Lamanite kin strictly keep "the commandments of God," while most—though not all—Nephites live "in great wickedness." The righteous Lamanites are the fruits of a handful of Nephite missionaries, in particular the direct descendants of the first Nephi and the caretakers of the Nephite archive. These Nephites help establish a "church of God" among the receptive Lamanites.[93] And within the church of God, doctrinal unity—"one faith and one baptism"—cuts across all divisions, knitting "hearts . . . together in unity and in love."[94]

The Book of Mormon consistently teaches that the church of God, and later the church of Jesus Christ, is universal. But when a Lamanite knits his heart together with righteous Nephites, does he still remain—racially as well as spiritually—a "Lamanite"? The Book of Mormon does not indicate the color of Samuel's skin when he scales the walls of Zarahemla. But in the interlude between Samuel's prophecies and Christ's arrival to the New World (between 6 B.C. and A.D. 34), Mormon writes that the Lamanites like Samuel who "had united" with the few righteous Nephites have their "curse . . . taken from them." Their children's "skin became white like unto the Nephites" and were even "called Nephites."[95]

In other words, a change of heart from wicked to righteous, the Book of Mormon teaches, leads to reconciliation and reunification of the races. Through conversion, the Lamanite can overcome his own Lamaniteness to form spiritual—and likely marital—covenants with the Nephites, which leads to an eventual whitening of skin. Within a few generations the cursed Lamanite completely disappears into the white, universal Nephite identity. Membership within the Book of Mormon's two racial divisions is mutable. The Lamanite and Nephite identities are outward racialized expressions of individuals' interior religious persuasions. Samuel is nominally a Lamanite when he preaches from atop the walls of Zarahemla, but perhaps only because his dark skin color has not caught up to his pure heart. Likewise, Samuel's wicked and prideful Nephite audience might still be white-skinned. But if the Lord had not leveled their cities and smote them at the moment of Jesus's death—as Samuel prophesied that the Lord would—their skin might have eventually turned black as a marker of their accursedness.[96]

Samuel, the Lamanite is rarely mentioned in the early Mormon archive.[97] Nevertheless, Samuel embodies the principles of Joseph Smith's early church and its hermeneutic of restoration. In the Book of Mormon's most idealized vision, it is not the white Gentiles who will lead the building up of New Jerusalem. Instead this responsibility and authority will pass to yet-to-be named Lamanite leaders. Like Samuel, these future leaders will transcend their own supposed racial limitations to rediscover who they are: lost and then found descendants of God's covenantal people, latter-day Lamanite Israelite prophets and priests of the New Jerusalem.

What's more, Samuel's case raises more questions—which I explore throughout much of the rest of this book—about how the Book of Mormon's hermeneutic of restoration played out in early Mormon history as its earliest "Gentile" adopters attempted to bring the book's message of (white) universalism first to the Lamanites and later to "all nations, kindreds, tongues, and people." If, as prophesied, dark-skinned descendants of the Lamanites accepted the Book of Mormon as gospel, would their increased righteousness lead to the whitening of their skin? And what of other cursed peoples, including people of African descent? Did they have a place in the newly restored church and newly mended white, universal human family? And finally, would white Latter-day Saints accept their formerly cursed, dark-skinned brethren as full partners in the creation of New Jerusalem?

How Words Become Scripture

Christ's commandment that Samuel's prophecies "should be written" into the records suggests that the Book of Mormon's narrators are aware of the need to include the voices of marginalized historical subjects in the Nephite archive. Or perhaps more accurately, Christ makes these ancient historians and their modern-day translator aware of this need. Yet Samuel's case also raises perhaps the most critical question about the historical archive as a place of racialized authority. What else have the Nephite archivists and historians omitted in the Plates of Nephi?

A careful reading suggests that there is no easy answer to this question. The Book of Mormon's narrators repeatedly remind their readers that the history they recount, and perhaps the racialized hermeneutic through which they recount this history, is of human origin. It is thus susceptible to human limitations and even failings. For example, the first Nephi does not claim to be an omniscient narrator. And his description of other figures is decidedly selective. Tellingly, Nephi does not treat his perfidious older brothers, Laman and Lemuel, as individuals. Even though he lived with them for more than thirty years, and thus must have had different interactions and relationships with them, Laman and Lemuel almost always appear in his telling of the family's history as a single, traitorous unit.[98] Instead of creating a comprehensive history with fully fleshed-out characterizations, Nephi states clearly that the history he leaves behind is meant to be faith promoting. He hopes that his words "speaketh of Jesus, and persuadeth [his readers] to believe in [Christ]," and "to do good."[99]

The same is true for the other two Book of Mormon narrators. Before his own demise, Mormon writes what is essentially an explanation of his own historical method—that he chooses what he believes are the most salient events and leaves out the rest. Mormon also writes with his "own hands" and based in large measure on the events he has seen with his "own eyes." As such, his perspective is embodied and limited. And understandably, for a man who has witnessed the brutal slaughter of hundreds of thousands of his Nephite people at the hands of Lamanites, his perspective is subjective.[100] In fact, Mormon completes his narrative after he, too, has been gravely wounded. His physical and mental state raises doubts about his reliability as the definitive narrator of the Nephite and Lamanite histories.[101]

It is unfruitful, and perhaps unfair, to hold the Book of Mormon narrators to standards of inclusive and balanced history writing to which they do not claim to aspire. Nevertheless, highlighting how and why the Book of Mormon falls short as a complete record of ancient America, as the case of Samuel, the Lamanite does, can be productive for scholars of Mormonism. The contested place Samuel occupies in the Book of Mormon provides lessons about how dark-skinned and other historically marginalized subjects are written (or not written) about in the narration of early Mormon history.

For example, beyond accusations of ethnocentrism on the part of the Nephites, one reason why one of Samuel's prophecies did not make it initially into the Nephite archive is that they are oral in nature. In 6 B.C., Samuel did not send a letter to the Nephites of Zarahemla to admonish them for their wickedness. Instead, Samuel "*spake* upon the walls of the city . . . [and] many . . . *heard* the words of Samuel."[102] To be sure, there are Nephite prophets in the Book of Mormon, not to mention the resurrected Christ himself, who do not write their own narratives. The spoken words of these historical figures are thus subjected to the editorial and narrative prerogative of the Nephite historians.[103] Yet Samuel's case is unique. No other prophet's words does Christ deem so important that he explicitly trumps the Nephite record keepers' authority to decide what gets written down and what does not. As such, the division between the oral and written archive highlights a division between "white" and "dark-skinned" history keeping. Because whites, be they Nephites, Puritans, or Mormon pioneers, control the means of the production of history—the written word, the printing press—whites control what gets recorded in the archive and thus remembered as history. Oral histories, if they survive, are deemed folktales, family lore, and given a second-class status as reliable archival sources for the writing of history.[104]

The Book of Mormon itself repeatedly highlights the importance of literacy as a key line of demarcation between Christian and unbeliever. The first Nephi writes that the Lord promised him "these things which I write shall be kept and preserved, and handed down unto my seed," and thus *not the seed* of his brother Laman—"from generation to generation."[105] King Benjamin (ca. 130 B.C.), the second of the great Nephite kings of Zarahemla, teaches his own sons "the language of his fathers" so that they can discern the recorded prophecies of their ancestors. According to Benjamin, literacy differentiates between the faithful Nephites and the faithless Lamanites. Benjamin explains to his sons, "Were it not for these things—which have been kept and preserved by the hand of God, that we might read and understand of his mysteries, and have dwindled in unbelief, and we should have been *like unto our brethren the Lamanites*, who know nothing concerning these things, or do not believe them when they are taught them."[106]

Were it not for the ability to read the histories of their fathers and to write their own, the Nephites would have become no better than the unbelieving Lamanites. Tellingly, the Nephites whose racial identities remain stable are figures like Benjamin—the direct descendants of the first Nephi who are charged with safeguarding the Nephite archive, which forms an unbroken chain of custody that is passed down through the generations all the way to Mormon and Moroni. Their proximity to this sacred family record, which they read and add to, inculcates them against the failings of pride, greed, and forgetfulness that led to the downfall of both the Lamanites and most Nephites.[107]

Literacy here is next to godliness. Literacy is also power. Those who control the written word get to narrate the losers and winners of war, to portray who is civilized or savage, heathen or Christian. We can and will ask these same questions about what—or who—gets excluded from the narration of Mormon history in the latter days. What racialized prerogatives do the all-white official record keepers of the Church of Jesus Christ of Latter-day Saints bring to the recording of the history of the early church? Likewise, what racialized prerogatives do the (all but) all white Mormon people—whose journal keeping and family history writing become performances of (white) Mormon identity—bring to the recording of the history of the early Mormon people?

Samuel, the Prophet on the Wall

Back to Samuel on the wall of Zarahemla. How can Samuel see so much more clearly the future of Jesus's birth, death, and resurrection than any of his white-skinned contemporaries, even better than the Nephite record keepers and historians who narrate the Book of Mormon? Perhaps the first way to answer this question is by way of comparison with other marginalized, antebellum prophets who were critical of American religious and political culture. To be sure, early Mormons believed that the Book of Mormon was an authentic, historical account of ancient Native American origins. Yet its 1830 publication means that the prophecies of Samuel, the Lamanite enter the antebellum world in the same period as, for example, the 1836 autobiography of the itinerant black Methodist preacher Jarena Lee. To substantiate her authority to preach and to challenge the prohibition against female ministers, Lee wrote that God directly called her to "Preach the Gospel." Such a divine calling served as assurance that she was not relying on her own abilities. Instead, God told her, "I will put words in your mouth, and will turn your enemies to become your friends."[108] Likewise, from the beginning of his testimonies, Samuel makes clear that he does not preach to the Nephites of Zarahemla using his own words. He uses the words of the Lord. Lee's and Samuel's self-ascribed humble (racial and gendered) positions make them particularly receptive vessels for the Lord's words. Their status as outcasts makes them uniquely qualified to speak for God, or more aptly to have God speak through them.

Yet a second way to understand Samuel's prophetic acumen is to assert that God chose Samuel as a prophet because of the particular point of view on American history that Samuel's racialized marginalization affords him.[109] Again one must proceed with caution when making comparisons between the ancient (and/or mythical) Samuel and other antebellum Native American authors. Still, Samuel is far from the only Native American who leverages his marginalized position to criticize white America's treatment of indigenous peoples. In his 1833 essay, "An Indian's Looking Glass for the White Man," the Pequot Methodist minister William Apess transforms the "Indians'" status as "the most mean, abject, miserable race of beings in the world" into a lens of self-reflection in which he can see clearly the causes of Indian degradation. And Apess implores his white readers to turn this mirror on themselves.[110]

Apess belongs to the literary lineage of Native American Christian converts who penned excoriating critiques of some of the very missionaries who brought them to Christianity. This includes Samson Occom, the Mohegan Presbyterian preacher and erstwhile cofounder of what would become Dartmouth College. Occom famously wrote in 1768 that when it comes to purposeful deceit, "pretended Christians are seven times worse than the Savage Indians."[111] In his 1826 *Address to the Whites*, Elias Boudinot argues that that Cherokees had demonstrated that they have achieved the standards of civilization long required by Anglo-Americans to covenant politically with white citizens. And yet the Republic had demonstrated its duplicity by insisting that Cherokees are still "Indians." Thus, like all other Indians, the Cherokee, too, must be removed from their ancestral lands.[112] Apess agreed with Occom and Boudinot.[113] When they take the "red" as well as "black" skin "as a pretext to keep [the Natives and black slaves] from our unalienable and lawful rights," white Christians in America prove themselves to be hypocrites who fail to recognize Native and African Americans as inherently like themselves—members of the universal family of the children of God.[114]

Samuel, the Lamanite shouts from the walls of Zarahemla to the Nephites below, accusing them of rejecting him *"because* I am a Lamanite." On the pages of his *Short Narrative*, Samson Occom describes observing a white farmer beat an indentured Indian boy—likely an allusion to the illtreatment he experienced at the hands of white ministers—*"because* I am a poor Indian." Yet both Samuel and Occom suggest that their Lamaniteness and their Indianness are divinely ordained identities.[115] Their marginalization, even dislocation, ironically frees these Native Americans to become fierce, prophetic critics of their fellow white Christians. Occom "can't help" the fact that he is a "poor Indian . . . God has made me so." But as this poor Indian, he can see better the abuses of a society that claims Christian identity but fails to uphold Christ's (second) highest commandment: to love thy neighbor as thyself.[116] Apess challenges his white readers along the same lines: to interrogate their own position relative to the Native neighbors whom they treat with disdain and inequality. "I would ask you if you would like to be disenfranchised from all your rights, merely because your skin is white?"[117]

Yet Occom, Apess, and Samuel assert that white men are not fully capable of such self-reflection. Their vantage point from the inside of American culture limits their vision. As Apess puts it, they cannot see that the "principle" of racial hierarchies, which white Americans consider divinely mandated or biologically predetermined, are in fact themselves "black" and "unholy."[118] On the other hand, from atop the walls of segregated Zarahemla, Samuel can look to both heaven and earth. He can see God's will and look over an American city at odds with it. He can see all this "because [he is] a Lamanite" *and* because he is "a prophet" who "testifieth of . . . [the] sins and in-iquities" of the ancient white American ruling race, the Nephites.[119] He can also see Jesus coming on history's horizon and, following him, the Nephite apocalypse.

Nevertheless, while the Book of Mormon appears forward thinking—the oppressed have a privileged place, even a privileged sight—it also adheres to its own decidedly ancient, and perhaps arcane, ideas of the process of the restoration of the human family. To regain their past and future glory, the Lamanites must shed "their scales of darkness from their eyes."[120] Samuel, who somehow overcomes these visual limitations innate to his race, is thus an exception to the rule. Or perhaps he is a racially ambiguous figure, tran-sitioning from one racial identity to another. The Book of Mormon professes that "all are alike unto God," including "black and white, bond and free, male and female." No soul, even those whose skin is the color of "flint," is lost.[121] Yet universal redemption involves a return to the purity and unity of Adam's and Lehi's white family. If faithfulness to the gospel is the standard of righteousness, this righteousness manifests itself in skin that in "many generations shall not pass away among them, save they shall be a white and delightsome people."[122]

The Race of the Archive

Samuel, the Lamanite serves as a case study for the racial politics within the Book of Mormon. In particular, Samuel highlights the instability of how Mormonism's foundational text understands who is righteous and who is wicked, and how this instability maps onto white-skinned and dark-skinned bodies. Because of this instability—because nonwhite peoples can be righteous and prophetic—Samuel's case underlines the import of locating the voices of nonwhites in the Mormon archive. Such voices can serve to correct and even revise the dominant narrative of Mormon his-tory. And yet, because of the tension between the oral and written archive, Samuel's case also helps contextualize why nonwhites are often excluded both from the historical records of the Book of Mormon and from histori-cal records of nineteenth-century America. We will see that when Native and African Americans make it into the archive, they rarely add directly to the archive themselves. To borrow from literary theorist Gayatri Chakra-vorty Spivak's seminal work, a subject like Samuel can "talk back" or even "write back" to criticize the hegemonic culture that marginalizes him and excludes his prophecies of ultimate, even salvific import, in Mormon his-tory. But he can rarely write his own unmediated way into the archive, a domain that remains racialized, coded in a (white) universal form.[123]

William Apess understood the power of the written word as a tool of racial oppression wielded against the marginalized. "The Indian character . . . has been greatly misrepresented. Justice has not, and I may add, justice cannot be fully done to them by the historian. My people have had no press to record their sufferings, or to make known their grievances; on this account many a tale of blood and wo[e] has never been known to the public. And during the wars between the natives and the whites, the latter could, through the medium of the newspaper press, circulate extensively every exaggerated account of the 'Indian cruelty,' while the poor natives had no means of gaining the public ear."[124] Apess's case was itself unique. He is an exception to the rule that the early American historical narrative remained the domain of white Americans who had the prerogative to shape the "Indian character" to fit their cultural and political expectations and ambitions. Rarely did Native Americans, and for that matter African Americans, have the means to archive their side of the story, to air their grievances, to "gain the public ear."

What was generally true for the marginalized in antebellum culture is particularly true in early Mormon history and history writing. Samuel, the Lamanite's case serves as a cautionary tale that even when they do appear—from the Delawares in Kansas in 1831 to Chiefs Arapeen and Wakara in Utah's Sanpete Valley in the 1850s to Jane Manning James in Salt Lake City in 1893—"red" and "black" subjects do not directly add their own voices to the written archive. Instead, their voices are mediated by their white scribes and archivists. Nonwhite subjects can and do "talk back," and they do so against their objectification or exclusion from the Mormon community. But as historian Gary Ebersole might put it, they often remain "captured" in the texts produced by white record keepers. As such, they remain "captured" in the cultural conventions about nineteenth-century conceptions of race, religion, and literacy.[125] What's more, because in early Mormon history literacy signifies whiteness and worthiness, when a Mormon historical subject becomes a writerly self he or she also becomes—figuratively, and the Latter-day Saints believed, perhaps even literally—a white self.[126]

2 MARKETING THE BOOK OF MORMON TO NOAH'S THREE SONS

It was March 1830. Broadsheets hung from the rafters and the sweet, metallic smell of drying ink filled the air of E. B. Grandin's third-floor printing office located on Main Street of Palmyra, New York, a bustling Erie Canal town of some five thousand residents. As he set type for the March 26 edition of the *Wayne Sentinel*, the twenty-four-year-old newspaperman was racked with anxiety and doubt.

In the previous week's edition, Grandin printed the bloodless announcement, "*We are requested* to announce that the 'Book of Mormon' will be ready for sale in the course of next week."[1] Grandin's rhetorical passivity hints at his state of mind. On the eve of the Book of Mormon's debut, perhaps Grandin wished to distance himself from Joseph Smith's "Gold Bible." Against his better judgment, Grandin had agreed to print the book in the same office where he produced the *Wayne Sentinel*. The year before, when Joseph Smith approached Grandin about publishing his translation of a long-lost record of an ancient American people and new Christian gospel, Grandin refused. He called "the whole affair . . . a wicked imposture." Grandin and Smith eventually agreed to terms—but only after Smith convinced Grandin that the book would be published, either in his shop or elsewhere. And only after Martin Harris, a local farmer who had helped transcribe portions of the book, mortgaged his farm to raise three thousand dollars as collateral to pay for the audacious printing run of five thousand copies.[2]

By March 1830, almost everyone in and around Palmyra had heard about the Book of Mormon. But notoriety did not assure sales. Many Palmyrans believed that the book was fraudulent and blasphemous. Some threatened a boycott. It was one thing for Smith to claim that he had discovered a history of the Israelite origins of America's Native peoples. It was another thing to claim that the risen Christ had visited this American house of Israel in A.D. 34. And it was downright outrageous to prophesy that the Indians—tens of thousands of whom would soon march west into government-mandated exile—would unite with believing Gentiles to build New Jerusalem in America before Christ's imminent second coming and the accompanying global calamities. The rest of "the world . . . would come to an end in two or three years," another Palmyra newspaper mockingly summarized the Book of Mormon's apocalypticism. "The state of New York would (probably) be sunk."[3]

Setting type for the March 26 edition of the *Wayne Sentinel*, in which he announced that the Book of Mormon was available for purchase in the bookstore on the first floor of his building, Grandin could steal a glance outside his printshop window to Palmyra's Main Street below. There, carriages full of local produce and dry goods—including books and newspapers—came and went to the canal that passed just a few hundred feet to the north.[4] As he did so, Grandin might have wondered whether he had made a terrible mistake. Would anyone show up at his store to buy the book when he unlocked the front door?

In terms of a business venture, Grandin's fears were realized. The Book of Mormon did not sell well. Martin Harris soon lost his farm. He complained to Joseph Smith that, despite his efforts to sell copies of the book door to door throughout western New York, "no Body wants them."[5] And Grandin soon closed his shop. Nevertheless, the publication of the Book of Mormon, and the founding of a new church less than two weeks later on April 6, 1830, immediately elevated Joseph Smith to the stature of a latter-day prophet in the eyes of his earliest followers. It also made him a dangerous blasphemer in the eyes of his enemies. As the number of Mormons and anti-Mormons multiplied, so did interest in (and antipathy for) the Book of Mormon, or more precisely its message of a restored Christian church, a restored priesthood for all (male) believers, and a restored prophet on earth to whom God continued to speak. By the time a mob killed Smith in Carthage, Illinois, on June 27, 1844, the church he had established fourteen years earlier had grown into an international religious community and an expanding market for the Book of Mormon. Yet Mormonism had also become a national controversy and would soon be debated at the highest levels of American political culture.[6]

And yet how did Joseph Smith and his earliest followers market both their own new religious movement and what Smith called the "keystone" of this movement, the Book of Mormon? And who would become the consumers of the new Mormon scriptures and converts to the new Mormon religion?

Between the church's founding in the spring of 1830 in New York State and the Mormons' expulsion from Jackson County, Missouri, in the fall of 1833, the earliest Mormons engaged in marketing campaigns to bring the "blessings" of this new gospel to "all the families of earth." In other words,

Joseph Smith and his first followers imagined a universal market for their new faith and their faith's foundational text. In an era when Americans were increasingly divided along political, religious, economic, and racial lines, the Book of Mormon prophesied what Joseph Smith called "a restoration of all things." When fulfilled, this restoration would end all schisms within the human family—at least for all those willing to believe. The Book of Mormon, along with Joseph Smith's other early translations and revelations, thus not only served as a lens through which the Mormons envisioned the reconstitution of the Body of Christ—then divided by sectarian battles over the proper place of baptismal waters, the sacrament table, and the clergy, as well as the proper place for Native and African Americans in the American Republic. This hermeneutic of restoration also served as a lens through which the Latter-day Saints envisioned the restoration of the human family to what they believed was its original, white form.

During the first three years of the church's existence, however, the Mormons marketed their universal gospel in specific ways to the branches of the human family presently separated into distinct races. In 1831, Joseph Smith and other leading members of the church met in western Missouri to make plans for the building of their Zion in America. During this time, early Mormon newspaperman and key figure in the early Mormon missionary outreach W. W. Phelps described the races that the Saints hoped would populate New Jerusalem as the American-based progeny of Noah, human history's (second) first family: the "Lamanites . . . descendants of Shem," "Negroes . . . descendants of Ham," and Gentiles, descendants of "Japheth."[7] The Christian world had for centuries accepted that these three sons of Noah were the postdiluvian progenitors of the "Gentile" peoples of Europe, the Semitic peoples of Asia (including the Holy Lands), and the Hamitic peoples of Africa.

Japheth, Shem, and Ham's shared parentage did not mean that the descendants of Noah were equal. To be sure, migration brought all three branches of Noah's family tree from the Old World to the New. Japheth's Gentile offspring came as religious refugees, missionaries, and colonizers. Ham's sons and daughters came as slaves. And according to the Book of Mormon, Shem's Israelite descendants fled the Babylonian destruction of Jerusalem to settle in America six centuries before Jesus's birth, eventually becoming the people whom the Book of Mormon names Lamanites and whom most Americans named Indians. To borrow from Michel Foucault, this is how the Mormons "named and ordered" the current state of the three branches of Noah's descendants they encountered. The early Latter-day Saints marketed the message of a restored gospel according to each lineage's spiritual and intellectual characteristics as well as the racial politics of Jacksonian America. To put it another way, while the Latter-day Saints understood that humanity was in essence one family, to make the restoration appealing and efficacious to this family's current (racialized) lineages—the "Lamanite," the "Gentile," the "Negro"—required targeted marketing.

New Jerusalem "among the Lamanites"

Joseph Smith founded the "Church of Christ" on April 6, 1830, at a small farmstead in Fayette, New York, some thirty miles southeast of Palmyra, where the Book of Mormon had gone on sale ten days before. This Church of Christ began as a family affair.[8] With perhaps as many as sixty members, it consisted mostly of Smith's immediate and extended family, along with local boosters like Martin Harris and Oliver Cowdery, Smith's chief Book of Mormon scribe and the early church's second leading official. Smith's 1830 revelation promising that the Book of Mormon missionaries would find that "the field is white already to harvest" came to fruition in the quick growth of the church among white, "Gentile" populations.[9] Even though the Book of Mormon did not become the best seller Smith, Grandin, Harris, and Cowdery hoped it would, it played a vital role in the conversions of many early Saints who became key figures in the restoration. During the church's first year in existence, copies of the Book of Mormon that were sold or given away passed from hand to hand among networks of families and neighbors. Before ever meeting church members, Smith's successor to the church's leadership, Brigham Young studied a borrowed copy of the Book of Mormon. So did early Mormon missionary and theologian Parley P. Pratt, and Smith's future plural wife, poet Eliza R. Snow. By the end of 1830, the size of Smith's church had grown to an estimated 280 members.[10] According to Smith, it was this success that drew the ire of his persecutors. As Smith later explained, anti-Mormon mobs, lawmen, and jealous sectarian "priests" conspired against him because he and his followers had set "the country in an uproar by preaching the Book of Mormon." After he was briefly imprisoned on charges of being a "disorderly person," Smith and his wife, Emma Hale Smith, fled to her family's home in Harmony, Pennsylvania. Soon after, anti-Mormon mobs chased the rest of the young religious community out of New York.[11]

Even before the early Mormons left the birthplace of Mormonism, based on the prophecies contained in the Book of Mormon, Joseph Smith revealed the future role of Native Americans in the restored church. For the Latter-day Saints, America's indigenous peoples were much more than

"Indians"—seen by many white Americans as a burden to the Republic and a hindrance to the nation's westward expansion.[12] In the Book of Mormon, the Indians are literal descendants of ancient Israelites. And it was the responsibility of the Gentiles to whom the Book of Mormon would first come to restore the Indians to the knowledge of their true selves. Following the Book of Mormon mandate, Smith sent the first official Mormon mission to the Indians. In a September 1830 revelation, Smith commanded Oliver Cowdery to "go unto the Lamanites and preach [the] gospel unto them." If the Lamanites accepted these "teachings" contained in the newly rediscovered American gospel, the Lord told Cowdery through Smith, then "thou shalt cause my church to be established among them."[13]

Smith and Cowdery expected that this gospel would naturally appeal to the Indians. After all, the Book of Mormon was the Indians' own long-lost family history. It was, explained the title page, "a record of the people of Nephi and also of the Lamanites." And in the Book of Mormon–prescribed order of Zion, it was the people of this "broken off" branch of Israel who would be the principal members of a restored covenant of the latter days. Not only would the Gentiles return the Lamanites' history to them, the Book of Mormon prophesied, but they would also help elevate them from their current depraved "Indian" state, restore them to the faith of their forefathers, and shape them into citizens of New Jerusalem. For this work, the Gentiles would also be invited to join the covenant that the Lord had established with the Lamanites' most ancient forefather, Abraham.[14]

This vision of restoration stood in contrast with Andrew Jackson's vision for the nation's future, in which the Indian played no part. "What good man would prefer a country covered with forests and ranged by a few thousand savages," the president declared in his annual address to Congress in December 1830, "to our extensive Republic, studded with cities, towns, and prosperous farms and filled with all the blessings of liberty, civilization and religion?"[15] Mormon millennialism built Zion around the Lamanite. Emerging Manifest Destiny pushed the Indian out of the Republic. The Lamanite would be a Mormon; the Indian could not be an American.[16]

In mid-October 1830, two months before Jackson delivered his speech celebrating the "happy consummation" of Indian removal, Oliver Cowdery, Parley P. Pratt, Peter Whitmer Jr., and Ziba Peterson left Upstate New York and headed west. The four were well suited to participate in this first mission in Mormon history. As Smith's chief Book of Mormon scribe, Cowdery knew the Book of Mormon better than anyone, perhaps even better than Smith himself. In the last pages of the Book of Mormon's first edition, Cowdery and Whitmer were listed as eyewitnesses to the golden plates from which Smith supposedly translated the new scripture.[17] Cowdery baptized Ziba Peterson in April 18, 1830, twelve days after the Church of Christ was established. And Pratt's chance encounter with a copy of the Book of Mormon in the summer of 1830 led to his almost immediate conversion.[18] Westward was both the prophesied and logical trajectory of the church. Before Cowdery departed for the mission, Joseph Smith revealed to him that the Mormons' millennial city "shall be [built] among the Lamanites."[19] And following the passage of the Indian Removal Act in 1830, hundreds of thousands of Native Americans were forced west to Indian Country. If New Jerusalem was to be built "among the Lamanites," then this city would be built on the Lamanites' lands on the westward side of the new, ragged edge of the United States.

Between October 1830 and February 1831, the four twenty-something-year-old missionaries trekked more than a thousand miles. They searched for potential Lamanite converts and potential locations for New Jerusalem. Along the way, they preached to both Indian and white audiences in New York, Pennsylvania, and Ohio. Ohio's Western Reserve proved to be particularly fruitful. This was a region already alive with the great religious awakening that had begun in the early 1800s in western New York.[20] Parley P. Pratt brought word of the new prophet and copies of the new gospel to his former minister, Sidney Rigdon, the leader of a Campbellite church in Kirtland, Ohio. Within weeks of the missionaries' arrival, almost the entire membership of Rigdon's church was converted. Rigdon became one of Mormonism's highest-ranking officials and eventually Brigham Young's chief rival to the succession of church leadership after Joseph Smith's death in 1844. The addition of these Ohioans doubled, if not tripled, the Church of Christ's membership. These conversions also injected vital enthusiasm for the Saints' restorationist vision. And Ohio became a geographic base that would sustain the church during much of its tumultuous first decade.[21] What's more, as Cowdery suggested in a November 1830 letter sent to the Mormons still in New York, the Ohio converts were likely a lucrative market for the Book of Mormon. "There is considerable call here for books." Cowdery instructed his brethren to send "five hundred immediately."[22]

Missionaries among the Delawares in Diaspora

These unintended "Gentile" converts were a boon to both the Mormon movement and Book of Mormon sales. Yet Cowdery and the other missionaries were anxious to bring the gospel to the Lamanites.[23] The missionaries thus left the embryonic Kirtland community and headed west to seek out their divinely mandated target audience: the American remnant of Israel. In early February 1831, Cowdery, Pratt, and a convert from Ohio, Frederick Williams, walked across the iced-over Kansas (Kaw) River and into a Delaware village, a two-day trek from the last American settlement at Independence, Missouri.[24] The highlight of the Mormons' first venture west of the U.S. border was a visit with Chief William Anderson (Kikthawenund), the sachem of the ten Delaware nations in diaspora.[25] The missionaries believed that, if the venerated chief could be brought to accept the Book of Mormon, then he could help introduce other Delawares to it.

A little more than a year before the missionaries met him, on September 24, 1829, the aged and illiterate Anderson put his mark (an "X") on a treaty document with the federal government. The treaty annulled the Delawares' rights to land that ran along the James Fork in Missouri.[26] Anderson hoped to prevent further disputes with white Missourians who had accused the starving Delawares of stealing hogs. These western Missourians were migrants themselves. They had moved north from Mississippi to squat on land the Delawares had been granted in the 1818 Treaty of St. Mary's (land that was also the ancestral home of the Osage Indians). Tensions with the white settlers were so high that Anderson did not wait for the arrival of the spring thaw or the federal government's promised provisions to make his exit. In November 1830, through late fall snows, Anderson and a large body of the Delawares trudged out of Missouri and into their newly allocated lands between the Kansas River to the south, the Missouri River to the east, and Fort Leavenworth to the north.[27]

This move west was the latest chapter in the Delawares' long exile from their ancestral lands. Two centuries earlier, Anderson's forefathers governed a huge expanse of the Delaware River basin, from southern New York to northern Maryland. The Delaware Indians had their own patrilineal origin story quite distinct from the Indian-as-Israelite saga that the Mormons would present to them in early 1831. Revered as the progenitors of all Algonquian tribes, the Delawares were called "Lenape," the "original" or "real men." Yet when the English settlers began colonizing their land in the late seventeenth century, the Delawares were reduced to nomads, divided by war, religion, and poverty. The Iroquois, whom the Delawares blamed for colluding with the English, signaled the Delawares' reversal of status by renaming the "real men" with the epithet "women."[28]

The century before the Mormons brought their own pan-Indian message west, the Delawares and other Indian tribes attempted to unify Native Americans to resist further displacement. Almost a half century before the Second Great Awakening reached western Ohio, the Delaware prophet Neolin led a religious revival among the Native Americans in that region.

Beginning in 1761, Neolin began receiving revelations from the "Master of Life," who implored the Indians to reject the trappings of European culture, including Western dress, food, firearms, alcohol, and Christianity, and to return to the traditions of their forefathers of hunting, fishing, and worshiping the Master of Life. Neolin even told the Indians to refuse to shake hands with whites. And when greeting each other, he instructed them to extend the left hand instead of the right, as was the white custom. The left hand, after all, "is nearest to the heart," Neolin explained.[29] Neolin also created his own scripture, which missionary observers dubbed "the Great Book of Writing." But this "book" was not a book that could be read like the Book of Mormon, another supposed Native American prophetic scripture. Instead it was a map of Neolin's cosmology sketched out on deerskin. It charted a path by which faithful Indians could retake their lands in this lifetime and find salvation in the life to come. In the Great Book of Writing, the Master of Life explained to the Indians that America was, by divine right, the land of their inheritance. "The land on which you are," the Master of Life revealed through Neolin, "I have made for you, not for others."[30]

Described by a Moravian missionary as a "half-breed" son of a Delaware princess and a Swedish Indian trader and interpreter, Chief Anderson became the leader of the Delaware tribes when another pan-Indian revivalist, Tenskwatawa, "the Prophet," the brother of the military leader Tecumseh, accused then Delaware chief Tetepachksit of witchcraft. The Moravian missionaries, who since the 1740s had moved westward with the Delawares, looked on with horror while Tetepachksit and a few of the Moravians' Indian converts were burned alive.[31] After the tumult created in the wake of Tecumseh and the Prophet's defeat first at Tippecanoe and then during "Tecumseh's War" of 1812, Anderson made peace with the Americans and began to unify much of the Delaware people in diaspora.[32]

Anderson was less belligerent toward the missionaries than Neolin and Tenskwatawa were. Yet he also proved less accommodating than some of his predecessors, including his uncle, the Delaware chief Gelelemend (William Henry Killbuck Jr.), who joined the Moravian missionaries' Indian Christian village at Goshen, Ohio.[33] Decades before Mormon missionaries would try to market their gospel to Anderson, the Moravians remarked on the sachem's resistance to Christianity, referring to Anderson's village near the White River (now Anderson, Indiana) as "the heathen town, four miles away." Conversations between Anderson and the Moravian and Baptist missionaries recorded in the missionaries' journals hint at why Anderson preferred to remain a "heathen." Anderson likely believed that while missionaries peddled Christianity, other white men, who would surely follow close behind, would peddle the white man's whiskey, the white man's cattle and clothing, and the white man's land treaties. Even Anderson's resistance to English-language education appears to have been deliberate. According to the journal of Baptist missionary Isaac McCoy, in June 1818, McCoy met Anderson at his Indiana settlement and offered to teach Anderson and his community "to read and write, to raise corn, and to make our clothes." Anderson told McCoy that the chief recognized the "great benefit to our children" of a "good education." But Anderson suggested that other Delaware leaders were skeptical about the missionaries' true intentions. Perhaps white Americans wished to separate young Indians from their families and place them in white homes and schools. "My chiefs say perhaps the white people desire to educate more Indians, so that they can kill them."[34]

Where Tenskwatawa and the Moravians had, for the most part, failed to unify Native Americans, the confident and naive Mormon missionaries expected that their pan-Indian message would succeed among Anderson's Delawares. Although decades later the Mormons' own relations with Native Americans would resemble those of the Moravians, at least in the beginning the Mormon and Moravian understandings of the Native Americans' place in their respective religious communities could not have differed more. The Mormons believed that they and their Native converts would create an integrated, covenantal community. And in due time the Natives would even assume the prophetic leadership of New Jerusalem. The Moravians kept their Indian converts at arm's length. They created separate villages for them away from the missionaries' settlements. And they required that Indian converts adhere to strict moral and behavioral codes, including "prohibitions against native practices" such as dancing, sacrifices, and "heathen festivals."[35] Even when the converts followed the Moravians' paternalistic rules, the missionaries were cautious in accepting them as full brothers in Christ. For example, the missionaries only agreed to baptize Anderson's uncle Gelelemend thirteen years after he first expressed interest in Christianity and only after the chief renounced his leadership of the Delawares.[36] With Christ scheduled to return at any moment, the Mormons' theology required more immediate application. They could not wait decades for Indians to prove their fidelity to the gospel. The goal was to teach the "Indian" how to become a "Lamanite" and then a Mormon. And to do so with great haste.

A Restored Gospel for Chief Anderson

On April 18, 1831, a few days after the missionaries ended their visit with Anderson, returned to Missouri, and began preparing for the arrival of the prophet and other leading Mormons, Oliver Cowdery posted a letter to Joseph Smith. The Church of Christ's second elder gave an upbeat assessment about the missionaries' success. Even after the Mormons' departure from Indian Country, "the Delaware Nation of the Lamanites" remained very interested in the Book of Mormon. Cowdery was glad to report that Anderson had pledged his faith in the new gospel, even if the illiterate chief and many of his nation had to rely on the missionaries' interpretation to understand the words written on the pages. Cowdery wrote that part of the Lamanites' interest in the book was that in it, they heard a name they recognized. "Every [Lamanite] Nation have now the name of Nephy." And this name had been "handed down to this very generation."[37] The Delawares might have forgotten the pre-Colombian American Christian gospel itself. Yet, an important vestige remained in the Natives' collective memory: Nephi, the name of the faithful son of Lehi whose descendants protected and added to the archive that would become the Book of Mormon. Perhaps the name "Nephy" would serve as the welding link between these Indians' Lamanite past and their Mormon future.

Despite this optimism, Cowdery's letter also highlighted potential barriers to the mission's success. One was the missionaries' struggle to communicate the Book of Mormon's message to non-English-speaking Indians. After all, Cowdery's information about the Delawares' continued interest in the Book of Mormon is hearsay. Anderson did not write a letter to Cowdery about his budding faith in the Book of Mormon. Instead, this information came from the interpreter, James Poole. Between Saint and Indian, the "fulness of the gospel" had to be mediated and translated. Another barrier was what the Mormon missionaries called unconstitutional governmental interference. Cowdery wrote that Richard W. Cummins, the Delawares and Shawnees' federally appointed agent, had prevented the Mormons from exercising what Cowdery called their "liberty" to visit "our brethren the Lamanites." The inexperienced missionaries failed to secure the proper governmental approval to travel into Indian lands. The Mormons' more seasoned rivals did not make these mistakes. For example, the Baptist missionary Isaac McCoy had acquired licenses to trade with and preach to the Delawares in the newly formed Indian Territory.[38]

It is also likely that the Mormons suspected that federal Indian agents colluded with these more established religious groups wishing to proselytize to the Indians. And not without cause. In a letter dated February 15, 1831, not only did Indian agent Cummins explain to the superintendent of Indian affairs William Clark that the Mormons lacked the proper paper work to preach in Indian Territory. He also reported that they "act very strange" and belonged to a suspect "sect." The Mormon missionaries told Cummins that government bureaucrats would not deter them from fulfilling their mandate to bring "a New Revelation" to the Indians. If they did not receive permission to "go among the Indians," Cummins wrote to Clark, then missionaries planned to "go to the Rocky Mountains."[39] Cummins, who would later be a signatory of the July 1833 "manifesto," which accused the Mormons of meddling with both Indians and blacks and demanded that they leave Jackson County, Missouri, wanted more than simply to uphold the letter of the law. It is possible that Cummins also wanted to remove competition to other missions in the area, perhaps including McCoy's Baptist mission and that of Methodist missionaries, which other Indian agents in the area supported.[40]

From this failed first mission to the Lamanites—and their great success among the Campbellites in Ohio—the Mormons learned that for now they would find their prophesied "white fields" ready to harvest among white American Gentiles. This market was culturally more prepared to accept the gospel than unlettered Indians. Yet unlike other Protestant missionaries who also struggled to win converts in Indian Country in the 1830s, the Mormons did not attribute to the Indians some permanent intellectual or spiritual inability to accept civilization and Christianity. Instead, the Saints insisted that Indians need only be taught the right gospel message—and to read this message for themselves—to be restored to the religion of their ancient forefathers. And they needed to be taught this gospel without interference from the government.[41]

Parley P. Pratt among the Delawares

Despite the failure of the 1831 mission to the Delawares, the Book of Mormon–inspired hermeneutic of restoration required the Latter-day Saints to hold out hope for mass Lamanite conversion. There is no better example of the longevity of the Mormons' expectation for Lamanite redemption than Parley P. Pratt's retrospective account of the Mormon missionaries' encounter with the Delawares. Pratt recorded this encounter in his autobiography, which he wrote in the 1850s and which was published in the 1870s. In writing about his memories of this first mission to the Lamanites, Pratt details how he conceptualizes the white Mormons' own understanding of themselves and their relationship with the Indian peoples with whom they hoped to create a New Jerusalem on the frontier.[42]

Pratt recalls how in February 1831 when the missionaries met with Chief Anderson and a group of his councillors, the lead missionary, Oliver Cowdery, explained to the Delaware chief that their recent difficulties were not the result of American malice. Instead, it was the fulfillment of Book of Mormon prophecy. The "Great Spirit" used the "pale faces" to displace the "red men" westward from their ancestral lands and bring them to Indian Country. To be sure, these were traumatic experiences. Yet, Pratt explained to Anderson, this forced exile should really be thought of as an exodus—a divine act that would serve "to restore [the Indians] to the knowledge of the will of the Great Spirit and to His favor." This exodus would also bring them into the lands that the Lord had designated as the site of their new millennial city. And this fulfillment of prophecy "will do the red man good as well as the pale face."[43]

According to Pratt's recollection, this exile-as-exodus was just one Book of Mormon prophecy that was being realized. The other was the restoration of the Indians' own history to them, which was contained in the Book of Mormon itself. Cowdery described the rise of great pre-Columbian Amerindian civilizations whose citizens built great cities and cultivated the land. They also worshiped the Great Spirit, who revealed his gospel to wise men and prophets. These prophets recorded this sacred history on golden plates handed down from fathers to sons. Cowdery also told of the ultimate destruction of this civilization. Apostasy led to wickedness. And the loss of knowledge of how to read and write led to the oblivion of the Indians' true Israelite parentage. Yet this sacred history was preserved so that a "pale face" prophet—Joseph Smith—could unearth it centuries later and translate it into English, "the language of the pale face." The preservation of this history was also the result of divine intervention. God had instructed the last two ancient American prophets and historians, Mormon and Moroni, "to hide the Book in the earth, that it might be preserved in safety, and be found and made known to in the latter days to the pale faces who should possess the land."[44]

Pratt recalled that Cowdery also explained that Joseph Smith translated this book not for the pale faces but for the red men. This is why he sent his missionaries "to bring some copies of it to them" and tell them of the good news. "The Book" could "restore them" to the ways and knowledge of their forefathers. According to Pratt, Cowdery framed this potential restoration in the conditional tense: "*If* the red man would then receive this Book and learn the things written in it, and do according thereunto, they should cease to fight and kill one another; should become one people; cultivate the earth in peace, in common with the pale faces, who were willing to believe and obey the same Book, and be good men and live in peace . . . *then* should the red men become great and have plenty to eat and good clothes to wear."[45]

This particular formation of "if . . . then" is the reoccurring discursive mechanism by which the early Latter-day Saints explained and offered the universal salvation that Christ's sacrifice created. Pratt here presents what I call a "covenantal contract."[46] If Indians followed the gospel that the "pale face" restored to them in the form of the Book of Mormon, then the red men would enjoy not only material blessings but spiritual ones, too. However, before the red men could become "great," they had to end their nomadic wanderings and become landed farmers and ranchers. They had to "obey" the same book as the pale faces and, based on this shared worldview, covenant with them. This covenanted people would also be a literate people: literacy was essential for "learning the things written in [the Book of Mormon]" and for recording God's providential hand in the unfolding history of this last dispensation.

Though Pratt does not leave a record that Cowdery taught the Delawares this lesson, the "Book" also teaches that if the red men do all this, then not only could they become one with the pale faces, but they, too, could become "pale face" themselves. The Cowdery-led mission to the Delawares parallels that of the Book of Mormon Nephite missionaries who brought the gospel to the Lamanites in the years before Christ's birth. Those Lamanites who "united with the Nephites" had their curse removed, and "their skin became white like unto the Nephites." Just as these Lamanites disappeared "and were called Nephites" (3 Nephi 2:14–16), so the missionaries foresaw the disappearance of the "red men." For example, in 1861 early Mormon newspaperman W. W. Phelps wrote a letter to church president Brigham Young claiming that in July 1831, Joseph Smith disclosed a confidential revelation to Phelps, Oliver Cowdery, and other missionaries to the Indians. Through Smith, the Lord told the Saints that it was his "will, that in time, ye shall take unto you wives of the Lamanites." The goal was to breed out the Lamanites' curse, so "that their posterity may become white, delightsome, and just."[47]

Phelps's report of a thirty-year-old revelation has an apocryphal ring. It echoes Utah-era views of Mormon-Indian relations. Then, church leaders encouraged Mormon missionaries to take Indian women as their plural wives as means to acculturate the Indians into Mormon culture and create matrimonial allegiances with Indian peoples. Yet the revelation is not entirely out of place in the early 1830s. Though many missionaries like the Moravians discouraged intermarriage between white missionaries and their Indian initiates, the practice was a long-standing tradition for other missionizing Europeans. This was especially true among the French who, like the Mormons, saw marriage as a means of creating kinship between Europeans and indigenous Americans.[48] What's more, the decade preceding the founding of the Mormon movement was marked by a national debate over the efficacy and morality of Indian-white marriages. Best-selling novels by the likes of Lydia Maria Child and James Fenimore Cooper, and a "scandalous" marriage between the Cherokee writer Elias Boudinot and his white wife, Harriet Gold, made marriages between Native Americans and whites the talk of the nation.[49] And while it supposedly came more than a decade before Smith received formal revelations requiring elite male Saints to practice what they would call "celestial marriage," the 1831 revelation echoes other anecdotes about Smith's early interest in and theological ruminations about polygamy.[50] Whatever or whenever its origins, the revelation reflects an early Mormon desire to create familial bonds between leading male Mormons and those they believed to be literal daughters of Israel. Such covenants were seen as a vital step toward the restoration of Christ's church among the Lamanites and the Lamanites' restoration to the white, original, universal family.[51]

According to Pratt's recollection, Cowdery's sermon convinced Chief Anderson that the Mormons' intentions were benevolent. "We are truly thankful to our white friends who have come so far," the chief said through translation, "and [having] been at such pains to tell us good news, and especially this new news concerning the Book of our forefathers." Pointing to his heart, Pratt recalls the chief declaring, "It makes us glad in here."[52] The Delaware chief promised that when the winter's deep snow receded, his tribe would build a meetinghouse. They would also erect fences, homes, and farms. For the chief and his people, these structures would serve as ramparts against the harsh climate of their new and unfamiliar home. These proposed infrastructures also had symbolic significance. They would mark the nomadic Delawares' transition to a landed and civilized people.

As did Cowdery in his April 1831 letter to Joseph Smith, in his autobiography Pratt recalls the missionaries' time in eastern Kansas as one of great excitement among the Delawares.[53] It seemed that the retail marketing—bringing word of the restored gospel directly to the Delawares—worked. Within several days of teaching, "nearly the whole tribe began to feel a spirit of enquiry and excitement," writes Pratt.[54] "Several among them could read the language of the pale faces," perhaps the fruits of previous Baptist and Moravian missions. "To them we gave copies of the Book of Mormon." Those who could translate written English into oral Delaware "began to rejoice exceedingly, and took great pains to tell the news to others, in their own language." But for the majority of Delawares who could not read, the book remained an icon. It was an illegible totem whose stories were accessible only to those who had the power of literacy.[55]

In 1831 as soon as the Mormons left, what seemed to be a quick sprouting of seeds of faith among the Delawares quickly died out. Like Cowdery before him, Pratt did not blame the Native Americans for some inherent inability to understand and accept the gospel. Instead he faulted jealous "Indian agents and sectarian missionaries." They worked to prevent the Indian excitement around "The Book" from progressing to the point where the church could be established among the Lamanites.[56] Yet perhaps Cowdery and Pratt were wrong for faulting missionary competitors and conspiring federal agents. If Chief Anderson's actions in the spring and summer of 1831 are any indication, perhaps Anderson himself was responsible for not allowing Mormonism to take root. Instead of the great excitement about which the missionaries boasted, Anderson's efforts reflected what John C. McCoy, who helped settle and develop nearby Kansas City, later called the Delawares' "indifference" to the Mormon message, or at least the prioritization of different needs.[57]

Anderson did not erect farms or a Mormon meetinghouse. He worked to move the rest of his people over the Missouri River and ensure provisions for their settlement in Indian Country.[58] In late summer of 1831, Anderson dictated a letter to Andrew Jackson's secretary of war Lewis Cass, the man most responsible for implementing the president's Indian Removal Act. He petitioned Cass to supply "a pension of $100 annually to each of his four sons." Beyond this small cash infusion, it seems that the chief wanted little to do with white Americans. The descendant of the Lenapes had his own ideas about protecting his people's lineages into the future. The year before, on September 22, 1830, in another dictated message, Anderson told Cass: "I hope that if the Government fulfill all its promises that before many years the balance of my nation who are now scattered . . . will all come here on this land." Like the Mormons, Anderson envisioned the creation of a pan-Indian nation gathered near the border of Indian Country and the United States. But he did not foresee a place for white Americans—Mormon or non-Mormon—in this new nation. In another letter to Cass, Anderson offered to "shake hands with" the secretary of war. Yet perhaps this handshake would occur with Anderson on the Indians' side of the border between Indian Territory and the United States and Cass on the other. Anderson continued, "I pray the Great Spirit to preserve you *where you are* for the good of the Red Skins."[59]

A Mission Postponed

The importance of this first Mormon mission to the Lamanites cannot be overstated. It changed the course of Mormon history and arguably American history as well. But it did so in a way that the early Latter-day Saints did not envision.[60] Early Mormons (and historians of early Mormonism) naturally focused on the unexpected missionary success among the Campbellites in Ohio.[61] Yet there are lessons to be learned from the missionary failures among the Lamanites in Indian Country. The first lesson is about how early Mormons conceptualized, and attempted to realize, their Book of Mormon mandate to restore Native Americans to the faith of their supposed Israelite forefathers. The optimism of Pratt's 1850s-era description of the first Lamanite mission shows that the Saints' millennial vision to covenant with the Lamanites did not go away during the decades between 1831 and the Mormons' arrival in Utah's Great Basin.

The conversion of the Kirtland community also shaped how the Latter-day Saints came to understand proper restorationist hermeneutics and behavior. John Whitmer, the first official church historian, recorded with more than a little dismay that some of the Kirtland Saints began acting out Book of Mormon historical dramas by imitating stereotypical Indian behavior. Some pantomimed an "Indian in the act of scalping." Others "would slide or scoot on the floor, with the rapidity of a serpent, which they termed sailing in the boats to the Lamanites, preaching the gospel." Another observer reported witnessing some converts engaged in glossolalia, which they believed allowed them to speak Indian languages. "[They] fanc[ied] themselves addressing a congregation of their red brethren."[62]After his arrival in Kirtland in the late winter of 1831, Smith used this outburst of religious fervor to differentiate between true religious experience and dangerous enthusiasm. In May 1831, Smith revealed that white converts were not expected to act more like Indians. Instead, in the restored church, the Indians were expected to act more like white Saints. Imitations of the Indians, Smith revealed, were "abominations in the Church which professes . . . [Christ's] name."[63]

A third lesson gleaned from this first mission is less about history and more about history writing. Pratt and Cowdery captured on paper the words of the illiterate Indian chief whom they tried to convert. This is particularly true for Pratt, who served as scribe for both sides of the encounter between the Mormons and their nonwhite interlocutors. Although Anderson authorized white Indian agents to compose letters and interpret treaties on his behalf, Pratt functioned as Anderson's unauthorized amanuensis. And he re-created the interaction between the Mormons and the Indians long after the encounter.[64] This allowed the Mormon missionaries to accomplish on paper what they could not in the flesh. In his autobiography, Pratt molded the Delawares into the Mormons' conception of Lamanites, their conversion thwarted not by a lack of Indian interest but by unbelieving Gentiles' anti-Mormon persecution. The missionaries thus had the power to "name" "Lamanite" Anderson and place him in the "order" of the Mormons' hierarchical hermeneutic of restoration. Anderson's words become a written record in order to reflect this vision. Here the archive becomes a racialized space. To be sure, Anderson is a historical subject with his own historical prerogatives. Yet because he does not write down his version of the 1831 encounter with the missionaries, in the Mormon archive he is reduced to an object lesson for Mormon faith-promoting history of the continued potential to restore Indians to their Lamanite selves.

The Publishing House of New Jerusalem

Naming and ordering affected the medium that early Latter-day Saints used to market the Book of Mormon to different racialized populations in antebellum America. Joseph Smith knew that reaching the Lamanites, who were both geographically and culturally on the margins of American society, required direct visits from missionaries. And because they shared neither a spoken nor a written language with their audience, these missionaries had to recount the Book of Mormon history and prophecy orally and through translators. Naming and ordering also affected the message brought to the Delawares. Though the early missionaries imagined that the Lamanites would soon occupy places of esteem in God's millennial city, the missionaries told them that they were not yet elevated to such vaunted positions. Even these heirs to the Israelite covenant had to contract into Christ's restored covenant of the latter days. Their contract required that they unify with other "red men" as well as with the "pale face." It also required that the Indians become land-cultivating, law-abiding citizens of the yet-to-be established New Jerusalem. Perhaps most importantly, as Pratt tells it, the Indians had to become literate so that they could learn to "obey the . . . Book [of Mormon]."

When it came to marketing to American Gentiles, the early Mormon missionaries sought audiences with religious communities who they believed would find their message of a covenantal, restored Christian church appealing.[65] And although fewer than expected actually bought it, early missionaries sold or gave away copies of the Book of Mormon that subsequently circulated through family, religious, and even economic networks in New York, as well as in communities in Ohio, Vermont, and Massachusetts.[66] After reading the Book of Mormon, many early Mormon leaders, including future church president Brigham Young, apostle Heber C. Kimball, Mormon newspaperman W. W. Phelps, and Relief Society presidents Eliza R. Snow and Zina D. Huntington Young, claimed to have been convinced of the book's historical and prophetic assertions.[67] The Book of Mormon became the early church's most effective "literary missionary."[68] Still, as Joseph Smith and other church leaders realized, door-to-door marketing was not the most efficient way to spread the restored gospel. Nor was it always the safest, as Smith learned from his run-ins with anti-Mormon mobs. So the Mormons did what many new religious movements in the early Republic did. They founded a publishing house. On their own press, the early Mormons created a medium and shaped a message specifically targeted to Gentiles.

Publishing was designated a principal activity of New Jerusalem. In late July 1831, Joseph Smith and some sixty converts from Coleville, New York, arrived in Jackson County, Missouri. On July 20, the small community gathered in the unsettled land just west of Independence. There Smith revealed that his followers were to purchase "every tract [of land]" between the Indians located across the Missouri River in Indian Country and the "gentile" Americans living to the east in Independence. Through Smith, the Lord proclaimed that this land, "between Jew"—meaning here "Lamanite"—"& gentile," was the land "appointed & consecrated for the gathering of the Saints . . . the place for the city of Zion." Smith next indicated where a temple, in which the Saints would perform yet-to-be-revealed sacred ordinances binding families together for eternity, was to be built. And he appointed Sidney Gilbert to establish a store to provision the city.[69] Smith also called on W. W. Phelps to run the Saints' newly established printing office.[70] Phelps was a seasoned newspaperman. Before his conversion to Mormonism, Phelps had established the anti-Mason *Ontario Phoenix*, among other short-lived newspapers. The Mormons' first newspaper, the *Evening and the Morning Star*, printed on the Mormons' printing press in Independence, was intended to be a marketing tool for the promotion of the Mormons' sacred texts as well as a literary vehicle to reach those Gentiles willing to join the Mormons and to help establish Zion in Missouri.

The Mormons' desire to become publishers of their scriptures was a natural one for an evangelizing, antebellum religious movement. The Latter-day Saints joined a robust market of religious printers, which developed exponentially during the first three decades of the nineteenth century. Methodists, Baptists, Universalists, and Millerites all had their own presses on which they printed hundreds of denominationally specific newspapers and pamphlets.[71] Like the Latter-day Saints, religious missionaries from these communities also became colporteurs, peddling both their religion and their religion's devotional literature.[72] Moreover, lackluster Book of Mormon sales meant that the Saints hoped to find another means of distributing their new gospel. Unfortunately, the *Evening and the Morning Star*'s subscriber lists are no longer extant. They were possibly destroyed along with the Mormons' printing office during the anti-Mormon attacks in Independence in July 1833. However, some surviving records from the early 1830s suggest that Smith considered these lists of an estimated few hundred names an invaluable resource for distributing church news and scripture.[73] After all, in the earliest years of the church, it is likely that more people— both the Saints and their enemies—read sections of the Book of Mormon in the pages of the *Evening and the Morning Star* than in the hardback first edition of the book. And certainly the *Evening and the Morning Star* was the most widely distributed source of Smith's revelations. Because of the newspaper, converts did not need to be within earshot of Smith to hear divine messages about the development of Zion.

The medium of the newspaper also shaped the early Saints' message to their hoped-for Gentile converts. The *Evening and the Morning Star* printed specific excerpts from the Book of Mormon, which functioned as reading guides for how early church leaders hoped both the faithful and potential church members might consume the new gospel. In particular, Phelps aimed to shape how the paper's consumers would read the Book of Mormon in relation to the prophet's revelations.[74] For example, in the *Evening and the Morning Star*'s first edition in June 1832, Phelps published "The Articles and Covenants of the Church of Christ," which were established at the church's organizational meeting at Fayette on April 6, 1830. Through the pages of the *Evening and the Morning Star*, readers could participate in that auspicious day's events when, through revelation, Joseph Smith and Oliver Cowdery were named the church's first and second elders. Readers could learn that Smith had been given "the means" to translate the Book of Mormon, which contained the history of the "fallen" Lamanites and the future restoration of the "Gospel of Jesus Christ to the Gentiles; & also to the Jews [the Lamanites.]"[75] Readers could learn the proper means of conferring the priesthood and the duties and powers of specific offices, including how to conduct baptisms and administer the sacrament.

Smith's revelations reprinted in the *Evening and the Morning Star* often matched word-for-word passages from the Book of Mormon.[76] These intertextual connections between the Book of Mormon and Smith's early revelations signify that the early Church of Christ leaders did not see themselves as belonging to the theological lineages of Augustine, John Wesley, and John Calvin. After all, the Book of Mormon implied that such theologians and prophets of "sectarian" churches had corrupted the early Christian faith.[77] Instead, the early Mormons believed that their writings joined an uncorrupted scriptural patrilineage stretching back to the Book of Mormon's American prophet-historians as well as to the Bible's own original prophets, historians, and archivists. In other words, these early Mormon leaders believed that they picked up where their textual forefathers—Nephi, Mormon, and Moroni, Moses, Mark, and Paul—left off. The *Evening and the Morning Star*'s message to its Gentile readers was that when they joined the Church of Christ, they could rest assured that they were covenanting into Christ's one true church. Because sectarians like the Baptists, Presbyterians, and Methodists based their theologies and ritual practices solely on their interpretation of the Bible—and an incomplete Bible at that—the Saints' competitors could not make such assurances.

A Relational Covenant

Phelps's editorial decisions about which revelations and Book of Mormon passages that he chose to print in the *Evening and the Morning Star* also demonstrate that the early Mormons thought of this covenant as relational. The reunification of the human family in the latter days required the American descendants of Noah's sons Shem and Japheth to cooperate in building up New Jerusalem. As the patrilineal heirs to the Abrahamic covenant, the Lamanites would be the primary peoples in New Jerusalem. Yet the restored gospel would come to the Gentiles first, in large measure because they were already literate.[78] As Cowdery and Pratt did for the Delawares, the reading-and-writing Gentiles would bring the Book of Mormon to the Lamanites. And with it, they would bring the message that literacy is key to the restoration of the white, original family.

Gentiles and Indians can be redeemed, but only in relation to one another. Christ explained as much in a sermon he delivered during his mission in America, which was recorded in the Book of Mormon and from which Phelps quotes in the December 1832 edition of the *Evening and the Morning Star*. The "house of Israel" and the "Gentiles" will be brought together because of the Book of Mormon, which Christ declares "shall be a sign unto [the Lamanites]," signaling that the Heavenly Father had again begun the work of fulfilling the promises of the ancient Abrahamic covenant. Oliver Cowdery and the other missionaries to the Lamanites brought this sign and message of a renewed covenantal contract to the Delawares in early 1831. To

Gentiles reading the *Evening and the Morning Star*'s passages of the Book of Mormon directly addressed to them, Christ also offers a covenantal contract: "*If* they will not harden their hearts, that they repent and come unto me, and be baptized in my name, and know the true points of doctrine," which the Book of Mormon restores, "[*then*] that they may be numbered among my people, O house of Israel."[79]

Covenanted together, believing Gentiles and restored Lamanites will build New Jerusalem. As printed in the June 1832 edition of the *Evening and the Morning Star*, Joseph Smith's revelations regarding this sacred city contain a vision of Zion as "a city of refuge, a place of safety for the saints." This one-square-mile "plat of the City of Zion" included housing for the expected twenty thousand residents. It also included plans for church, governmental, and commercial enterprises.[80] In this city, the "righteous"—both Lamanite and Gentile—will be safe from the calamities of the outside world. In the days before Christ's return, unbelieving Gentiles will experience an "overflowing scourge" of apocalyptic earthquakes, conflagrations, and wars.[81] What's more, this millennial community will not be ghettoized. Absent from Smith's plans for New Jerusalem are the types of transitional housing for Indians that were popular with the Moravians, who believed that the Indians had to prove that they could live as Christians before they would be admitted into civilized settlements. Instead, Gentile and Laminate will live and govern together. Religious redemption will also lead to racial unification. A white (raceless) people will emerge, ready to greet Christ on his return.

Marketing to the Sons and Daughters of Cain and Ham?

To be sure, the vast majority of Gentiles did not accept Christ's offer—or at least the Book of Mormon's description of it—to join the newly restored covenant. Many were indifferent to this new covenantal contract. Others violently rejected it. According to leading Latter-day Saints, this was especially true for the jealous "sectarian priests" who were fearful that the Mormons would attract converts from their churches.[82] A few months after the Mormons were expelled from Jackson County, in a March 1834 article in the *Evening and the Morning Star*, which had temporarily set up shop in Kirtland, Ohio, Oliver Cowdery compared the "righteous" Saints' treatment in Jackson County to "the horrors of the Inquisition."[83]

Cowdery focused on the religious persecution that the Mormons endured at the hands of the "mob," which he insisted were led by "professor[s] of religion." But according to the old Missouri settlers who opposed the Saints' presence in Jackson County, religion was only one factor in their increasing Mormon animus. In July 1833, Jackson County's non-Mormon leaders circulated a petition to remove the Saints from the area. The hundreds of signatories of this "manifesto" included the Mormon missionaries' old foe, Indian agent Richard Cummins. The old settlers worried that these "lazy, idle and vicious" people, who openly professed "that their God hath given them this county of land," would soon monopolize the levers of power in the county.[84] At least in terms of changing demographics, the old settlers' worries were not without cause. By the end of 1833, the Mormons numbered some twelve hundred in Jackson County. This was far less than the twenty thousand Smith had envisioned in his city planning for Zion. But it was still approximately one-third of the county's population.[85]

In their manifesto, by referencing the Latter-day Saints' belief that Jackson County was their God-given "inheritance," the old settlers made it clear that they were reading the Book of Mormon passages and Smith's revelations printed in the *Evening and the Morning Star*. And they were reading them carefully. Though they did not hold to this belief as literally as the Saints, the old settler Missourians also saw Jackson County as a kind of second Eden. They had designs on making it a cultivated, pastoral region where slave owners could manage their farms and plantations and create localized, Jeffersonian democratic communities without interference from abolitionists or religious fanatics wishing to make citizens out of their slave property.[86]

Thus, along with concerns about the Mormons' religion and politics, old settler Missourians were also alarmed that the Mormons were "tampering with our slaves," as they wrote in their manifesto, "and endeavoring to sow dissentions and raise seditions among them." The old settler Missourians' best evidence for these accusations was printed in the Mormons' own newspaper, the *Evening and the Morning Star*.

In a July 1833 article entitled "Free People of Color," W. W. Phelps spelled out the conditions under which "free people of color, who may think of coming to the western boundaries of Missouri" could do so. The article was mostly a verbatim reprint of the Missouri statute that permitted only those "negroes" and "mulattos" who carried documentation stating that they were citizens of "one of the United States" to settle in Missouri.[87] Yet the old settlers read "Free People of Color" as an explicit invitation to "free negroes and mulattoes from other States to become mormons and remove and settle among us." The old settler Missourians interpreted the article as an attempt to agitate both free and enslaved blacks.[88] In a way, the old settler Missourians imagined the dystopian underbelly of the Mormons' vision for the utopian New Jerusalem in Jackson County. The Mormons hoped to create a racially diverse and productive community, unified in their covenant to create a great city worthy of Christ's return. Old settlers, including the Mormons' old competitor among the Delawares the Baptist missionary Isaac McCoy, envisioned a horde of religious fanatics, savage Indians, and blacks whose zealotry would threaten the social and political order. The old settlers also professed fear of the threat to sexual security and racial purity that they believed such a diverse set of new neighbors presented. "We are not prepared . . . to receive into the bosom of our families, as fit companions for our wives and daughters," the manifesto read, "the degraded and corrupted free negroes and mulattoes that are now invited to settle among us" by the Mormons.[89]

Phelps quickly recognized that he had created a crisis. Within a week of the publication of "Free People of Color," Phelps printed an "Extra" edition of the *Evening and the Morning Star* (fig. 2.1). In it, the paper's editor expressed "extreme regret" that the article had been "misunderstood." "Our intention was not only to stop free people of color from emigrating to this state," Phelps wrote, "but to prevent them from being admitted as members of the Church." Phelps also pledged loyalty to "the laws and constitution of our country." He hoped that their neighbors would recognize that the white Latter-day Saints shared with them the same political patrilineage, stretching back to the Republic's founding "sons of liberty," and "through the favorable auspices of a Jefferson and Jackson."[90] Appeals to white American constitutional republicanism did not work. On July 23, 1833, church leaders relented to the old settlers' demands that the Mormons not vote in local elections, that they cease printing their newspaper, and that they leave the county within six months. Yet there would be no organized, peaceful exodus out of Jackson County. During the summer and early fall of 1833, Mormon homes and businesses, including Phelps's printing office, were attacked or destroyed. One Mormon and two Missourians were killed in a shootout.[91]

Even if "Free People of Color" was not the cause of the Mormons' expulsion from Jackson County, it was certainly the catalyst. And even if Phelps was at least somewhat correct in his assertion that his intended message was misread, the old settler Missourians' reaction raises an important question: what were the Saints' intentions toward "people of color"? What place could the least favored of biblical lineages, the supposed sons and daughters of Cain and Ham, occupy in New Jerusalem? To begin to answer this question, it is worth revisiting the early Mormon universalistic impulse to see how, if at all, this impulse translated into the Saints' efforts to market their new religion to African Americans.

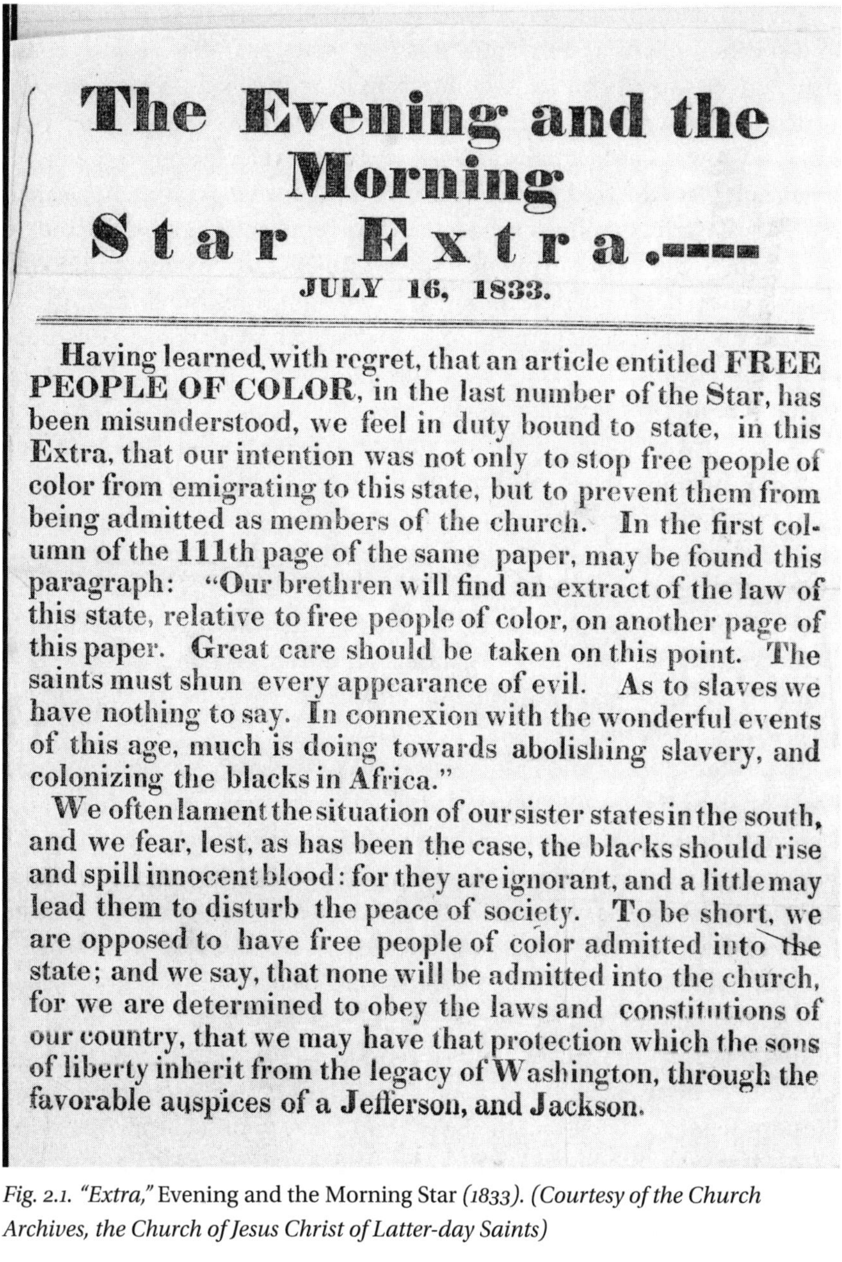

The Evening and the Morning

Star Extra.——

JULY 16, 1833.

Having learned with regret, that an article entitled **FREE PEOPLE OF COLOR**, in the last number of the Star, has been misunderstood, we feel in duty bound to state, in this Extra, that our intention was not only to stop free people of color from emigrating to this state, but to prevent them from being admitted as members of the church. In the first column of the 111th page of the same paper, may be found this paragraph: "Our brethren will find an extract of the law of this state, relative to free people of color, on another page of this paper. Great care should be taken on this point. The saints must shun every appearance of evil. As to slaves we have nothing to say. In connexion with the wonderful events of this age, much is doing towards abolishing slavery, and colonizing the blacks in Africa."

We often lament the situation of our sister states in the south, and we fear, lest, as has been the case, the blacks should rise and spill innocent blood: for they are ignorant, and a little may lead them to disturb the peace of society. To be short, we are opposed to have free people of color admitted into the state; and we say, that none will be admitted into the church, for we are determined to obey the laws and constitutions of our country, that we may have that protection which the sons of liberty inherit from the legacy of Washington, through the favorable auspices of a Jefferson, and Jackson.

Fig. 2.1. *"Extra,"* Evening and the Morning Star *(1833). (Courtesy of the Church Archives, the Church of Jesus Christ of Latter-day Saints)*

Though perhaps not the main attraction, concern over the temporal and spiritual plight of nonwhites was one factor that drew some prominent converts to the faith. For example, in 1830, five years before she converted to Mormonism, future plural wife of Joseph Smith and famed poet Eliza R. Snow published in local Ohio newspapers elegiac poems bemoaning the plight of the "red man" under the "white man's" tyranny. In particular, Snow described Andrew Jackson's Indian removal policy as a fraudulent land grab. Under noms de plume such as "Tullia" and "Pocahontas," in her poems Snow, then a member of Kirtland's Campbellite church, also articulated sentiments similar to the Book of Mormon's providential expectations of Indian redemption.[92] Likewise, in his autobiography, Parley P. Pratt described the Indians as a pure people, free from the corruption of "sectarian divisions" that plagued white communities, albeit certainly less advanced than the Gentiles. When reading the Book of Mormon for the first time, Pratt recalls finding "to my great joy" that Christ had come and preached to the "remnant of Joseph on the continent of America." Such a discovery, Pratt writes, "greatly enlarged my heart. . . . Surely, thought I, Jesus had *other sheep*, as he said to his Apostles of old; and here they were, in the wilderness of the world called new. . . . Truly, thought I, the angels sung with the spirit and with the understanding when they declared: *We bring you glad tidings of great joy, which shall be to ALL PEOPLE.*"[93]

To be sure, Snow's and Pratt's universalism was colored. Many antebellum Christian communities shared an ambition of converting Indians. Missionizing blacks, especially by a suspect religious community and especially in a newly established slave state, was something else altogether. As an abolitionist, W. W. Phelps was more explicit than most Mormons in his distaste for slavery, which he believed was a threat to the realization of a true American, Christian republic.[94] Still, abolitionism was not the same as religious integration. And even if we read Phelps's "Free People of Color" article as the old setters did—as an invitation for free blacks to "become mormons"— the scant to nonexistent free black population in both Missouri and Ohio's Western Reserve meant that the Saints had limited contact with blacks. As such, Pratt's 1839 proclamation that, during the first decade of its existence, "[no more than] one dozen free negroes or mulattos never have belonged" to the church is probably accurate.[95]

Yet lack of opportunity was not the only factor. After all, Joseph Smith's first mission involved sending some of his most trusted followers on a thousand-mile trek to seek the Native American "remnant of Joseph." Likewise, though not as directly as it did with the Lamanites, the Book of Mormon's hermeneutic of racial restoration—that even those cursed with dark skin can be restored to the white, original human family—also played an important role in the precarious place African Americans occupied in the Saints' new covenantal community. To put it plainly (once again), there are no people of African descent in the Book of Mormon. Yet, the inclusion of biblical-sounding curses led many readers to apply standard antebellum biblical hermeneutics to the text. The Book of Mormon's curses resulting in divisions within that scripture's first family (Lehi's offspring) resemble the divisions within the Bible's first family (Adam's offspring as well as Noah's). Yet the Book of Mormon curses do not involve the same populations. The Bible and biblical pseudepigrapha were written in and around (Old) Jerusalem, the crossroads of the Old World, where the peoples of Europe, Asia, and Africa met. As such, its protagonists reflect this diversity.[96] However, diversity in Book of Mormon history is limited almost completely to the progeny of the sons of the Israelite Lehi in exile in the New World. Ham's progeny are absent from the Book of Mormon's millennialism. Instead the book envisions Shem—initially understood to be the Lamanite remnant of Lehi—covenanting with Japheth's Euro-American Gentiles, who together would build New Jerusalem in America.

Keeping this in mind helps us to understand the inconsistent public positions—from implicit abolitionism to staunch defenses of human bondage— that Joseph Smith and other Latter-day Saints put forth during the church's first decade.[97] Phelps wrote in "Free People of Color" that "as to slaves we have nothing to say." Yet Phelps believed that the *Evening and the Morning Star* had something to say about slavery or, more precisely, about its coming demise. In the May 1833 edition of the *Evening and the Morning Star*, Phelps printed reports of the American Colonization Society's efforts in Liberia. And in July of that same year, Phelps exclaimed, "in connection with the wonderful events of this age, much is doing towards abolishing slavery, and colonizing the blacks, in Africa." For Phelps, abolishing slavery and returning Africans to Africa were signs of the millennium. If the progeny of Cain and Ham returned to their homeland, then the United States would be clear of the people who, at least according to the Book of Mormon's hermeneutic of restoration, did not belong there in the first place. The nation would be freed from the divisive politics of slavery. And the Saints would be more at liberty to build New Jerusalem.

That being said, in the early 1830s Joseph Smith thought a lot about the supposed biblical lineages of Africans. Smith was particularly interested in the origins of the curse of Cain and their implications for Cain's African progeny. Between August 1832 and July 1833, the *Evening and the Morning Star* printed large sections of Smith's revelations and translations of the Old

Testament. In particular, the paper published Smith's revisions and additions to the book of Genesis. He completed this work as part of his mandate to restore those "plain and precious things" essential for salvation that had been stripped from the Bible by two millennia's worth of ignorant and corrupt translators.[98] The revisions of Genesis contain an extended visionary experience during which God revealed to Moses knowledge about the nature of God and Christ, the purpose of creation, and Moses's future role in the Israelite covenant. The revised book also elaborates on the biblical story of Adam and Eve and describes human history's first generations after Adam and Eve's first act of sin.[99]

It is this last element of what would be canonized as the book of Moses that seemed most to interest Phelps. The August 1832 edition of the *Evening and the Morning Star* contains a description of Cain in which the eldest son of Adam and Eve does not fare well. In it, Cain is cursed for some undisclosed sin, though most readers would certainly recognize it as the murder of Abel.[100] It is hard not to read Cain's sin against his brother, Abel, intertextually with Laman's sin against Nephi. This is especially true since the book of Moses was Smith's first translation project after the Book of Mormon. Motivated by envy, both Cain and Laman act violently against their brothers. Although only Cain is guilty of murder, both Cain's and Laman's sins result in curses of black skin. In the book of Moses, God expresses willingness to look past the transgressions of the "sons of Adam," which resulted in Adam and Eve's exile from the Garden of Eden. Yet one lineage of Adam, namely "the seed of Cain," was not welcome to mix with their kin: "for the seed of Cain were black, and had not place among [the other sons of Adam]."[101]

Smith's translations reflected standard antebellum biblical hermeneutics linking the origins of black-skinned Africans to Cain, a people named as cursed and divinely ordered as separate from and unequal to the other children of Adam. As such, in the book of Moses, the sins of their fathers, which Cain's seed carried on their skin, were so egregious that a covenantal contract was not available to them. Smith's first translation, the Book of Mormon, teaches that those named Gentiles and Lamanites would "mix" and covenant with one another and build New Jerusalem. Smith's next translation, the book of Moses, suggests that those who belonged to the most inferior of the ancient lineages, those of Cain, "had not place" among the Saints of Zion.

Yet the purpose of publishing this passage of the book of Moses in the *Evening and the Morning Star* had more to do with marketing Smith's new translations and his authority than excluding the seed of Cain from the early church. It was only in the 1880s that church leaders frequently began to cite the book of Moses as a justification to exclude people of African descent from full participation in the Mormon community. In the 1830s, Smith, Phelps, and the other early Saints were focused on implementing the Book of Mormon and book of Moses prophecies to, as the August 1832 edition of the *Evening and the Morning Star* spelled out, gather the elect "from the four quarters of the earth unto . . . a holy City." From inside this "New Jerusalem," the elect would "be looking forth for the time of [Christ's] coming."[102]

"Black Pete"

What's more, it seems that the book of Moses's anti-Cain theology did not shape early Mormon policy toward its early black membership. Written records on early African American Saints are scarce, in part because black members were so rare. Yet the history of one African American convert, "Black Pete," who appears only briefly in the Mormon historical record, speaks to the Mormon archive as a place where race, literacy, and prophetic authority intersect. In the 1830s, Ohio and Missouri, the two states in which the Mormons tried to build permanent settlements, counted only a small number of free blacks, largely because of the states' restrictive black codes.[103] A former slave, Pete became one of the first nonwhite converts in the Mormons' Ohio settlements.[104] In February 1831, an article in one Western Reserve newspaper described "Black Pete" as "a man of colour, a chief [Mormon] man, who is sometimes seized with strange vagaries and odd conceits."[105] A neighbor of Pete's Kirtland-based Mormon community described him as "a low cunning illiterate negro [who] used to run over the hills and say he saw holes of fire."[106]

Setting aside the ridicule of this "illiterate negro" among non-Mormon Ohioans, Pete's conversion occurred literally at the crossroads of the early Mormon outreach to the Lamanites and Gentiles. Pete was a member of the Morley Family, a communitarian Christian society gathered on Isaac Morley's farm outside of Kirtland. Along with many other members of this millenarian community, Pete converted to Mormonism when the missionaries to the Lamanites visited the Kirtland area in the fall of 1830.[107] Already preparing for the return of Christ, the Morley Family was primed to accept the four missionaries' message of a restoration of the true church, of prophetic revelation, and of the priesthood. Yet because they were anxious to get to the Lamanites, the missionaries left Ohio before the new Mormon community had been adequately instructed about who could claim prophetic authority.

Before they left, the missionaries did explain to the Ohio converts that Joseph Smith had translated the Book of Mormon through a mysterious combination of translation and revelation. Mimicking Smith's process, Black Pete was among a group of early Mormons in Ohio who also began receiving written messages from heaven. Both Mormon and non-Mormons provide recollections of the process by which Pete and his prophetic colleagues obtained their divine communiqués. One Ohio newspaper reported that the converts received letters "directly from the God of Heaven." "[Their] credentials [as prophets were] written and signed by the hand of Jesus Christ."[108] Another anti-Mormon Ohioan reported that these divine letters "came on parchment . . . [and the recipients] had only time to copy them before they vanished from their sight." As was the case with Joseph Smith's golden plates, God restricted who could see such "commissions" and for how long. "With such papers in their pockets," the report continued, the prophets "went through the country, preaching, and made many converts."[109] Decades later, Mormon apostle George A. Smith remembered the letters Pete and others received as signs of unauthorized fanaticism. Smith recalled that, in early February 1831, "they had a meeting at the [Morley] farm, and among them was a negro known as Black Pete who became a revelator." On one occasion, "Black Pete got sight of one of those revelations carried by a black angel." Trying to catch up with the angel, Pete "ran off a steep wash bank twenty-five feet high, passed through a tree top into the Chagrin River beneath. He came out with a few scratches, and his ardor somewhat cooled."[110]

Despite their thinly veiled dismissal of Pete's ecstatic behavior, these descriptions of Pete's "letters from heaven" reveal two important points about Pete and the early 1830s Western Reserve that he traveled as a self-appointed Mormon prophet. First, although there is no extant record of the supposedly illiterate Pete's writing in the archive, his composition of divine communications suggests at least that Pete understood that the written word trumped the oral in terms of asserting prophetic authority.[111] It is possible that, as one Native American who was baptized by the Mormons would do in Utah (chapter 6), Pete merely mimicked writing—scrawling lines on paper—without actually composing discernible messages. Second, such divine commissions would have been of vital importance for Pete because of the legal restrictions on free blacks in Ohio. As was the case in many free states in the antebellum period, Ohio law required free blacks to travel with "free papers." Black Pete, less than a decade removed from slavery, might have believed that traveling with a letter from heaven would give him the legal cover to avoid imprisonment or expulsion from the state.

Black Pete disappeared from Mormon history as quickly as he arrived. There is no evidence that he remained with the Latter-day Saints after 1832. However, it is possible that Black Pete's departure from the early church was related more to his claims to be a "revelator" than with his race. On his arrival in Kirtland in February 1831, Joseph Smith found a nascent Mormon community in which many claimed to have prophetic powers. Through a revelation, Smith made it clear that he alone was God's "appointed" prophet, and thus he alone had the authority "to receive revelations from [God's] hand." Black Pete was probably among other Ohio revelators who were tried by church leaders for apostasy and "cut off" from fellowship. In a May 1831 revelation, later printed in the *Evening and the Morning Star,* Smith attempted to distinguish for his community the boundaries between true religious experience and unholy enthusiasm. The revelation proclaimed that the act of spiritual revelation was one of "reason[ed]" discourse between the "ordained" prophet and God. Running off riverbanks in attempt to capture letter-carrying angels was a sign of madness or even demonic possession.[112]

And yet Black Pete's appearance in the Mormon record highlights the racialization of the archive. Black Pete understood the power of the written word, even if what he wrote was rejected as religiously inauthentic. What's more, the naming of "Black Pete" within and outside the Mormon community—his racial identity attached to a moniker that lacks a family name and thus lacks a clear patrilineage—fits into a Mormon pattern that begins with the Book of Mormon prophet "Samuel, the Lamanite" and repeats throughout the archive in the naming, for example, of Jane Manning James as "Black Jane." Those seen as white are named without a racialized adjective, emphasizing the assumption that whiteness is a racial category that is, in fact, empty of race. And whites have the authority to bestow these racialized names on those outside this raceless, white identity.[113]

Marketing to "Free People of Color"

Yet the case of Black Pete is only one example—and an ambiguous one at that—of how the early Mormons marketed their new faith to people of African descent. Once again, what was printed in the *Evening and the Morning Star* provides more concrete detail. In the October 1832 edition, Phelps published an extract from a February 1831 revelation in which Joseph Smith called on his faithful to prepare themselves and the world for Christ's return. The "elders" of the church should "teach the children of men" about the restoration of the gospel. "Call upon the nations to repent, both old and young, both bond and free," and invite them all to join the

Latter-day Saints.[114] This missionary exhortation echoes the Book of Mormon's most racially universalistic passage. In 2 Nephi 26:33, the first Nephi states plainly that if they are faithful, the Lord does not exclude any of the (racialized) lineages to which the early Mormons marketed their message. The Lord "inviteth them all to come unto him and partake in his goodness . . . black and white, bond and free, male and female." Even "the heathen" is remembered. "All are alike unto God."

Phelps might have been right to claim that the July 1833 edition of the *Evening and the Morning Star* was "misunderstood," that the Mormons were not attempting to agitate free and enslaved blacks. Yet "Free People of Color" is undeniably a direct address to free people of color "who may think of coming to the western boundaries of Missouri, as members of the Church." By quoting from the "laws of Missouri" regarding emigrating freemen, Phelps forewarns those potential black church members of the legal ramifications that they face by entering the state. "*If* it shall appear that such person is a free negro or mulatto . . . and such a person shall not produce a certificate . . . evidencing that he is a citizen of such state, [*then*] the justice shall command him forthwith to depart from this state."[115] Yet this warning—composed in the conditional construction of the Mormons' own covenantal contract—is political, not religious, in nature. In "Free People of Color," Phelps presents no theological objection to free blacks coming to Jackson County. In other words, *if* free blacks want to covenant with the Mormons and take part in building New Jerusalem, *then* they must overcome the high hurdles created by the laws of man but not the laws of God or God's church.

Phelps's invitation to the sons and daughters of Cain and Ham is a narrow one; slaves were "real estate" in Jackson County and thus not welcome in the church. Nor were freemen permitted without free papers.[116] The law might have stood in the way of people of African lineage who sought to gather with the Mormons in Missouri. But Christ's covenant, it seems, was open to all: to the Lamanite "heathen," to the white Gentile, and even to the people the book of Moses names the "seed of Cain," as long as they were "free people of color" and have the documentation to prove it.

Noah's Three Sons in Indian Country

In July 1831, Joseph Smith and an entourage of trusted followers arrived in Jackson County. There they marked off the land where the Latter-day Saints would build their New Jerusalem. Smith pointed about him, performing a land survey guided not by compass but by revelation. The Mormons' general store would be *here*. The printing office *there*. And the temple, "not far from the court-house" in Independence.[117] On the first Sunday after their arrival, the *Evening and the Morning Star*'s editor W. W. Phelps crossed a more secular boundary. He left "the United States" to preach "to a western audience" in Indian Country. There, Phelps found "specimens of all the families of the earth . . . for there were several of the Lamanites as descendants of Shem, quite a respectable number of Negroes as descendants of Ham; and the balance was made up of citizens of the surrounding country their great progenitor, Japheth."[118] In those first three years of the church, Phelps's Sabbath sermon in Indian Country was a rare opportunity to preach to the supposed descendants of Noah's three sons all at once— racial lineages the Latter-day Saints hoped to unify in a new covenant of the latter days. For the most part, the Saints had to reach out to these three populations through tailor-made mediums and messages.

And yet this targeted marketing—this particular means—was in the service of a more expansive end. The Book of Mormon's message challenged the standard theological and political views of the potential for reconciliation of these three main racial populations of antebellum America. When the Saints looked out onto the landscape and the people who inhabited it, they did not see simply "white," "black," and "red"—fixed identities with fixed characteristics that made racial reunion impossible. Instead, the Mormons saw one human family only *temporarily* separated by literal and symbolic skin color.

3   FROM GENTILE TO ISRAELITE

By the summer of 1833, the initial wariness that the old settlers of Jackson County, Missouri, felt toward the county's new residents turned to outrage. Days after the publication of "Free People of Color," the county's political leaders met at the Independence courthouse, just across the street from W. W. Phelps's printing office. There they penned their anti-Mormon manifesto. The Mormons had shown "their true colors" with the July issue of the *Evening and the Morning Star*. They sought to build their New Jerusalem—populated by Indian, Gentile, and "free negroes and mulattos"—in the Missourians' backyard. The old settlers believed that this act would spoil "our beautiful county" and "corrupt our [enslaved] blacks, and instigate them to bloodshed" against their peace-loving owners.[1]

The Latter-day Saints' audacious marketing campaign to the descendants of Noah's three sons in America was upsetting news not just on the western frontier. In Mormonism's birthplace, Upstate New York, on the pages of the Palmyra-based *Reflector*, which he established to discredit his neighbor-turned-prophet, Abner Cole noted that the "zeal in this new religion" was spreading just as "Jo" Smith had expected. In February 1831, Cole reported that Smith's followers had grown "from 1 to 200 (whites)." These "Mormonites" were also interested in converting Indians, who they believed "were the ten lost tribes [of Israel]." A few had "already been dipt" in baptismal waters.[2] Cole's reports came from Eber D. Howe. Howe was the editor of another anti-Mormon newspaper, the *Painesville Telegraph*, based just twenty miles west of the Mormon community in Kirtland, Ohio. Howe had his own correspondent, the Mormon defector Ezra Booth, who sent him dispatches regarding the troubling events in Jackson County. Booth claimed that the Mormons were preaching the Book of Mormon's apocalyptic prophecies to "inflame the minds of the Indians." The Mormons' goal was to enlist large numbers of Indian warriors to "expel the white inhabitants [of Jackson County], or reduce them to a state of servitude." "The enthusiastic spirit which Mormonism inspires," Booth warned, might indeed result in the Indians "going forth among the white people," as the Book of Mormon promised—and from which Booth directly quoted (3 Nephi 20:

16)—"as a young lion among the flocks of sheep, who, if he goeth through, both treadest down and teareth to pieces."[3]

Word of the Mormons' ambitions to covenant with black and Indian Americans also crossed the Atlantic. In a report of his tour of the United States, published in London in 1835, English legal scholar and abolitionist Edward Strutt Abdy wrote that the Mormons "maintain the natural equality of mankind, without excepting the native Indians or the African race." Abdy highlighted the scriptural source of the Mormons' "extraordinary" belief in racial equality. "He inviteth them all to come unto him," Abdy quoted directly from 2 Nephi 26:33, the Book of Mormon's most inclusive passage, "black and white—bond and free, male and female, and he remembereth the heathen; and all are alike unto God." Abdy recognized that such egalitarianism would be poorly received in the United States, where white supremacy was a bedrock principle of the nation's political and religious culture. "The preachers and believers [of this doctrine] were not likely to remain unmolested."[4]

Just as news of Mormon racial meddling quickly spread eastward, so did news of violent attacks that the Mormons endured at the hands of the old settler Missourians. In August 1833, E. B. Grandin's *Wayne Sentinel* reported mob violence against Mormons in Independence. W. W. Phelps's printing office and the Mormons' general store were destroyed, and Mormon leaders were tarred and feathered. Grandin decried this "illegal and riotous" response to the "nuisance" that the Mormons presented.[5] Following their expulsion from Jackson County, when the Saints crossed the Missouri River into neighboring Clay County, even Eber Howe's *Painesville Telegraph* voiced support for the Saints' constitutional rights. "The Mormons are as much protected in their religion, their property, and persons, as any other denomination, or class of men."[6]

Joseph Smith also understood Mormon persecution as a failure of American citizens to abide by the political covenants of the Constitution. A document that the Mormons would come to believe was inspired by God, the Constitution guaranteed (white) citizens the right to establish religious communities without fear of molestation by other (white) citizens or the government.[7] Yet the Latter-day Saints realized that the local and state officers sworn to uphold the Constitution would not prevent further anti-Mormon violence. As such, in response to their expulsion from Jackson County in 1833, and in response to the politics of Indian removal and slavery during the rest of the 1830s, the Mormons' original ambitions to make Christ's restored covenantal contract universal *contracted*—at least for a time.

After they failed to build their racially diverse millennial city in Jackson County, the Latter-day Saints interpreted their trouble as a sign from heaven that they were not ready to build New Jerusalem. "Zion cannot be built up unless it is by the principoles [*sic*] of the laws" of the kingdom of God, Joseph Smith revealed at a June 22, 1834, gathering of the Saints in their temporary home in Clay County, Missouri. While they waited "a little season for the redemption of Zion," the Mormon people needed to learn more about the laws of God's kingdom.[8] They soon discovered that these laws were not fundamentally about municipal organization. Instead, the kingdom was organized around a network of family trees, at the center of which were (male) priesthood holders. And the Saints found that their own family trees—starting with Joseph Smith Jr. to Joseph Smith Sr. and even extending back to the biblical (and Book of Mormon) patriarch Joseph— connected them not only in spirit but also in blood to the ancient Israelite patriarchs with whom God had established the original covenant and to whom God had given the original priesthood.

To be sure, the Latter-day Saints were not alone in their belief that Anglo-Americans might actually be themselves the descendants of the ten lost tribes of Israel. This "British Israelism" explained—and reinforced—English and American triumphalism. After all, Anglo-Saxons brought democracy, Christianity, and economic progress to the once barbaric and heathen American continent, Pacific Islands, parts of Africa, and Indian subcontinent. Yet perhaps more than any other Anglo-American religious or political community, the Saints would come to believe that such descent from ancient Israelite patriarchs was not speculation. It was fact. The covenantal blood of Jacob, of Joseph, and especially of Ephraim—the most favored of the lost tribes—literally ran through their veins. The proof was that converts in America (and soon, in the British Isles and Scandinavia, too) accepted Mormonism in the first place. Mormons would come to believe that converts' patrilineage made them naturally predisposed to receive the good news that the ancient Abrahamic covenant had been restored in the latter days.[9]

It is important not to assume causality. The Latter-day Saints' exile from the prophesied site of New Jerusalem in Missouri in the early 1830s, along with the failure of the first missions to the Lamanites, did not lead them to abandon dreams of Indian redemption in favor of the reality of the growing number of white converts. In fits and starts, over the next century, the Mormons continued to expend great resources toward the conversion of Native Americans, who remained in the Saints' collective imagination a remnant of a fallen, but destined to be redeemed, branch of Israel. Yet, even though the Missouri trials did not cause them to reconfigure their theology, the trials did prompt the Saints to clarify *who* was literally *who* in the theological schema of Zion—namely, who was truly a Gentile and who an Israelite.

Relatedly, during this period, instead of seeking out a lost branch of the house of Israel among America's Indians, church leaders sent one missionary, church apostle Orson Hyde, overseas to bring the gospel to the Jewish remnant of Shem's descendants in the Holy Land and in diaspora scattered throughout Europe. They also began sending missionaries to the British Isles. There they found receptive audiences among a people whom the Saints increasingly believed were not, in fact, "Gentile" descendants of Japheth but instead themselves descendants of lost tribes of Israel. For the moment, the Saints could not establish the community of New Jerusalem among the Lamanites. But they did find that they could establish covenantal families with Israelites whom they discovered were scattered among their own supposedly Gentile converts.

What's more, during the mid-1830s Smith revealed that the priesthood authority—the office that all Mormon males were required to hold for church leadership positions in this world and for exaltation in the world to come—flowed from their connections to this ancient Israelite genealogy. The Israelite sons of Shem were naturally born with this authority, though they still had to be judged worthy and ordained to the priesthood before they could exercise it. The Gentile sons of Japheth could gain the authority through adoption into the covenant. During this period a mixed-raced African American named Elijah Abel also joined the church, became a missionary, a priesthood holder, and even an adopted member of the Mormon covenant. Yet the new translations of ancient scriptures that Smith produced in the mid-1830s revealed a more ambiguous place for the sons of Ham's priesthood eligibility, a place that would become much less ambiguous after Smith's death.

Antiabolitionist Converts

Before their troubles in Jackson County, many leading Latter-day Saints expressed misgivings about the morality of the Republic continuing to exist as half slave and half free. The Saints brought their ambivalent or antagonistic attitudes toward slavery with them when they moved from the Northeast to Missouri.[10] Joseph Smith's own Upstate New York was a hotbed of abolitionism. Before she and most of the rest of the Smith family joined her son's Church of Christ in April 1830, Joseph's mother, Lucy Mack Smith, was a member of Palmyra's Western Presbyterian Church, which in the 1840s served as a stop on the Underground Railroad.[11] Even when they reached Utah and began excluding blacks from full participation in the Mormon sacred community, leading Latter-day Saints were far from uniform in their views on the issue of slavery. In 1852, with the backing of territorial governor and church president Brigham Young, Utah's first legislature legalized a form of "African" slavery in the newly formed territory. Yet church apostle and member of the legislature's upper chamber Orson Pratt not only denounced slavery. He also called for the enfranchisement of black men.[12] Eight years later, on the eve of the outbreak of the Civil War, during a speech in the Salt Lake Tabernacle, Brigham Young himself spoke about Joseph Smith's famed 1832 Civil War revelation in which the prophet had revealed that the demise of slavery was a prerequisite for the millennium.[13]

Yet after the first set of troubles in Jackson County in the summer of 1833, church leaders realized that their slave-owning Missouri neighbors would not abide ambiguity when it came to the Saints' public views on abolitionism. As such, W. W. Phelps published his "Extra" on July 16, 1833, in the *Evening and the Morning Star*, denying that his "Free People of Color" article signaled the Saints' intent to convert and free slaves. Phelps's effort to stamp out fears of Mormon meddling with slaves failed. Phelps could not unprint what had already been printed. Nevertheless, the Mormons wanted their neighbors in Ohio and Missouri to know that they would abide by the race laws of the land.[14] And for the rest of the 1830s, the Mormons' printing press was typeset to assuage their enemies' fears that the Saints wished to topple America's precariously balanced racial politics.

The following year, the Kirtland-based *Messenger & Advocate*, which replaced the *Evening and the Morning Star* as the Mormons' newspaper of record, dedicated its April 1836 edition to denounce the abolitionist movement. The prophet himself wrote the lead article. It included the lengthiest public pronouncement on slavery and the place of African Americans in the church that Smith would make during his lifetime. Smith was compelled to put his feelings in print after an abolitionist named James Watson Alvord established an antislavery society in Kirtland. Non-Mormon observers noted that Alvord had some success. An abolitionist newspaper in Cincinnati reported that by April 1836, the society counted some eighty-six members on its Kirtland roster.[15] Smith wanted to avoid even the appearance that Mormons were supporters of abolitionism. In his *Messenger & Advocate* article, Smith made sure to mention that, at least among the Saints, Alvord, who was studying at the nearby abolitionist stronghold of Oberlin College, had garnered little interest. Smith also stated proudly that his followers did not abuse the abolitionist. This stood in sharp contrast with the non-Mormon antiabolitionists in the area, who reportedly pelted

Alvord with stones, snowballs, and rotten apples.[16] Smith agreed with the nation's chief law enforcement officer, President Andrew Jackson, who in the 1830s described abolitionism as a threat to the stability of the Republic. Five years after Nat Turner's rebellion, in which more than fifty whites and one hundred blacks were killed, Smith faulted abolitionists like Alvord for instigating "the slave to acts of murder" by teaching them that slavery was against God's will.[17]

According to Smith, slavery was legitimate in the eyes of both the law and the Lord. To justify his position, Smith did not turn to the Book of Mormon. After all, Smith's intended audience was not his Mormon flock but his enemies. They demonstrated that they read the Saints' newspapers, searching for any religion or politics that they perceived as threatening. Sounding like any number of antebellum Christian defenders of human bondage, Smith cited Genesis 9:25–27—the passages that describes the curse that marks Ham's descendants off from the rest of postdiluvian humanity. Smith declared that since "he was perfect in his generation and walked with God," Noah was justified when he cursed Ham for sinning against him. And because of this sin—what antebellum racial theorist Jacob Flournoy described in an 1835 treatise on the origins of the "African Race" as the "second fall"— Ham's progeny were destined to remain the servants of the seed of his more righteous brothers, Shem and Japheth.[18] Human bondage was biblical. For Smith, and for many antebellum Bible believers, this meant that it was also legal and moral.[19]

"Our Worthy Brother"

At the same time that he was espousing support for the institution of slavery, Joseph Smith also sent off on an extended mission—with a blessing and a preaching license—the racially mixed Mormon named Elijah Abel. If the presence of the early Kirtland convert Black Pete in the Mormon archive is faint, Abel left an indelible mark on the history of the church's relationship with its black membership, one that speaks to the changing racial politics within Mormonism. In 1832, the twenty-year-old Elijah Abel joined the Mormons after migrating to the church's Kirtland settlement from his home in Maryland. The details of Abel's pre-Mormon existence are sketchy. Some scholars suggest that he was a freed slave; others believe that he ran away. But as a Mormon, Abel's life is well documented. During his half century as a Latter-day Saint until his death in 1884, Abel was a priesthood holder, a Smith family confidante, and an indefatigable missionary. While Joseph Smith was alive, Abel even served in the Third Quorum of the Seventy of the Mormon hierarchy.[20]

On March 31, 1836, in Kirtland—days before his antiabolitionist harangue first appeared in the *Messenger & Advocate*—Joseph Smith signed a missionary license confirming Abel's status as "an elder" in the church and praised him for his "good moral character, and his zeal for the cause of righteousness." This license, which was intended "to serve as proof of [the Mormons'] fellowship and esteem" in him, Abel likely kept on hand during his mission in the Mid-Atlantic states and Canada.[21] Unlike Black Pete's "letter from heaven," written "by the finger of the almighty," such a letter of recommendation written by the hand of the church's prophet—or more likely by the hand of one of the prophet's many scribes—probably served as more effective de facto free papers for Abel. Even in the antebellum North, a man of Abel's ambiguous racial background would have faced difficulty traveling freely.[22] This document signified that Abel did belong to somebody, namely the Mormons. On the pages of the Mormons' newspaper of record, Smith voiced his public support for the subjugation of the sons and daughters of Ham. On the paper on which Abel's license was written, Smith voiced his support for a mixed-race Mormon whom he named "our worthy brother in the Lord."[23]

Lamanites in the West

In February 1834, the *Evening and the Morning Star*, then briefly relocated to Kirtland, published another "Extra." This time the author was Parley P. Pratt, the onetime missionary to the Delawares. And this time Pratt denied accusations that the Mormons were "colleguing [*sic*] with the Indians, and exciting them to hostilities against the whites."[24] Despite these denials, rumors of Mormon Indian meddling dogged the Saints for the rest of the decade. On June 29, 1836—almost three years to the day after the Jackson County leaders met to write up their anti-Mormon manifesto—Clay County's elite met at Liberty, Missouri, to voice their concerns about their Mormon neighbors' true intentions.

The resolution passed at Liberty was less bellicose than the Jackson County statement. In fact, the Clay County leaders made note of the abuse the Saints had faced in 1833. "[The Mormons] were expelled from their homes in Jackson county . . . like Noah's dove without even a resting place for their feet." Clay County had provided the Saints with the metaphorical dry land. But the Mormons had outstayed their welcome. And they had demonstrated that they were "Eastern men" who opposed slavery in a slaveholding state where "the haggard visage [of abolitionism]" was not welcome. More disturbing, the Mormons continued "keeping up a constant communication with the Indian tribes of our frontier, with declaring, even from the pulpit, that the Indians are part of God's chosen people, and are destined, to inherit this land, in common with themselves."[25]

Together, Sidney Rigdon, Joseph Smith, Oliver Cowdery, and other leading Mormons took to the pages of the August 1836 edition of the *Messenger & Advocate* to refute these accusations. Like the area's non-Mormon residents, these leading Mormons wrote that they, too, were well "acquainted with the barbarous cruelty of rude savages." And they pledged that if the "Indians should break out" into warfare against western Missouri's white citizens, then the Mormons would "be among the first to repel any invasion, and defend the frontier from all hostilities."[26]

There is no reason to question the Saints' sincerity here. The citizens of Clay County—not unlike the citizens of Jackson County before them—provided a fair accounting of the Mormons' views of the Indians, the Indians' role in the final dispensation, and the location of Zion in Missouri. Yet by 1836, the Mormon leaders recognized that, for the time being, neither they nor the Lamanites were ready to establish New Jerusalem. And they also learned from the Jackson County ordeal that if their proselytizing efforts toward the Indians were too ambitious—or even perceived as such—their enemies would seek to destroy them.

Thus, instead of trumpeting their millenarian vision of a racially inclusive New Jerusalem, the Saints presented themselves as fully supportive of the national policy toward Indians. In a January 1836 article in the *Messenger & Advocate*, W. W. Phelps made clear that he believed that President Jackson's policy to move "the remnants of this race which are left within our borders" west of the Mississippi was sound. Incapable of being Americans, the Indians should gather in their own country. There they would be provided with clothes, fertile land, arms, and ammunition. But it would be up to the Indians to feed themselves, either by farming or by hunting the "countless herds of Buffalo" who roam "the skirts of the great prairies." Phelps did put a Mormon spin on Jackson's policy. He hoped that this future "nationalizing" of the Indians would create a pan-Indian civilization. As they unified, the Indians would begin to see themselves as the Mormons saw them: not as disparate tribes, warring with one another and with the Gentiles, but as a *people*, a rediscovered branch of "Israel . . . upon this continent." Once the "gathering by the government" was completed, Phelps imagined a time when the Indians could "be gathered by the gospel." But until then, Phelps supported Jackson's decision to leave the Indians to their own devices.[27]

Yet even before the Mormons were expelled from Jackson County, changes made to Joseph Smith's revelations regarding the Lamanites reflected more circumscribed expectations for Native Americans within the sacred Mormon community. Sometime between the return of the first mission to the Delaware Indians in the spring of 1831 and the Mormons' expulsion from Jackson County in late 1833, Joseph Smith's revelation declaring that New Jerusalem would be built "among the Lamanites" was edited. In the original revelation, dated September 1830, which Oliver Cowdery wrote in the ledger book containing most of Smith's early revelations, a strikethrough line runs through the preposition "among." And a caret indicates the insertion of the prepositional phrase "on the borders by."[28]

Revelation was scripture sent to the prophet from heaven. But revelation could be amended to reflect changing realities on earth. The Mormons interpreted the federal prohibitions against their settlements in Indian Country, as well as the lukewarm reception from the Indians themselves, as a sign that the Book of Mormon–prophesied covenant with the Lamanites was not in the immediate future. According to the edited revelation, New Jerusalem would be built near the Lamanites—on their borders. Indian converts would join the Saints in due time. But New Jerusalem's center would lie somewhere east of Indian Country.

The Saints were quick to reevaluate the *where* of their new covenantal community. They were also quick to recalibrate the *who* of the Lamanites. In fact, as soon as the first missionaries to the Lamanites realized that they would not be permitted to proselytize in Indian Country, they began to fix their gaze not on the Lamanites in their neighborhood but on more western horizons. Writing from Kaw Township, Missouri, in his May 7, 1831, letter to the brethren back in Kirtland, Oliver Cowdery suggested that it was not the "local" Indians like the Delawares that the Saints were destined to redeem. Nearby Independence was the easternmost stop on the Santa Fe Trail. And through the news that the trail brought east, Cowdery heard of "another Tribe of Lamanites." The "navahoes" were successful ranchers and manufacturers of high-quality textiles. Cowdery suggested that in the future, the Saints should send missionaries west, where among these more civilized tribes they might find more receptive audiences.[29]

Jews and Judah

American politics of Indian removal as well as local Indian indifference to the Mormon message meant that at least for "a little season," the Saints could not hope to covenant with the Lamanites. Yet, this did not mean that the prophesied unification of Israelites with Gentiles would have to wait. After all, the Lamanites were just one branch of Israel. The modern-day Jewish people, who already called themselves religious and ethnic descendants of Abraham, were the logical second choice to complete the

Book of Mormon mandate that "Gentile" Saints find other patrilineal heirs to the Israelite covenant with whom they could unify.[30]

The early Mormons were certainly interested in the plight of the Jews. They shared with many other antebellum Christian communities the belief that their return of the Jews to Israel was an important precursor to the millennium.[31] And as the Mormons worked toward building New Jerusalem in America, they felt it their duty to do their part to restore the Jews to Old Jerusalem in Palestine. To that end, early in the 1830s, Smith gave a special blessing to Orson Hyde, an original member of the Quorum of the Twelve Apostles. Smith revealed that it was the quorum's responsibility to oversee the governance of the church and to conduct missions "first unto the Gentiles and then unto the Jews."[32] Hyde would lead the Jewish mission. Smith prophesied that Hyde would one day go to Jerusalem "and be a watchman unto the house of Israel," facilitating there "the gathering together of [the Jewish] people."[33]

In 1841, Hyde set off on a mission across Europe and the Near East. With stops in England, the Netherlands, and Palestine, Hyde's mandate was to bring the gospel to the people he called the modern-day remnant of "Judah." He was also charged with encouraging them to leave "Gentile" cities of Europe, which would soon be laid to waste in the global calamities before the return of Christ.[34] Despite their outward expressions of philo-Semitism, the early Saints' view of the Jews was not without its complications. Like the Hebrew Bible, the Book of Mormon also emphasizes the divide, even antagonism between the tribes of Israel and Judah.[35] The Book of Mormon recognizes that the Jews were once a covenantal people. Yet it also espouses long-standing views of deicide, blaming the Jews for Christ's death, a communal sin that led to their exile from their own promised land. The Jews had rejected the universalized gospel offered by Christ. And in doing so, in the eyes of the Mormons (along with many other nineteenth-century Christians), this once covenantal people broke the covenant of their forefathers.[36]

Orson Hyde brought these sentiments with him on his 1841 mission and expressed them during his audiences with leading rabbis in London, the Netherlands, and Jerusalem. The Jewish people had lost their "kingdom— a land flowing with milk and honey," Hyde wrote in a letter to England's chief rabbi, Solomon Hirschel. Because of their fathers' idolatry and because they caused the "shedding of [Christ's] innocent blood," God meted out the appropriate punishment for their crimes, namely the Babylonian conquest, the destruction of the temple, and exile "to the four quarters of the earth." Like the seed of Cain, because of the sin against the family—in this case, sin against God's only begotten son—these sons of Judah were separated from the rest of humanity and forced to live in ghettos in Europe and Eurasia. There they were reduced to the state of shylocks, "buying and selling the stale refuse with which their fathers would never have defiled their hands." Yet Hyde's message was that the Mormon gospel gave the Jews a new chance at redemption and restoration to their own lands. Hyde's mission was to call them to "repent" and return to the covenant "as in the days of old."[37]

Like the first Mormon mission to the (Native) American branch of Israel a decade before, during his mission Hyde made no Jewish converts. And like that first mission to the Delaware Indians, Hyde blamed interference from unfriendly Christian missionaries whom he encountered in the mission field as well as the unpreparedness of the Judaic branch of Israel to accept the restored gospel.[38] But according to Hyde, his visit to Jerusalem was still a success. On October 24, 1841, Hyde climbed atop the Mount of Olives. There he prayed to the Lord to facilitate the Jewish gathering to the Holy Land. He also built a simple stone shrine to memorialize the event.[39] For the next half century, in their newspapers the Mormons reported on events in Palestine, often citing the "gathering" of the Jews as fulfillment of Hyde's rededication of Palestine to Judah.[40] Yet in the near term, besides Hyde's mission to the Holy Land, the Mormons watched Old World Jerusalem at a physical and theological distance. The Mormons discovered that a more important remnant of Israel was even closer at hand.

Three Josephs

With the Lamanites at least temporarily out of reach, and with the Jews a less than favorable and less than enthusiastic alternative, the Latter-day Saints began emphasizing the implicit Israelite lineage already in their midst. And the patrilineage that the Saints hoped to follow back to the ancient Abrahamic covenant ran through Joseph Smith Jr. and his first converts, his immediate family. On its title page, the Book of Mormon is described as having "come forth . . . by way of the Gentile," namely "Joseph Smith, Jun." However, within the Book of Mormon's actual text, Mormon describes finding evidence on the ancient Hebraic plates, which Lehi's family brought with them when they fled Jerusalem, that Joseph Smith's complete identity is not so self-evident. Mormon cites a vision from history's first Joseph, the son of Jacob (Israel) and great-grandson of Abraham. While a captive in Egypt, the ancient Joseph foresaw that "out of the fruit of his [own] loins" a Joseph of the last days would be born. This latter-day Joseph would write down the words of the Lord. He would then bring these written words to the Lamanites, which would help restore them to the covenants of their forefathers. The ancient Joseph foretold not only that this future Joseph's "name shall be called after me" but that he would be named "after the name of his father."[41]

More so than either the Lamanites or even the Jews, these three Josephs—the ancient Joseph, Joseph Smith Sr., and Joseph Smith Jr.—formed an Abrahamic patrilineage that survived over three millennia. Joseph Smith's dual identity, a Gentile *and* a seed of Abraham, reflected what would come to be typical of many early converts who would be named as descendants of ancient Israelite patriarchs. According to the Book of Mormon, Joseph Smith Jr.'s "Gentile" identity was a political designation; Smith belonged to the "nations of the Gentiles" where Nephi prophesied the true church would be established.[42] While Smith and his successors pledged fealty to the constitutional principles of the Republic, their patrilineal identity as sons of Joseph and Abraham would supersede their identity as Gentile citizens of the United States. For the rest of the nineteenth century—especially once the Mormons reached Utah—the line between the Gentile American nation and these Israelite Mormon families would become more explicit and more contentious.

The Patriarch of the Latter Days

According to the Book of Mormon, the three Josephs shared more than a name. The family resemblance among son, father, and ancient progenitor was literal. "He shall be like unto me," declared the first Joseph.[43] These genealogical connections among these three Josephs were established in the Book of Mormon and thus were present well before the founding of the church. Yet the true import of the latter-day Joseph Smith's literal link to the ancient Joseph was only articulated after the failure to attract Lamanite descendants of Israel with whom the early "Gentile" Saints expected to covenant. At that point, Smith and his early followers went searching for other heirs of the Abrahamic covenant. And they found them in the Smiths' own family tree. Starting in the mid-1830s, the ritual of naming of Mormons' descent from ancient Israelite patriarchs increasingly became part of the familial, even ethnic identity that defined membership in the Mormon people.[44]

Just a month after the expulsion of the Mormons from Jackson County, on December 18, 1833, by revelation the prophet of the restored church named his father "Patriarch." This office empowered the elder Joseph to bless individual Mormon converts and, if such a connection existed, proclaim their connection to the house of Israel.[45] In 1834, these blessings were limited mostly to the patriarch's immediate family and their spouses. But by 1835, Joseph Smith Sr. began blessing many more Saints. And by the time they were driven out of Nauvoo in late 1846, Smith Sr. and his successors and sons, Hyrum and William Smith, along with the other patriarchs appointed to provide blessings within their regional stakes, had performed thousands of blessings. Modeled after the blessing that the Hebrew prophet Jacob (Israel) gave to his sons before his death, the Mormons' patriarchal blessings ritualized the naming of individuals and the ordering of them according to the hierarchy of the lineages.[46]

Joseph Jr. and Joseph Sr. described their Israelite family tree as a literal connection between the modern Josephs and the ancient Hebraic patriarch of the same name. But this family tree was also allegorical. On December 18, 1833, when Joseph Smith Jr. blessed his father, the younger Joseph declared that the elder Joseph was akin to "an olive tree whose branches are bowed down with much fruit." A year later, Joseph Sr. described his son "as a fruitful olive and choice vine . . . laden with precious fruit."[47] As for those Gentile converts not deemed to have a literal connection to the Israel covenant, they could be grafted onto this allegorical olive tree by accepting the covenantal contract of belief in Christ as humanity's messiah.

In the first decades of the church, this grafting of converts became an elaborate theology of adoption into Abrahamic patrilineal families. This adoption theology echoed the Book of Mormon precedent, which understood that "all mankind" who seek to participate in Christ's covenant "must be born again." This new birth necessitated a change from a "carnal and fallen state, to a state of righteousness."[48] In his 1837 *Voice of Warning to All People*, perhaps the most systematic treatise of Mormon theology written in the nineteenth century, Parley P. Pratt echoed this belief. As it was in Christ's first church, in this last dispensation no one could become a citizen of God's kingdom without being adopted into it. And yet Pratt also suggests the existence of a hierarchy within this citizenry. Divinely appointed disciples were charged with unlocking "the door of the kingdom and adopt[ing] strangers and foreigners into it as legal citizens, by administering certain laws and ordinances." These ordinances included baptism and adoption.[49] Pratt's *Voice of Warning* hinted at a shift in early Mormon epistemology, which led to an evolution in Mormon ontology. At least for those discovering that they were firstborn members of the covenant, baptism into the restored church did not lead to a new birth. One was not needed. By dint of their descent from Israel, the most sacred of bloodlines flowed in their veins. And the patriarchal blessing became the ritualized mechanism to sort out the patrilineal divisions in the human family. Before the creation of a restored and expanded covenantal family tree could proceed, the patriarchal blessing named and ordered converts' relationships to the most favored and least favored lineages of Noah.

This naming and ordering had to be recorded, too. The physical and oral performance of the patriarch's blessing—in which the patriarch laid his hands upon the head of the recipient and, increasingly as time went on, pronounced his or her lineage—was compiled in patriarchal blessing books.[50] The first entry in the first of these special ledgers is dated December 9, 1834. It records the patriarch's blessing for Joseph Smith Sr.'s oldest surviving son, Hyrum. Joseph Sr. named Hyrum a "true descendent" of Joseph. He also foresaw that Hyrum's "posterity shall be numbered with the house of Ephraim."[51] That same day, the patriarch blessed several of his other children and their spouses. For example, Joseph Smith Sr. blessed his son William as the "seed of Joseph." In his blessing for William's wife, Caroline, Joseph Sr. declared that her union with William meant that her "seed shall be numbered with the chosen seed." Because of Emma Hale Smith's devotion to her husband, Joseph Smith Jr., the patriarch declared that Emma would enjoy Joseph's blessings "and rejoice in the glory which shall come upon him."[52]

As for Joseph Smith Jr., in the first patriarchal blessings book, the patriarch's blessing for his son-turned-prophet noted that the Lord had selected him to bring forth "a marvelous work"—the Book of Mormon—"which shall prepare the way for the remnants of [the Lord's] people to come in among the Gentiles, with their fulness, as the tribes of Israel are restored." Joseph Sr.'s blessing shows that, despite their initial failure to convert the Indian "remnant of Jacob," the early Saints held out hoped that some covenant between Gentile and Israelite would still be formed. Yet the definition of Gentile and Israelite had been clarified and expanded. Instead of finding it only among the Lamanites, the covenantal connection to the ancient patriarchs could also be located within many white Saints' family lines. Joseph Sr. declared that Joseph Jr. was no Gentile. Instead he was the biblical Joseph's "seed, scattered *with the* Gentiles" and counted among the "sons of Ephraim."[53] This pronouncement of the Smith family's literal connection to Ephraim was not unexpected. It reinforced Joseph Smith Jr.'s earlier revelations that the progeny of Ephraim were destined to receive the greatest blessings and fill the most important roles in the restoration.[54]

However, before the patriarch's blessings began to reveal something different, many if not most early converts thought of themselves as Gentiles. For example, in the May 1833 edition of the *Evening and the Morning Star*, W. W. Phelps published a letter written by Eliel Strong and Eleazer Miller from Rutland, Pennsylvania. "Above all," the two converts noted, they were most grateful "that we, as Gentiles, have the privilege of receiving the light manifested" for the "restoration" of God's elect. Strong and Miller also referenced the Book of Mormon allegory in which Gentiles are grafted onto Israel's olive tree so that the fruit produced from such unions is "like unto [the tree's] natural fruit." "By entering into the covenant, we may become the spiritual children of Abraham," wrote the two "Gentile" converts, "and with Israel partake of the fatness and the fulness of the olive tree."[55]

Smith's early revelations supported the belief that Gentiles could join this family tree. The early Saints were to seek out those Gentiles like Strong and Miller who, as Christ describes in the Book of Mormon—a passage reprinted in the December 1832 edition of the *Evening and the Morning Star*— "will not harden their hearts, that they repent and come unto me . . . and be numbered among my people, O house of Israel."[56] At least according to available records, in his first year as patriarch, Joseph Smith Sr. rarely named a Saint to a particular lineage, reinforcing the notion that the early Saints believed that most converts were made up of Gentiles like Strong and Miller.[57] For example, in his March 19, 1835, blessing of early Mormon convert and California pioneer Samuel Rolfe, Joseph Smith Sr. did not name Rolfe to any Israelite lineage. Instead Joseph Smith Sr. told Rolfe that because he had that day received "the blessing of Abraham," he was "now numbered with [Abraham's seed]." On occasion, Joseph Sr. even declared that a blessing recipient was "an orphan," most often indicating that they did not have any parents who were members of the church. Such was the case for John Allen, an early member of the church hierarchy, whom the patriarch described as not having a "father to bless thee." The senior Joseph thus took on the role of adoptive father. Through his blessing, the patriarch transformed Allen into "the seed of Joseph."[58]

In terms of the insight it provides into early Mormon views on race, perhaps the most significant of the several dozen extant orphan blessings that the first Mormon patriarch pronounced was on behalf of Elijah Abel. In 1836, the same year Joseph Smith Jr. gave him a missionary license, Abel received a blessing from Joseph Smith Sr. Laying his hands on Abel's head, the elder Joseph made no mention of Abel's lineage, which might have traced the mixed-race missionary back to Ham or Cain. Instead, Joseph Sr. declared, "I seal upon thee a father's blessing, because thou art an orphan."[59] As part of this blessing, the patriarch noted Abel's perilous journey to join the Mormons: "The Lord hast his eye upon thee, and brought you through straits and thou hast come to be rec[k]oned with the saints of the most high." Since Abel had been brought into fellowship, even an adoptive kinship with the Mormons, the patriarch also noted that Abel had "been ordained an Elder." The patriarch did not foresee that this ordination would become a source of contention decades later when the Saints settled in Utah and established limitations for black participation in the Mormon covenant. Instead, Joseph Sr. prophesied that Abel would travel on behalf of church until a "good old age." Joseph Sr. even declared that Abel's blessing was archived not only in the earthbound patriarchal blessings book. Abel's name would also be "written in the Lamb's Book of Life," the heaven-bound registry of the names of the Saints who will have eternal life.[60]

Abel was not the only Mormon of African descent to be blessed by the early church patriarchs. In 1844, Hyrum Smith, who succeeded his father as patriarch after Joseph Sr.'s death in 1840, blessed the black Mormon pioneer Jane Manning James. Hyrum named James as the "seed of Ham," a lineage that by the time the Saints reached Utah would be deemed ineligible of full inclusion in the Mormon sacred community. The absence of such proclamation in Abel's blessing might be the result of Abel's ambiguous racial background; church leaders described Abel as an "octoroon."[61] Other possibilities must also be considered. During the eight years between the two blessings, much had evolved in the Saints' theology of race and lineage. For one, the distinction among the other branches of Noah's progeny became well established. Pronouncing the difference between Japheth's Gentiles and Shem's Israelites had become ritualized in the patriarchal blessing. Likewise, as it was for those Saints born Gentiles, before the descendants of Ham could be adopted into the Israelite covenant, their original lineage had to be named so that they could be adopted into the covenant and then renamed members of Zion.[62]

What's more, during this period the Latter-day Saints' public pronouncements regarding the proper place of African Americans within the restored church and in the Republic also came into sharper relief. In the mid-1830s during their exile from Jackson County, the Mormons repeatedly denied any interest in converting blacks. And Joseph Smith himself pledged fealty to slavery's status quo. Yet in 1844, from the relative safety of Nauvoo, Illinois, Smith welcomed black converts like James and Abel into the Mormon community—even into his home (chapter 4). As a candidate for the presidency of the United States, Joseph Smith declared himself a gradual abolitionist. In his presidential platform, Smith even described both the persecution of the Saints and the perpetuation of slavery as affronts to the principles of liberty enshrined in the Declaration of Independence.[63]

And yet, mention of Abel's African parentage, indirect though it might have been, did make it into his 1836 blessing. Joseph Smith Sr. declared that Abel "must seek first the kingdom of heaven and all blessings shall be added thereto." For Abel these blessings included overcoming his blackness in the hereafter: "Thou shalt be made equal to thy brethren, and thy soul [will] be white in eternity and thy robes glittering."[64] Thus for Joseph Smith Sr., Abel's African blood did not make him existentially ineligible for exaltation, as would be the position of later church leaders. Abel could be made worthy, and even made white, by seeking out the kingdom of heaven and serving the church.

In his blessing of Abel, the patriarch made clear that grafting onto the tree of Israel resulted not simply in spiritual changes but in physical changes, too—changing the color of souls, for example, from black to white. Three years after his father blessed Abel, in June 1839, Joseph Smith Jr. explained that white Gentile converts experienced changes to their blood as they are grafted onto the tree of Israel. "The effect of the Holy Ghost upon a gentile is to purge out the old blood, and make him actually of the seed of Abraham," Smith explained. "That man who has none of the blood of Abraham (naturally) must have a new creation by the Holy Ghost." And when such a change occurs to a Gentile convert's blood, the change would result in "a [more] powerful effect upon the body, and visible to the eye, than upon a [natural-born] Israelite [convert]."[65] The patriarchal blessing became perhaps the most efficient mechanism to bring about such changes. Take, for example, John Landers's July 17, 1840, blessing. Through the authority vested in the patriarch, Landers, an "orphan," was renamed a "literal descendent, and of the covenant seed of Abraham." Joseph Smith Sr. declared that the blessing he bestowed upon Flanders cleansed the convert so completely that "little or no gentile blood remain[ed]" in his "veins."[66]

As the number and import of patriarchal blessings increased, the frequency of declaration of Israelite lineages also increased. According to one estimate, by 1838 the vast majority of blessings contained some kind of declaration of biblical patrilineage.[67] This suggests that during the second half of the 1830s, the Saints grew more confident in their belief that most early white converts were not in fact Gentiles. Instead, they were members of the house of Israel scattered in politically defined Gentile nations. These converts shared more than a new religion. They were literally long-lost kin, making the covenantal bonds between them both spiritual and familial.

To be sure, the Mormon temple sealing ceremonies, developed mostly during the Nauvoo period, with significant changes occurring throughout Mormon history, became the most important covenantal rituals. Temple endowments sealed family members together, sealed families with other families, and sealed the Saints to their heavenly father.[68] These rituals created networks of families that the Mormons believed would survive and expand in the heavenly kingdoms to come. However, before the temple became the most sacred site for Mormon ritual performance, Joseph Smith Jr. and Joseph Smith Sr. established the patriarchal blessing as a ritualized performance of ordering Mormon converts based on their ancient patrilineage, naming them eternal Saints, and recording these names for posterity. And the patriarch's blessing books became archived repositories of the names of those who belonged to this covenantal Mormon family.

Postmodernist scholars—along with skeptics of Mormonism—might call the ritual of patriarchal blessing an act of "invention" of both traditions and ethnicities.[69] Joseph Smith Jr. would certainly reject the notion that he invented the office of the patriarch. Instead, the younger Joseph would say that the precedent that Jacob established in the Bible proved that he was restoring the patriarch's authority to bless and seal family members to each other and to God. Likewise, the older Joseph would say that when he laid his hands upon a Saint, he did not invent that blessing recipient's lineage. Instead, this ritual restored to these Mormon converts' consciousness something that their bodies already knew—that they were literal descendants of the most ancient of covenants.[70]

And yet scholars of early Mormonism can understand Mormon identity as an "invented" Israelite ethnicity without evoking, as Werner Sollors has written, "a conspiratorial interpretation of a manipulative inventor who single-handedly makes ethnics out of unsuspecting subjects."[71] Instead, rooted in extant Anglo-American ideas of British Israelism—that scattered among the British were long-lost descendants of the lost tribes of Israel—the Mormons created *first* their own conception of a literal covenantal family. And like the emergence of other national or ethnic groups in the eighteenth and nineteenth centuries, only *later* in Utah did they create a specific Mormon ethnicity. This ethnicity was fashioned at the intersection of shared ancient kinships, shared interpretation of sacred texts, shared participation in sacred rituals, and shared experiences—most notably persecution, exodus, and gathering to their new Zion in the Great Basin.

Soon after the assassination of Joseph Smith Jr., the once universal Mormon covenant became more particular. In Utah, the Saints found that true Gentiles showed their true Gentile nature through their indifference or antipathy to the Mormons' message. African Americans wore their less-than-worthy lineage on their skin. And increasingly, the Saints found that most Indians were by nature unrepentant savages, antagonistic to their own Israelite kin and to their own Israelite selves. Yet a decade before the beginning of the Mormons' exodus to Utah, as white "Gentile" Mormons began to discover their own connection to the most ancient and favored covenant, the seeds of this new Mormon ethnicity were already planted.[72]

Believing Blood and the British Mission

The discovery found in the early Mormon patriarchal blessings that many, if not most Gentile converts "naturally" belonged to Abraham's family tree, as Joseph Smith himself put it, had implications for how the Mormons understood their missionary successes in the late 1830s and the 1840s. Many of Smith's earliest American-born converts were of English heritage, some with family still in the old country. As such, Smith and other Mormon leaders believed that, based on shared linguistic, religious, and familial roots, the English would be receptive to the Mormon missionaries' message. In the spring of 1837, Smith sent Apostles Heber C. Kimball and Orson Hyde to establish a mission in England, in order to "open the door to salvation" for that nation.[73] Soon after making landfall in England in the summer of 1837, the missionaries met with immediate success, especially in the mill town of Preston in Lancashire. In particular, the missionaries made inroads with members of the family of the Mormon missionary Joseph Fielding. Fielding's brother, the Methodist minister Rev. James Fielding, and Fielding's brother-in-law the Rev. Timothy Mathews, lent the missionaries their pulpits, leading to many in their congregations to convert. Soon, word of the new gospel spread throughout Preston. Before he left in the spring of 1838, Joseph Fielding estimated that there were nearly 1,000 members organized into twenty branches around the city.[74] Over the next three years, subsequent missions grew the number of British Saints to over 3,500. Parley P. Pratt and Brigham Young oversaw the development of the mission's infrastructure, including the founding of the Manchester-based *Millennial Star,* as well as the printing of five thousand copies of the Book of Mormon and three thousand hymnals.[75] American and newly ordained local missionaries distributed this literature and preached before church congregations, temperance organizations, and the merely curious in rented social halls throughout the urban centers of the British Isles. English cities like Manchester and Liverpool quickly became home to Mormon congregations that rivaled in numbers the Mormon communities in America.[76]

Why such a bountiful harvest? To be sure, part of the answer is that Mormonism responded to practical concerns. As was the case among the converts from New England and Upstate New York, the Mormons were successful in England because their message was well suited for a rapidly industrializing culture experiencing sweeping economic and social change.

The missionaries' willingness to welcome all those interested in the gospel contrasted sharply with English denominations that increasingly divided along class lines. The possibility of emigrating was also an attraction. After all, the United States was a nation where even the "poor and the ignorant," but industrious and ambitious, as Young later described the British converts, could buy land, start businesses, and vote.[77]

Yet according to the Mormon missionaries in England, Mormonism's true appeal was more spiritual than practical. As was the case with Sydney Rigdon's Kirtland-based Campbellite community a decade earlier, the missionaries found great success among British-based movements that also stressed immediate religious experiences, social reform, and a lay clergy. For example, Wilford Woodruff claimed that over a span of several months in 1840, he converted and baptized all but one of the six hundred United Brethren of the Gadfield Elm Chapel in Worcestershire, including dozens of the movement's lay leadership.[78] The success of the British mission guaranteed the survival of the church during a period rife with internal dissention and external persecution in the American branches of the church. By the end of 1840, nearly one in four Mormons lived in England, a proportion that would steadily increase during the next decade.[79]

As natural a fit Mormonism's message was to religious communities already spiritually primed to receive it, Mormons would come to believe that the reaction to the gospel from the British converts was equally natural, perhaps even biological. Though not as common as the belief that Native Americans were the unredeemed descendants of the lost tribes of Israel, in the first half of the nineteenth century, some Anglo-Americans promoted a belief in British Israelism. In 1840, just as the Mormon missionaries were converting thousands of Englishmen, the Scotsman John F. Wilson published *Our Israelitish Origin*. Wilson became a popular speaker on the lecture circuit in England and in America. To his audiences, he proclaimed a literal connection between the contemporary population of the British Isles and the lost tribes of Israel. The Mormons shared with Wilson this belief in British Israelism, in particular that their new converts were heretofore "invisible" Israelites whose acceptance of Mormonism was not only a matter of faith.[80] As many Mormons would later describe it, because they were born into the Abrahamic covenant, these converts had "believing blood"; their blood was predisposed to believe in the Mormons' gospel.[81]

However, the scant interest in Mormonism among the Jews whom Orson Hyde encountered in Europe and in Jerusalem as well as the failure of the early missions to the Lamanites proved that not all-believing blood is created equal. After all, as Orson Hyde made clear in his letter to England's chief Rabbi, Solomon Hirschel, the Jews were descendants of Judah, the benighted betrayers of "Jesus of Nazareth," who called for his crucifixion by declaring, " 'let his blood be on us and on our children.' "[82] Likewise, the Lamanites, who showed their antipathy toward the gospel during Book of Mormon times by slaughtering their more righteous kin, the Nephites, and seeking to destroy the Plates of Nephi on which the New World gospel was archived, would come to be associated with Joseph's less favored son, Manasseh.[83] However, at the stake conference in Manchester on April 6, 1841, celebrating the eleventh anniversary of the church's founding, the British church counted 5,814 members—with 800 having already emigrated to the United States. Such great missionary success demonstrated that the gathering of Ephraim's branch of Israel was occurring as prophesied.[84] Judah, Manasseh, and Ephraim might all be named Abraham's seed. But each branch of Abraham's tree confirmed their hierarchical order by their relative receptivity to the gospel.

And yet, it is important to remember that the Mormons rejected the Calvinist concept of irresistible grace. Onetime editor of the *Millennial Star* Orson F. Whitney described belief in Mormonism in racialized terms. "As well might the leopard hope to change his spots, or the Ethiopian his skin, . . . [It is impossible] for a child of Israel to rid himself in this life of the blood that flows in his veins. . . . Believing blood will believe in the Church." Still, even those who belong to such sacred lineages can reject it. "If spirit can rebel, surely blood can, even the blood of Israel, and forsaking its first love, turn away from the God of Abraham, Isaac, and Jacob."[85]

Yet in the second half of the 1830s, the importance of shared lineages named in patriarchal blessings became an increasingly important marker of church membership. The Mormons were not just a covenantal community of believers. They belonged to an ever-expanding network of family trees. And during the nineteenth and twentieth centuries the most important branch of this tree was Ephraim. "It is Ephraim that I have been searching for all the days of my preaching," declared the former head of the British mission and then church president Brigham Young in 1855, "and that is the blood that ran [through] my veins when I embraced the gospel." In 1893, another onetime British missionary leader and then church president, Wilford Woodruff, made the connection between the Saints and Ephraim even more explicit: "Ninety-nine out of every hundred of this people are descendants of Ephraim that have been scattered among the nations."[86] Not all of Ephraim became Mormon. But almost all Mormons were Ephraim.

The Patriarch and the Priesthood

The ritualized naming of patrilineage defined the hierarchal order in the restored church. And patrilineage defined the priesthood. In 1835, Joseph Smith Sr. began performing patriarchal blessings for Latter-day Saints outside his immediate family. That same year, Joseph Smith Jr. revealed that "the order of [the restored] priesthood was . . . handed down from father to son, and rightly belongs to the literal descendants of the chosen seed." The prophet specified that this priesthood order was established at the beginning of human history with Adam. Adam passed the priesthood to Seth, his firstborn. Adam also ordained his great-grandson Methuselah. And "under [his] hand," Methuselah ordained his grandson Noah.[87]

This 1835 revelation was certainly not the first time that Joseph Smith Jr. spoke about the central role that the priesthood would play in the building the kingdom of God.[88] Smith explained that the true Christian priesthood had been lost to the apostasy of the Lamanites in the New World and the corruption of the abominable church in the Old. Yet it had been restored in this last dispensation when the Lord sent Peter, James, John, and John the Baptist to ordain Joseph Smith, who in turn ordained his first followers. On April 6, 1830, the day the Church of Christ was established, Smith taught the Mormons' first priesthood holders how to baptize and ordain others.[89] Early the next year, Smith revealed that it was the law of the church that only those Latter-day Saints properly ordained by priesthood holders have the authority to preach the gospel and teach the scriptures.[90] Yet, beyond baptism into the restored church and ordination by the laying on of hands, no special training was required to hold the priesthood. As such, the Mormon priesthood stood in sharp contrast with what Saints often derided as the "priestcraft" of the professional Protestant clergy as well as the priests of the Catholic Church. The Mormons believed that theirs was a restoration of the primitive church's priesthood in which all (male) believers had the authority to serve the people of Christ and to expand the kingdom of God.

As much as the priesthood was to be expansive, Smith realized that it also required order. In the first three years of the church's history, Smith structured the priesthood into an elaborate hierarchy. Priesthood officers were assigned specific duties, ordained with appropriate authorities, and organized into quorums according to their offices. Smith revealed that the prophet and two other "High Priests," who would serve as councillors to the prophet, formed the First Presidency of the Church. Along with this First Presidency, Smith charged the Quorums of the Twelve and the Seventy with overseeing the national and international missions. High priests along with lower-ranking deacons, teachers, and bishops were called to manage the affairs within Zion.[91] Smith also revealed that within the priesthood itself, there existed two divisions. The higher "Melchizedek" priesthood would administer "spiritual" ordinances and would hold "the key of mysteries of the kingdom." The lesser "Aaronic" priesthood would administer "outward" ordinances, like baptism and the sacrament.[92]

Though it was an essential building block of the Mormon hierarchy, the priesthood was more than an administrative office. It was also the organizing principle of the Mormons' reimagined conception of Israel's covenantal family, an ancient family restored in this lifetime and bound together for the eternal life to come.[93] As early as September 1832, Smith first revealed that, through their ordination, priesthood holders of the latter-day Church of Christ became "sons of Moses and of Aaron and the seed of Abraham."[94] For the first five years of the church's history, because most Saints were believed to be Gentiles by birth, such patrilineal bond between latter-day priesthood holders' and their Israelite forefathers was believed to be the fruit of spiritual adoption into the restored covenant. But in April 1835, when Joseph Smith expanded the hierarchical organization that he established in 1831, the distance between patrilineage and priesthood collapsed. To be sure, the laying on of hands of one Melchizedek priesthood holder conferred the same priesthood to another worthy (male) Saint, whatever the lineage. Yet the Saint who was "a litteral [sic] descendant of Aaron"—Moses's brother and the first high priest of the Israelites—had the "legal right" to the priesthood.[95] And through their patriarchal blessings more and more Saints who had believed themselves to be Gentiles discovered that they were birthright heirs to the Israelite covenant.

As such, the priesthood increasingly became a family business. It was passed down from ancient Israelite fathers to latter-day Mormon sons. At the same time that Joseph Smith Jr. was articulating the import of Israelite patrilineage for the priesthood within the church-wide hierarchy, his father's patriarchal blessings revealed how individual Latter-day Saints' genealogies related to their priesthood authority. For example, on April 30, 1835, Joseph Smith Sr. declared that Jonathan H. Hale, a future bishop of Nauvoo, was already "of the blood of Israel" and thus already had "the power of the Melchizedek Priesthood." Likewise, because Wilford Woodruff was a descendent of Joseph and "of the blood of Ephraim," the patriarch declared that Woodruff's "great blessings" included the "power and authority of the Melchisedeck priesthood." These inherited authorities would extend into future generations. "Thy sons shall receive the priesthood," the patriarch told Woodruff.[96] Such blessings reveal that the early Saints understood that rights to the priesthood were a result of birth and not simply a condition of belief.

The Book of Abraham

Revelation and patriarchal blessings were not the only sources for the knowledge that priesthood and patrilineage were intricately connected. In 1835, when both Joseph Smith Jr. and his father began declaring the priesthood a birthright for those named descendants of Abraham, the younger Smith began yet another ambitious translation project, which decades later would be canonized as the book of Abraham. This new translation reinforced Smith's belief that a Saint's priesthood authority was inherited from his ancient forefathers.[97]

After Jean-François Champollion used the Rosetta Stone to decipher ancient Egyptian hieroglyphics in 1822, interest in all things Egyptian spread across Europe and America. In an attempt to profit from the public's great demand for Egyptian antiquities, the Irish-born Michael H. Chandler purchased a set of mummies. Over the next two years, Chandler and his mummies toured the United States. According to Chandler's advertisements, in cities like Philadelphia and Baltimore people lined up to see "strangers" from ancient times who "may have lived in the days of Jacob, Moses, or David."[98] In July 1835, Chandler traveled to Kirtland, Ohio, in hopes of employing Smith's translation skills to help him decipher ancient Egyptian papyri that he had purchased with the mummies. After all, Smith had already translated one ancient record—the Plates of Nephi—from their original "Reformed Egyptian" into the Book of Mormon. Chandler may also have hoped to tempt Smith into purchasing his collection. When Smith inspected Chandler's papyri, to his prophetic eye the hieroglyphics spelled out "the writings of Abraham while he was in Egypt, called the Book of Abraham, and written by his own hand, upon papyrus."[99] Though the community was already financially overleveraged from building the Kirtland Temple, Smith raised $2,400 to purchase the papyri and four of Chandler's mummies.[100]

Half a century later, the histories of the papyri and the temple would converge again. By the 1880s, the exegesis of a few passages of the book of Abraham served as a popular scriptural justification for banning black men from the priesthood and all blacks from the most sacred parts of the temple where such rituals as marriage sealings and other ordinances were performed.[101] In the 1830s, however, the book of Abraham served a more immediate function. It provided ancient scriptural support for Smith's evolving views on the connection between priesthood and descent from biblical patriarchs.[102] Like the Book of Mormon and the book of Moses, the book of Abraham expands on familiar biblical themes. In Joseph Smith's translation, Abraham is more than the father of many nations. He is also the first patriarch to articulate the origins of the patrilineal priesthood. Abraham explains that the priesthood "was conferred upon me from the fathers; it came down from the beginning of time . . . [from] the first man who is Adam, our first father." Describing the genesis of ancient Egypt, in the book of Abraham, Abraham also writes that "Pharaoh" was "the eldest son of Egyptus, the daughter of Ham." Despite receiving "blessings of the earth, and . . . blessings of wisdom," Pharaoh and his descendants were "cursed as pertaining to the priesthood" because they were of the lineage of the cursed Ham.[103]

The priesthood authority was patrilineal. Although Ham's (and Pharaoh's) descendants would not have access to it, God explained to Abraham that his own "seed" was synonymous with the priesthood. "In thy seed (that is, thy priesthood) for I give unto thee a promise that this right [of the priesthood] shall continue in thee, and in thy seed after thee (that is to say, the literal seed, or the seed of the body)." Yet the book of Abraham also presents the potential for an ever-expanding priesthood. The Lord promises to make of Abraham "a great nation," a nation that would not only include his own descendants. His progeny "shall bear this ministry and Priesthood unto all nations . . . for as many as receive this Gospel shall be called after thy name, and shall be accounted thy seed."[104]

The book of Abraham thus presents the priesthood as both particular and potentially universal. The priesthood is an inherited authority. But it is also an authority that is intended to be shared: to restore, through the act of adoption—ritualized first in the patriarchal blessing and later in the temple—the less favored biblical lineages into the heavenly father's good graces. The book of Abraham also makes clear the limitations to this universalism. Certain lineages—namely, that of Ham—would not be eligible for the priesthood, even through adoption.

There is no evidence that during his lifetime Smith or any of his followers cited the book of Abraham to deny black Mormon men the priesthood. In fact, just months before Smith began translating the book of Abraham, the February 1835 edition of the *Messenger & Advocate* again articulated the early Mormon message of universal salvation. "Whether they are descendants of Shem, Ham, or Japheth, in Christ they should be blessed."[105] The book of Abraham reflects Joseph Smith's ambivalent views on black spiritual potential, views that Smith recorded in his revelatory translations but did not act on in his relationships with African Americans. Pharaoh and

Ham in the book of Abraham, Cain in the book of Moses, and Laman in the Book of Mormon present a caveat to Smith's theological universalism even as he insisted that every individual enters this world without shouldering the sins of his or her fathers. Not until the 1880s, when the book of Abraham was canonized, did Pharaoh's priesthood curse become the scriptural linchpin of black exclusion from the priesthood and the temple.[106] By then, church leadership had been teaching for some thirty years that the sons and daughters of Ham wore on their skin markers signifying curses that even patriarchal adoption could not overcome.

From Gentile to Israelite

It is important not to overstate how quickly the Latter-day Saints' covenantal contract *contracted* from its universal beginnings. What would become in the Utah period a peculiar, even an ethnic Mormon identity, remained in the 1830s and early 1840s largely inchoate. As Jan Shipps has argued, in the first decades of Mormon history, the formula for "making Saints" appeared to differ little from the process of "making converts to Protestant churches." Acceptance of the Mormon gospel, obedience to Joseph Smith's revelations, acceptance of the authority of the priesthood, and baptism into the Church of Christ were enough to make anybody a Mormon. Yet unlike members of many other evangelical traditions, Mormons began to understand conversion into their church as the result of heretofore undiscovered descent from biblical patriarchs. Save for the few Gentiles whose conversions made them into "new creations"—even with new blood of Abraham coursing through their veins—the Holy Spirit did not have to "renovate" many converts' whole beings, as Charles Grandison Finney might have said about evangelical rebirth and sanctification.[107]

Conversion was not the cause of new life. Instead it was the effect of descent from ancient biblical forefathers.[108] The missionaries in America and in the British Isles found receptive audiences because these converts had an inborn yearning to hear and accept Mormonism. As much as their minds and hearts, the Mormons began to believe that these converts' blood was predisposed to the message of the gospel. Likewise, other Gentiles seemed to prove their true Gentile ontology by their indifference or antagonism to Mormonism. Writing in his journal in June 1840, Wilford Woodruff made the distinction between unbelieving Gentiles and Saints unequivocal. At that time, Woodruff witnessed increased levels of "Gentile" persecution in England and heard troubling reports from the United States. In the two previous years, anti-Mormon Missourians attacked a Mormon settlement at Haun's Mill, in Caldwell County, killing eighteen. The Saints' were finally expelled from Missouri. And Joseph Smith and other leading Mormons had been imprisoned in the Liberty, Missouri, jail for five months. In response, Woodruff wrote that "England & America" would not be "excepted" in the final judgment before Christ's return. Instead these nations "are ownly fuel for the fire & tinder for the Breath of the Almighty." The Mormons' Gentile persecutors had "trodden" down the two branches of Israel, "Judah & Ephraim." But, Woodruff warned, Israel "will rise again & fulfill the word of God on thee!"[109] For Woodruff, a "Gentile" shows his true colors in response to the gospel; a Gentile rejects it, an Israelite embraces it.

This belief that the embrace or rejection of Mormonism was somehow an inherited family trait existed in tension with a universalistic, covenantal community to which the Mormons dedicated themselves in the first three years of the church's history and to which, in principle, they remained committed through the early 1840s. In June 1840, as Heber C. Kimball described the nature of the British converts in Preston, "the Saints, in general, as they have been baptized into one body are partakers of the same spirit, whether they be Jew or Gentile, bond or free."[110] And yet, despite Kimball's paraphrase here of Paul's universalistic message to the Galatians (and its echoes of Nephi's description of the universal covenant open to "black and white, bond and free"), lineage and its corollary, race, mattered when it came to the creation of the restored house of Israel. And lineage and its corollary, race, would matter even more in the coming years and decades.

British and, later, Scandinavian converts passed with relative ease into the "universal" category of American whiteness. These converts from supposed Gentile nations were easily renamed the seed of Abraham.[111] And their new, or rediscovered, names allowed these (male) converts to be appointed to the priesthood. As the Latter-day Saints made the priesthood a birthright reserved for those who could claim Abrahamic lineage, the difference between black and white did affect who could participate fully in the Mormon covenant. Those who wore their biblical lineages on their skin—the cursed descendants of Cain, Ham, and Canaan—could not so easily be renamed as Abraham, Joseph, or Ephraim.

4 "AUNT JANE" OR JOSEPH'S ADOPTED DAUGHTER?

In late 1843, Joseph Smith's wife Emma Hale Smith greeted Jane Manning and nine of her family members at the front door of the Mansion House in Nauvoo, Illinois.[1] The two-story Greek Revival building served as the Smiths' private home and guesthouse for visiting dignitaries to the Latter-day Saints' booming city-state built on the banks of the Mississippi in western Illinois. The travelers were exhausted. To join their new spiritual brethren, the Mannings had trekked from their home in Connecticut, where the black converts first heard and accepted the Mormon gospel. Yet before he sent them to bed, Joseph Smith ushered the Mannings into the Mansion House's sitting room. There he gathered the house's other residents, including the prophet's personal physician, John Bernhisel, and perhaps even his secret plural wives, Eliza and Emily Partridge and Sarah and Mariah Lawrence, who lived in the house as servants. Smith was anxious to hear from Jane Manning, whom he called "the head of this little band," about how Manning and her family managed to make the thousand-mile trek, much of it on foot. Jane Manning did not disappoint. She regaled Smith with the story of how, on their way to Nauvoo, her family overcame destitution, race-based persecution from both Mormons and non-Mormons alike—even threats of imprisonment for traveling without free papers—and early autumn snows. Jane Manning explained that they were guided only by their faith in the Lord and the promise of fellowship at the end of their voyage.

This harrowing story, which won Jane Manning the admiration of Joseph Smith as well as others who heard it, was written down, not in 1843 in Nauvoo, but a half century later in Salt Lake City. In 1893, Elizabeth J. D. Roundy helped Jane Manning James—she would take the surname James after marrying another black Mormon, Isaac James, in the mid-1840s—to record the black Mormon pioneer's autobiography. By then, James was no longer a young convert or a stranger to most Mormons. Instead she was the elderly "Aunt Jane," the most famous black Mormon in Salt Lake City (fig. 4.1). She was respected for her indefatigable faith in Mormonism and for her memories of Mormonism's first prophet, whom she called "the finest man I ever saw on earth."[2]

Fig. 4.1. Jane Manning James (center and inset), 1847 Pioneer Jubilee (1897). (Courtesy of L. Tom Perry Special Collections, Harold B. Lee Library, Brigham Young University, Provo, Utah)

In the 1890s, despite her advanced age, James's face belied her seventy-one years. It lacked the deep creases and liver spots that marked the faces of most of Salt Lake City's "old folks," as they were known, who first settled the valley a half century before. It also helped that she still had most of her teeth. Yet an illness had left her thin. And her eyesight was all but gone. James could no longer read or write. So she asked Roundy to help her create a written record of her "verbal statement," as Roundy wrote in the preface to the original copy of the narrative. Over the next several years, the women worked together to archive more than simply the story of James and her family's conversion to Mormonism and the trials of their trek to Nauvoo, which she first told the Mansion House residents in 1843. James also told her scribe about the life events that came after: how James became a servant to Mormonism's first two prophets, an early Mormon pioneer, a matriarch to a large Mormon family, and a faithful, tithe-paying Latter-day Saint throughout the second half of the nineteenth century, a time during which she, her husband, and their children worked alongside their white brethren to build up the Mormons' Zion in Utah.[3]

For her part, Roundy was perhaps more interested in James's memories of Joseph Smith than she was interested in James's own history. An English convert who settled in Utah in 1870, Roundy had spent the previous two decades championing efforts to document and commemorate the life of Mormonism's founder. Sometimes accompanied by her friend, the poet and Joseph Smith's widowed plural wife Eliza R. Snow, Roundy traveled the Salt Lake Valley collecting firsthand accounts of the life and words of the prophet from his earliest converts before this first generation of Mormons died.[4] In the last decades of the nineteenth century, Roundy was one of a number of prominent Latter-day Saints who worked to preserve the Mormon people's peculiar identity in a postpolygamy era. These Mormons emphasized their faith's origin myths, especially around Joseph Smith, his mandate to restore Christ's church, and the authority of his prophetic successors to continue to speak in the present tense on God's behalf.[5] In contrast, James's stake in affirming Joseph Smith as the exemplar of prophethood was at once more personal and political. She composed a revisionist history about Smith's attitudes about and actions toward Mormons of African descent.

According to James, such a revision was needed. In turn-of-the-century Utah, James was publicly celebrated as a Smith family confidante. And she was lionized as a pioneer of 1847, the year that the Mormons settled in the Great Salt Lake Basin. For the last two decades of her life, when the church gathered for General Conference and other special occasions, James and her brother, Isaac Manning, occupied a cushioned seat at the front of Salt Lake City's tabernacle.[6] Just hours after her passing at noon on April 16, 1908, the *Deseret News* rushed to publish an obituary of "Aunt Jane" on the front page of its evening edition. The church-owned paper lauded the "aged colored woman" for remaining "loyal and true to [Smith's] memory" since the prophet's death in 1844. Five days later, the *Deseret News* reported that Joseph Smith Jr.'s nephew and namesake, church president Joseph F. Smith, spoke at James's funeral, during which she was praised as a woman of "undaunted faith and goodness of heart."[7]

Yet the great fanfare with which the Mormon leadership marked James's death belies the fact that because she was black, James was excluded from full participation in the most important rituals of the church to which she had shown unbound dedication from the moment of her conversion in the early 1840s until her death in the spring of 1908. For the last several decades of her life, James engaged in a letter-writing campaign, petitioning church presidents to allow her access to the temple. Before she died, James desperately wanted to participate in the sacred temple ordinances that Mormons believe are required for exaltation in the life to come. But, as she makes clear in her autobiography and in her letters to the prophets of Zion, she was not alone in her desire that she be raised above the lowly, cursed station into which she was born. James claimed that in Nauvoo, Smith offered to adopt her as his spiritual child, which would allow James to join his family for eternity. James did not just want a seat in the tabernacle. She wanted a place in the prophet's eternal household. Joseph Smith Jr.'s successors, notably Joseph F. Smith, declared this impossible. Even for the faithful Jane Manning James, there was no place for a black woman in the eternal family of the prophet—except, perhaps, as a servant. The doors to the temple and to the highest levels of heaven were closed to James and to all sons and daughters of Cain and Ham.

James chronicled a time in Joseph Smith's Nauvoo Mansion House when the Mormon covenant was not so racially circumscribed, memories that she recounted to Roundy and that Roundy recorded with pen and paper. This archived memory of a more racially inclusive first Mormon prophet—and a more racially inclusive period in Mormon history—stood in sharp contrast with the opinions of the Mormon brethren in late nineteenth-century Utah. Joseph Smith's successors insisted that the ban on the priesthood and temple access for blacks had been in place since the beginning of the restoration. And with the canonization of Joseph Smith's translation of the books of Moses and Abraham in 1880, which contained descriptions of divine curses placed on Cain, Ham, and their progeny, church leaders argued that these curses extended back to history's first family, Adam and Eve, and carried through to the establishment of the Abrahamic covenant itself. Smith's successors were actively working to marginalize or redact Joseph Smith's racial open-mindedness. James, however, had the advantage of having lived with the prophet. She was thus a firsthand witness to and, she would argue, a beneficiary of Smith's racial magnanimity. And for James, such a privileged experience carried authority. James deployed this authority to subtly challenge the hierarchy's theologies regarding the incompatibility between full church membership for blacks and black accursedness. And she did so by writing herself into the Mormon archive that was being generated in order to exclude her black kind in general as well as to exclude her—as an individual, historical subject—in particular.

The experiences of Jane Manning James are singular in the history of Mormonism. But the act of studying this singular life story reveals the experiences of people of African descent more generally in the restored church during the Nauvoo period, roughly from 1839 to 1846. It was in this short-lived era—when Joseph Smith oversaw the largest and most successful Mormon community established during his lifetime—that the early Latter-day Saints most fully expressed and, to a degree, acted out an inclusive attitude about the potential for reconciliation of the supposedly cursed sons and daughters of Cain and Ham with the original, white human family. When it came to racial mutability, many leading Latter-day Saints in Nauvoo—notably the Smith family—held to the Book of Mormon's anti-Calvinistic precedent. Even for those born of lineages burdened with the curses of their forefathers, paternity was not destiny. During the Nauvoo period, the inverse was also true. By persecuting God's chosen people and by rejecting God's designated prophets on earth, even people born white could become cursed.

However, the Nauvoo period is not the only point of entry to understand early Mormon relations with black people. The most detailed source for Nauvoo in the 1840s is James's autobiography, which was recorded in Salt Lake City a half century removed from the events that she remembered. To compose it, James looked back on the relationship between black and white Mormons in Nauvoo through the lens of Salt Lake City. By chronicling her own thoroughly Mormon life, James also attempted to correct the vision of Joseph Smith's successors on the potential for blacks to become full members of the sacred Mormon community.

Nauvoo: A Place of Refuge, a City on the "Border of the Lamanites"

The city of Nauvoo was the closest that Joseph Smith Jr. came to establishing a New Zion in the New World. Out of a wilderness of thick bushes and bogs, which made the ground "so wet," Smith later recalled, "that it was with the utmost difficulty a foot man could get through," beginning in 1839, Nauvoo rose out of swampland. At its height Nauvoo became a bustling, frontier metropolis, home to some fifteen thousand residents. It also became home to a new temple where the Saints performed sacred ordinances intended to bind families together for eternity. Horrified by the abuses that the Mormons endured at the hands of Missouri's government, in December 1840 the Illinois legislature established a generous city charter for Nauvoo. It granted the city's leaders all but complete autonomy, including provisions for a university and a militia, which the Mormons would name the Nauvoo Legion. Nauvoo became the gathering place of Mormon converts from the eastern United States and British Isles. It was also a place of refuge for the thousands of Mormons who streamed out of Missouri in the fall and winter of 1838–39 during the so-called Mormon Wars, which culminated in Missouri governor Lilburn Boggs's October 1838 executive order declaring that the Mormons "must be exterminated or driven from the State."[8]

To avoid further bloodshed, in late 1838, Joseph Smith and a few other Mormon leaders, including Hyrum Smith and Sidney Rigdon, surrendered to Missouri officials who had charged them with treason. They were imprisoned from November 1838 to mid-April 1839. Before he could escape from the small jailhouse in Liberty, Smith dictated a letter to his followers already at work building Nauvoo. In the letter, Smith revealed that for their "dark and blackening deeds . . . cursed are all those that shall lift up the heel against mine anointed."[9] Those cursed included the Mormons' political enemies in Missouri, a state that, in a September 1840 *Times & Seasons* article, was compared to "Western Egypt" and occupied by people worse than "Goth and Vandals, the Cruel Arabs, or the Savage Indians." Those cursed also included Mormon apostates Oliver Cowdery, W. W. Phelps, and David and John Whitmer.[10] This group of Smith's most trusted followers had challenged the prophet's authority in response to the failure of the Kirtland Safety Society Bank in 1837, as well as to the growing rumors that Smith had taken a plural wife.[11] Like the curses pronounced on the progeny of Cain and Ham, Smith's revelation revealed that these curses—including for the first time in Mormon history a declaration of a priesthood ban—would follow the offenders' posterity "from generation to generation." Repentance, Smith also revealed, could bring them back into the fold.[12]

By the early 1850s in Utah, the priesthood ban would become synonymous with people of African descent. Yet the first priesthood restriction was not placed on blacks for their supposed inferior lineages. It was placed on whites for their perfidy and anti-Mormon violence. In the late 1830s and early 1840s, as the Saints were once again forced to find another location to build their millennial city, curses and blessings were not birthrights. According to Joseph Smith, they were earned by being "servants of sin" or by being faithful "servants" of God, of God's church, and of God's prophet.[13] And after Joseph Smith was assassinated in Carthage, Illinois, by an anti-Mormon mob whose members had painted their faces black with gunpowder and mud, Parley P. Pratt described the assassins as "artificial black men." One non-Mormon told the *Nauvoo Neighbor* that the Smith brothers' killers must have been ashamed of their "white skin" to disguise themselves in such a manner. "They wished to make their faces correspond with their hearts."[14]

In the early 1830s, Smith prophesied that the City of Zion would be built "on the borders by the Lamanites" in Jackson County, Missouri, where the Missouri River separated the United States from Indian Territory. In the early 1840s, Nauvoo, Illinois, was another Mormon frontier city built directly across the Mississippi River from Indian settlements in Iowa Territory.[15] The proximity to large populations of Native Americans led to unprecedented contact between Mormons and the Indians whom they still hoped to convert. Delegations of Sac and Fox Indians—who had themselves been forced west from their ancestral lands in the Great Lakes by European colonization—crossed the river to visit the prophet. During these meetings, Joseph Smith taught the chiefs the essentials of the Book of Mormon, including the Indians' true Lamanite identity. Smith also offered them the same covenantal contract proposed to the Delawares in 1831; their redemption was in reach if they "cease killing each other and warring with other tribes" and if they "keep peace with the whites."[16]

Yet unlike the early 1830s, during the Nauvoo period, the Saints invested few resources to bring the gospel to the Lamanites. Instead, the missionaries sent into Indian Country were more explorers than proselytizers. They scouted for possible Mormon expansion opportunities or, if need be, locations for an exodus out of the United States. Proposed sites included the Rocky Mountains as well as what was then the Republic of Texas. Both regions held the promise of distancing the Saints from potential Gentile American persecutors and bringing them closer to large populations of Indians.[17] A few Native Americans did settle in Nauvoo, including a set of brothers of Shawnee and European heritage, Joseph and George Herring. Joseph Herring along with the Oneida Lewis Dana were ordained to the Melchizedek priesthood. And in October 1845, in the Nauvoo Temple, Brigham Young performed a marriage sealing between Dana and Mary Gont. As Heber C. Kimball explained it in his journal, this unprecedented union of the Lamanite Dana and "a white woman," Gont, was sanctioned because Dana "was civilized and had been an Elder about four years."[18]

But the assimilation of Indian converts into the Nauvoo community was, at best, of mixed success. Dana became the first Lamanite to join the church hierarchy. He later became a trusted emissary to the Native American communities whose lands the Saints crossed on their way to Utah. Yet after Joseph Smith's assassination, Joseph Herring grew frustrated with the church leadership and refused to follow the Brigham Young–led Mormons west. According to Mormon pioneer Hosea Stout, Joseph Herring even threatened to take the life of apostle and future church president Wilford Woodruff. Herring's heavy drinking, Stout recorded in his journal, certainly did not help the Indian's demeanor. Before the Mormons reached Utah, the Herring brothers disappeared from the Mormon community (as well as from the Mormon archive). They either left of their own volition or were forced out by the Mormons, who refused to abide bodily threats to their apostles. Hosea Stout was disappointed in the two brothers' inability to mold themselves to the exigencies of membership within the Mormon covenantal community. "So it appears that all the trouble & expense laid out in [the Indians]," Stout wrote in January 1847, "will prove futile, because they have not integrity and stability enough."[19]

Black Brothers and Sisters in Nauvoo

The Mormon archive suggests that the Lamanites who joined the Latter-day Saints in Nauvoo proved to be unworthy of membership in the restored covenant. Yet during the same period, records indicate that, of the forty or so African Americans who lived in Nauvoo from 1839 to 1846, a few black converts established themselves as respected members of the city.[20] Likewise, during this period, Joseph Smith and some of his family members worked to create a more inclusive covenant of which at least some blacks were invited to become full members.

Soon after the first black Mormon priesthood holder, Elijah Abel, moved to Nauvoo from Kirtland, Ohio, Joseph Smith appointed him the city's official undertaker. In 1840, Abel also joined the House Carpenters of the Town of Nauvoo, an informal guild comprised of prominent white Saints including Levi Jackman, who would become a member of Brigham Young's vanguard pioneering company to Utah in 1847, and Joseph Smith's younger brother William Smith, who would replace his brother Hyrum as the church's presiding patriarch after Hyrum and Joseph were assassinated on June 27, 1844.[21] Before he was sent to Cincinnati to support that city's burgeoning Mormon population, Abel joined his fellow carpenters in the construction of the Mormon temple.[22] "Men were as thick as blackbirds busily engaged upon the various portions [of the temple]," wrote Wandle Mace, a mechanical engineer and convert from New York City whom Brigham Young appointed to speed up construction efforts after the Smiths' assassination and before the Saints' impending exodus. "All [were] intent upon its completion: although we were being in constant expectation of a mob."[23]

In Nauvoo, not only did Abel become a respected member of the city's economic culture. He also joined the Mormons' evolving religious community. In 1841, Abel was reordained a member of the Quorum of the Seventy.[24] And starting in late summer of 1840, Abel gathered with other Latter-day Saints on the banks of the Mississippi River, where the faithful performed a newly established Mormon ritual: proxy baptism for the dead. In the early 1840s, Joseph Smith began teaching that in this last dispensation the living and the dead could be reunited, creating one eternal family "from the days of Adam to the present time."[25] Vicarious baptisms by the living would allow those dead who during their mortal lives did not have the opportunity of baptism into the restored church to participate in this first principle of the restoration. Baptism for the dead expanded Mormon universalism across time, permitting the creation of a covenant of all God's chosen people unbound by the strictures of history. Implicitly, baptism for the dead expanded this universalism across the races, too. It allowed even those cursed descendants of the Book of Mormon's Laman, as well as the descendants of the Bible's Cain and Ham, to be reconnected to the eternal chain of human belonging. Like the Mormon notion of conversion, Joseph Smith's understanding of baptism diverged from the Pauline theology of rebirth into a new form. Smith's intention was less progressive and more restorative. His vision was to return the whole of humanity to the ancient days before the first and second falls—before Adam's sin against God separated the first man from his heavenly father, and before the sins of Adam's son Cain, Noah's son Ham, and Lehi's son Laman sinned against their (white) human families, creating a hierarchy of distinct lineages in which the less worthy were marked off by dark skin. Early black Mormons like Elijah Abel participated in this restoration. They vicariously baptized their own dead loved ones into the covenant of the restored church. For his part, Abel performed three baptisms for the dead, including for a friend, John F. Lancaster, for his mother, Elisha, and for a daughter named Delila.[26] These baptisms collapsed the transcendent and the bureaucratic. Witnesses to the baptisms were instructed to write down the names that Abel and other Saints temporarily took as their own as they dunked themselves in the shallows of the Mississippi. Smith revealed that doing so added names to book of records of church members on earth, which mirrored the "book of life" in heaven.[27]

Elijah Abel also became a Smith family intimate. In 1840, Abel was at the deathbed of Joseph Smith Sr. Four years earlier, the church patriarch had blessed Abel and told him that his dedication to the gospel would allow him to transcend his own blackness in the afterlife.[28] In June 1841, after Joseph

Smith Jr. was arrested on another warrant from Missouri, Abel, along with six other men including Hosea Stout, set off to rescue the prophet from his captors.[29] A few years later, in 1843, the prophet publicly praised Abel as a model for his downtrodden race, an "educated negro . . . a man who has risen by the powers of his own mind to his exalted state of respectability."[30] While most Negroes "come into this world slaves mentally and physically," if they are given the chance to "change their situation," the prophet explained and cited Abel as his example, then they can become like "the white[s]." After all, "[Negroes, too,] have souls & are subjects of salvation."[31]

Jane's Joseph

Whereas Elijah Abel came to Nauvoo in 1840 as a respected member of the Mormon community, in late 1843 young Jane Manning and her family arrived as strangers on the prophet's Mansion House doorstep.[32] Penniless and road weary, the black Mormon converts had little more than the clothes on their backs. Yet according to her autobiography, the twenty-one-year-old Jane Manning did carry with her something of great value: a story of conversion to the Mormon gospel as well as perseverance in the face of adversity for which she would win the admiration of the prophet himself. Yet perhaps more importantly for James, her autobiography tells a story of the first prophet for whom James's cursed race was not an insurmountable barrier to acceptance in the restored covenant. James added this portrait of a racially benevolent Joseph Smith to the Mormon archive in the late nineteenth century, a period during which Smith's views on the matter, as well as his translations of the book of Abraham, became canonical and normative.

Jane Manning James's autobiography is, by nature, retrospective. When she and her scribe, Elizabeth Roundy, sat down to compose the short—some 2,300 words—but detail-rich narrative, James looked back on her life as a young black servant in a wealthy New England home, as a convert to Mormonism, as a confidante to Joseph Smith and his family, and as an intrepid Mormon pioneer. James's autobiography thus bridges two nineteenth-century literary genres: the slave narrative and the Mormon conversion narrative. James was born free to a formerly enslaved mother. But because her life experiences at times crossed the blurred boundary between slavery and freedom, elements of her life story—especially those over which she lost control—parallel slave narratives.[33] As is the case in the narratives of Frederick Douglass and Harriet Jacobs, because she often functioned as an object of racial exclusion and patronizing condescension in her own community, in her writings Jane Manning James demonstrates keen awareness of the distance between her (black) experiences and those of her (white) readers. And yet like Parley P. Pratt's archetypal nineteenth-century Mormon autobiography, James's narrative also moves in the other direction: toward her Mormon readership by adhering to tropes of Mormon conversion narratives.[34] In other words, in her autobiography James creates credibility about her more fantastic claims—including her would-be familial connection to Joseph Smith—by repeating Mormon verisimilitudes. James presents herself at once as a racial other *and* as a fellow Mormon convert. Still, although James tentatively tries to collapse her black self into her Mormon self, she makes sure to not pass over the line where her race would make her story intolerable for her white Mormon audience.

In this sense, James's autobiography is polemical. To be sure, James compliments the church's five prophet presidents, "Brother Brigham, Taylor, Woodruff, Snow," and Joseph F. Smith, whom she praises for "rul[ing] this great work" since the martyrdom of Joseph Smith Jr.[35] And yet this public profession of reverence and submission creates the space in James's narrative in which she can author an implicit critique—what James C. Scott calls a "hidden transcript"—of the antiblack theologies and practices developed after Joseph Smith's death.[36] James's narrative challenges Joseph Smith's successors who claim that Mormonism's original prophet believed that the sins committed by blacks' biblical ancestors put their contemporary progeny beyond the pale of full acceptance in the Saints' covenantal community. For James's Joseph Smith, the categories of black and Mormon were not mutually exclusive, or at least they need not be so.

Jane's Nauvoo

Despite its half-century remove from the Mormons' exodus from Illinois, in her autobiography Jane Manning James creates a sense of immediacy with the time she spent in the Smith family's Mansion House in Nauvoo. She does so by rhetorically relocating when and where she narrates much of this history. The first part of the autobiography is an embedded narrative. In her home in Salt Lake City in the late nineteenth century, James repeats for Roundy (and for her future readers) the story that she first told to Joseph and Emma Smith, along with the Mansion House's other residents, after the Manning family completed their thousand-mile trek through the cold fall and early winter of 1843 from Wilton, Connecticut, to Nauvoo.[37]

Soon after the company was gathered in the Mansion House's sitting room, Jane Manning recounted at the prophet's behest what brought her family of black converts to the Mormons' bustling capital. Jane Manning explained that since the age of six she had lived in the home of the wealthy Fitches of Wilton, Connecticut, and had been raised by the couple's daughter. A year and a half before her conversion to Mormonism, she became a member of the local Presbyterian church. "Yet I did not feel satisfied," she explained. "It seemed to me there was something more that I was looking for."[38] Over the objections of the pastor of her church, Jane Manning attended a Mormon meeting, likely in nearby Norwalk, where the missionary Charles Wandell had established a branch of the church.[39] After hearing the Mormon elder speak, "I was fully convinced that it was the true Gospel he presented and I must embrace it."[40] Jane Manning explained to her audience in the Mansion House that she quickly immersed herself in Mormon culture. The first Sunday after she heard the missionaries, she was baptized and confirmed a member of the church. A few weeks later, while praying, "the Gift of Tongues came upon me." Though this ecstatic encounter with the Holy Spirit initially "frightened [my] whole family who were in the next room," soon seven members of her family also converted. Jane Manning told Joseph Smith that within a year, this extended family joined a large group of converts led by Wandell heading west to gather with the Saints in Nauvoo.[41]

Jane Manning's expression of dissatisfaction with the "sectarian" offerings from antebellum Protestant churches, her immediate adoption of Mormonism, her powerful experiences with the gifts of the Holy Spirit, and the conversions of several members of her family follow closely the conventions of early Mormon conversion narratives. For those predisposed to it, once introduced to the gospel truth of the restored church, rejection of all other churches as false and adoption of Mormonism came quickly.[42] The Mormon missionaries' great success among large numbers of families in England during this same period led Mormons to develop a belief that converts carried in their veins "believing blood," an inherited predisposition to Mormonism. Jane Manning's description of her family's quick adoption of Mormonism subtly challenged the idea that blacks' supposed descent from a spiritually inferior lineage made them less capable of recognizing what the young Jane Manning called the "true Gospel."

In her autobiography, Jane Manning James also establishes her Mormon bona fides in order to demonstrate the strength of her faith in the face of persecution. For example, in the Mansion House's sitting room, Jane Manning explained to the prophet that her family experienced racial discrimination as they made their way west. After taking the Erie Canal across New York State, the migrating Mormons arrived in Buffalo. There, Charles Wandell refused to pay the Mannings' fare for the ferry that was take the

Saints across Lake Erie. Though he was eventually acquitted of any wrong-doing, a few months after the Connecticut Mormons arrived in Nauvoo, Wandell was charged by the church's High Council for "unchristian conduct towards certain colored brethren."[43]

Jane Manning did not mention Wandell by name. Yet she did explain to Joseph Smith that, after the missionaries "would not take us further," her family continued on foot the eight hundred miles to Peoria, Illinois. "We walked until our shoes were worn out," Jane Manning recounted, "and our feet became sore and cracked open and bled until you could see the whole print of our feet with blood on the ground." To heal the pain caused by their fellow Mormons' refusal to recognize her as a member of their community—pain manifested in real physical suffering—the black Saints prayed to God, "and our feet were healed forthwith."[44] In the embedded narrative of her autobiography, James thus details how even before she joined the Mormon exodus to Utah, she had already experienced persecution, which led to bodily suffering and, in turn, to faithful prayers and Heavenly Father's response of miracles of deliverance.

In Peoria, the Mannings were again forced to stop their trek when they encountered the region's legal and political turmoil over slavery. Though Illinois was officially a free state, its black codes were similar to those found in the Mormons' former home in the slave state of Missouri. Illinois forbade African Americans without a certificate of freedom to settle in the state. And to ensure that they would not become a financial burden, they were required to register a bond of one thousand dollars in the county in which they wished to settle. Blacks who could not produce such a certificate and bond would "be deemed a runaway slave or servant" and subject to arrest by the local sheriff, who was empowered to hire them out "for the best price he can get."[45] Though the Mannings "had never been slaves," because they could not produce "free papers," Jane Manning explained that a local official threatened to throw them in jail.[46]

Jane Manning told the prophet that the official in Peoria eventually "concluded to let us go." Yet after trekking the last hundred miles west, when the Mannings finally reached "beautiful Nauvoo," they faced another round "of hardship, trial, and rebuff." Though she did not specify the form that these difficulties took, James's description indicates that Nauvoo was far from a utopia of racial inclusion and equality.[47] To be sure, the Mormons' great missionary success at home and abroad led the church's leadership in October 1840 to envision Nauvoo as the gathering place for converts from around the world, including "the polished European, the degraded Hottentot, and the shivering Laplander."[48] Yet in reality, Nauvoo's free black

Mormons were never full members of the Mormons' growing civil or religious community. Although Elijah Abel baptized his dead in the Mississippi River along with white Saints, in January 1841, God revealed through Joseph Smith that the river's waters were provisional, acceptable only "in the days of your poverty, wherein ye are not able to build a house unto me."[49] Thousands of baptisms were performed in the river in 1841. Yet once the Saints finished the temple's font that November, baptisms for the dead moved inside the "House of the Lord." And this sacred ritual became, for the most part, inaccessible for black Saints, whom Joseph Smith's successors would deem unworthy to enter into the Mormons' holiest spaces. According to extant records, no black Saints performed temple rituals in Nauvoo after the temple was completed in 1845. This includes Abel, who years later, like Jane Manning James, petitioned church leaders without success to receive his endowments and to be sealed to his wife and children, endowments that if he had received in Nauvoo he would not have needed to ask to be repeated in Utah.[50]

Full black citizenship was also out of the question. The Nauvoo city charter limited voting rights in municipal elections to white male citizens.[51] Interracial marriage was outlawed. Offenders faced criminal sanctions in the city's court.[52] And at least one black resident of Nauvoo was the victim of mob violence. In March 1844, a man named Chism was savagely whipped after being accused of robbing a local store. When the city court failed to convict his attackers—just months before he became the victim of a lynch mob himself along with Joseph and Hyrum Smith—the editor of the *Nauvoo Neighbor*, John Taylor, excoriated the court and the perpetrators of vigilante violence for making a "mockery of justice": "Lynch law will not do in Nauvoo, and those who engage in it must expect to be visited by the wrath of an indignant people, not according to the rule of Judge Lynch, but according to law and equity."[53]

In Nauvoo, even the line between freedom and slavery was blurry. In 1842, Joseph Smith advised southern slave-owning converts "to bring slaves into a free country and set them free."[54] Two years later, Smith ran for president of the United States as a gradual abolitionist. In the preface to his presidential platform, Smith claimed that the only group of Americans who had been more systematically denied their rights to "life, liberty, and the pursuit of happiness" than the Mormons were enslaved blacks.[55] And yet Smith did not believe that the solution to the "Mormon problem"—Smith wanted the federal government to ensure the Mormons' access to full constitutional rights and protections—was the same as the "Negro problem." In a March 1844 speech, Smith proposed that freed slaves be sent to live in Texas or

Mexico, where they might create their own communities or assimilate with the existing mixed-race populations in those regions.[56] What's more, at least some of the black "servants" whom southern converts brought into the nominally free state of Illinois between 1843 and 1846 were still enslaved by the time Brigham Young and the Utah territorial legislature legalized "African" slavery in 1852.[57] In Nauvoo and later in Utah, positions of employment open to free black Mormons were the same as those performed by non-Mormon free blacks and slaves: house servants, washerwomen, coachmen, manual laborers, and field hands. Even his "calling" to be Nauvoo's undertaker was perhaps a more elegant term for what occupied most of Elijah Abel's time performing his office: digging graves. In the first three years of the Mormons' sojourn in Illinois, this work kept Abel busy constructing coffins and interring Saints lost to plagues of malaria during the summers of 1839, 1840, and 1841.[58]

Jane's Mormon Trail and Mansion House

As for her own family, Jane Manning told the prophet that only when they reached the Mansion House did this group of black converts finally find sanctuary and acceptance. In her autobiography, the Mannings' arrival at the Mansion House also concludes the embedded narrative of her family's faith-testing journey. Shifting the narrative perspective from the Mansion House sitting room in 1843 to her home in Salt Lake City in the 1890s, James recalls for Roundy's dictation the prophet's reaction to Jane Manning's story. Joseph Smith was so impressed by the black converts' dedication to the Mormon gospel that he turned to Dr. John M. Bernhisel, who was also present, "slapped [him] . . . on the knee," and asked him, "Isn't that faith?" James tells Roundy that Bernhisel, who in 1851 would become Utah's first delegate to Congress, responded, "Well I rather think it is." According to James, this respected white physician, politician, and Mormon leader acknowledged that a black Mormon woman's faith was stronger than his own. "If it had have been me I fear I should have backed out and returned to my home!" exclaimed Bernhisel. The prophet next blessed the Mannings and promised to protect them from further trials. "You are among friends now," Smith declared.[59]

In her autobiography, Jane Manning James hopes to do more than to detail her own exceptional faith. And she hopes to do more than to demonstrate how this faith won her some impressive admirers. After all, the prophet's nephew and church president Joseph F. Smith himself praised the depth of James's commitment to Mormonism at her funeral in 1908. Yet her faith alone had not proven enough to gain her access to the temple, the most sacred space in Mormon culture. Thus in her autobiography, James creates her own place by writing herself into some of the most sacred spaces and events of the Mormon origin story.[60] In turn-of-the-century Salt Lake City, the image of an intrepid, industrious, and faithful Mormon pioneer was certainly a key part of this myth. And as a member of the first wave of pioneers to enter the Salt Lake Valley in 1847, James was counted among the most revered members of the Mormon pioneering generation.[61] In 1897, Salt Lake City marked the fiftieth anniversary of the founding of the Mormons' Kingdom of Zion in the High Plains desert with a grand jubilee. James was among the 250 remaining pioneers of 1847 (see fig. 4.1) who were able to make the trip to the state capital, where they were paraded on floats down Salt Lake City's main streets with golden badges made by Tiffany and Company in New York pinned to their chests.

Jane Manning James records her own pioneer credentials in her autobiography. When they left Nauvoo in the spring of 1846 for their yearlong journey to Utah, James and the other pioneers of 1847 did not follow a well-established trail, as later Mormon pioneers would. Instead, they put their faith in the Lord, believing that he would "be with us and protect us all the way" as they trekked toward the "Great and Glorious [Salt Lake] Valley."[62] And the Lord did protect them, James recalls. A cattle stampede created the only real moment of concern. According to James, giving birth to her son Silas during the trek across the hot, exposed plains was treated as a matter of course for the hardy pioneer. The midwife Patty Sessions, who helped James deliver Silas, identifies her as "black Jane" in her own Mormon trail journal. Yet in her autobiography, James hopes that before her readers identify her by her race, they will recognize her as a pioneer of 1847 who was among the first Mormons to make the thirteen-hundred-mile journey from Nauvoo to the Salt Lake Valley.[63]

Yet James claims an even more exclusive history and, for that matter, an even more exclusive space than the Mormon trail—the Nauvoo Mansion House. And by chronicling this history, she asserts the strongest challenge to her exclusion from the most sacred of Mormon rituals and sacerdotal spaces. When she lived under the prophet's roof, James's race did not prevent her from ascending to ever increasing levels of intimacy with members of the Smith household: from houseguest to live-in servant to family confidante and even to would-be family member. Absent the testimonies of others—including the testimonies of the Smiths—it is James who controls how her place in the Nauvoo home of Mormonism's first family gets remembered and archived.[64]

James recalls that Emma Hale Smith was not alone in greeting her family at the Mansion House's front door. Joseph Smith himself coordinated his newly arrived guests' sleeping arrangements. "Brother Joseph said to some White sisters that was present, Sisters I want you to occupy this room this evening with some brothers and Sisters that have just arrived." James remembers that the Mormon prophet integrated the Mansion House's living quarters without a thought about the racial implications of placing black and white Mormons in the same room.

James also remembers that soon after she arrived, Joseph Smith found her in tears one morning. She was upset because every other member of her family had secured housing and employment, yet she had none.[65] Joseph told the young Jane Manning, "You have a home right here if you want it, you must[']nt cry, we dry up all tears here." Emma and Joseph Smith also gave her a job as a laundress. In this position she came into contact with some of early Mormonism's most sacred objects and indirectly witnessed some of the faith's most defining events. Soon after she began working, James recalls: "[Emma Smith] brought the clothes down to the basement to wash. And among the clothes, I found Brother Joseph's robes. I looked at them and wondered—[as] I had never seen any before—and I pondered over them and thought about them so earnestly, so sincerely that the Lord made manifest to me that they pertained to the new name that is given the saints that the world knows not of."[66]

James here describes a mystical experience with the prophet's dirty laundry—the robes Smith and other Latter-day Saints wore when performing rituals in the Nauvoo temple. By pointing out that she knows that the Latter-day Saints are given a "new name" as part of these rituals, James implies that she knows something of the secret ceremonies that go on inside the temple, ceremonies in which she would never be permitted to participate.[67] Young Jane Manning also became a confidante to other members of the household, including the prophet's mother, Lucy Mack Smith. James recalls that one day "Mother Smith" invited her into the Mormon matriarch's room, where she allowed Jane Manning to hold the Urim and Thummim, the instruments with which her son had translated the Book of Mormon. James recalls that Mother Smith wanted the Mormon convert to recognize the significance of holding these objects: "You will live long after I am dead and gone," Mother Smith said, "and you can tell the Latter-day Saints that you was permitted to handle the Urim and Thummim."[68] Although she could never set foot in the most sacred chambers of a Mormon temple, in Mother Smith's bedroom and in the mansion's basement, James handled the sacred artifacts that helped bring about the Mormon dispensation.

Houseguest, servant, confidante. All of these identities solidified James's claim that she should be recognized as a witness to many of the elements and events that make Mormon origin myths. But it is her claim that she is—or at least should have been—an adopted daughter of Joseph and Emma Smith that becomes the most important identity to which James lays claim. James tells Roundy that in the Mansion House, her intimacy with the Smiths developed to the point that "Sister Emma asked me one day if I would like to be adopted to them as their child? I did not answer her. She said I will wait awhile so you can consider it. She waited two weeks before she asked me again. And when she did, I said No ma['a]m! because I didn't understand or know what it meant."[69] "What it meant" was that, in Mormonism's evolving soteriology, such an adoption would have allowed a lowly black laundress to ascend to the same levels of heaven as the prophet himself.

In the early 1840s, Joseph Smith began teaching that husbands and wives could be "sealed" to each other, and children sealed to their parents, creating bonds among family members that would endure in the heavenly kingdoms. Smith's vision for such families exploded the bounds of Victorian era nuclear kinships. Baptism for the dead reached back in time. By descending first into the waters of the Mississippi and later into the font in the temple basement, living Saints rescued from oblivion generations of dead family members and brought "multitudes of their kin into the Kingdom of God," as Smith taught in 1841.[70] By entering into the temple's upper rooms, where they gave themselves as children to leading members of the church, Latter-day Saints became the celestial kin and legal heirs of their adoptive parents.[71] What's more, adoptive children born outside the Abrahamic covenant completed the grafting, which began with their conversion and, if they were men, continued with their ordination into the priesthood, onto the Israelite family tree. Such grafting was more than metaphorical. Jane Manning James believed that a temple adoption to Joseph Smith would have separated her from her cursed ancestral lineage and connected her to the lineages of her adopted parents. Born the daughter of Cain, Ham, and Canaan, by becoming the daughter and legal heir of Joseph Smith Jr., James would have become the daughter of Abraham, Jacob, and his son, Joseph, the ancestor and namesake of the prophet of the latter days.[72] Lamenting the decision to reject Emma's offer of adoption, a decision that would become one of the greatest regrets of her life, James tells Roundy that her younger self "did not know my own mind[.] I did not comprehend."[73] But James's older self did comprehend. Joseph and Emma Smith were offering to make her their spiritual daughter and provide for her in this lifetime and the next.

James's claim that the Smiths offered to adopt her also has implications for Joseph Smith's treatment of other black Mormons. James's portrayal of Joseph Smith can also be read as a challenge to the notion that, as his nephew Joseph F. Smith would assert in 1908, "the Prophet himself" stripped a close and trusted servant like the indefatigable missionary Elijah Abel of his priesthood because Smith discovered that Abel was "tainted with negro blood."[74] As Joseph Smith's appraisal of Abel as a respectable "educated negro" suggests, the prophet believed that even those born into the lowliest of lineages could, through faith in the gospel, obedience to Christ's church, and self-improvement, join the restored Abrahamic covenant and even rejoin humanity's original, white family.

A Reliable "[Auto]biography"?

The "Biography of Jane E. James"—the title that Elizabeth Roundy scrawled atop the handwritten narrative—makes a case for James's inclusion in the present by highlighting her inclusion in the past. Because her history is a polemic, the question of the narrator's reliability must be raised. James herself acknowledges that during the sixty or more years since her time in Joseph Smith's household, "many incidents has [sic] passed from my memory." Yet the narrative is fairly consistent with timelines and contemporary accounts of her arrival in Nauvoo, her recollection of who also lived in the Mansion House during her time there, and the Mormon exodus to Utah.[75] However, regarding her more fantastic claims, most importantly Emma and Joseph Smith's invitation of spiritual adoption, the archive begins and ends with James's words.

And yet, are these actually James's words? After all, James's autobiography is an "[auto]biography." The verbal memories of James became part of the Mormon archive—and thus part of Mormon history—only when Elizabeth Roundy transcribed them and, when she felt it necessary, when she corrected them. The narrative was not "written by [James] herself," as was so important to the authorial authority of other nineteenth-century African American narratives.[76]

Why did James not write her own autobiography? There are two interrelated answers to this question. The first is practical. The long-held assumption among scholars who have studied Jane Manning James's life has been that James was illiterate.[77] When she and Roundy met to record James's life story, this was true. But there is ample evidence to suggest that James's illiteracy was the result of the loss of physical ability, and not due to an absence of aptitude. After all, in another interview about her memories of Joseph Smith published in 1905, James stated, "I used to read in the Bible so much and in the Book of Mormon and Revelations." James also claimed that the Smiths expected the Mannings' arrival "because I wrote them a letter."[78] And yet in her old age, James could no longer read. As she states in her autobiography, "I am nearly blind which is a great trial for me."[79] Federal census records from 1860 to 1900 correlate with James's statements that she lost the ability to read and write sometime between 1880 and 1900.[80]

The second reason is racial. Like most prominent nineteenth-century slave narratives, James's story required a white Mormon to validate its claims. William Lloyd Garrison attested to the authenticity of Frederick Douglass's *Narrative of the Life of Frederick Douglass* (1845) by providing a preface. Harriet Jacobs's *Incidents in the Life of a Slave Girl, Written by Herself* (1861) was validated twice, once by Amy Post, who is credited with helping Jacobs write the text, and a second time by Lydia Marie Child, who edited the narrative. And though he wrote letters seeking assistance from New York benefactors during his enslavement, when it came to compose *Twelve Years a Slave* (1853), Solomon Northup verbally recounted his experiences to a white scribe and editor, David Wilson, who in the book's preface testified to the narrative's accuracy.[81] The cultural exigency to validate these narratives reinforces the connection between literacy and race in the nineteenth century. To write is to be white. And the assumption of James's illiteracy—and the tendency to disregard her own statement and either ignore or fail to examine other archival evidence about her ability to read and write—emphasizes the intractability of literacy as a signifier for whiteness. What's more, the assumption of James's illiteracy underscores the challenge for nonwhites to add their own, unmediated written voices to the historical archive. Even if Jane Manning James actually put pen to paper, her words remain in the liminal space between the oral and written until a white writer intervenes to testify to the words' historical credibility.

Because James is functionally illiterate, her symbolic inability to add her own words to the archive becomes literal. Her text became subject to direct intervention by her scribe, who believed it was her responsibility, as the white validator of a black woman's testimony, to correct the text. Thus, before asking whether Jane Manning James is a reliable narrator, we must ask the same question of Elizabeth Roundy.

In describing the members of the "little band" of black Mormon converts that she led from Connecticut to Illinois, James did not name her eldest son, Sylvester, born around 1834. Sylvester's absence is conspicuous. By the time his mother dictated her autobiography to Roundy, Sylvester James was a wealthy farmer in Utah. He was one of just two African Americans listed in the popular biographical encyclopedia *Pioneers and Prominent Men of Utah*.[82] Why does James not mention that her successful son was born in

Connecticut? Why not mention that as a small boy, Sylvester, too, made the harrowing trek halfway across the country to gather with the Saints in Nauvoo and then became a member of the 1847 pioneers who first made the trek to Utah?

Elizabeth Roundy also wondered about James's "reticence pertaining to one of her children," as Roundy put it. Thus, after recording James's verbal account of her life story, Roundy steps away from her role as faithful scribe. And she interjects her own prerogative into the narrative. In a one-page epilogue that she attaches to James's statement, Roundy implies that she believes almost all of what James told her. For example, Roundy finds no cause to challenge James's claims that she was the beloved servant and even the potential adopted spiritual daughter of the Smith family. She does not question James's claim to have handled the prophet's temple robes and the sacred Book of Mormon translation aids, the Urim and Thummim. Yet Roundy believed that it was her responsibility to correct the statement's "only error, or you may call it evasion," as she explains on the last page of the handwritten original document. This error was the true paternity of Sylvester James, who was often described as a "half-breed."[83] Roundy writes that she "could not get any thing out of Jane" about Sylvester. But Roundy learned from James's brother, Isaac Manning, that Sylvester "was born in Conn . . . that he was the child of a white man[,] a preacher." Roundy writes that "Jane was nearly eighteen or quite that old when the child was born" and that she left the infant in the care of her own mother to return to her work as a servant in the Fitch household.[84]

The consensus among contemporary Mormons who celebrate Jane Manning James's faith by performing reenactments, plays, and fictionalizing her life in historical novels is that the "preacher" whom Isaac Manning claims was the father of Sylvester was Jane Manning James's onetime Presbyterian pastor. The consensus is also that James did not consent to this sexual relationship.[85] To be sure, it is plausible to connect the unsympathetic pastor whom James describes in her narrative with the preacher whom her brother Isaac Manning told Roundy was the father of Sylvester. It is also plausible to imagine that this minister used his position of authority to abuse a young black servant in his flock—especially when such an image heightens the contrast between this religious and perhaps even sexual tyrant and Joseph Smith Jr., the beloved Mormon prophet and fatherly figure who, in James's own telling, fulfilled his promise to protect her, both in this lifetime and in the next. In antebellum America, even in a free state like Connecticut, the laws protecting African American women against rape by respected white men were all but nonexistent. Yet twenty-first-century understandings of sex and power make a truly consensual relationship between two people of such different social standings all but impossible.[86] What's more, such an implied depiction of Joseph Smith as a protector of young female virtue also subtly challenges the common non-Mormon view of Mormonism's founder as a sexual predator who used his authority to coerce dozens of young women to enter into polygamous marriages with him.

As was the case more than a century ago when Roundy interjected family gossip into James's "[auto]biography," any attempt today to determine the nature of James's relationship with Sylvester's father is an act of speculation. But what is not speculation is that Roundy's addition to the autobiography alters the identity that James constructed for herself at the point of her conversion. Roundy adds experiences of great pain into James's purposefully optimistic, faith-promoting narrative. After Roundy's intervention into the text, James is no longer simply a spiritual seeker, dissatisfied with the local religious offerings, who finds a spiritual home in Mormonism, then becomes a would-be adoptive daughter to the prophet Joseph Smith, a celebrated Mormon pioneer, and a mother to a large Mormon family. She becomes the young, unwed mother of a mixed-race son, looking for a new community that would not know her past and thus not hold it against her. After Roundy's intervention, James also becomes the Mormon mother who failed to keep her family within the church. In her autobiography, James declares that she convinced her family to leave their homes in Connecticut and join the Mormons in Nauvoo. Yet she does not mention that the only other family member who eventually settled in Utah and remained Mormon was her brother Isaac, the source of the family gossip about Sylvester's paternity. In fact, by the time of James's death in 1908, Sylvester had been excommunicated for "unchristian like conduct." All of her other children had either died or left Utah. None of her grandchildren were active members of the church.[87]

James "evades" the question of whether she lost control over her own sexual self in Connecticut.[88] But there is no question that because she could not write her own autobiography, James could not maintain control over her writerly self. Like Samuel, the Lamanite in the Nephite archive, and the Delaware Indians in Parley P. Pratt's autobiography, James is captured in the very text in which she attempted to fashion her Mormon self—a self that, despite its blackness, she believed had proven worthy of a place in the sacred Mormon community, even in Joseph Smith's eternal family. When she tacked her unsolicited epilogue onto the end of Jane Manning James's autobiography, Roundy made it clear that, at least when it came to discussing the paternity of Sylvester, the white scribe believed that her black narrator was unreliable. And yet, putting aside her motives, Roundy's interrogation of James's potential interracial relationship in fact relates to another question regarding James's reliability on the most important claim in her narrative: that the Smiths wished to adopt her as their spiritual daughter.

In the last few decades of her life, Jane Manning James grew concerned over her spiritual future. Beginning in the 1880s, James wrote several letters to a series of church presidents in an effort to secure her exaltation. She petitioned the church to allow her to enter the temple and obtain her own endowments and those of her family members. For the most part, James pegged her hopes that the church would grant her the necessary temple privileges on the notion that the church's current leaders would accept what she claimed were the wishes of Mormonism's first prophet. Yet James also tried different approaches in what she recognized was an uphill battle to convince church leaders to grant a black woman access to the temple. As she explained in an 1884 letter to church president John Taylor, James accepted the church's position that, because Cain sinned against humanity's original family in killing his brother, his seed's curse would be removed only, as Brigham Young taught in the early 1850s, "when all the other children of Adam have had the privilege of receiving the priesthood," a privilege that also included temple access.[89] "I recognize that my race and color [mean I] can[']t expect my endowments as those who are white," James wrote to Taylor. From Cain to Ham and Canaan, "my race was handed down through the flood." Still, James asked for a special dispensation. "You know my history," she reminded Taylor, "& according to the best of my ability I have lived all the requairments of the Gospel." Because she had proven herself worthy—the evidence for which she would provide in her autobiography—James pleaded, "Is there no blessing for me[?]"[90]

Six years later, in 1890, James wrote to then apostle Joseph F. Smith. She asked that church officials seal her as a wife to the long-deceased, early black priesthood holder Walker Lewis.[91] Not surprisingly, Joseph F. Smith ignored this request. To grant it would have been a tacit recognition that a "seed of Cain" had been ordained to the priesthood in the early years of the church. Yet James's choice of Lewis as a prospective posthumous husband shows that James understood the Mormon leadership's antipathy for and fear of miscegenation. Had James been white, as a widow—in 1870 she divorced Isaac James, and he died in 1891—she would have likely become a plural wife to a living priesthood holder. This man would have been responsible for her earthly and heavenly well-being. The Mormons had long argued that plural marriage was the ultimate fulfillment of the Abrahamic covenant because it enabled God's chosen people to "multiply and replenish the earth" and to reach the highest levels of heaven.[92] According to the Saints, plural marriage was also moral and humane. In 1885, at the height of the federal government's antipolygamy campaign, church leaders argued that plural marriages functioned as a safeguard against the prostitution, infanticide, and disease produced by a surplus of poor women and overly libidinous men—social ills that the Saints asserted plagued monogamous societies but were absent in their desert kingdom.[93]

Yet in Utah, for a black woman like James to be sealed in marriage to a white Mormon man—dead or alive—was out of the question. To be sure, external pressures shaped the church's antagonism toward interracial relationships. In 1856, on its first presidential platform, the Republican Party named polygamy and slavery the two "twin relics of barbarism." The Republicans accused Mormon polygamists of committing similar types of sexual abuse—leading to similar types of race contamination—as white southern slave masters who bedded their black slaves. During the Civil War, the church's newspaper of record, the *Deseret News*, responded by claiming that in fact it was northern abolitionists' ideals of equality of the races, ideals which the Mormons rejected, that led to "miscegenation without hesitation."[94] Two decades later, in 1885, when the federal government was enacting its most sweeping antipolygamy legislation, the *Deseret News* published a missionary's dispatch from the South. The Mormon elder described "the result[s] of miscegenation" in the region that considered itself the sentinel of white political and cultural power. "A [train] ride through the Southern States tells a fearful tale of the moral degradation which is rapidly setting its seal upon the entire community," the missionary wrote. "At every station the sight of hordes of mongrels of all shades from the sickly white to the seven-eights black" was evidence that "colored blood" and with it the "spreading curse" was everywhere, even in the blood of the South's supposed "best citizens." After witnessing this state of racial denigration, the missionary felt compelled to "thank heaven that a beneficent Providence has permitted his soul to be born upon the earth through the medium of parents who realize the true nature of the curse of Cain and so far removed from its damning influence that any thing like an inter-marriage with the colored race is looked upon with aversion." Northerners and southerners alike attacked Mormon polygamist marriages for producing offspring with degraded bodies, minds, and souls. The Saints responded by asserting that their marital unions were in fact more holy and biblical. As the missionary in the South put it, because of divine "revelation," more than any other people, the Mormons "are able to comprehend the awful consequences of disobeying that great commandment given by the children of God, Seth's posterity, not to mix with the children of men, as Cain's offspring."[95]

Yet this traveling elder's retort to what he considered the hypocrisy of one southern "anti-Mormon" who deigned to call Mormon men "whore masters" but whose own children were issues "of the lowest negro families in the neighborhood" also suggests that fears of race mixing were internal to the Mormon racial project. After all, it was the Saints' mandate to restore and grow the priesthood. And the slightest presence of black blood in their immediate or ancient "genealogies," they believed, could threaten the success of this mission.[96] As Brigham Young explained in an 1849 council meeting on whether the "African Race" has "a chance for redemption," "the curse remains on" Cain's descendants because their ancient forefather "cut off the lives of Abel to hedge up his way & take the lead." As punishment, the Lord gave Cain's African race "blackness, so as to give the children of Abel an opportunity to keep his place with his descendants in the eternal worlds."[97] Young's first explicit mention of a race-based priesthood restriction would come in 1852, when the Utah territorial legislature debated whether to legalize a form of "African" slavery. Yet, as historian W. Paul Reeve has written, in this 1849 pronouncement Young presented "the core of the argument Mormons used to ban black men from the priesthood and black men and women from temple worship. Blackness was a curse from God, a consequence for Cain's murder of his brother Abel. By killing a competing patriarch in Adam's family line and attempting to usurp Abel's position in the 'Kingdom of God,' Cain fractured the eternal human network and broke the great chain of belonging." Young believed that by placing a mark on Cain, the Lord was also placing Cain outside the great chain of belonging that bound together the family of God through time and eternity.[98]

Preserving these distinct—and distinctly unequal—divinely mandated lineages was of paramount importance. As Brigham Young explained in 1863, "under the law of God" relative to the "African race," "if the white man who belongs to the chosen seed mixes his blood with the seed of Cain, the penalty . . . is death on the spot."[99] No chances of blood corruption could be tolerated. The restoration of Ephraim, whom God had elected to be God's "holy nation, a kingdom of priests, a people to receive the covenants," as Apostle Erastus Snow declared in 1882, was central to the Saints' covenantal contract. To allow the "[seed of] Cain" into Mormon bloodlines, explained church president John Taylor that same year, would corrupt the blood increasingly purified by unions among Ephraim's sons and daughters in Utah.[100] In the early 1890s, this is likely why Elizabeth Roundy was so concerned with learning the truth about Sylvester James's true paternity. And this is likely why Jane Manning James sought to "evade" Roundy's questions. Whether her relationship with the white minister in Connecticut was consensual or not, James had transgressed the sexual boundaries between white and black, the flesh and bone evidence of which was her "half-breed" son, Sylvester.

Relatedly, James's efforts to observe Mormonism's rigid boundaries between the most and least favored lineages also likely affected her ability to narrate reliably what exactly transpired between her and the Smiths during her time in the Mansion House. According to extant records from the Nauvoo period, James's claim that the Smiths' offered to adopt her in 1843 appears to be suspect. Although certain important rituals, including baptisms for the dead and marital sealings, took place in temporary locations—for example, the Mississippi River and the Mansion House—the evolving "Law of Adoption" theology required a completed temple for adoption sealings. When the temple was finished in December 1845, in the flurry before the impending exodus from Illinois, 211 individuals were adopted to sixteen prominent Mormon couples. Only one person was adopted to (the deceased) Joseph Smith in Nauvoo. The adoptee was not Jane Manning James but her onetime Mansion House housemate, John M. Bernhisel. According to the Nauvoo "Book of Proxey Sealings," on February 3, 1846, Bernhisel presented himself to the "sacred Alt[a]r" in the most sacred room of the "House of the Lord." There he became the martyred prophet's "legal heir to all the blessings bestowed upon Joseph Smith pertaining to exaltations," the same blessings that a half a century later James petitioned Joseph Smith Jr.'s nephew Joseph F. Smith to grant her.[101]

With this in mind, what are we to make of James's claim that she should have been the spiritual daughter of Joseph and Emma Smith? Of course, one possibility is that the Smiths offered nothing to James. In this case, perhaps a contrived memory of the adoption offers dates not from 1840s Nauvoo but from 1880s Utah when, following the opening of the first Utah temples, Joseph Smith became the adoptive father to thousands of living and dead Mormons. In fact, on December 4, 1885, in the Logan Temple, James's scribe, Elizabeth Roundy was adopted to Smith. "Anxious" as she was for the spiritual well-being of her dead and for her own "welfare for the future," as she explained to Joseph F. Smith in two letters written in 1890, James also hoped that she, too, could participate in the rush of Saints eager to seal themselves to the first prophet.[102]

And yet, a second possibility must be considered: that the offer made was to seal young Jane Manning to Joseph Smith not as his daughter but as his plural wife. In Nauvoo, with almost no exceptions, the ritual of spiritual adoption was reserved for men, whereas plural marriages united the female faithful to what Smith envisioned would be the ever-multiplying heavenly family.[103] Would-be plural wife or not, Jane Manning James was not a stranger to polygamy. In her autobiography, James claims to have been a witness to the early, secretive days of what the Saints called "celestial marriage."[104] James recalls that while "discussing Mormonism" with four other servants in the Mansion House, the sisters Emily and Eliza Partridge and Maria and Sarah Lawrence, " 'Sara said [to me] what would you think if a man had more wives than one? I said that it is all right! Marie said well we are all four Brother Josephs wives!' " Jane Manning responded with glee and approval. "I jumped up and clapped my hands and said that's good."[105]

Setting aside the critical question of race, little differentiated Jane Manning from these other female servants in the Mansion House. All five were single. All five were in their late teens or early twenties. All five were fatherless. All five lived in Joseph Smith's home, where the prophet pledged to care for their material and spiritual well-being.[106] And yet the question of race is critical to this potential offer of marriage. But which race? Recall that, since the earliest years of the church, leading Latter-day Saints had encouraged white missionaries to take Indian plural wives. Such unions would join the two most favored Israelite bloodlines, the (mostly white) progeny of Ephraim and the (mostly red) sons and daughters of Manasseh. Such unions would also help civilize the Indians so that they could fulfill the Book of Mormon precedent to become "white, delightsome, and just." "We will have intermarriages with [the Indians]," Brigham Young purportedly taught, so that "the curse of their color shall be removed, and they [shall be] restored to their pristine beauty."[107]

The creation of covenants—in this case, marriage covenants—between white Latter-day Saints and Native Americans was the fulfillment of Book of Mormon prophecy.[108] A marital union between the seed of Cain and any Mormon man, let alone Joseph Smith, was beyond the pale of acceptability. Thus, if Joseph did ask James to marry him in Nauvoo, half a century later in Utah, James had to perform a sleight of memory. She had to forget marriage and remember adoption. James understood that in the minds of Utah's late nineteenth-century Mormon hierarchy, she would never be welcomed into the heavenly household of the prophet as a wife. Yet James believed that, if she could write herself into the history of Joseph Smith's Mansion House as a faithful convert, then Smith's successors might accept her as the prophet's adopted daughter.

A Covenantal Contract for a Daughter of Cain, Ham, and Canaan

Decades removed from the Mansion House, in her letters and autobiography composed in 1890s Utah, Jane Manning James provides the only firsthand testimony of her would-be adoption to the prophet. Yet James's writings are not the only archival sources from the Nauvoo period that shed light on how Joseph Smith Jr., and those church leaders closest to him, viewed the potential for spiritual redemption of people of African descent. On May 11, 1844, less than six weeks before he was assassinated alongside his younger brother, church patriarch Hyrum Smith performed for Jane Manning James the first of two patriarchal blessings she would receive in her lifetime. As is the case in her autobiography, from the contents of the blessing, young Jane Manning was clearly worried about her material and spiritual welfare. And yet, according to Hyrum's blessing, Jane Manning had the ability to ensure that her concerns about "food and Raiment and habitations to dwell in," as well as her desire to know the "Mysteries of [God's] Kingdom," would be met. "If you will keep the commandments of God [then] you shall be helped Spiritualy and Temporaly."[109]

This "if" appears in many patriarchal blessings of the era. The blessings of the Lord were conditional, a covenantal contract. This was not the Calvinism of the elect, who could not resist God's grace even if they tried.[110] Although God's providence was paramount, Joseph Smith taught that God gave humanity agency to choose right from wrong. As such, men and women create their own destiny: to follow the path of sin or the path of righteousness through "obedience to the gospel," as Hyrum described it in Jane Manning's blessing. Hyrum's blessing to William Rufus Rogers Stowell of Oneida County, New York, dated January 31, 1844, also included such a covenantal contract that emphasized Stowell's agency: "Therefore I say unto you, William, *if* you will continue faithful as you have begun [*then*] you shall be a bright and shining light unto this generation."[111]

Yet Jane Manning did not enter into this world on equal footing with her fellow white Mormon convert Stowell. According to the blessing that Hyrum gave to him, Stowell was born into the favored "lineage of Ephraim," and he was "blessed with the Priesthood." In the blessing he gave to her, Hyrum revealed that Jane Manning came "down in the lineage of Cainaan the Son of Ham which promise the fullness thereof is not yet revealed." Only after his death did Canaan's progeny become excluded from the Mormon priesthood. Yet Joseph Smith did teach that Canaan's sons and daughters carried with them the burden of their forefathers' misdeeds, even if the full extent of this burden was not yet known. The March 1, 1842, edition of the Nauvoo-based *Times & Seasons* contained the first published version of Smith's translation of the book of Abraham, which includes the vague reference that the descendants of Canaan's father, Ham, were "cursed . . . as pertaining to the priesthood." By the 1890s this passage became popular among church leaders as a justification for the priesthood ban. Ironically, the same edition of *Times & Seasons* also first published the church's Articles of Faith. "We believe that men will be punished for their own sins," Smith explained, "and not for Adam's transgressions."[112] Jane Manning was not born guilty of Adam's sin. But she was born guilty of Ham's. And she carried the mark of this sin on her skin.

And yet Hyrum Smith's blessing does not end with the naming of Jane Manning's lineage. For Hyrum—and for his brother Joseph—Jane Manning's inferior birth did not determine her spiritual destiny. Hyrum Smith promises Jane Manning that through faith and obedience, she "shall have a place and a name in the midst of the people of zion." The Saints would not turn her out because of the sins of her ancestors. In fact, Hyrum Smith offers Jane Manning a covenantal contract that would allow her to secure her place and her name in Zion by parting ways entirely with the sinful forefathers—Ham, his son Canaan, and perhaps most importantly, Cain—that have cut her off from the rest of her fellow (white) Saints.

Cain is not explicitly named in Jane Manning's patriarchal blessing. But by reading Manning's blessing intertextually with Joseph Smith's early translations, Cain's shadow becomes present. To be sure, it was Smith's successor Brigham Young who implemented the restriction against black men holding the priesthood and against black men's and women's access to the temple. "Any man having one drop of the seed of [Cain] . . . in him cannot hold the priesthood," Young famously declared in his January 1852 address to the Utah territorial legislature, "and if no other Prophet ever spake it before I will say it now."[113] Yet, in the church's first years, Joseph Smith too was particularly interested in the origins of the curse of Cain and the implications of this curse for Cain's supposed African progeny. Ten years before *Times & Seasons* published Smith's translation of the book of Abraham, in its August 1832 edition the *Evening and the Morning Star* printed large sections of Joseph Smith's translation of the book of Moses. These excerpts contain Smith's revisions and expansion of the first six chapters of the book of Genesis. It also contains prophetic visions of who would inhabit the millennial city. Zion would be populated by "a mixture of all the seed of Adam," with the exception of the "seed of Cain." The fallout from history's first murder—Cain killing his brother, Abel—would remain until the end of time. "For the seed of Cain were black, and had not place among" the other sons and daughters of Adam.[114] Elsewhere in the book of Moses, even though Cain is exiled both from God's presence and from his family, the Lord protects Cain from other children of Adam who wish to avenge the death of Abel. But the protection comes in an ironic form—"a mark upon Cain"—a mark that many leading Latter-day Saints insisted for the next century and a half only God could remove.[115] In Smith's translation of the book of Moses, which reflected standard antebellum ideas of immutable African accursedness, the mark placed on the seed of Cain rendered them ineligible for full membership in the human family. And according to Smith's revisions of Genesis even at the end of time, they would have no place in the city of Zion.

And yet in Jane Manning's patriarchal blessing, Hyrum Smith indicates that all is not lost. Like the potential redemption of the Native American descendants of the Lamanites, whose cursed dark skin could be made "white and delightsome" through faith and piety, Hyrum Smith comforts Jane Manning, "for he that changeth times and seasons and placed a mark upon your forehead, can take it off and stamp upon you his own linage."[116] In Nauvoo, the church's prophet offered Jane Manning the chance to be adopted into his family. And the church's patriarch told Manning that she could part ways with her inherited identity as a daughter of Canaan, Ham, and Cain. She, too, could join the blessed lineage of Heavenly Father's chosen people.

Yet such a change was conditional on Jane Manning's decision to properly exercise her agency. In the conclusion of the blessing, Hyrum Smith establishes a pathway toward this alternative lineage by offering Manning a very tailored, racially specific covenantal contract: "Behold I say unto you jane if thou doest well thou shalt be accepted; if thou doest not well Sin lieth at the Door." The import of Hyrum's choice of words here cannot be overstated. Hyrum cites word for word Moses 5:23, which is his brother Joseph's translation and slight alteration of Genesis 4:7.[117] In the Bible and in the book of Moses, this passage is part of the conversation between God and Cain that comes directly before Cain rises up against his brother and slays him.[118]

By citing this passage, Hyrum Smith reads Jane Manning into the Cain and Abel narrative. He places her at the scriptural precedent right before the second fall—at the moment before Cain sins against the first human family, for which God curses him with dark skin and segregates Cain and his seed (including his postdiluvian progeny, Ham and Canaan) from the rest of the children of Adam. In other words, Hyrum Smith provides Jane

Manning with the opportunity to write her own conclusion to the Genesis story. She need not follow Cain into sin. By doing "well," she can be accepted as a Latter-day Saint. "Shun the path of vice," Hyrum tells Jane Manning earlier in the blessing, "turn away from wickedness be fervent unto prayer without ceasing and your name shall be handed down to posterity, from generation to generation."[119]

Jane Manning James: "Aunt," Servant, or Daughter?

Near the end of her life, when she met with Elizabeth Roundy to compose her life story, Jane Manning James sought to demonstrate that she had successfully adhered to Hyrum Smith's half-century-old covenantal contract. She turned away from the wickedness of her black ancestors. She chose a more righteous path. And in James's autobiography, literal paths—a journey to Nauvoo and a trek to Utah—become metaphors for her devotion to the restored church and obedience to the church's divinely appointed leaders. James believed that she made herself worthy to have her name handed down to posterity, as Hyrum Smith foresaw. And this name should not be "Aunt Jane," the "colored" servant to the prophet, as the *Deseret News* described her in her obituary.[120] She should be remembered as Jane Manning James Smith, the prophet's adopted daughter, until, that is, her new temple name is revealed to her. And this name should be written not only into the archives of the (earthbound) temple but also into the (heaven-bound) Book of Life.[121]

After all, in Nauvoo, the prophet and his brother, the patriarch, taught young Jane Manning that her blackness, and the spiritual and intellectual limitations that her blackness signified, did not define her destiny. She was born into the least favored of lineages. But James believed that she had successfully disassociated herself from her cursed biblical forefathers. And she had restored herself to God's favor and to God's original, white human family. For James, this restoration was all but total. In 1899, James declared to her longtime friend, fellow Mormon pioneer, and medical doctor Elvira Stevens Barney, "I am white with the exception of the color of my skin."[122]

Dr. Stevens, along with Elizabeth Roundy, were just two prominent Mormon women in late nineteenth-century Utah whom James could count as friends. During her sixty-one years in Salt Lake, James built a network of sisters in the gospel on whom she relied for social, spiritual, and sometimes financial support. For more than three decades, James was a weekly presence in the Eighth Ward's Relief Society, the women-run educational and philanthropic arm of the church.[123] She was also involved in meetings of the church-wide Relief Society. And in these meetings James was frequently invited to speak about her experiences in the prophet's household, and indirectly about her unique but precarious place within the Mormon community.

For example, in December 1893, the influential suffragist magazine and unofficial news organ of the Relief Society, the *Woman's Exponent*, reported that during a recent Relief Society gathering, James declared that she maintained hope that the "light [of the gospel] would yet reach her people" as it had reached her. James also recounted a half-century-old conversation that she had with Joseph Smith in Nauvoo. She prayed that her son, most likely the prosperous but by then excommunicated Sylvester James, might serve as the intermediary between white Mormons and potential black converts, "as the Prophet Joseph had predicted."[124] The *Woman's Exponent* also provided James with the written, public space to articulate the same implicit polemic of her autobiography. The published minutes of an October 1896 Relief Society meeting included the report: "Sister James felt to bear her testimony and rejoice that she had beheld the Prophet and Patriarch Joseph and Hyrum Smith, and wished she could go into the Temple; but she felt to wait in patience on her Heavenly Father. [She] prayed to be faithful unto the end and alluded to the time she embraced the Gospel, and how she rejoiced even until today in the same."[125] In January 1894, Relief Society president and the widow of both Joseph Smith and Brigham Young, Zina D. Huntington Young even wrote to then church apostle Joseph F. Smith to support James's request that she "be adopted into Joseph Smith's family as a child."[126]

Joseph and Hyrum Smith's prophetic male successors did not see James the way her female supporters saw her, let alone how James saw herself. As Brigham Young first began teaching in the 1850s, the leaders of the church's hierarchy believed that she was born into a class of "the human family that are black, uncouth, uncomely, disagreeable and low in the habits, wild and seemingly deprived of nearly all the blessings of the intelligence that is generally bestowed upon mankind." And James, along with all other seeds of Cain, would remain so until "all the rest of the children [of Adam] have received their blessings in the Holy Priesthood."[127] In other words, not any time soon.

For James this also meant she was deemed unworthy to enter the most sacred places in the temple. In her autobiography, James does state with pride, "I have had the privilege [*sic*] of going to the Temple and being baptized for some of my dead."[128] Yet James was never granted permission to receive her endowments or to be sealed to her husband and children. In May 1894, church leaders did grant James's request to be sealed to the prophet—with the exception that she would be Joseph Smith's "servitor," not his adopted daughter. The Salt Lake Temple records indicate that James herself was not permitted to participate in her own circumscribed sealing. Instead, famed suffragist and Relief Society leader Bathsheba W. Smith served as James's proxy during the ceremony, an unusual occurrence because proxies were employed almost exclusively for dead participants. President Joseph F. Smith stood in for his uncle. He also officiated the ceremony, declaring the "Negro Woman" Jane Elizabeth Manning James would be a "Servitor to Joseph Smith . . . and to his household for all eternity."[129]

Jane Manning James's minor personal victory may have played an ironic role in the hardening of membership restrictions for current and future black Saints in the Mormon community. Her quest to receive her temple endowments—one she herself framed as a special exception for her special case—may have encouraged the church leadership to form a more formal racialized sense of who was worthy of admission to the temple and ordination in the priesthood. According to available records, the practice of banning blacks from the priesthood and the temple was well established by the first decade of the twentieth century. Yet it was only in August 1908, just a few months after James's death in April, when the Quorum of the Twelve Apostles first met to discuss a formal policy of exclusion. During the meeting, Joseph F. Smith raised the case of "Aunt Jane" and her adoption to Joseph Smith "as his servant," a relationship that "did not satisfy her."[130] Such a gray area in the church's stance toward "descendants of Cainan" could not continue, the current church president and prophet declared. The Quorum of the Twelve thus passed a motion—without opposition—stating that "if negroes or people tainted with negro blood apply for baptism themselves they might be admitted to Church membership in the understanding that nothing further can be done for them." In particular, this meant that from August 1908 forward, it was the church's official policy that although membership would be open to people of African descent, the church would not seek out black converts. And those black Saints who did join the church would not be admitted to the temple, nor could they hold the Mormon priesthood.[131]

At the beginning of the twentieth century, the church not only moved to remove the possibility of a black Mormon future. It also dismantled the memory of a black Mormon past. There is no evidence that Joseph Smith Jr. ever cited his translations of the books of Abraham and Moses to justify black exclusion during his lifetime. Yet the curses against Cain and Ham described in these texts became the de rigueur scriptural defense of the exclusionary policies until the 1950s. Even Joseph Smith's attitudes toward specific black Mormons were rewritten to fit the attitudes of the day. At the same August 1908 meeting during which the priesthood and temple bans were formalized, Joseph F. Smith asserted that his uncle declared the ordination of the "octoroon" Elijah Abel "null and void" when he discovered that Abel was "tainted with negro blood." This perspective contradicted Joseph F. Smith's own assertions from 1879 on the same question about whether the prophet supported Abel's ordination.[132] What began as a practice in the 1850s and was formalized as church policy in 1908 became doctrine by the mid-twentieth century. "The attitude of the Church with reference to Negroes remains as it has always stood," the First Presidency asserted in an August 17, 1949, "[a] direct commandment from the Lord, on which is founded the doctrine of the Church from the days of its organization."[133]

In life and even in death, Jane Manning James subtly challenged the church leaders on this bad history by writing herself into the Mormon archive. She left a record of her direct, personal experiences that she believed were demonstrably authoritative, even more authoritative than the abstract justifications for her exclusion issued by the church's hierarchy. On the first page of the original handwritten autobiography, Roundy writes that James "wishes [this statement be] read at her funeral by EJD Roundy." And on April 21, 1908, five days after James's passing, the *Deseret News* reported that Roundy fulfilled this instruction. She read "a sketch of her life as dictated by Mrs. James" at "Aunt Jane's" memorial service, a service at which Joseph F. Smith also eulogized James. This means that the Mormon president and prophet most responsible for institutionalizing the racial restrictions against black membership had to sit and listen as James—from the grave—told the story of a pioneering black Mormon woman who shook the prophet's hand, washed the prophet's robes, handled the Urim and Thummim, and should have become the spiritual daughter of Joseph Smith Jr.[134] Turn-of-the-century Mormon officials might not have allowed her to enter the "House of the Lord." But at her own funeral, by asserting her intimate relationship with the objects and bodies that brought about the Mormon dispensation, James claimed that her place among the Saints was recognized in another cherished house in the communal Mormon memory: in the Smiths' Nauvoo home and perhaps even in the Smiths' eternal household.

5   PEOPLE BUILDING, ON BODIES

During the first week of May 1854, the daguerreo-typist and portrait artist for John C. Frémont's final Rocky Mountain expedition, Solomon Nunes Carvalho, traveled south from the Salt Lake Valley with Brigham Young, the president and prophet of the Church of Jesus Christ of Latter-day Saints, Utah's territorial governor, and its ex-officio superintendent of Indian affairs. Young had invited Carvalho, a Sephardic Jew from South Carolina, to join his Mormon cavalcade. The large party, which was making a late spring swing through the growing communities south of the Mormon capital, included Young's first counselor Heber C. Kimball, apostle Parley P. Pratt, and future church president Wilford Woodruff. Fifty mounted militiamen kept watch over a train of more than a hundred wagons. The show of force was also a show of largesse. The Mormons brought with them sixteen oxen and several wagons stuffed with blankets, clothing, arms, and ammunition—all gifts intended for the Ute peace delegation that the Saints would meet in the Utah Valley.

During the weeklong journey, Carvalho scaled rocky outcrops to take in the vista. With an artist's eye for landscape, he watched as the company lengthened to more than a mile along the Mormons' well-maintained wagon road that ran some 250 miles from Salt Lake City in the north to the missionary and mining outposts of Parowan and Cedar City in the south (fig. 5.1). Carvalho observed the convoy "winding leisurely along the side of a mountain, or trotting blithely in the hollow of some of the beautiful valley through which we passed, to the sound of musical choruses from the whole party, sometimes ending with: 'I never knew what joy was / Till I became a Mormon.'"[1]

The Saints' high spirits contrasted with the solemnity of the trip's purpose. On May 11, the Mormon company met a large contingent of Utes, led by their military chief, Wakara, at his camp on the banks of Chicken Creek, a mile off the main road and fourteen miles south of the settlement at Nephi. The purpose of this parley was to end the hostilities between the settlers and the Natives, a conflict later dubbed the "Walker War." Neither Wakara nor Young—the two most powerful men in Utah Territory—wished to fight.[2]

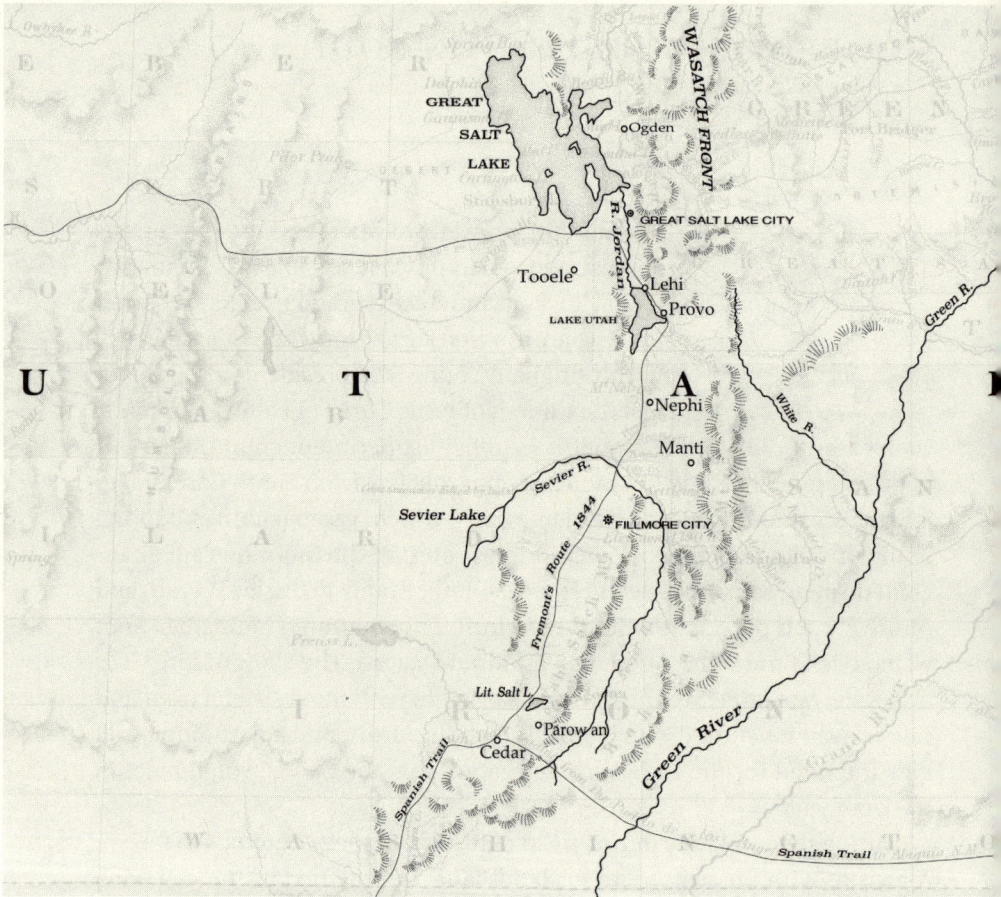

Fig. 5.1. The Territory of Utah, 1855. (George Woolworth Colton, "The Territories of New Mexico and Utah," in Colton's Atlas of the World Illustrating Physical and Political Geography *[New York: J. H. Colton, 1855]; courtesy of Special Collections, University Libraries, University of Nevada, Las Vegas. Thanks to Sarah Murray for updating this map to make it more readable.)*

Since arriving in the Great Basin in 1847, Young had pledged to live in peace with the Indians, to trade with them, and to convert them. Young recognized early that fulfilling this pledge involved handling Wakara with care. As did the Spanish, the Mexicans, and the American trappers with whom the Ute chief often traded and sometimes fought, the Mormons described Wakara—his name, translated as "yellow," referring to the face paint he frequently wore to complement the dye-colored clothing that distinguished him and his horsemen—as intelligent and ruthless. Wakara was the leader of a disciplined cavalry made up of Ute, Shoshone, and Paiute fighters and, for a time, the renowned mountain men Jim Beckwourth and Thomas "Peg-leg" Smith. Wakara became famous for horse thieving along the Old Span-ish Trail, which ran east from the California missions across present-day Nevada, Utah, and Colorado to Santa Fe, New Mexico. In 1840, at the San Luis Obispo mission, the chief and his men reportedly stole more than a thousand horses. This and many other raids earned Wakara the moniker "the greatest horse thief in history."[3]

For his part, Wakara was probably ambivalent about the Mormons' ar-rival. The Mormons tried to differentiate themselves from the Spanish and Gentile Americans who had colonized Ute land by force, initially staking their territory in the Salt Lake Valley to avoid the Wakara-led Timpanogos Utes' hunting and fishing grounds around Utah Lake. But Wakara knew that white men's promises of peace and civilization in this lifetime and salvation in the next presaged the spread of white men's farms and fences in all direc-tions across the lands that had been the Utes' ancestral home for the pre-vious millennium. The Mormons' arrival was also likely to spread disease and warfare that threatened the Ute way of life and Ute life itself. Yet Wakara also saw the Mormon gathering as a new market for trade in horses, pelts, and his most valuable commodity, Indian slaves. Wakara had become well known as a skilled military commander and horse raider and trader. But he had become rich and feared as a purveyor of humans whom he bought or stole from weaker Utah tribes and sold in New Mexico's slave markets.[4] Soon after the Mormons' colonization of Utah, Wakara and his men de-manded that the Mormons participate in the slave trade. When the Mor-mons refused, Wakara and his men tortured and even killed their human property to break the Saints' resolve. In June 1853, just before the outbreak of violence between the Mormons and Wakara's Utes, Brigham Young re-ported to the Bureau of Indian Affairs in Washington that "one of Walker's brothers, lately killed an Indian prisoner child, because the trader would not give him what he asked for it."[5]

Wakara had initially decided that diplomacy was best for business. He pledged to live in peace and trade in friendship with the Saints. In 1850, soon after the Mormons' brutal conquest of the Utah Valley, he was even baptized a Mormon and encouraged his people to do the same. By the sum-mer of 1853, however, Wakara turned against his would-be brethren. In July, a Mormon man killed one of the chief's relatives during a trade deal gone bad. And frustrations over Mormon encroachment into Ute land and the Saints' continuing efforts to disrupt the chief's slave-trading operations led to open conflict. Over a ten-month period, Utes sporadically attacked Mormon communities in southern Utah—communities that Wakara had helped establish only a few years before. Though not always under Wakara's direct orders, Ute warriors engaged in what the Saints called "Indian depredations," pilfering Mormon cattle, stealing crops and horses, destroying the settlers' infrastructure, including fences, farmhouses, and mills, and terrorizing the Mormon settlers themselves. Along with an untold number of Indians, perhaps a half dozen Saints were killed. Mormons living in outlying areas abandoned homes and crops still in the ground to find shelter in fortified towns.[6] At the same time, the Nauvoo Legion went on the offensive. They attacked Ute villages with undiscriminating violence. A mile from Wakara's camp in the Utah Valley, a group of Ute noncombatants sought shelter in the Mormon fort at Nephi. Instead of finding refuge, they were "shot down like so many dogs," remembered Adelia Wilcox, one of Heber C. Kimball's plural wives, who witnessed the massacre. Their bodies were "picked up with pitch forks, put on a sleigh and hauled away" to be dumped in a mass grave. "The squaw they took prisoner" and sent north to Salt Lake.[7]

To end the war, Wakara demanded that Young come to him. Wakara wanted to work out his difficulties with the Mormon prophet, not through couriers and lieutenants, but in person and chief to chief. While Wakara was making his yearly visit to the Timpanogos band's fishing grounds near Utah Lake during the spring spawning season, he sent a letter through the Provo settler George Bean. Wakara told Young to come south bearing presents. Oxen, flour, guns, ammunition, "& a little Whiskey" would be a good start. Young should also come bearing promises to end all restrictions on Wakara's slave trade in New Mexico. And "if [Brigham] wants [Wakara] to be good friends with the whites," the Ute chief explained, he must also be ready to buy the Indian slave children Wakara had just acquired.[8]

According to Carvalho, Young obliged the summons south. "If the mountain will not come to Mahomet, Mahomet must go to the mountain," Young reportedly quipped.[9] After the Mormon company arrived at Wakara's camp, Carvalho accompanied Young and the brethren into Wakara's lodge. There they found the Ute chief seated on a buffalo robe, wrapped in his blanket, and surrounded by his council.

During a two-day-long series of meetings, Carvalho drew likenesses of Ute chiefs, including Wakara (fig. 5.2) and Kanosh, "the chief of the Parvain Indians," the Mormons' most trusted Paiute ally and the sole Paiute chief invited to participate in the peace council that ended the Mormon-Wakara conflict.[10] Young and the Utes negotiated terms. Young told the chiefs that he "loved them like a father, and would always give them plenty of clothes and good food." However, Young's paternalistic generosity was conditional. It was based on the Indians' promise to cease "slay[ing] any more white

Fig. 5.2. Solomon Nunes Carvalho, Portrait of Wakara; Later Chief of the Utah Indians, 1854. (Courtesy of the Gilcrease Museum, Tulsa, Oklahoma)

men." As a token of goodwill, Young presented Wakara with the oxen, which the chief happily accepted. Like the Mormon prophet, Wakara explained that he, too, talked "with Great Spirit; Great Spirit say—'Make peace.'" Yet Wakara had his own conditions. The Saints could settle on the Utes' lands as long as Young reciprocated by "giving Wakara plenty of bread, and clothes to cover his wife and children."[11]

After the peace pipe was smoked, there was more gift exchanging and trading, but not only in beef, bread, and cloth. Young granted Wakara's request that the chief be given a letter certifying that peace had been established, which the chief could show to other Saints so that Wakara could pass unmolested through the Mormon colonies.[12] Before the Mormon company left the Ute camp, Young also purchased two Indian toddlers—Wakara's spoils of war from the Utes' ongoing battles with the "Snake" (Shoshone) Indians. Carvalho wrote that Wakara provided so little sustenance to his captives that Young found the two "living skeletons" "digging with their fingers for grassnuts" in the ground, still hardened from the winter's snows. Young sent them north to "have them cared for and educated like his own children."[13]

Carvalho was shocked by the state of these slaves. Yet he also acknowledged that it was the "whites" who were at fault for creating the conditions for the declining health and wealth of Utah's Natives, which led to Mormon-Ute hostilities. The Natives had become "much aggrieved and injured people" since the Mormons had moved to the area.[14] The Mormons could sing their songs of joy in celebration of the growth of their colonies. But it was Wakara's Utes whose flora and fauna the Mormons had disrupted or destroyed and whose trading in slaves and other goods in New Mexico the Mormons had greatly curtailed. Out of existential desperation more than innate brutality, the Mormon incursion increased Ute reliance on human trafficking, encouraged the cruel treatment of slaves as a sales tactic in the new Mormon market, and led Wakara and his allies to attack Mormon settlements to reclaim control over what the chief called "his country."[15]

After the meeting near Nephi, Young, Wakara, and their respective entourages traveled south to Parowan, the regional capital of the Iron Mission established four years before to exploit the area's ore and rich soil. According to Parowan's clerk, James H. Martineau, Young told Wakara, "The war is over," and over for good. Young brought Wakara to Parowan to show him why. The Mormon prophet's implicit message to the chief was that the Mormons' victory had less to do with military conquest than it did with proper cultivation of the Utah land. "Wakara had long considered himself President Young's equal," wrote Martineau. The Ute chief would demonstrate this belief in his broken English, which he accented with exuberant gesticulation. He held "up his forefinger and say[ing] 'Brigham: Great Chief!' Then placing his other forefinger beside the first [and] would say, 'Me Walker! Me big chief all same as Brigham!'" But from Martineau's perspective, any Saint, Indian, or Gentile who examined "Little Salt Lake," as Parowan was sometimes called—a bustling town of a hundred houses laid out in the square-shaped Mormon plat, with an irrigation system that supplied water to vegetable and flower gardens that ornamented each home, as well as the four-hundred-acre field outside of town that produced bounties of wheat and corn—had to acknowledge that this was not true. Since they had established the Iron Mission in 1850, the Saints had done more with southern Utah in four years than Wakara and his people had done in a thousand.[16]

According to the Latter-day Saints and other Gentile observers, Wakara had misunderstood the value not only of Utah land but of Utah people. Inside the modest but dignified homes of Parowan could be found "one or more Pah-Utah [Paiute] children," observed another western explorer, Gwinn Harris Heap.[17] Young instructed the Mormons that whenever they could, they should purchase Indian slaves from slavers like Wakara who thought of them as no more than commodities to be bought, sold, and abused. It was the Mormons' divine Book of Mormon mandate to turn these slaves into people, or more specifically into Lamanites. Treat them with kindness, teach them to farm, to blacksmith, to keep house, Young instructed his faithful. Teach them to read and write, so that they might learn for themselves about their own true ontology and to do so from their own sacred scripture, the Book of Mormon. As the Saints had mastered the Indians' land, it was time that Wakara and other Indians like him were "made to understand" that the Saints were the Indians' paternalistic "masters," as Brigham Young explained during the 1854 Mormon-Ute meeting at Parowan.[18]

Body-Building Project

In Utah, the Mormon leadership dedicated blood and treasure to build up a Lamanite people with whom they could finally covenant. The Mormon leadership also dedicated blood and treasure to build up new kinds of race-based slavery and indentured servitude (chapter 6) that further distinguished in the body politic of Utah and in the Mormon Body of Christ the difference among white, black, and red. The Mormons' efforts to physically transform the Native Americans of the Intermountain West were focused on transforming the Indians' bodies into the standards of the white Saints. The Mormons worked to restore the Indians to their true selves—to make them Lamanites, and then white and delightsome Latter-day Saints. These efforts manifested in efforts to physically transform he Native Americans whom the Saints encountered, attempted to convert, or bought into freedom, into service, and on occasion even into marriage. This work was literal, taking place on the bodies of Utah's Native peoples; it was also literary, taking place on the paper on which the Latter-day Saints chronicled Mormon-Indian encounters.

In both body and paper work, "Walker"—described as a onetime friend and brother in the Mormon gospel, as well as an unrepentant slave trader, horse thief, and Indian marauder—serves as a synecdoche for the volatile Mormon-Indian relations in early Utah. In the history of early Mormon encounters with Utah's Native peoples, to invoke his name is to invoke the project of "people building" in which the Saints engaged during Brigham

Young's tenure at the head of the church and state of Deseret, the long-prophesied New World Zion of the latter days.[19] When they arrived in Utah, the Saints did not doubt that they had located a remnant of Israel about which the narrators of the Book of Mormon had written. Yet in the expanding archive of their people-building enterprise—in journals, letters, and ecclesiastical and territorial legislature minutes and laws—the Mormons asked, out of this remnant, what portion could be "nursed" up to the standard of the white Saints, as the Book of Mormon had prophesied?[20] Who could be made into Lamanites? And who would prove to be too Indian—too far gone into savagery—to be redeemed?

According to the Mormons, the answers to these questions were mostly found in the ways that the Native people acted in response to the Mormons' people-building projects. Within the borders of what was first envisioned as a sovereign, theodemocratic kingdom of Zion and then, after the Mexican-American War, what was envisioned as a semisovereign U.S. state of Deseret, the Saints believed that they enjoyed a monopoly on coercion—even violent coercion—to build their infrastructure and people according to the (Mormon) rule of law. As such, the Mormons narrated Indian violence as an assault on more than Mormon lives and property. They also narrated it as an assault on the Mormon state's authority with which, the Mormons believed, Wakara (and many of his followers) had politically allied themselves and to which, in the baptismal waters, Wakara (and many of his followers) had religiously submitted.

The archive is almost—but not quite (chapter 6)—devoid of any records that contain Wakara's own, unmediated viewpoint on his mercurial relationship with the Saints. His words enter the archive only when white Mormon and Gentile scribes and narrators see fit. And these words were mostly translated, modified, and redacted to fit the scribes' and narrators' prerogatives. Thus, to glean Wakara's perspective on Mormon-Native relations—to separate the Mormon archive on people building from the Indian archive—the historian must interpret Wakara's words in relation to his actions: to create peace through the bonds of political, economic, and religious connection, to deploy violence to break those bonds, or, perhaps more accurately, to deploy violence to renegotiate the terms of the relationship. In times of friendship, Mormons viewed Wakara as a subject, though not quite a citizen, in their new theodemocratic kingdom in Utah. In times of war, Mormons viewed Wakara as an incorrigible savage who demonstrated perfidy by attacking the very hand that blessed and fed him. Wakara, however, viewed himself as a leader of a sovereign people who expected acts of reciprocity in exchange for allowing the Mormons to live in peace on the Utes' ancestral lands. As such, when he recognized that the Mormon project of building the Indians into Lamanites *by definition* involved the deconstruction of the Ute (hunting, fishing, and slaving) way of life, Wakara used violence in attempt to regain control over the Utes' land and to protect the Utes' very lives.[21]

"A Good Place to Make Saints"

The problem of how to deal with Wakara had troubled the Latter-day Saint leadership long before the outbreak of Mormon-Ute violence in the summer of 1853. In fact, even on July 24, 1847—now celebrated annually in Utah as Pioneer Day, marking the arrival of the first Saints to their Rocky Mountain Zion—Wakara was probably on Brigham Young's mind. According to Mormon pioneering mythology, on that day Wilford Woodruff drove his wagon out of a canyon that opened onto the northeastern edge of Utah's Great Basin. Young, who was fighting off the flu, was laid out in back. But the prophet arose from his sickbed to take in the view of the snow-capped Wasatch Front to the west and the Great Salt Lake to the east. Young told Woodruff that the Saints in exodus had trekked far enough. "This is the place," Young reportedly proclaimed, the place that the Lord had appointed to "make Saints."[22] Within six months of their arrival, the conclusion of the Mexican-American War brought the region under U.S. control. Nevertheless, Young still believed that in the Great Basin, the Mormons would finally be able to establish their Zion homeland, free of persecution from Gentile Americans that had dogged them since the founding of the church in Upstate New York. In 1849, Young petitioned Washington to create the state of Deseret (the name for "honeybee" in the Book of Mormon). Statehood would allow the Mormons to control the levers of political power with little interference from the federal government. Yet as a result of the Compromise of 1850, Utah became a territory. Young officially became the first territorial governor in 1851, though the Saints continued to petition for statehood for the next half century.

The Great Basin, however, was not an empty wilderness waiting for the Saints to cultivate it, gather their people to it, and build their homeland on it. In the vicinity lived diverse communities of Native Americans with an estimated population of between twelve thousand and thirty-five thousand. As their new neighbors moved in, the Natives surveyed the Saints, seeing them as potential trading partners and threats to their land and resources.[23] The Saints surveyed the land to lay down their plat while keeping an eye on the Natives. The famed western explorer Jim Bridger told Brigham Young that the Salt Lake Valley was caught between the often-warring Utes to the south and Shoshones to the north.[24] In particular, Young was careful not to cross paths too soon with the Ute chief known as "Walker." The Mormon leader understood that Wakara could either ease or obstruct the building up of Zion.[25]

More than many other Native tribes, Wakara's Utes had successfully adapted, even flourished after the arrival of European missionaries and colonists to the American Southwest. In the seventeenth and eighteenth centuries, the acquisition of horses and firearms from Spanish traders, along with an alliance with the Spanish colonial regime, helped some Ute bands transform from pedestrian tribes subsisting on what they could hunt, fish, and gather on foot to become formidable equestrians. Ute cavalries deployed violence against Comanche and Navajo horsemen to expand their territories and trading networks across Utah, Colorado, and New Mexico. By the mid-eighteenth century, equestrian Ute bands including Wakara's Timpanogos also began participating in the long-standing Spanish slave trade. They captured women and children from weaker, nonequestrian tribes and sold them in New Mexico. There, captives often became domestics, farmhands, and sexual servants. By the time the Mormons arrived in 1847, in Utah, even among bands that spoke the same language, the difference between equestrian and pedestrian had led to the formation of all but fixed ethnic categories—the Utes traveled by horseback, whereas the Paiutes (Piedes), whom the Utes often enslaved, traveled on foot. Ute chiefs like Wakara raided and traded flesh—horse and human—without seeming to distinguish much between the two.[26]

The Mormons in exodus also had to contend with potentially dangerous Gentile trekkers moving west. In 1846, the historian Francis Parkman wrote about his firsthand experience with the tension created by the triangle of Mormon-Indian-Gentile populations on the overland trails. The Indians presented enough worry for westward-bound companies of whites. But Parkman declared that adding Mormons to the mix meant that "no one could predict what would be the result when large armed bodies of these [Mormon] fanatics should encounter the most impetuous and reckless of their old enemies on the prairie."[27] Once they arrived in the Great Basin, the Saints erected squares to protect themselves from the dangers of Parkman's triangle. On July 28, 1847, four days after the main body of Brigham Young's Vanguard Company entered the Salt Lake Valley, Young ordered the construction of "a foart . . . 40 rods squir 10 ft high," in which the Saints would live, "that we might not be surprised by the Indians." The Mormons believed that these infrastructural improvements staked their claim to the land, over which, by Anglo-American tradition, nomadic Indians had not established ownership and which other white pioneers were legally, or at least honor bound, to respect.[28]

The Old Fort housed some seventeen hundred Mormons who arrived the first year of the migration, making the settlement one of the largest white communities in the Rockies. Green Flake, Hark Lay, and Oscar Crosby were the first African American Mormons—or at least the first African Americans owned by Mormons—to arrive in the valley. Jane Manning James, her son, Sylvester, and her husband, Isaac, and their son, Silas, also lived in the fort. They were the first free blacks to settle in Utah.[29] Over the next decade, similar forts were erected in many early Mormon settlements. Utah's urban sprawl started with log cabins built on the lands farther afield from the strongholds. These lands were cleared of trees and rocks and, when necessary, unfriendly Indians. For the first decades of Mormon Utah, to frighten children who wandered too far into the diminishing but not vanquished Utah wilderness, mothers warned, "Old Sanpitch will get you!" Long after the Mormons killed the famed Ute brave and Mormon foe during the so-called Black Hawk War of the mid-1860s, Sanpitch—or at least his specter—lurked in the shadows.[30]

In Utah the building of Zion was to go apace on three fronts. The first was the expansion of a built environment fit for the Mormon people. The second was the creation of a missionary network to the Natives. And when the Natives proved too savage to participate in these first two fronts, a third front would open to root out Indians who opposed the expanding Mormon civilization.[31] On July 28, 1847, the same day that he ordered the construction of the Old Fort, Brigham Young told the Saints to "form connections with the different tribes of the Indians." These connections would braid together religious, political, and familial lines with the Natives, linking them into the chain of covenantal belonging that Joseph Smith inaugurated and Brigham Young was called on to extend. Once they were taught to accept their true origins and destinies, Indians-turned-Lamanites would throw off the curses of their forefathers and become, as Young explained in 1847, "white and delightsum." They would unite with their white brethren and build one kingdom of the latter days.[32]

Connections originated with communication. Brigham Young's first goal was to communicate the message that the Mormons were different from the "Americats," as some Indian leaders named the Gentile pioneers who, at least according to the Mormons' message to the Indians, took both Native territories and Native lives with little regard to their land claims or even to their humanity. Young's basic belief that the Saints were called to redeem the Indians was in fundamental conflict with what Young (among many others) characterized as the American policy—that the only good Indian was a dead Indian.[33]

Theology informed policy. Unlike many Americans who foresaw no place for Natives in their vision of a Columbia destined to stretch from sea to sea, the Mormons understood their exodus from the United States as a providential move toward the Indians, their would-be covenantal partners in the building of Zion. To be sure, the Mormons were neither the first nor the last people of European descent with ambitions to Christianize and civilize the Natives of Utah. In the summer of 1776, the Franciscan friars Silvestre Vélez de Escalante and Francisco Atanasio Domínguez journeyed from Santa Fe through central Utah. Their goals were to establish a more northerly route to the Spanish missions at Monterey, California, and to bring the gospel to the Natives whom they encountered along the way. In September, Escalante and Domínguez preached to Utes in present-day Colorado and Utah. The friars urged their Native audiences to accept instruction in "the way of living that would lead them to baptism" as well as in "how to farm and raise livestock, whereby they would then have everything necessary in food and clothing just like the Spaniards." Escalante and Francisco described being warmly received by "friendly" Utes. Two Timpanogos served as their guides through much of Utah. According to the expedition's journal, the Timpanogos "fish-eaters" at Utah Lake even offered to provide fertile land on which future Spanish settlements could be built. Despite this promising initial contact in 1776, the friars never returned. The Spanish crown focused expansion efforts in California. And none of their Ute "friends" joined the Catholic Church. However, the friars' *entrada* into Utah did integrate Wakara's ancestors more fully into the Spanish trade system, especially the trade in flesh—horses, pelts, and slaves.[34]

The Mormon vision of Natives' place within a society of the Saints was also similar to the "friends of the Indian" ideology developed during the mid- to late nineteenth century. Protestant social reformers lobbied the federal government to dismantle the reservation system and to integrate Natives into white farming communities. By providing Natives educational opportunities comparable to those afforded to white children and by granting them full citizenship, the Friends of the Indians believed that the Natives could be transformed into agrarian, republican, Christian (all but white) Americans.[35] However, the Saints were unique in their belief that the ultimate success of their own covenantal community was incumbent on turning Indians into Lamanites, who would eventually become (literally and figuratively) white Mormons. After all, the Indians were "the house of Israel," as prolific pioneer diarist and Vanguard Company member Levi Jackman called them in late July 1847, "the children of the covenant seed unto whom belongs the priesthood and the oricals of God." The attempt to covenant with the Indians, which began almost two decades before with the unsuccessful 1831 expedition to the Delawares, was finally at hand. Jackman acknowledged that the Utah Indians were currently little more than "filthey, degraded and miserable beings." However, it was in the Great Basin where the Saints would find "a people to commence" this work with. Unlike the tribes in the East, "[They] have not been paisoend with sectarian impositions" of other Christians missionaries. The stakes were high. Jackman recognized that nothing less than the creation of "Zion [to] be built up no more to be throne down" was contingent on building up the "Lamonites."[36] In the interest of both their particular Christian duty and economic practicality, Young's axiom was that it was "cheaper to feed them, than to fight them." As such, the Mormons reached out to the Indians as the Book of Mormon taught them they should: to nurse them up to the standards of their would-be white brethren.[37]

Young wanted to clearly communicate this divine mandate of paternalistic redemption to the Natives. When he did not meet with them himself, Young sent emissaries with letters in hand to be read to Native chiefs. For example, as the Saints moved south in the late 1840s, Young sent Indian interpreter Dimick Huntington to Fort Utah. The settlement was built near the fishing villages of the Timpanogos Utes in the Utah Valley, which served as the gateway through the mountains between the Great Basin and the fertile plains to the south. In the spring of 1849, Huntington reported to Young that he was working to distinguish in the minds of "influential Indian[s]" the difference between the Mormons and the Americans. Huntington also worked to distinguish between Indian friend and foe. Despite the many "very friendly" Indians in the area, the mood was precarious. A large number of the settlers at Fort Utah were converts who came from southern and frontier states, including Missouri, and were familiar with trading and fighting with Indians. Through Huntington, these settlers told Young that they needed both carrot and stick—more guns to forge Indian friendship as well as a stronger show of force to frighten the fence-sitting Indians into compliance. "We fired the [fort's] cannon once and it had good effect," Huntington wrote to Young.[38] In response to Indian attacks in the Utah Valley, in January 1850, Young ordered the creation of a company of "minute men" drawn from the best fighters in the Nauvoo Legion. After the first skirmish with the Timpanogos that produced a body count, General Daniel H. Wells authorized the legionaries to "act as the circumstances may require exterminating [Indian fighters] such as do not separate themselves from their hostile clans."[39]

Of course, the Saints had personal experiences with orders of extermination. When he announced his 1838 "extermination order," Missouri governor Lilburn Boggs deemed the Mormons enemies of the state. In contrast, Wells cautioned his minutemen that when possible, "sue for peace" and "exercise every principle of humanity compatible with the laws of war."[40] Yet as the makers of the laws of the land, the Mormons believed that they could deploy violence as a tool of state formation. In February 1850, the militia swept through the Utah Valley. They tracked down and killed several dozen Timpanogos, along with a few Utes not involved in the fighting. According to John Gunnison, a military officer and explorer who surveyed Utah for throughways for the transcontinental railroad, Mormon fighters coaxed a group of Indians into surrendering. The Mormons then executed them en masse. One of Gunnison's expeditionary colleagues, the surgeon James Blake, helped the Mormons decapitate the Indians. Blake wanted to box up the forty to fifty Indian heads and send them back to Washington for study. The headless bodies were left to freeze and then to rot in the warming Utah spring air. During the fighting a Mormon-friendly Ute named Antonga took shelter in Fort Utah. Antonga, whom the Mormons would later dub "Black Hawk," watched with horror as his tribesmen's heads were prepared for shipment east, a gruesome scene that he and other Utes would not soon forget.[41]

For his part, Gunnison approved of this use of violence as an act of state-sponsored "chastisement" of "insolent" Indians who refused to recognize the Mormons' authority. "This thorough work makes such an impression" on the surviving Indians that in the future, Gunnison predicted, "they will fear to offend, which is the humane policy."[42] However, the Mormons' claim that they had the right to deploy violence because they were representatives of the state was based on a fallacious tautology. The Mormons could use violence to suppress threats to their settlements not because they enjoyed state authority but because they enjoyed superior tools of war. Such tools included bullets, cannons, forts, and well-trained militias. Such tools also included a seemingly unending stream of migrants who brought with them communicable diseases against which the Indians had no immune defense. The migrants also brought with them oxen, plows, seeds, and irrigation systems, which remade the Utah landscape in the name of an American Zion and in the image of the Mormons' ancestral homes of New and Old England. These changes to the land eventually led to famine among the game- and fish-eating Utah Natives as well as the desertification of much of the once-verdant Utah landscape.[43]

Amid their first Indian War, the Mormon military leaders understood the seeming incongruity between their mandate to bring the gospel to the remnant of Israel and the massacre of these very same people.[44] Yet the message from the Mormon leadership was that the Saints need not cry over a few dead Indians. During a February 1850 meeting of church and legion officials, Young cited a previously unrecorded prophecy from the Mormons' first prophet. In the process of restoring the Lamanites, Joseph Smith himself foresaw that "many of the Lamanites will have to be slain by us." These unredeemable Indians would be "better off on the other side of the vail [sic]" than continue to live in open opposition to Zion.[45] During this meeting, the onetime missionary to the Delawares Parley P. Pratt agreed that it was "best to kill the Indians." By Indian, Pratt meant male Indians. Unlike an Indian "brave," women and children were malleable to the civilizing will of the Saints. "I would take the women and clothe them and dictate [to] make them do what we want," Pratt said. Young agreed to limit this extermination to Indian men. While "we have no peace until the men are killed off," Young proposed to "let the women and children live if they behave themselves."[46]

The Nauvoo Legion executed this plan. After turning the "squaws & children" into widows and orphans, the militiamen brought several north to Salt Lake. There, John Gunnison observed, they were "placed [in Mormon homes] as servants to make white people of them."[47] Gunnison was half right. The Saints had even greater aspirations for the captives: to make them into Lamanites with whom the white Mormons could covenant. Yet the Mormon leadership soon recognized that it overestimated these Indian women and children's ability and desire to be made into Lamanites. After being fed and cared for through the winter, many "ran back to their Indian camps," while others died, recalled Daniel Wells.[48] Utah's Great Basin proved to be a good place to make Saints. Making Lamanites proved to be a more challenging enterprise.

Wakara: Lamanite Elder

Brigham Young and his councillors recognized that it was both impractical and unchristian to kill off all male Natives. The fulfillment of the gospel and the realities of diplomacy dictated that the Latter-day Saints attempt to negotiate peace and friendship with at least some leading male Indians. During the first few years in Utah, the Saints hoped to turn Wakara and other members of his family, which constituted the elite of the Northern Utes, into exemplars to which lesser Indians would aspire.[49] After all, as Parley P. Pratt observed in 1850, Wakara and his men had shown that they were different from other, more belligerent Timpanogos.[50] To be sure, the Mormons abhorred Wakara's slave trading. Yet they recognized that Wakara's travels on the Old Spanish Trail had refined him. Conversant in several Indian dialects as well as Spanish and English, Wakara was viewed as something of a cosmopolitan Indian. He occupied a state between savage and civilized, a liminality exemplified in his dress (fig. 5.3). In March 1850, the Mormons' chief Gentile ally, Thomas L. Kane, told the Historical Society of Pennsylvania that Wakara wore "a full suit of the richest broadcloth, generally brown and cut in European fashion, with a shining beaver hat and fine cambric shirt." To this ensemble, the chief added "his own gaudy Indian trimmings."[51]

In the late 1840s, Young frequently met in person with or sent letters to Wakara. Young hoped to win the Ute chief's support for Mormon plans to expand into the warmer, more fertile land of southern Utah as well as to missionize southern Utah's Natives. In a November 1849 letter, which Dimick Huntington read to the Ute chief, Young explained what Wakara might gain from an alliance with the Mormons. Young offered him a practical as well as spiritual covenantal contract. If the chief allowed the Saints to settle the Utah Valley, then the Saints would instruct Wakara's people on how to cultivate the land. The Utes could then cease to live and die by the vagaries of the valley's wildlife.[52] "Deer are few, and you must make corn this year, and learn to work like white men," Young told Wakara in a May 1850 letter. The Indians must put down their guns, bows, and arrows and take up the hoe and plow and build farms.[53]

Young's didactic messages point to a second goal of early Mormon-Indian relations. Not only did the Saints want to prove that they were distinct from the "Americats." They also wished to become teachers to their Indian pupils, bringing knowledge of both modern civilization and the truth of the Indians' Israelite identity. Echoing the Mormon message to the Delaware Indians from 1831, in another November 1849 letter that he had Huntington read to Wakara, Young explained, "We are sent here by the Great Spirit to teach you, and do all of you good." If you cease the fratricide and begin to "love one another," "[then you will] become a great, united, and good people . . . and you will realize all the blessings that have been told [to] you by your forefathers."[54] Young expected that Wakara would accept this lesson as would a child. After all, in May 1849, Huntington reported to Young that after spending a peaceful night with the Utes in the Utah Valley, during which they displayed their happiness by singing "around the Fort"

Fig. 5.3. Sketch of Walker, Chief of Utah's *(1852). The Mormon artist and early Utah pioneer William Warren Major made this sketch and many others of leading Utah chiefs. (Courtesy of the Peabody Museum of Archaeology and Ethnology, Harvard University, Cambridge, Mass., PM# 41-72-10/427 [digital file # 99050027])*

and warming themselves by a fire, "Walker lay[ed] in my arms. . . . I told [the Utes] of the Book of Mormon [and that] they must be our friends, & we yours."[55]

Most of the Timpanogos Utes had proven that they were unable and unworthy to be given such instruction. And Young predicted this would hold true for most Indians who were too set in their heathen, horse-stealing ways to respect Mormon property, let alone to enter into an "everlasting covenant" with the Saints.[56] As such, Young responded to Huntington's campfire dispatch with a letter admonishing the Utah Valley settlers to finish the fort and cease the unnecessary fraternizing with the Indians.[57] To Young's mind, the subsequent Indian attacks at Fort Utah demonstrated that he was right not to confuse Indian kindness with weakness. However, soon after the Fort Utah battles, followed by a measles outbreak that killed a large number of his tribe, on March 13, 1850, Wakara asked Isaac Morley, the head of the new Manti settlement in the Sanpete Valley, to baptize him in Manti's City Creek. Following this, Wakara began what the Saints likely viewed as missionary work, encouraging other Indians to enter the waters and "wash away [their] sins." In fact, with Wakara's blessing, Manti was established ostensibly as a mission to cultivate the Indians: to convert them from nomadic hunters, gatherers, and horsemen into landed Mormon farmers. The hope was that a peaceful Lamanite neighborhood would be in place when white Mormons moved in.[58]

The plan seemed to work. By summer, more than one hundred Indians followed Wakara into the baptismal waters and were confirmed members of the church branch in Manti.[59] Fellow Ute chiefs Arapeen and Sowiette were also baptized. And in May the three chiefs were ordained church elders. Morley was overjoyed. Two months after they were forced to exterminate troublesome Indians in the Utah Valley, in Manti the Saints found that "the [gospel] door is open," as Morley wrote to Young in April 1850, "and they are coming in with expression of good feelings, and kindness as could probably be expected from uncultivated minds."[60] Young was equally elated. He saw these baptisms as fulfillment of ancient prophecy. "The spirit of the Lord is beginning to operate upon the hearts of the Lamanites," Young wrote to Morley. The prophet hoped that the spirit's work would be so complete that these Lamanites would leave their Indian ways behind and only "do good."[61]

The Book of Mormon taught that Wakara's ancient ancestors had periodically been good, too. But Wakara's ancestors did not record the gospel's truths in a manner that could be passed down from generation to generation. Their illiteracy meant forgetting the ways of the Lord. For the incipient goodness to endure in the hearts of Wakara and other modern-day Lamanites, these new members had to be further converted: from an oral people to a people of the book. Young explained to Morley that Wakara must learn to read. "The Book of Mormon might be a great blessing to [him] . . . & through him to many of his kindred." Young instructed Morley to do all he could to assist Wakara to become literate. Morley should translate the Book of Mormon into the Indian language. And as any attentive tutor would, Morley should see to it that Wakara "apply himself diligently by study & also by faith."[62]

A month later, when the Ute chief was making the annual spring visit to his band's fishing grounds along the Timpanogos (Provo) River, Young traveled south to tell Wakara in person how the Indians could learn to form an "everlasting covenant" with their white brethren. In Wakara's tipi, cramped full of Mormon apostles and Indian chiefs, including the other two Ute priesthood holders, Arapeen, and Sowiette, Wakara told Young that he was a friend and loved the Mormon chief. "I don't want you to throw me away," the Ute chief exclaimed. With Dimick Huntington acting as interpreter, Young told Wakara that he felt the same way. He also explained, however, that his love was conditional—based on how much effort the Indians put into achieving literacy and agrarian respectability. Indian children needed to learn to read and write. Indian women needed to learn to keep house. And Indian men needed to learn to farm and trade. Young concluded the meeting with the Ute chiefs by gathering them into "a large round ring." "My friends I want you all to be brothers tho we are strangers now," Young explained. "We expect to be intimately acquainted (yes) We have come here to settle on your land but our Father the Great Spirit has plenty of land for you and for the Mormons. We want you to learn to raise grain and cattle and not have to go and hunt and be exposed to other Indians, but build houses, raise grain and be happy as we are." The chiefs said that they understood Young's message. For his part, Wakara told Young that he wished to settle and build a home in "Sanpete close to [the] Mormon's house."[63]

Wakara: Ute Chief Negotiator

The early Mormon archive presents a clear view of how the Latter-day Saints understood the respective roles that the Mormons and Wakara were to play in the venture to build a certain portion of Utah's natives into Lamanites. The Mormons were the mothers and fathers, teachers and masters to their would-be Lamanite sons and daughters. The few Indians who proved themselves redeemable were the Saints' obedient children, students, and servants. The same archive presents a less clear view of Wakara's actual feelings about his relationship with the Mormons. It's worth pausing here to consider how Wakara's perspective on this people-building project likely differed from that of the Mormons.

Some records indicate that Wakara never wanted whites—be they Mormons, Mexicans, or other Gentile Americans—to settle permanently on the land he considered "his country."[64] Wakara had witnessed in New Mexico and in California the destructive effects of European incursion into Native lands; when "friendly" friars arrived, less-than-friendly armed settlers were almost certainly not far behind. The Utes had succeeded in the Spanish colonial economy in part because the Spanish had chosen to expand their settlements to the Utes' south and west. This allowed the Utes to maintain control over their ancestral lands longer than most other Native communities. Until the arrival of the Mormons in 1847, Wakara and his predecessors had mostly enjoyed free passage along the Old Spanish Trail. They raided horses in California and Indian slaves in southern Utah. They traded their spoils in Santa Fe, Taos, and Abiquiu for more horses, metal wares, and European clothing. And every spring, they returned to their fishing grounds in the Utah Valley, where they fed their bodies and souls on the fish that they revered. However, after taking stock of the Indian Battle at Fort Utah of 1849–50—in which many Utes lost their lives to what Gunnison described as the Mormons' "gunpowder and measles"—Wakara chose to negotiate with the newcomers. Perhaps he hoped that playing the role of ally instead of antagonist in the Mormons' efforts to build Zion might enable him to direct Mormon growth away from the more sensitive and sacred sites of the Utes' spiritual geography. In the face of the Mormons' superior tools of war, perhaps Wakara believed that by deploying the tools of accommodation and compromise, the destruction of the Ute way of life could be avoided.[65]

Wakara's first negotiation tactic was to give the Saints permission to settle on—but not to purchase—Ute land. Wakara invited the Saints to build settlements in the Sanpete Valley but, tellingly perhaps, not near the Timpanogos' treasured hunting and fishing grounds. To be sure, the Mormon footprint in the resource-rich Utah Lake region was already sizable and certain to grow.[66] However, perhaps Wakara's efforts to promote development farther south—including his pledge to contribute labor of Ute men to assist in building houses and raising grain, to allow Ute children to attend planned schoolhouses, and even to relocate himself to Sanpete "close to [the] Mormon's house"—was a way of shifting Mormon attention and resources away from his beloved Utah Lake region.[67] In return for land use, Wakara expected reciprocity in the form of material goods. In May 1854, after the Mormon-Indian war that would come to bear his name, Wakara proposed a twenty-year lease "for portions of his lands" in exchange for yearly payments of cash and "cattle & horses." However, he would no longer direct his tribesmen to contribute labor to the building up of Zion. "He is at present averse to farming & building houses" on the land, George Bean explained Wakara's 1854 lease offer to Brigham Young, "unless the Whites will do [it] all themselves."[68] In contrast, the Paiute chief Kanosh adopted the Mormons' sedentary farming lifestyle on his band's lands located on the

Mormon road between Salt Lake City and the southernmost settlements at Saint George. Kanosh, who was baptized and ordained a Mormon elder, also publicly supported the Mormons' claims to private land ownership, for which he was compensated in cattle, farming equipment, and clothes.[69]

For Wakara, baptism was a second tactic of negotiation. The Saints might have interpreted Wakara's choice to be dunked in Manti's City Creek as an act of acceptance of the truth of the Mormon gospel and as an act of submission to the authority of that gospel's prophets on earth. In Wakara's mind, his act of stepping into the creek likely did not set him on the path away from being an Indian and toward becoming a Lamanite. Instead of submissive, the move was perhaps more incorporative, adding Mormon religious symbols and rituals to his own Native worldview.[70] Even Wakara's choice of baptismal locations—the waters of Manti in Sanpete instead of the rivers and lakes of the Timpanogos region—hints at an expansion of Wakara's sacred geography. After all, Isaac Morley named Manti after the hill in the Book of Mormon whose summit was said to be "between heaven and earth" (Alma 1:15). Or perhaps the choice of Manti was instead one of misdirection, pointing the Saints away from his Timpanogos waters, which he hoped the Saints would not further pollute with their ritual bathing and agricultural runoff. Or perhaps for Wakara, the baptism held no spiritual meaning at all. Instead it was simply another building block in his effort to construct an alliance with the Saints—a familial covenant more than a religious one, and thus more horizontal in nature than vertical. Wakara repeatedly demanded that the Mormon leadership give him a "white wife," likely a privilege of reciprocity that he believed he earned when he became a Mormon elder.[71]

The third tactic of negotiation was violence. Wakara did not wage a war in the traditional sense against the Saints in 1853–54. Instead, he waged a war of terror, intended to send a message more than sow destruction. Wakara explained as much in a letter he sent to George A. Smith, the Nauvoo Legion's colonel and founder of Parowan. The chief upbraided Smith for failing to understand the purpose and scope of the Utes' attacks against the southern settlements. "The Mormons were d——d fools for abandoning their houses and towns, for he did not intend to molest them," the chief explained. Instead, "his intention was to confine his depredations to their cattle." Wakara urged the Mormons to return to their crops, "for if they neglected them, they would starve, and be obliged to leave the country, which was not what he desired, for then there would be no cattle for him to take."[72] Dissatisfied with the state of Mormon-Ute relations, Wakara used violence to force the Mormons to renegotiate terms. In the early May 1854 letter he sent to Young through George Bean to invite the Mormon prophet south for peace talks, Wakara explained that he had "been a little mad" with the Mormons for trying to end his slave trade in New Mexico. However, he warned, "when he gets very angry, there will be no more travel on the roads" between Salt Lake and the southern settlements. Allowing him free trade, the chief wrote, as well as bringing "many presents . . . much more than common," could assuage his anger, alleviate his fear of violent Mormon reprisals, and reestablish friendship.[73]

Indian Dependents, Lamanite Farmers

Well before the fallout with Wakara, Young had been less than sanguine about the prospect that many of the Rocky Mountain Natives could be made into Lamanites. In December 1850, Young told the representatives of the incipient state of Deseret that the Indians' inability "to leave off their habits of pilfering and plundering" and work like civilized white people, was a failure of physiology. Many Indians who had tried to live like and with the white man had died trying. The Indians' "physical formation," Young explained, made them ill-equipped for the hard work of a white man's existence. Another interpretation could be that the Indians' immune systems were ill-equipped to fight off the white man's diseases, especially measles and smallpox, which decimated Utah's Native population in the late 1840s and 1850s.[74]

Young believed that the few redeemable Indians, like the Wakara-led Utes, would be made into Lamanites and then absorbed into the growing Mormon kingdom. Young predicted that the more savage element of Utah's Natives would fight violently against the expansion of Mormon settlements. Yet, as had been the case for their Native cousins east of the Mississippi, these Indians would eventually be rendered benign, if not extinct. In the interim, hostile Indians posed a threat to the peace and prosperity of the Mormon settlements. For example, during a spring 1851 visit to Parowan, Young warned the southern Utah settlers to prepare to defend themselves against "the children of the Gadianton robbers," a secretive band of thieves from the Book of Mormon. Young explained that ever since this particularly wicked group had united with the Lamanites at the end of the Book of Mormon's history to annihilate the Nephites, they "had infested the mountains for more than a thousand years and had lived by plundering all the time."[75] Thus, while they were working to form religious and familial covenants with the few Indians capable of change, church leaders tried to form political covenants with Washington. They petitioned federal lawmakers to apply Jacksonian era logic to the Indian problem in Utah and authorize and fund the Saints' efforts to remove antagonistic Indians from the territory's most fertile lands.[76]

The Mormons' request to displace the Indians went unanswered. As such, Mormon leaders sought to make Utah safe for the building up of Zion by engaging in a particular form of pedagogy. If the white men in Washington would not disentitle the Indians, the white Mormons in Utah would teach them to be dependent on the white Mormon ways of living.[77] To secure peace and establish friendship in the short term, as well as to remove the Indian threat in the long run, the Mormons needed to teach the Indians "to depend upon us until they eventually will not be able to get along without us," Young said soon after the end of the 1853–54 conflict with Wakara. The way to the Indians' heart, however, was not through their minds.[78] The Mormons' paternalistic generosity—gifts of cattle, grains, guns, medicine, and clothes—would educate the Indians' bodies by changing what they ate, how they dressed, and where they lived. Those few Indians who survived these changes would then naturally want to learn for themselves how to live as white Mormons did.

During the 1850s, church leaders established three points of contact where the work of adapting the Indians' bodies and minds took place. First, out of community storehouses located in Mormon villages, many destitute Indians were provided with essential commodities. The rebirth of the women-led Relief Society in Utah came initially in the form of "Indian Relief Societies," which were established to feed and clothe Indian women and children dislocated during the conflict with Wakara.[79] Yet the Saints did not want to create an Indian welfare state. Young explained that the Mormons should "require the Indians to pay in labor for every article" that they received. Physical effort, Young believed, "learns them to work upon their own exertions for a subsistence."[80] As such, the second point of contact was the so-called Indian farms. On lands that the territorial government set aside for Indian use, Mormon overseers taught their Indian pupils the art of agriculture so that one day they could run the farms themselves. As the Mormons dug deeper in and spread farther out—disrupting the Indians' hunting grounds and fishing stocks—the Indians would be forced to stop watching the Mormons "throw the dirt," as some Indians called plowing and hoeing, and start throwing dirt themselves.[81] The same goals held true for the third point of contact: Indian mission outposts established in the wake of the conflict with Wakara and in the far-flung regions of Mormon Country.[82] Young tasked the missionaries with establishing permanent settlements among the Indians, learning their languages, and creating covenants of trade as well as covenants of marriage. Through preaching the gospel, feeding and clothing the Indians, and teaching them agricultural skills, these missions would further cleave local Natives to the Saints. These Lamanite brethren would then serve as emissaries to other Natives in the region. And if needed, they would also serve as defensive forces, protecting Zion from Indian as well as American enemies.[83]

Some early records suggest that the strategy was working. In late May 1854, after leaving the peace meeting near Nephi, Solomon Carvalho traveled south with Young's cavalcade before Carvalho and the rest of the Frémont company headed west to California. At Cedar City, Carvalho made note of the improved state of the Indians since the arrival of the Saints to the southwest corner of present-day Utah. The "Piedes" (Paiutes) had been "considered the most degraded" in the region, subsisting on "reptiles, insects, [and] roots." Yet under the care and tutelage of the Saints, they had become more civilized. They dressed in manufactured clothes and ate the cultivated grain and meat that the Saints provided. They were also learning "the arts of agriculture and husbandry." Many had been baptized into the Mormon faith. A few days later, Carvalho was able to take the true measure of the Mormons' influence on the Paiutes. A group of the tribe who had not yet benefited from Mormon patronage paid a visit to his camp on the banks of the Santa Clara River. There the Indians begged for food, and did so "almost in a state of nudity."[84]

Carvalho's encounter with the Paiutes at Santa Clara came just before the Saints founded there the most successful and long-lasting missionary Indian outpost in Utah. This "Southern Indian Mission," headed by "the Apostle to the Lamanites," Jacob Hamblin, was established to proselytize the Southern Paiutes, Utes, and Goshutes. It later expanded to include the Hopis, Navajos, and Zunis of modern-day Arizona and New Mexico.[85] Early in 1854, the Mormon missionaries' assessment of the Indians at Santa Clara matched Carvalho's. They were little better than "dogs" or indigent "children," one missionary observed. They survived on a hand-to-mouth diet of porridge, ants, and roasted heads of porcupine, "brains and bones" not excluded. The prospects of redeeming such depraved creatures, the mission's official recorder, Thomas D. Brown, believed, were slim.[86] And yet ironically, perhaps the Indians' destitute state led to the missionaries' success. After years of enduring attacks from Wakara and other Indian slave traders who took advantage of their poverty to steal their women and children, the Paiutes turned to the Mormons for protection and training in farming. According to Mormon records, some even handed over their children to the Mormons' care. Better they grow up as the Mormons' adopted children and servants—clothed, fed, and taught to farm, read, and write—than in the hands of Wakara, who would sell them to the highest bidder or kill them if he did not get his price.[87] Even the Paiute chief Tutsegavit recognized that his tribe's future as a civilized people was embodied in these children. "We cannot be good," he told Jacob Hamblin. "Some day, maybe, our children will be good. Now we only Paiutes."[88]

On occasion in the Southern Indian Mission, adopted children became wives of Mormon missionaries. Jacob Hamblin's fourth wife, Eliza, was a Paiute girl who had grown up in his household. Hamblin's longtime missionary companion, Ira Hatch, married Sarah "Maraboots," the adopted daughter of missionaries Andrew and Rispah Gibbons.[89] From the 1850s through the 1870s, Hamblin, Hatch, and their Native American wives served as economic and cultural intermediaries between the Mormon settlers and the Indians of southern Utah and northern Arizona, working to secure peaceful trading relations as well as some Native converts.[90]

Indians at Home, Lamanites (Again) on the Horizon

Yet the success of the Southern Indian Mission was an exception to, not the rule of, the Mormons' efforts to establish permanent points of contact with Native Americans during much of Brigham Young's time as church president. Neither church leaders nor the Indians showed much interest in the Indian farms, which were poorly financed and maintained. They were abandoned a few years after they were established.[91] For the most part, the same held true for the Indian missions. Like the first missionaries to the Delawares in 1831, missionaries to the Indians in Utah described great enthusiasm for the Mormon message among the Natives they encountered, only to report that their hopes for Lamanite conversions were dashed when anti-Mormon agitators—in Utah these agitators most often took the form of other Indians—began to interfere. For example, on July 22, 1855, missionaries who were sent to Elk Mountain in central Utah baptized fourteen men and one woman. Four of the new converts were renamed after the Book of Mormon prophets Nephi, Lehi, Samuel, and Joseph. They were also ordained Mormon elders. Yet by late summer, a handful of local Indians who objected to the Mormon presence began stealing the missionaries' crops, horses, and cattle. And they even attacked the missionaries. By October, the missionaries fled Elk Mountain for the safety of the Mormon settlement at Manti.[92]

By 1858, most of the missions had been deserted due to Indian ambivalence or outright hostility. The impending arrival of the U.S. Army in 1857 also contributed to church leaders' decisions to close ranks around Mormon Country's north-south cordon.[93] Yet even the more established and better-protected settlements from Salt Lake to Cedar City were not immune to Indian raids.[94] Young promised his people that the Nauvoo Legion would protect them. But he also made clear that the militia was charged with "preserv[ing] peace," not seeking vengeance. Not only was an eye for an eye not effective at "check[ing] their depredations." "To retaliate for every outbreak" would also be to "descend to their grade of conduct."[95]

And yet by 1857, and certainly by 1865, when Black Hawk (Antonga) organized a pan-Indian resistance to Mormon encroachment, it was clear to Brigham Young that his 1850 predictions about the inability of the Utah branch of Israel to be redeemed had proven prophetic. These Indians had demonstrated that they were simply incapable of becoming a peaceful and productive people living within the ever-expanding Mormon Kingdom.[96] Yet the failures of the Utah Indians to become Lamanites did not end the white Saints' quest for their Book of Mormon–promised red brethren. Instead, church leaders looked to find Lamanites on more distant horizons. To the east, in 1855 the church sent missionaries to proselytize among the "civilized tribes," notably the Cherokees, who had been forced to settle in the Indian territories in Oklahoma after the Indian Removal Act of 1830.[97] To the south in Arizona, in 1858 and 1859 Young sent Jacob Hamblin to bring the gospel to the Hopis, whom, five years earlier, Wakara had described as blond haired and blue eyed. Some Saints thought that these "white" Indians were in fact the descendants of a twelfth-century king of Wales who, according to Welsh folklore, sailed to the New World in 1164 with a dozen ships and three thousand men, never to be heard from again.[98] Though their language seemed to contain remnants of Gaelic gutturals, interpreter and missionary James Davies failed to communicate with the Hopis in his native Welsh. The missionaries found Spanish a more effective common tongue.[99]

To the north, in Idaho and Wyoming in the early 1870s, Mormon missionaries found a religious awakening among the Shoshones despite (or perhaps because of) Mormon expansion in prior decades, which had disrupted vital food and water resources.[100] The combination of prophecies of millenarian pan-Indian movements—arising in response to continued cultural and demographic annihilation—and Book of Mormon theologies of Lamanite people building circulated among the first Ghost Dance participants.[101] According to Orson Pratt, the visions that one Indian convert recounted, in which three strangers appeared to him and explained that the Mormons' Heavenly Father was also the father of the Indians, and as such the Indians must be baptized and learn to live like white men, matched the descriptions of the Book of Mormon's fabled "three Nephites" who were destined to roam the earth as immortal missionaries until Christ's return.

Pratt declared that the white Saints had laid the foundation of Zion. "We have succeeded in building many cities, towns, villages, &c., for some four hundred miles north and south," Pratt explained to a Salt Lake City audience in February 1875. "We have got our farms fenced and our water ditches dug." It was time, Pratt declared, that the white Saints turn their minds to fulfilling the Book of Mormon promise to fold into this infrastructure the "remnants of the house of Israel."[102] That same year, the excitement about the Shoshone revival even pulled an aged Dimick Huntington out of retirement to perform baptisms in a font that he built himself. "How I do rejoice in [this work!]," Huntington exclaimed. "They are coming in by the hundreds to investigate, are satisfied and are baptized."[103]

Finally, to the far west, Mormon missionaries' success among Polynesians expanded the definition of the Lamanite and extended the geographic boundaries described in the Book of Mormon to include the Polynesian Islands. In 1851, Mormon missionaries generated a fair amount of interest among the Native population, though the white population in the Sandwich Islands ridiculed them. Years later, mission leader George Q. Cannon recalled receiving a revelation that the Hawaiians were in fact the long-lost progeny of the Israelites' first patriarch in America, Lehi. As the number of Polynesian Saints grew in the nineteenth and twentieth centuries, the Saints began to view these converts as they did those supposed descendants of Ephraim from the British Isles. By dint of their birth into the lineage of Manasseh, the Polynesians were already favored members of the covenant. Exposure to the gospel led their minds to discover what their believing blood already knew.[104]

With the exception of the large number of converts in the Polynesian Islands, the Mormon missionaries had only moderately more success among the Indians whom they found on Utah's horizons than they did within the territory's borders. In 1855, a Cherokee chief promised the missionaries that he would read the Book of Mormon. By 1860, the Cherokees told the missionaries to leave their nation.[105] Among the Hopis, the missionaries never found their white Indians. However, by the 1870s, one convert, Hopi chief Tuba (Tuuvi) helped Jacob Hamblin and other missionary leaders establish their first permanent settlement in Arizona, later named Tuba City. Tuba also oversaw the construction of a short-lived wool factory in the settlement, which was dedicated to "benefit the Indians and the [LDS] Church."[106] Though there remains a Hopi Mormon presence in Arizona to this day, some Hopis and Navajos saw the Mormon settlers not as teachers of the gospel but as invaders with little regard to Native land claims. These competing claims to the land, brought by the Mormons, Native Americans, and the federal government, eventually led to the expulsion of the Mormons from their settlement at Tuba City in 1903, when the Navajo Nation reservation was created.[107] Even the great fervor among the Shoshones died out quickly, though a small Shoshone Mormon community survived into the twentieth century. By the end of the 1870s, the priorities among Saints had also shifted. Integrating the great bounty of white British and Scandinavian converts arriving by the trainload was the main concern. Legal battles with Washington over antibigamy laws, which sent many Mormon polygamists to jail or into hiding, also drew the Mormon leadership's attention away from Lamanite people building.

A half century after the failed first mission to the Delawares, the would-be Lamanites' would-be white brethren resigned themselves to the fact that this generation of Indians was simply not ready for redemption. John Nicholson, a Scottish convert, a long-serving missionary in the British Isles, and a convicted bigamist who in the mid-1880s spent time in Utah's territorial penitentiary, explained as much in an 1881 speech at Salt Lake's Assembly Hall marking the fiftieth anniversary of the first mission to the Lamanites in 1831. Since its earliest days, the church had sent missionaries to Native Americans "to endeavor to bring them to a knowledge of their fathers," Nicholson explained. And yet, unlike the great number of Israelite Saints found scattered in Europe, these efforts among "the portion of Israel on this continent," but for a few exceptions, had been fruitless. The Indians "had fallen so low in the scale of being, so depraved that it seemed next to impossible for the rays of truth to penetrate their minds." Because of their current state, Nicholson, a rhetorician by trade, interpreted the Book of Mormon prophecy regarding Lamanite restoration to read the exact inverse of the earliest church leaders' interpretation. In the early 1830s, Joseph Smith, Oliver Cowdery, and Parley P. Pratt taught that the restoration of Israel was to begin with the Lamanites. In 1881, Nicholson asserted that the Lamanites would be the last children of Abraham to be restored, not the first.[108]

6 PEOPLE BUILDING, ON PAPER

On January 23, 1852, Brigham Young took to the podium in the central chamber of the Council House built at the southwest corner of what would become Salt Lake City's Temple Square. Utah's newly constituted territorial representatives had gathered in the stately two-story, granite and adobe edifice. There they listened to the Mormon prophet and territorial governor call for the passage of laws that would sanction slavery in Utah. Young urged his brethren and fellow lawmakers to legalize the enslavement of "Africans" whom wealthy southern converts, including a few territorial legislators, had brought as slaves into their Zion of the Intermountain West. Young also wanted legal sanction for the Mormons who had been buying Utah's most vulnerable Native Americans from powerful Indian slave traders—traders whom the Saints had at first befriended and baptized and would soon war with—since the Mormons arrived in the Great Basin in July 1847.

In Young's proposed legislation, the African slave would not be the same as the Indian. The laws would require Utah's territorial government to view the potential for Native and African Americans to take part in the civil life of the territory in the same way that the Church of Jesus Christ of Latter-day Saints viewed the potential of these two branches of the human family to take part in the Mormon community. It was the Mormons' duty to Christianize and civilize the Indians so that they could covenant with the white Saints. People of African descent, however, should not be permitted to participate in the affairs of the Mormons' incipient theodemocracy. Be they slave or free, Young declared that Africans were, by dint of their birth, "servants of servants" and should remain so "until the curse is removed from them."[1]

Young argued that indefinite African servitude in Utah should be an end unto itself: to create a separate and unequal class of people. Yet Indian servitude should be a means to a particular end: to empower the Mormons to purchase the Indians legally in order to free them, care for them, and build up their spiritual, intellectual, and physical capacities so that they could become equal to their white brethren. Not all Indians were alike, however. By

1852, the Saints had found that although a handful had proven redeemable and could be built into a Lamanite people, most had proven through their acts of violence against both the Mormon built environment and Mormon human bodies that they were too Indian—too savage and too evil—to be saved from their Indian selves.

In the nineteenth century the Latter-day Saints mostly failed to build a Lamanite people in and beyond the Rocky Mountains. On paper, however, the Saints succeeded in creating Indians and Africans, too. And in the Saints' rhetoric and actions, these paper Indians and Africans took on flesh and bone bodies. Through the act of writing about Africans' cursed descent from Cain and Ham as a justification for their divinely mandated servitude, the Saints made Africans into a people inherently unfit for full political participation in Utah as well as inherently unfit for full participation in the Mormon covenant because they threatened the purity of the white Saints' sacred Israelite bloodlines. Likewise, through the act of writing about their savage "depredations," which many Saints understood as signifying their innate incorrigibility, the Mormons made most Indians into intolerable threats, ironically enough, to the few redeemable Lamanites as well as to the white Mormon communities in Utah. In particular, how Mormons wrote about the Indian slave trade created literary Indians who became literal Indians—and gendered Indians at that—on whom the Mormons could act: a (female) Indian to buy, a (female) Indian to free, a (female) Indian to civilize, a (female) Indian to marry, a (male) Indian to blame, and a (male) Indian to kill.

Almost as soon as they arrived in Utah, the Mormon pioneers confronted what they described as the horrors of Indian slaving. In his 1890 memoir, *Forty Years among the Indians,* the pioneer and Indian missionary Daniel W. Jones chronicled the lucrative slave trade along the Old Spanish Trail. A more powerful set of Indians, namely "Walker and his band," turned the women and children of the weaker Paiutes into a commodity, which they brought south to the slave markets of Santa Fe and other New Mexico cities. There, boys fetched "on an average $100, girls from $150 to $200." Jones explained that girls made better "house servants," though the potential for concubinage—providing both sexual comfort and offspring to perform invaluable labor—added to their value.[2] With the arrival of the Saints, the slavers hoped to create a new market for their human wares. The Mormon response to the enslavement, trading, and often brutal killing of Indian children was to purchase them. "Buy up the Lamanite children," Young told the settlers at Parowan in 1851, "and educate them and teach them the Gospel."

On its face this business of slave trading was pure evil. Yet below the surface, Young detected God's providential hand at work. "The Lord could not have devised a better plan, than to have put the Saints where they were, in order to accomplish the redemption of the Lamanites." Before the innocent were lost either to slavery or to savagery, the Mormons would purchase them and place them in Mormon homes where they would learn the truths of civilization and Christianity as well as the truths of their own Israelite parentage. This work would be done "so that many generations would not pass," Young pointed to the Book of Mormon's most famous passage regarding racial restoration, 2 Nephi 30:6, "ere they should become a white and delightsome people." Young explained the particular Mormon spin on what would become the dictum of the mid-nineteenth-century "friends of the Indian" movement—kill the Indian and save the man. "The Indians would dwindle away, but let a remnant of the seed of Joseph be saved."[3]

For a time, following his baptism and ordination, the Ute military chief Wakara, who had long been the most powerful slaver in the territory, was enlisted to assist in this salvific work. In March 1851, the founder of the Parowan settlement, George A. Smith, sent a "talking paper" north with Wakara, certifying that "Captain Walker" and his band of Utes had "showed themselves Friends and gentlemen." Those Saints to whom Wakara presented Smith's certificate should accord the Indians goodwill and trade with him for his "horses, Buckskins and Piede children."[4] Having helped the Saints settle southern Utah, having dedicated himself to the gospel, and having led other Indians into the baptismal waters, Wakara had been transformed, Smith reasoned, from an Indian purveyor of Indian flesh to a Lamanite protector of his Lamanite brethren.

And yet less than a year later, as Brigham Young testified in the January 1852 trial of the Mexican slave trader Don Pedro León Luján, "Indian Walker" proved himself not to be a Lamanite brother in the gospel. He was an unrepentant Indian who, instead of transporting Indians to freedom, continued to "traffic" in slaves. "He offers them for sale," Young testified during the trial, which served as a test case against the Indian slave trade in the Utah Territory—or, more accurately, any slave trading that the Mormons themselves did not control. "When [Wakara] cannot get what he thinks they are worth, he says he will take them to the Navahoe Indians, or Spaniards, and sell them, or kill them which he frequently does."[5] Mormons like Young and Daniel Jones, who described "Walker" as horrific and as "systematic in this [Indian slave] trade as ever were the slavers [of Africans] on the seas," were not alone in archiving their disgust for Indian slaving. Since the mid-1700s, Catholic priests in New Mexico preserved in writing the ill treatment of Natives, including ritualized public beatings and rapes of captives by "barbarians" like Wakara. Torture, the padres wrote in letters to the colonial authorities, was a bargaining technique used to exact a higher price from the soft-hearted Mexican priests. As would the Mormons, the priests justified their purchase of these slaves—almost always women and children—as a means to save their bodies and souls. In preparation for the baptismal font, the priests stripped the Indians not only of their Indian clothing but also of their "Indian" names and replaced them with Catholic ones before they were added to the church membership rolls.[6]

Luján lost the trial. An all-Mormon jury found him guilty of trading with Indians without a license, fined him five hundred dollars, and confiscated his slaves, who were placed with Mormon families. Within the year, Wakara lost, too. The Mormons succeeded in curtailing—but not ending—the three-hundred-year history of the Indian slave trade between New Mexico and Utah.[7] In April 1853 a licensed American trader named Dr. Bowman accompanied a group of New Mexicans, including Pedro León Luján, into Sanpete with the purpose of buying Indian slaves to take back to Santa Fe for sale and reasserting what they perceived was their legal right to do so. The Mormon settlers thwarted their efforts. Bowman threatened to order his New Mexican cavalcade, along with a sizable Ute contingent led by Wakara and Arapeen, to attack the Mormon settlements. Learning of the bellicose "horde of Mexicans . . . infesting the settlements, [and] stirring up the Indians," Brigham Young released a gubernatorial proclamation that empowered militiamen "to arrest, and keep in close custody every strolling Mexican party, and those associating with them." The irascible Bowman, whom Young met when he traveled south to quell the row, was eventually killed either by the Mormons or by Utes whom he had deceived in a trade.[8]

The Utah Territory, which included parts of Nevada, Colorado, and Wyoming, was too vast for the Mormons to police completely. So the slave trade with New Mexico went underground. Census records indicate that Luján had Paiute children in his household as late as 1870.[9] No longer free to send their human captives south, however, the Utes relied even more on the only remaining market—the Mormons. And when that market proved disappointing, the Indian slavers deployed violence as a sales tactic. The archive of Young's tenure leading U.S. Indian affairs in Utah and the memoirs of Daniel Jones describe one particularly gruesome incident. In the early summer of 1853, just before hostilities broke out between the Wakara-led Utes and the Saints, "Arapine, Wakara's brother," enraged that the Mormons had prevented the sale of Indian children to Mexicans, came to Provo to tell the Mormons "that they had no right to do so, unless they bought them themselves." The Mormons refused to give Arapeen the price he sought for the slave children. So, Jones recalls, Arapeen "took one of these children by the heels and dashed its brains out on the hard ground, telling us we had no hearts, or we would have bought it and saved its life." It was a strange argument, "the argument of an enraged savage." But it was often an effective one. Jones reported that after the summer of 1853, "I never heard of any successful attempts to buy children by the Mexicans. If done at all it was secretly." The Mormons became the (all but) sole purchasers of Indian slaves.[10]

Young hoped that under the Mormons' care, these child slaves could be raised up in the faith that would restore them to the knowledge of their Lamanite selves, "the children of Abraham, and belong to the chosen seed of Israel," the prophet explained in a speech given in May 1853 at the Tabernacle following the conclusion of the troubles with Bowman. In the same speech, Young declared that he believed that "Walker" had also "felt [the spirit of the Gospel] from time to time." Yet Young also said that he was not optimistic that even the gospel was strong enough to change Wakara from Indian to Lamanite. Young reported that Wakara had made his own attempt at finding a diplomatic solution to the tinderbox created by Bowman and his Mexican caravan. The leader of the Sanpete colony, Isaac Morley, had sent a letter to Young, which included a transcribed message from the Ute chief. "'Tell brother Brigham, we have smoked the tobacco he sent us in the pipe of peace; I want to be at peace and be a brother to him.'" Young told his audience that he interpreted Wakara's peace offering as exemplifying Indian duplicity. "It is truly characteristic of the cunning Indian, when he finds he cannot get advantage of his enemy, to curl down at once and say 'I love you.' . . . I am resolved, however, not to trust his love any more than I would a stranger's. I do not repose confidence in persons, only as they prove themselves confidential; and I shall live a long while before I can believe that an Indian is my friend, when it would be his advantage to be my enemy."[11]

Later that summer, when war broke out between the Utes and the Mormons, Young declared from the pulpit of the Tabernacle that these latest "Indian difficulties" had proven Wakara's incorrigible Indianness. Yet according to Young, embedded in Wakara's acts of terrorism was a message not just *about* the Indians but also *to* the Mormons. Instead of building forts strong enough so that the "Devil [and Indians] could not get into," as Young had instructed them to do, the Mormons in the southern settlements had relied on faith in the potential amelioration of the Indian and in God to protect them. Ironically, "the Lord is making brother Walker an instrument to help me," Young explained. "[What] Indian Walker . . . is doing with a chastening rod what I have failed to accomplish with soft words"—to demonstrate to his brethren the existential threat that the Indians posed and thus the need to build up their communities' defenses accordingly.[12]

Sally, the Lamanite

In the Mormon archive, if "Walker" signifies "Indian," then "Sally," a Paiute slave who became the adopted Indian daughter of Brigham Young, signifies "Lamanite." Sally's presence in the Mormon historical record and collective memory demonstrates that, along with the appropriate amount of paternalistic Mormon influence, even the lowliest Indian girl could be transformed into a faithful Lamanite woman. In his testimony at the trial of Luján, Brigham Young described how Sally ended up in his household through what was perhaps the first instance of Mormon participation in the Indian slave trade in Utah. In 1847, soon after the Mormons arrived in the Salt Lake Valley, an Indian warrior whom the Saints called Batiste brought two teenaged Paiute captives, one boy and one girl, to the Old Fort looking to trade humans for guns. Batiste responded to the Mormons' initial refusal by killing the boy. Charles Decker, who was married to Brigham Young's daughter Vilate, intervened to save the girl from a similar fate. He traded the "squaw" for a rifle. Decker then gave the girl to his sister Clarissa, who was one of Brigham Young's plural wives. In Young's household "Kahpeputz" was renamed "Sally." And according to Young's testimony against Luján, by 1852, Sally was "far[ing] as [well as the prophet's other] children, and is as free."[13]

Other contemporaneous written records indicate that Sally's body became the site of intense religious and cultural labor intended to remake the Indian girl into a Lamanite. In 1849, Zina D. H. Young, who would fifty years later petition church leaders to allow Jane Manning James to be adopted to Joseph Smith's family, recorded in her diary how she worked to bring Sally more fully into the Mormon sacred community. After singing in tongues, Zina Young was moved by the spirit to seek out "Sally (the lamanite that Charles Decker bought)" and bless her. Zina Young explained that while laying "my hands upon her head . . . my language changed in a moment and when I had finished she said she understood every word. I had talked in her mother tongue." Zina Young told Sally that soon "her mother and sisters were coming" to join Sally, "and she must be a good girl."[14] Sally did become a "good girl," at least according to Brigham Young. During his 1852 testimony, Young said that after being purchased and adopted, Sally initially continued to sleep outdoors and "preferred the meat she gathered from the gutters instead of good fried beef." But under the civilizing influence of the Saints, Sally became an excellent housekeeper and cook. Her aversion to her old Indian life was so strong that her body reacted viscerally to the thought of it. "[She is] ready to vomit now at the recollection of her former habits," Young said.[15]

Sally's Lamanite goodness and disdain for all things Indian was also captured in the collective memory of Utah's second generation of Latter-day Saints who were occupied with preserving and idealizing the Mormon pioneering past.[16] In her sentimentalized retelling of Sally's life published in the *Improvement Era* in 1906, Brigham Young's daughter Susa Young Gates writes that her adopted Lamanite sister became a regular fixture in her adopted father's Beehive House. One evening in Salt Lake City, Young met with a set of chiefs, including Wakara and Sowiette, to discuss the Mormons' intentions to settle the valley. During this meeting, Sally caught the eye of the Pahvant chief Kanosh. Kanosh was an exemplar of the noble savage, full of "rugged Indian manliness," writes Gates, "his dark proud face . . . a model of Indian power and sagacity." Kanosh was so smitten with Sally that he offered "a whole band" of ponies in exchange for the Indian girl. Young said no. As a "member of the white chief's family," Gates explains, "she should follow the customs of the white maidens and choose her own husband." By buying her from her slave master, who denied Sally her humanity, the Saints freed her so that she could exert her own God-given, human agency. And Sally, who under the influence of "nimble-fingered white women" had grown more "civilized," exercised this agency by refusing Kanosh's advances. After all, "He Indian!" Sally exclaimed, and thus, "He no beau to me."[17]

According to Susa Young Gates, along with forays into knitting, Sally's first tentative efforts toward literacy had a salutatory effect. Sally learned to overcome the prideful character innate to the Indian, which she inherited "from her progenitor, the proud Laman," by studying "the strange black lines and curves which spelled out this wonderful story [of the origins of her race], on the printed page of the Book of Mormon." Sally never learned to read the book. But physical contact with the ancient story was enough to make her understand that even Laman's cursed progeny could overcome their depraved state. As such, according to Gates, after Kanosh intervened to rescue Sally when she was captured by none other than the "brute, Wakara," who planned to sell her to other Indian braves, Sally's heart softened toward the noble savage. She began to see that Kanosh, too, had the potential to be redeemed and civilized. Sally eventually accepted Kanosh's proposal of marriage, and Brigham Young officiated at their wedding. Kanosh built Sally "a white man's cabin of trees, and glass." In turn, Sally made Kanosh a white man's home, decorated by needlework instead of bearskins and nourished with meals cooked on a stove instead of an open fire.[18] During their years together, Sally "did much towards civilizing" her husband, remembered another biographer of Sally, and he "died a faithful Latter-day Saint."[19]

Written at more than a half century's remove, when tales of brave Mormon pioneers and ferocious Indians became commonplace in pioneer memoirs, Susa Young Gates's addition to the archive of Sally and Kanosh's courtship is at best romanticized, if not completely contrived. The census records of 1860 do not list Sally as an adopted daughter of her "White Father" Brigham Young. Instead "Sally," to whom the census taker gave the family name of "Indian," not "Young," is grouped with the other female servants of the Young household.[20] What's more, there is no other record indicating that Wakara ever took Sally prisoner. And Sally and Kanosh were not young teenagers, expecting to find their mates through the performance of romantic gestures, when they officially married on June 8, 1877. Instead, both were in their fifties. And it was not Brigham Young but the Indian missionary Dimick Huntington who officiated at the marriage of "Kanosh (Indian)" and "Kahpeputz or Sally also an Indian," as the handwritten marriage certificate reads.[21] According to contemporary correspondence, Sally did not demonstrate her agency, as Gates would have it, by choosing Kanosh. Sally entered into the marriage reluctantly, if not unwillingly, as a bargaining chip with Kanosh in order to strengthen the alliance between Young and the Mormons' most trusted Indian ally.[22]

Yet the mythologies that built up around Sally, Kanosh, and Wakara reveal a long-held and deeply ingrained Mormon vision of the mutually constructed nature of the two Native American historical and literary characters created out of the same fallen branch of Israel: the redeemable Lamanite and the unrepentant Indian. Young believed that he and his followers were divinely called to purchase children like Sally from savage Indian slavers like Wakara and to feed, educate, and love them as their own. This system of buying Native children into freedom afforded the Saints the best opportunity to make Lamanite people out of the remnant of Joseph that they encountered in Utah.

Lamanite Servants, African Slaves

This millenarian ideal, however, had a real cost. In exchange for Indian children, the Mormons traded foodstuffs, sheep, oxen, horses, cash, ammunition, and guns—Charles Decker's rifle for Sally's life, for example. This at a time when the Mormons were still working to create sustainable economies of agriculture, goods, and currency in Utah.[23] In March 1852, the newly formed territorial legislature, composed mostly of high-ranking church leaders, passed "An Act for the Relief of Indian Slaves and Prisoners." The law's purpose was to provide a practical mechanism to make the ideal of buying Indian slaves into freedom a reality, and a cost-effective one at that. This new law was also explicitly gendered. It was designed to stop men like Luján, Arapeen, and Wakara from buying and stealing "women and children of the Utah tribe of Indians." In the act's preamble, the lawmakers stated that these women and children were treated with loathsome savagery by their male captors. "Frequently carried from place to place packed upon horses or mules; larietted out to subsist upon grass, roots, or starve . . . and, when with suffering cold, hunger and abuse they fall sick so as to become troublesome, are frequently slain by their masters to get rid of them."

To turn these "troublesome" poor creatures into "delightsome" Lamanites, while also not breaking the bank, the act authorized settlers to indenture for up to twenty years the Indians whom they purchased.[24] This law was meant to codify the compensation in labor for the "favors and expenses which may have been incurred on their account," explained Young to the territorial legislature in January 1852.[25] While working to pay off their debt, the children/servants were to be clothed, fed, and schooled for three months a year by their Mormon parents/masters.[26]

The act was designed to distinguish the Mormon home in Utah, in which Indian women and children would be legally and lovingly placed for a time-limited indenture, from what the Saints imagined were the brutal slave auction blocs of Santa Fe, where Natives were mere property to be bought, sold, abused, and killed. In reality, however, the ethos and the mechanism behind the Saints' slavery enterprise were similar to those of the Spanish colonial system. As Ned Blackhawk has chronicled, New Mexico officials and church leaders described the purchase of the mostly female captives as saving them from public torture and even ritualized rape, which their Ute captors performed at trade fairs "to exact greater sympathy as well as higher prices from colonial officials." As was the case in Mormon settlements, these slaves, once purchased, would be baptized, given Catholic names, and placed in the homes of settler families.[27]

"An Act for the Relief of Indian Slaves and Prisoners" was not the first law that the Utah legislature enacted in 1852 related to human bondage. Earlier in the session, the legislature passed "An Act in Relation to Service," which legalized a Utah-specific form of "African slavery." According to Brigham Young, Indians enslaving other Indians was not only abhorrent. It was also antithetical to Book of Mormon prophecies, which foresaw the reunification of the Lamanites as one people and foresaw this people's redemption as the American branch of the house of Israel. And yet, Young believed that the enslavement of Africans was also scripturally based. As he explained to the legislature in his January 23 speech, ever since "old Cain['s]" ancient act of fratricide, "the colored race have been subjected to severe curses . . . Until the curse is removed by him who placed it upon them . . . they must suffer under its consequences." Young explained that neither he nor any Bible-believing man was "authorized to remove the curse."[28] Such a position stood in contrast with the views of Joseph and Hyrum Smith. As was evident in Joseph's acceptance of Elijah Abel's ordination to the priesthood and in Hyrum's patriarchal blessing of Jane Manning James, the Smith brothers believed that Cain and Ham's progeny need not necessarily carry the sins of their fathers in their hearts or even on their skin.

What's more, like his distaste for Indian slavery, Young's "firm" belief in African slavery was cast in a particular Mormon valence. As he explained to the legislature, "The African enjoys the right of receiving the first principles of the gospel," including baptism. But he stated plainly what had not been so plain to his prophetic predecessor, that "Africans cannot hold the priesthood." For Young, the fact that Africans lacked the right to the priesthood meant that Africans lacked the right to self-rule. Young's views on spiritual and political freedom were based on the Mormon principle of God-given human agency, which Young believed blacks were incapable of using properly without the guidance of a white master. As such, Young called on the legislature to enact a bill that would codify in the law books the truth already written in the Bible: "[African] slaves serve their masters" in perpetuity.[29]

And yet, though he supported the legislature's efforts to legalize slavery, after reading over the bill initially entitled "An Act in Relation to African Slavery," Young offered "a few alterations." Most significantly, he replaced the word "slavery" with the word "service" in the bill's title and removed reference to "African" altogether.[30] In this he was advised by John M. Bernhisel, the Mormons' lobbyist in Washington and Jane Manning James's onetime fellow houseguest in Joseph Smith's Nauvoo Mansion. Bernhisel did not want Utah to draw the attention of the federal government when it had once again precariously balanced the nation into equal parts free and slave with the Compromise of 1850.[31] Yet this sleight of hand on paper—Young scratching a line through "slavery" on an early draft of the bill and inserting "service" in its place—did little to change the flesh and bone status of African Americans in bondage in Utah. African slaves were to be "servants" to their owners until the end of time.[32]

Yet Young also said that he objected to the word "slavery" because it poorly represented the system of bondage he hoped to establish. "Service," as opposed to slavery, connoted mutual obligation between master and servants. To be sure, many Christian defenders of American slavery, including Joseph Smith himself in the 1830s, asserted that slavery was a system of paternalistic benevolence. Masters treated their slaves as children because they were incapable of caring for themselves.[33] Yet according to Young, "service" signified biblical mutuality, as both master and servant fulfilled their biblically mandated duties. The white man governs and cares for his black servant; the black man serves his white master. But it is not biblical, Young insisted, to have masters knocking down slaves "and whipping them and breaking their limbs," as was often the reality in the slaveholding South. That form of slavery also led to abuse and misuse of the "negro" as a resource.[34]

Young and the Utah legislature, which passed the act on February 5, 1852, making Utah the first U.S. territory to legalize slavery, intended to differentiate African "service" in Utah from the peculiar institution practiced in the South in three concrete ways.[35] First, under the threat of prison, a hefty fine, and the loss of ownership of slaves, the "Act in Relation to Service" criminalized "carnal intercourse" with "servants of the African race." Sleeping with slaves was both a storied pastime for southern masters as well as a means of increasing slave owners' wealth through procreation. Yet this part of the law was as much about preserving the Saints' pure Israelite bloodlines as it was about protecting slave women from abuse. As Young made clear in his January 5, 1852, address to the legislature, the religious punishments for producing offspring with Africans were even more severe than those spelled out in the law. "Any person that mingles his seed with the seed of Canaan forfeits the right to rule and all the blessings of the Priesthood of God," Young proclaimed. "And unless his blood were spilled and that of his offspring he nor they could not be saved until the posterity of Canaan are redeemed."[36] Second, the legislature required masters to send their servants "to school, no less than eighteen months." Utah's compulsory education stood in sharp contrast with the practice of compulsory illiteracy in which many states in the antebellum South made it a crime to teach slaves to read and write out of fear that education might lead to slave revolts.[37] Third, the act even required that the masters demonstrate to a local court that they were "entitled lawfully to the service of such servant" and demonstrate that the "servant or servants came into the Territory of their own free will and choice." It's all but impossible to imagine that masters—and there is little evidence that they ever did—would give their slaves the opportunity exercise his or her "free will" and reject servitude. This is especially true if the masters believed that they owned the labor—if not the bodies—of their slaves and could demonstrate such ownership with a bill of sale. Yet even this provision was also likely influenced by Mormon theology. Young and his fellow Mormon lawmakers wanted the "African" slaves to exercise their (circumscribed) free agency by making the only affirmative choice that the ancient Law of God and the incipient law of the Utah Territory deemed available to them: consent to be servants to their masters for the rest of their lives.[38]

It is also possible that Young wanted to replace the term "slavery" with "service" because he wanted a legal code that encompassed the permanent state of African bondage as well as the temporary indentured servitude for white European immigrant converts who agreed to work off the cost of their transportation to Zion. Established in 1849, the Perpetual Emigrating Fund (PEF) aided poor converts from the eastern United States, England, and increasingly in the 1850s Scandinavian countries, to cover part or all of their travel costs. Such emigrants signed contracts in which they promised that, once in Utah, their labor would go toward repaying travel expenses to the PEF.[39] Thus "service" was one racially coded code word for two kinds of indenture. First, "service" was a euphemism for African slavery. It provided legal cover for Mormon slave owners in Utah, including territorial legislator John Brown and church apostle Charles C. Rich, to perpetuate slavery by another name. And second, "service" empowered the PEF to enforce contracts of labor for white migrants and immigrants until they settled their debts.[40]

The rhetoric contained within these two acts passed by Utah's first territorial legislature legalizing service—both the *time-limited* red and white kind as well as the *timeless* black kind—reveal the kind of Mormon people building in which the Saints were engaged during the early 1850s.[41] Utah's civil and religious leaders found the American branch of Israel in peril; the unrepentant Indian threatened the incipient Lamanite. God placed the white Saints in Utah to save the innocent sons and daughters of Manasseh, the Indians' supposed Israelite progenitor, who could still be redeemed from those Indian slavers whose wickedness put them beyond redemption. The Indians who could be saved were to be bought. And while they paid off their debts, they were to be brought up in Mormon homes, trained to be domestics, farmers, brothers and sisters in the gospel, and, sometimes, plural wives. Their former captors and other belligerent Indians were to be run off, corralled, or killed. For poor white converts from the eastern United States or northern Europe, the codification of service helped make the gathering not just a luxury of the rich. Instead, the "worthy poor," as Young described them, who pledged to prove their worth by repaying their debts could also come to Zion.[42] The "Act in Relation to Service" and the PEF created financial and religious covenants to cleave converts to the church. This system also imported manpower used to construct Utah's public buildings, telegraph and railroad lines, and mines, and cultivate Zion's fields. This system also imported sons and daughters of Ephraim. Once their debts were paid, these Ephraimites would buy up their own parcel of Zion. Then they would fill voting roles and public offices before Utah's Gentiles threatened the Saints' hold on the economic and political levers of power in the territory.[43]

Yet the "Act in Relation to Service" also created black Africans on paper. They were enslaved for (all but) eternity because the sins of the cursed originators of their race could never be fully repaid. An early version of the act's text even included references to the standard biblical justification for African slavery: masters were entitled to the services of their servants "until the curse of servitude is taken from the descendants of Canaan."[44] Though such references were removed from the act's final language, the biblical precedent remained implicit. "The negro . . . should serve the seed of Abraham," Young explained on January 5, 1852, as the legislators worked on the act. The state of perpetual servitude prevented the "negro," free or enslaved, from holding civil or ecclesiastical positions of authority in Utah, where "the decree of God that Canaan should be a servant of servants unto his brethren (i.e. Shem and Japet [sic]) is in full force."[45] The Indian slavery act legalized the Mormon practice of buying Lamanites into freedom so that, in theory, they could fully realize their God-given agency and leave behind the curse of their forefather Laman. The Utah territorial legislature also sought to create laws to match leading Saints' beliefs that God curtailed blacks' agency through ancient biblical curses on their forefathers Cain, Ham, and Canaan with which blacks could never part. The white universalism preached by Joseph Smith and practiced by his church in Nauvoo did not accompany Brigham Young's Saints to Utah.[46]

The creation of this cursed "African" on paper translated directly into the Mormons' attitude to the embodied blacks in bondage. Until the Civil War officially ended slavery throughout the United States and its territories, even enslaved blacks in Utah who were members of the church were not free to act on their own agency. Green Flake and Oscar Crosby, who had been baptized into the church and were part of Brigham's Vanguard Company, were not permitted to settle and cultivate their own lands as did their white brethren. Instead they and the estimated several dozen to a few hundred other slaves brought into the territory between 1847 and 1862 labored for their masters. The slave-owning Saints often settled together in Utah and worked to create communities patterned after those they had left behind in the South.[47] Mormon slave owners sold their slaves like any other piece of property. They separated mothers and fathers from their children and husbands from their wives. In 1857, the leader of the Mississippi Saints, John Brown, even tithed an "African Servant Girl" whom he valued at one thousand dollars to the church.[48]

If this "Servant Girl" had been an Indian daughter of Shem instead of an African daughter of Ham, the Mormons might have valued her more, because her worth would have been measured not merely in her ability to serve her master or her master's church. At least in theory, Utah's territorial law against Indian slavery was designed to buy Native children out of the clutches of their Indian slave owners and place them in Mormon homes so that they could fulfill their Lamanite destiny: to join Mormon economic, religious, and matrimonial covenants. And as Brigham Young explained in 1851, the ultimate hope—and the Book of Mormon prophecy—was that "many generations would not pass" until the difference between red Lamanite and white Saint would cease to exist. And a unified, covenantal "white and delightsum people" would emerge.[49] "Africans," be they slave or free, could be baptized. But Mormon whiteness—and the spiritual exaltation it signified—became unattainable, at least not attainable anytime soon. As Young explained during the legislative debates over African slavery in January 1852—the earliest known articulation by a church president of a race-based priesthood restriction—the governmental laws and ecclesiastical dictates marginalized blacks from the priesthood, and from the priesthood holder's bed, so as not to corrupt the Israelite bloodlines to which the priesthood belonged and on which the building of the Mormon people rested.[50]

In at least a few well-documented cases, and in its holiest spaces, the church succeeded in keeping the prophesied fates of their African and Lamanite servants separate. After decades of missionary work throughout the United States and Canada, the priesthood-holding Elijah Abel settled in Salt Lake City in 1853. A former member of the House Carpenters of Nauvoo, Abel tithed his labor to work on Salt Lake's temple, as he had likely done in Nauvoo a decade before. Yet Brigham Young refused Abel's requests to enter Temple Square's Endowment House—a temporary space in which Saints performed some of Mormonism's most sacred rituals before a temple was completed—so that he could receive his endowments and "have his wife and children sealed to him." Young explained that these sacred ordinances were "privilege[s]" that were not available to black church members, no matter how worthy they had proven to be.[51] Near the end of her life, Jane Manning James was sealed in the Salt Lake temple as a "Servitor" to Joseph

Smith and his family "for eternity," not as Smith's spiritual daughter, as she claimed the prophet himself wished. However, in 1859, Ira Hatch was sealed to his Lamanite wife, Sarah Maraboots, in the Endowment House, and later their children were sealed to their parents. Four years later, Hatch's long-time missionary partner Jacob Hamblin was sealed to Eliza, his onetime adopted Indian daughter turned plural wife.[52] When she died in 1878, the year after Brigham Young's death, Sally Kanosh was buried in the temple clothes that Young, her "White Father," had given her.[53]

In the Mormon archive, Sally's is not the only recorded success story of adopted Indians remaking themselves into the Mormon image of the redeemed Lamanite. In his old age, Zenos Hill told a newspaper reporter that his white adoptive parents, the Hills of Ephraim, Utah, were "the only parents I ever knew." They provided him with fourteen years of education. He even attended Brigham Young Academy, the precursor to Brigham Young University. Zenos Hill so identified with the Mormons that he fought against (Antonga) Black Hawk during the mid-1860s Mormon-Indian conflicts. "I thought it my duty to do my part on the side of the whites," he explained. However, because he had the "instincts" for it, Hill put his supposed Indian nature to use on behalf of his white brethren, employing the tactics of his Indian enemies, including horse stealing and scouting. By 1880, Zenos Hill had his own home in Ephraim with his wife, Amelie, an English convert, with whom he was raising "'half-blood' children."[54]

It was rare for Indian men to take white women as wives. Leading Latter-day Saints responded with bemused disgust to Wakara's 1851 request that the Mormons give him a white wife as part of his status as an elder in the church. No white woman would demean herself with such a match, they told him.[55] Matrimonial unions between daughters of Manasseh and sons of Ephraim were also infrequent but more accepted. And on occasion, such unions were quite fruitful. Ira Hatch wrote in his journal that after he was sealed to Sarah Maraboots in the Endowment House on October 11, 1868, their five children would be "born-in-the-covenant."[56] According to historian Juanita Brooks, who was not only Dudley Leavitt's biographer but also his granddaughter, in 1860, George A. Smith offered a covenantal contract in the rhetorical register of a patriarchal blessing to convince a hesitant Dudley to take the Indian girl "Janet" as his fourth wife. "Brother Leavitt," Smith explained, "I promise you in the name of the Lord, that if you will take this girl, give her a home and a family, and do your duty by her, you will be blessed. You will count her descendants as among the choice ones of your offspring." Smith also promised Leavitt that these offspring would eventually be "white and delightsome."[57] Both Janet and Dudley Leavitt eventually agreed to the match and were married. They produced eleven children, eight of whom lived to adulthood. As George A. Smith promised, the children racially self-identified with their white father, not with their Indian mother. According to Brooks, the Leavitts' grandchildren and great-grandchildren, some of who held important church and governmental offices, either forgot or purposefully misremembered their Indian matriarch—at least in public settings and in public records, including in the U.S. census.[58] Janet and Dudley Leavitt's union, among others like it, represents a fulfillment of Book of Mormon precedent and prophecy. In not so many generations children produced from unions between whites and the remnant of Israel would dissolve their Indianness into the universal racial category of whiteness—a stepwise move toward the teleology of a Mormon people without "Lamanites, nor any manner of -ites" (2 Nephi 30:6, 4, Nephi 1:17), in essence a Mormon people devoid of race altogether.

The archive of early Mormon-Indian relations contains many such success stories of Indians-turned-almost-white-Lamanites, which are accompanied by testimonies of Mormon parents' unwavering paternalistic patience toward their Indian children.[59] Yet how these children were actually treated remains a question of debate. Juanita Brooks claimed that Brigham Young and others spoke with sincerity and accuracy when they declared that they treated their Native-adopted children as well as they did any white child. To be sure, Indian adoptees always maintained a sense of otherness within the white Mormon world (hence the motivation of offspring produced by Indian-white marriages to "pass" as white). Although they viewed the Lamanites to be a key part of their own millennial vision, many white Mormons also viewed Natives as did other Americans: an innately inferior race that was destined to disappear either through natural (or violent) annihilation or absorption into the expanding white Mormon people. Yet Brooks placed the maltreatment of Indian Mormon children outside the home and in public spaces like the schoolhouse, where "with characteristic thoughtlessness [of all young children], their playmates made sarcastic comments" about the Indians' supposed inferiority.[60]

More recently scholars have argued that, for the most part, Indian children remained "servants," not "brothers" or "sisters," in the homes of their adoptive Mormon parents. This was likely the case for Sally, who as late as 1870 was counted in the U.S. census as a servant, not as a child, in Brigham Young's household. And despite the legal and ecclesiastical requirements to send indentured servants to school, more than half of the Indian children that appear in the 1860 census had yet to receive formal education.[61] If Susa Young Gates is to be believed, despite her adopted Indian sister's attempts to read the Book of Mormon, Sally never learned to read.[62] As such, despite the Mormons' claims on paper that they were creating a more benevolent, even divinely inspired mechanism to remake Indian slaves into Lamanites than the cruel slave markets of New Mexico, the actual outcomes in the Spanish Catholic and Utah Mormon systems were often similar. The "freed" slaves rarely became fully assimilated members of the household. Instead, they often functioned as indentured laborers whose Mormon masters could barter or give them away. In 1854, the apostle to the Lamanites Jacob Hamblin noted in his journal that he had purchased a Paiute boy so "that I might let a good [Mormon] man have him that would make him useful." Likewise, not unlike the Indian slave girls purchased in New Mexico who became concubines of their supposed adopted fathers, Indian slave girls raised in Mormon homes sometimes became the paramours—but by a different name—of their adopted fathers. Hamblin's fourth wife, Eliza, for example, was his adopted Paiute teenaged daughter when they married in October or November 1860.[63] As such, these one-time slaves' bodies were just as much sites of labor—in the fields, in the home, and even in their wombs—as their souls were sites of conversion work.[64]

Whether they were truly beloved members of their Mormon homes or merely tolerated sources of work, if the narratives of the lives of Zenos Hill and Sally Kanosh are any indication, Indian children were certainly taught to hate the Indian—the one they read about in the Book of Mormon; the one they saw "marauding" through Utah's valleys and plains; the one they saw in the mirror. Though it is embellished if not altogether fictive, in her story of Sally's courtship with Kanosh, Susa Young Gates writes that, without understanding it in a literal sense, as Sally studied the Book of Mormon, which purportedly contained the history of her cursed, ancient lineage from Laman, Sally's "fear and dislike of her own race seemed rather to increase than to abate."[65]

The Mormon Narrator

The historical archive related to the Indian slave trade in early Utah contains few satisfactory answers to the question of how the untold number of purchased or adopted Indian women and children like Sally and Zenos were actually treated at the hands of their Mormon mistresses/mothers and masters/fathers/husbands. Yet this archive does contain answers to the question of how, in narrating the history of the Indian slave trade, the Mormons constructed the Indian and the Lamanite as mutually constitutive racial identities—along with the "African" as a fixed, immutable black point of reference. And as the narrator who gets to create his story in which he plays the white savior of red slaves, the white teacher of red savages, and the white redeemer of red heathens, the Mormon looms large, even if he is mostly absent from the narration's foreground.

For example, the white Mormon archivists and narrators of early Mormon-Indian relations in Utah can be located in how the early Saints depicted Wakara and Sally. When the Mormons held up "the Indian Walker"— their onetime fellow Mormon who demonstrated Lamanlike perfidy by waging war on his brethren—against the image of "Sally, the Lamanite," Sally appears pale in comparison. After all, in Susa Young Gates's telling, what made Sally the target of Wakara's wrath was that she had parted ways with her Indian self. When she is captured by Wakara and paraded in front of Indian braves whom Wakara hopes will purchase her, Wakara asks, "Who is she[?]," and then answers his own question, "Why does she wear the white squaw's dress?"[66]

In their respective relationships with white Mormon settlers and white Mormon narrators, the distinction between Sally's complexion and Wakara's is as evident in the stories of their deaths as it is in the stories of their lives. On January 29, 1855, Wakara died at Meadow Creek, seventy miles south of Chicken Creek, where Wakara and Brigham Young had reestablished peace in May 1854. The Ute chief, probably about fifty years old, had fallen ill ten days before after attending the trial of the Paiutes, most notably Kanosh, charged with the murder of John Gunnison. The explorer, railroad survey, and chronicler of early Mormon-Indian encounters had been killed in the fall of 1853. Gunnison and seven other men became collateral damage of the Mormon-Wakara conflicts when his party had been attacked by Pahvant Paiutes near Sevier Lake in central Utah. Some accused Young himself of ordering Kanosh and his men to carry out the assassinations, perhaps worried that Gunnison's findings would lead to the arrival of the railway and telegraph in Utah before the Mormons had a chance to establish their dominance over the land. Although an all-Mormon jury found three Paiutes of guilty of manslaughter, none were convicted of murder. And Kanosh, Young's most trusted Indian ally, was exonerated. The trial did have casualties. A violent epidemic spread through the gathering, likely leading to Wakara's death.[67]

George A. Smith reported that on his deathbed, Wakara once again pledged friendship to the Mormons and "expressed great anxiety for peace with the whites." But his burial ceremony shocked his would-be white friends. According to Smith, along with a letter from Brigham Young, Wakara was buried with fourteen of his best horses, which had been slaughtered for the occasion, along with "two or three Piede Squaws, and some prisoners."[68] Later retellings elaborated on the account. The horses were not killed but buried alive. So were "an Indian boy and girl," explained Peter Gottfredson, a Danish convert who became the Mormons' most prolific compiler of first- and secondhand accounts of nineteenth-century "Indian depredations." The captives were "secured near the corpse of the Chief at the bottom of a deep pit . . . and left until death brought them relief," wrote Gottfredson in 1919. Two Indians who passed by the pit heard the boy begging to be freed. "The boy said that Walker was beginning to stink." The Indians ignored the boy's pleas.[69]

According to Mormon narrators George A. Smith and Peter Gottfredson, at his burial, Wakara and his Utes showed their true colors by treating human slaves no better than horses. The story of Sally's death, and what followed it, is equally grotesque. But whereas in death Wakara demonstrated the depths of his savagery, Sally died a martyr to the Mormon way of life. In his memoirs published in 1920, Brigham Young's nephew John R. Young writes that after Sally and Kanosh's marriage, Sally spent several pleasant years living "in the white man's house which he built for her." Kanosh eventually took another plural wife, a traditional Indian, who grew jealous of Sally and "hated her because of her white man's ways." While Kanosh was away, she killed Sally and buried her in a gully. After locating Sally's body, Kanosh seized his Indian wife and would have killed her on the spot, "but white men interfered." Nevertheless justice—"Indian justice"—did come to the "murderess." John R. Young recalls that after the Indian woman confessed, she "offered to expiate her crime by starving herself to death. The offer was accepted, and on a lone hill in sight of the village, a 'wick-i-up' was constructed of dry timber. Taking a jug of water, the woman walked silently toward her living grave. Like the rejected swan, alone, unloved, in low tones she sang her own sad requiem, until her voice was hushed in death. One night when the evening beacon fire was not seen by the villagers, a runner was dispatched to fire the wick-i-up, and retribution was complete." A few days later, at Sally's funeral a caravan of one hundred carriages followed the hearse carrying Sally's casket. "For Sally had been widely loved among the white settlers for her gentle ways."[70]

Sally's death announcement, printed in the *Deseret News* on December 18, 1878, notes the white community's great affection for her. It also notes that even in death, Sally's body was the site of civilizing work. Heber C. Kimball's widow Adelia and other members of the Relief Society descended on the small settlement of Kanosh, named after its most famous resident and, ironically enough, located just a few miles from Wakara's grave. They took Sally's body from the Indians and prepared it for an interment in what the author of the obituary called "our burying ground." At the well-attended ceremony, "the old faithful chief, Kanosh," declared that Sally's death and funeral would produce a "good effect . . . upon his people, as contrasting a kind and Christian burial with the rude manner of disposing of the Indian dead." Sally had become all that the Mormons could hope of her. "Beneath that tawny skin," read the obituary, "was a faithful, intelligence and virtue that would do honor to millions with a paler face."[71]

Yet according to the *Deseret News*, Sally did not die at the hands of a sister wife, as John R. Young recalled. She died of a sickness.[72] A decade earlier, Kanosh had in fact lost an Indian wife to violence. According to a *Deseret News* report from 1869, Kanosh's wife "Mary," like Sally, was raised in a white Mormon home. And she lived separately from Kanosh's other wives, in a house kept in the "Mormoné fashion," with doors, windows, a high-post bed, and her own livestock and vegetable garden. Mary's sister wives became jealous. One cut her throat while she tended her garden. This wife was sentenced to a wickiup to die of thirst and hunger.[73]

In some ways, the conflation of Mary's death with Sally's is understandable. Both were wives of Kanosh reared by white Mormon adoptive parents. Both abandoned Indian wares and wigwams for "Mormoné" homes. And both of their deaths were noteworthy enough that the Mormon newspaper of record covered them.[74] What's more, unlike many other Mormon families in nineteenth-century Utah, the Kanoshes did not write their own history to provide clarity on this tragic but pivotal moment in the family's history. But perhaps just as important, Sally simply makes for a better victim. After all, she was the first Indian child whom the Mormons bought into freedom. She was the adopted daughter of Brigham Young and a cherished member of his Beehive House. She was the beloved and cultivated bride of an Indian ally, whom she herself molded into a faithful, Latter-day Saint. And she died because of her relative whiteness. Moreover, while in life Sally demonstrated her acceptance of her Lamanite identity, her death at the hands of uncivilized savage Indians reinforces the limits that the Mormons faced as they attempted to redeem the cursed branch of Israel. As Joseph Smith's (likely apocryphal) prophecy made clear, many if not most Indians would be killed, while only a few would prove worthy of joining the Mormon covenant.[75]

As did their spiritual predecessors Nephi, Mormon, and Moroni, the Mormon narrators of more modern histories of white-Indian relations abridge their histories. In doing so, Mary is remembered too little. Sally is remembered too much.[76] And while Mary all but disappears from the archive, Mormon narrators write her death onto the body of Sally. The construction of Sally's martyrdom masks how Sally actually became a member of Kanosh's household. Instead of the relatively horizontal progression of slave to servant to reluctant sister wife, in the writings of the white Mormon narrators who get to tell her story, Sally's life forms an arc; she moves ever upward from Indian slave to Mormon daughter to Mormon martyr. It is of little import to the Mormon narrator whether it was Sally or Mary who died so horrifically. Mary's story, which becomes Sally's, is reduced to a didactic tale of the Mormons' ability and limitations to redeem the Indians. Mary, Sally, Kanosh, and Walker (Wakara) are real people. But in these stories, they also become characters in a Mormon morality play.

Wakara Writes Back

In Utah, Native Americans encountered the Mormons, too. And when they did, they had things to say. To be sure, the Mormon-Indian dialogues often ended in violence, not words. But before arriving at this conclusion, Utah's Native Americans tolerated and sometimes welcomed the arrival of the Saints. They told their new white neighbors that they wanted to trade: blankets for grain, horses for beef, guns for humans. They were willing to share the land as long as there was fair recompense. Some of them even said yes when the Mormon missionaries asked if they would like to be baptized.

To contemporary scholars of such encounters between Native and Euro-Americans, it is axiomatic to acknowledge that whether by accepting, acquiescing, or resisting white Mormons' efforts to reshape them and their lands, Native Americans participated in the type of people building in which the Latter-day Saints were engaged during the second half of the nineteenth century. It is also axiomatic that, because Indians rarely wrote their own histories—preserving them instead in more ephemeral oral traditions—historians almost always have to pass through the highly mediated archive created on the white side of these encounters to locate and reconstruct an (approximation of an) authentic Indian perspective.[77]

The archive's asymmetries make it a racialized space. The written word weighs more than the spoken one, tilting the archive's floor in the direction of the white perspective. These asymmetries, however, also destabilize an older historiographical axiom. "History is written by the victors" proves inaccurate when the victor—at least of some battles—is an Indian. In the mid-1860s, Black Hawk (Antonga) and his pan-Indian alliance of Utes, Navajos, and Paiutes objected to the treaty agreements between other leading Utah chieftains (notably Kanosh) and the federal government in which Indians agreed to give up their land claims in Utah and relocate to reservations in exchange for cash settlements. During the so-called Black Hawk War, Black Hawk and his warriors halted and briefly reversed Mormon expansion in the southern Sanpete Valley.

Yet neither Black Hawk nor any another Native historian narrates the conflict's causes. Instead, one of Sanpete's many Danish Mormon converts, Peter Gottfredson, provides the most often-cited narrative of the Black Hawk War. In his *History of Indian Depredations in Utah* (1919), Gottfredson dismisses Native Americans' complaints that Mormons were "trespassers on their domain." He does the same with Indian accusations that white settlers "were to blame in some way for" smallpox outbreaks, which decimated native communities throughout Utah. Instead, Gottfredson portrays "Black Hawk" as an all but unprovoked aggressor whose perfidy against his one-time professed "friends" is manifested in stealing Mormon beef and murdering Mormon herdsmen and settlers. Throughout Gottfredson's narrated compilation of firsthand reports of the Black Hawk War and other incidents of Indian depredations, Black Hawk is virtually silent. He makes his mark in the archive through violence. In Gottfredson's history, only in defeat and near death from gunshot wounds received during the war is Black Hawk allowed to speak. According to Gottfredson, the chief spent his last days traveling to every settlement that he once attacked to beg for forgiveness for the "trouble" he had caused and to pledge peace with "the pale faces."[78]

Ambivalence characterized the Mormons' attitude to the lack of direct contribution from Black Hawk and other Indians to the written archive. The Saints professed a Book of Mormon imperative to make Indians into reading and writing people, with the same historical sensibilities—the desire to write down both personal and communal sacred histories—as those of the white Mormons. Yet the Mormons also located Indian apathy, even resistance to becoming a literate people in the Book of Mormon itself.[79] Even more than skin color, the Lamanites' disdain for the written record differentiated them from the record-keeping Nephites. Yet the Mormon archive shows that not all Native Americans whom the Saints encountered, befriended, attempted to convert, and killed were antagonistic to pen and paper. If we believe early Utah Mormon records, and there is evidence that we can, Wakara himself understood the authoritative weight the written word creates. From his earliest encounters with the Saints in the late 1840s to his death in 1855, Wakara and other chiefs witnessed Mormon emissaries and interpreters read letters that contained messages for them sent from Brigham Young. These chiefs then witnessed Mormon scribes transform the chiefs' spoken responses into written text to be carried back to the prophet.

His choice to be buried, along with his horses and Piede prisoners, with a letter from Brigham Young shows that Wakara understood the value and power of the written word.

As such, Wakara and other Ute chiefs recognized that words matter; words on a page matter even more. At the May 1854 peace meeting in which Young and Wakara promised to reestablish brotherly affection and trade, "Walker wished President Young to write a Letter," Wilford Woodruff recorded in his journal, "so [Walker] could show it to the people & let them know that we were at peace." Young obliged. (It is possible that this is the letter that Wakara took to the grave.)[80] Shortly after Wakara's death in January 1855, Wakara's heir-apparent, Arapeen, sought out the Mormon leaders of the Sanpete Valley. Arapeen asked them to transcribe the "visions" he had received and to share them with the Mormon leaders in Salt Lake. "Walker appeared unto me," Arapeen explained, "and told me . . . not to fight the Mormons but cultivate good peace." The Lord also spoke to Arapeen and charged him with preventing further hostilities. If the Indians stole the Mormons' cattle and horses, the Lord commanded Arapeen "to put a ball and chain on them [and] for me to whip them." But the Lord did not want Arapeen "to kill them or spill blood on the land." The Lord also promised that, once permanent peace was established and once "all people was good," the Lord would return to "earth and not go back." Arapeen also "saw three personages and their garments were white as snow and as brilliant as the sun," most likely a reference to the fabled Book of Mormon Three Nephites. "And by and bye," Arapeen continued, "all good people would seem as they did," becoming both as faithful and as white as the three immortal Mormon missionaries. Yet Arapeen's vision also contained a warning, which the Lord directed at the Saints: "If the Mormons throw away the lord's words," which the Lord instructed Arapeen to "have . . . written down," "the lord would not go to their meetings."[81]

The transcription of Arapeen's visions contains such particular biblical and Book of Mormon valences that the relationship between what the Ute chief actually said and what the scribe wrote down remains unclear, perhaps even dubious. In fact, in the summer of 1855 at another Ute-Mormon peace meeting held at the Provo Bowery, the Timpanogos chief Highforehead (Ton-om-bu-gah) not only accused the Mormons of purposefully misrepresenting the Utes' actions (the chief said that the Mormons had greatly exaggerated how much Utes had damaged Mormon property during the previous year's conflicts) but he also said that the Mormons had purposefully misrepresented the Indians' words. Through an interpreter, the chief complained, "Some of them pretend to understand their language when they understand but a few words, and they pretend that they understand more than they do, and owing to this many of them are apt to convey a wrong idea respecting the Indians, and they may influence the [Mormon] people against [Highforehead's] people."[82] Be they accurate records of Indian speech transformed into written words or not, the mere existence of the transcriptions of Arapeen's vision demonstrates that Arapeen (as did Highforehead) understood the power of the written word to contain messages and convey meaning. By February 1855, Arapeen and the recently deceased Wakara had been on the receiving end of dozens if not hundreds of missives of instructions, demands, and prophetic warnings. Arapeen wanted to send his own prophetic message—or more precisely the messages of Wakara and the Lord—back to Brigham Young. Arapeen hoped that the Saints, too, would be convinced to heed these written admonitions, and not simply "throw [Arapeen's words] away."[83]

In life as in death, Wakara also understood the authority that came with the performance of writing words on a page. In March 1850, during his lecture before the Historical Society of Pennsylvania, Thomas Kane provided the most colorful description of Wakara's oratory prowess. Having learned English, Spanish, and other Indian dialects, Wakara was also a "particularly eloquent master of the graceful alphabet of pantomime, which stranger tribes employ to communicate with one another." According to Kane, Wakara's linguistic faculties came in handy when he demanded from weaker Indians "black mail salary"—often in the form of Indian slaves. He also demanded "obsequious and distinguished attention" enforced by his troop of merciless equestrian warriors.[84] The records of his face-to-face meetings with Brigham Young also demonstrate that Wakara was a speaker who could hold his own with the most formidable of interlocutors.[85]

In his description of Wakara as an intelligent and ruthless leader, Kane does not mention whether Wakara's verbal eloquence extended to the "graceful alphabet" used by literate men and women. But there is no question that Wakara like Arapeen understood that the written word transcends its own materiality and embodies the letter writer's authority—especially when the recipient of this letter is at some remove. Thus in 1851, instead of calling on translators and scribes to compose a letter to Young, Wakara wrote one himself. Or tried to. Wakara's letter is illegible, at least to readers of English (fig. 6.1).[86] It is a set of looping lines, composed on a sheet of the yellow-tinted paper that the early Saints in Utah preferred because of its durability and thickness. Some of the lines appear to be Ws written in nineteenth-century cursive, as if a child attempted to imitate the writing of a

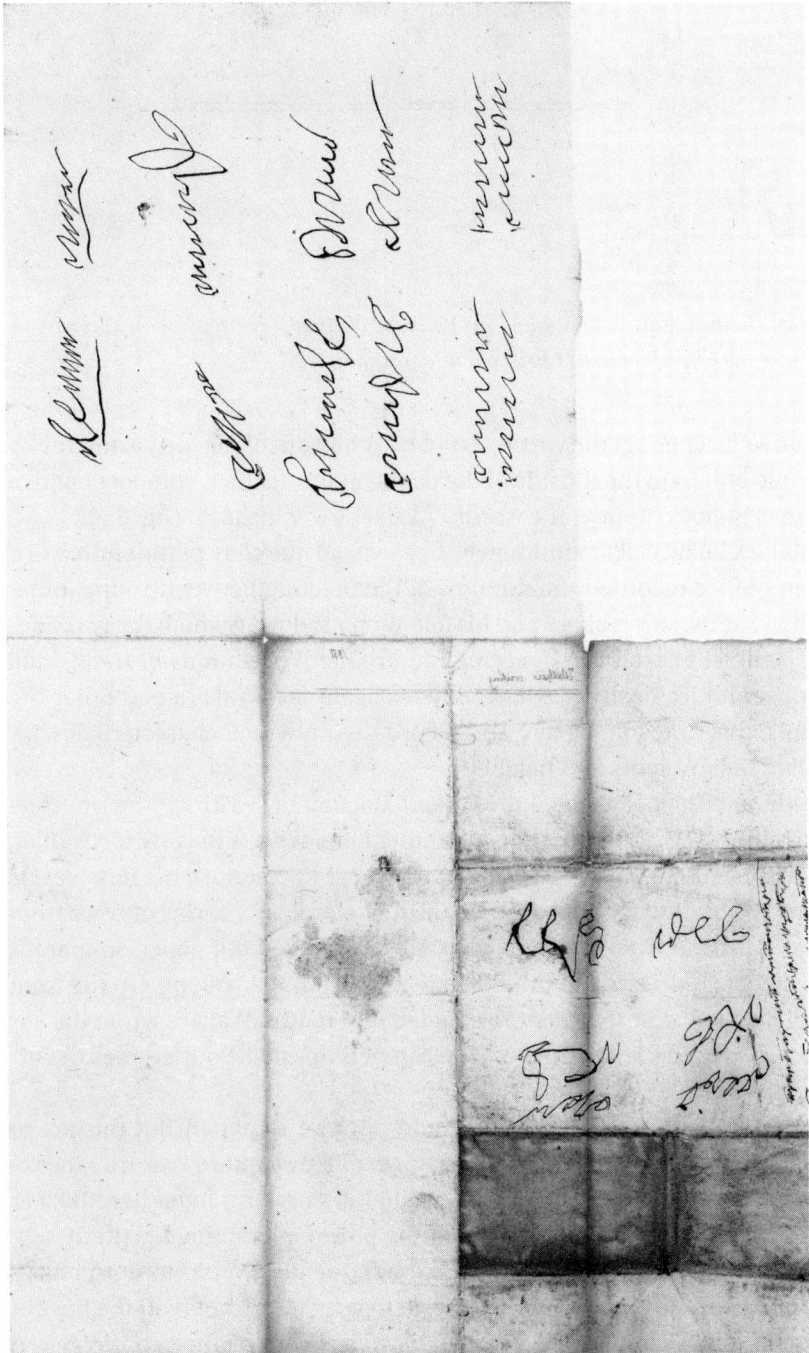

Fig. 6.1. Thomas Bullock, "Walker's Writing 1851." (Box 74, folder 44, Brigham Young Papers; courtesy of the Church Archives, the Church of Jesus Christ of Latter-day Saints)

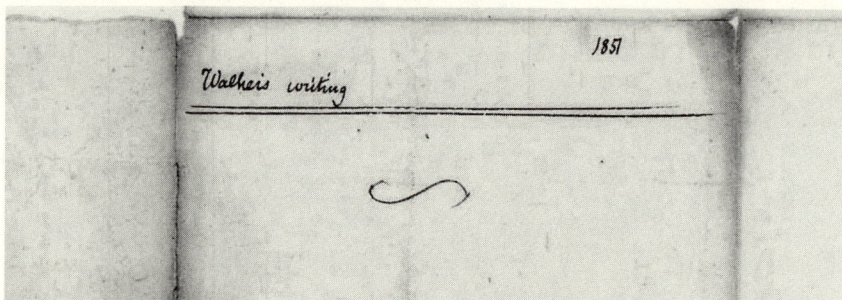

Fig. 6.2. Thomas Bullock's notation on "Walker's Writing." (Courtesy of the Church Archives, the Church of Jesus Christ of Latter-day Saints)

parent or teacher. Yet the writing is not of a child but of the forty-something-year-old chief. On the flipside of the paper, in the distinct, compact hand of Thomas Bullock, appear the words, "Walker's writing 1851" (fig. 6.2).

Bullock knew Wakara intimately. In May 1850, the clerk of the church historian's office recorded the minutes of the meeting between Young, other leading Saints, and Wakara and his fellow chiefs during which the two sides first pledged to establish peaceful and productive relations of trade, land sharing, and friendship. In 1852, Bullock again met Wakara and other Ute leaders, this time to measure and record their physical characteristics, including their weights and heights.[87]

Although Bullock labeled the Wakara document "writing," the Ute chief clearly intended it to be a letter. Like other letter writers in early 1850s Utah, Wakara used one half of one side of the sheet to compose his missive. He strung together what appear to be distinct words in a series of rows from left to right and from top to bottom. He then folded the paper, so that his one sheet could serve as both the letter and its own envelope. On the front panel, formed after the sheet was folded into tenths, Wakara wrote the address of the intended recipient. One can perhaps make out a series of cursive Bs.

Wakara demonstrated that he could put pen to paper. But this act of "pantomiming" words on a page did not explicitly capture Wakara's meaning. Even though it cannot be read in a literal sense, this letter has much to say about Wakara's understanding of the power of creating a writerly self, a self that the writer as well as the intended reader would have to recognize and contend with.[88] Thus, although historians cannot read the lines of Wakara's letter, perhaps we can read between them. Perhaps there, based on other, more legible archival material from the early 1850s, we can find in Wakara's writing a rebuttal to the Mormons' paper Indian: an ahistorical savage capable only of acts of depredations against the forward march of civilization and thus worthy only of removal, sequestration, or extermination.

Wakara was at the height of his power and wealth when he penned his letter in 1851. The previous decade had been a very successful and profitable one for him. From California, Wakara and his men had stolen horses by the thousands and brought them along the Old Spanish Trail for sale in Santa Fe. And from Utah between 1840 and 1849, records indicate that he and other slavers brought at least 225 captive Indians, most of who were Paiutes, to market in New Mexico.[89] And yet even by 1851, Wakara was also surely aware that his wealth and his people's way of life were under threat. Mormon growth along Utah's Wasatch Front had already begun to disrupt the fish and game resources on which Wakara's Timpanogos band relied for bodily and spiritual sustenance. By the time Wakara died four years later, disruption had been replaced by destruction. At the July 1855 Mormon-Ute gathering at Provo, Highforehead described the lush forests that had long grown next to the fish-eating Utes' streams. But now "the ground is hard and we cannot eat it." At the same meeting, Wilford Woodruff acknowledged the same change to the land. "Before the whites came, there was plenty of fish and antelope, plenty of game of almost every description," noted the future church president. "But now the whites have killed off these things, and there is scarcely anything left for the poor natives to live upon."[90]

By 1851, disease had also begun to decimate Wakara's Utes as well as the Paiutes. Measles had ravaged both the Natives and the Mormons during the first year of settlement in the Sanpete Valley. Mormon medicine saved many, but not most. After all, the Mormons brought a host of Old World pathogens—smallpox, scarlet fever, tuberculosis, perhaps even malaria and mumps—with them to the Great Basin. These microscopic pests, combined with the New World's own diseases, as well as colonialism, warfare, slavery, and forced migration, created an almost apocalyptic cocktail for Utah's native inhabitants. From a population of at least 12,000 when the Mormons arrived in 1847, by 1900 there were just 2,623 Native Americans in Utah.[91] As early as July 1853, during the first outbreak of conflict with Wakara, Brigham Young noted the precipitous fall in the Native population. "The Indians in these mountains are continually on the decrease. Bands that numbered 150 warriors when we first came here number not more than 35 now." Young most directly faulted Wakara's slave raiding for the decline, which left in "some of the little tribes in the southern parts of this territory, towards New

Mexico, not a single squaw amongst them." But even compared to the ruthlessly efficacious slave catching of Wakara, certainly viral and bacterial diseases killed many Indians.[92]

Of course, the recently arrived Saints had also already disrupted Wakara's slave trade. And they promised to end it altogether. For Wakara, Indian slavery was not the unmitigated horror that the Saints made it out to be. The Utes did not share the Mormons' view that all Indians were one people descended from one common Israelite ancestor. Centuries before, while the southern Paiutes remained pedestrian and thus forced to rely on local food sources, the Utes became respected and feared horsemen. They traveled throughout the Rockies and the Great Plains to hunt buffalo and to capture and sell other Indians, especially their poorer Paiute neighbors.[93] Brigham Young, too, believed in a hierarchy of peoples. He felt morally justified, even compelled to support the enslavement of people of African descent, who he believed were spiritually and intellectually inferior to whites. As such, Wakara might have viewed efforts to abolish Indian slavery as Brigham viewed efforts to abolish African slavery—an affront to the culturally and theologically prescribed order of humanity.

And yet the Latter-day Saints did not dismantle the Indian slave trade. Through their claims to legal and doctrinal exigencies as well as through displays of force, the Mormons usurped control over it from the Utes. They continued to purchase Paiute children and place them in Mormon homes long after they ended the Ute slave trade.[94] Thus, instead of trading partners and friendly neighbors, the Mormons became existential threats to the Utes' way of life. As the federal Indian agent in Utah Jacob Holeman explained in a series of reports that he wrote in the early 1850s to his bosses in Washington, the Mormons and other white settlers had destroyed the Utes' hunting and foraging grounds. As such, the Utes were forced to rely even more on trading humans for the guns and horses they needed to hunt increasingly scarce game, defend their lands, and steal Mormon cattle and grain.[95] The same year that Wakara penned his own letter, in January 1851 another Indian agent, H. R. Day, reported that the Utes considered Mormon thievery of land and resources, including Indian slaves, the cause of the escalating Mormon-Indian tensions. Day reported a conversation he had with Sowiette, a Ute chief who, along with Wakara and Arapeen, had been baptized and ordained a Mormon elder just a few months before. "The old chief . . . said to me, American-good! Morman-no good! American-friend, Morman-Kill-Steal," wrote Day.[96] As is the case with Mormon "transcriptions" of Indian speech, the "Gentile" Indian agent might have written his own anti-Mormon bias into Sowiette's words. And yet, the Ute chief's emphatic denouncement of the Mormons suggests genuine frustration with the effects of the expanding Mormon conquest of the Utes' lands.

For these Indians, what the Mormons called the "depredations" of unrepentant savages—stealing grain, horses, and cattle—could have been attempts to restore unjust imbalances in Mormon-Ute relations. When Brigham Young and other leading Saints met Wakara, Sowiette, and Arapeen in the Utah Valley in May 1850, the Saints and the Utes formed covenants of trade, land use, and friendship.[97] Such agreements established relationships of reciprocity. The Indians believed that they were entitled to the fruits produced on these lands—fat cows, golden grains—which they shared with the Mormons. What the Mormons called their Indian policy of largesse—feeding the Indians instead of fighting them—was to the Indians just deserts. If the Mormons broke the covenants by not providing the Indians their fair share, then the Indians were justified in taking what they needed, and with force if necessary. Even at the height of the Mormon-Ute conflict in 1853–54, Wakara told the Mormons as much. As he explained in a letter to Nauvoo Legion colonel George A. Smith, Wakara did not intend the Mormons' bodily harm. All he wanted was the share of cattle that he believed was his due for allowing the Saints to live on his land.[98] From this perspective, the Indians saw the Mormons, not themselves, as the dishonest, violent aggressors against whom the Indians had no choice but to fight back to protect their lands and lives once it was clear that the Mormons could not be held to their word.

On July 6, 1853, just days before the outbreak of Mormon-Ute conflict, a veteran Mexican fur trader named M. S. Martenas interviewed Chief Wakara. In the transcript of the interview, Martenas noted that he had known Wakara and his kin for more than three decades. "They talk freely with me," Martenas wrote, "and express their feelings and wishes without reserve." In Spanish, the polyglot Ute chief provided a counternarrative to what had already become the dominant Mormon view of Mormon-Indian relations in Utah. Though he did not employ the same ontological Lamanite lens through which the Saints read Wakara and other Indians of Utah, Wakara explained to Martenas that his claim to the lands of Utah was, in fact, inherited. These were the lands "on which his band resides and on which they have resided since his childhood, and his parents before him." Wakara acknowledged, "When [the Mormons] first commenced the settlement of Salt Lake Valley . . . [they were] friendly, and promised [the Indians] many comforts, and lasting friendship." The Mormons' neighborly behavior continued for a short time "until they became strong in numbers, then their conduct and treatment towards the Indians changed—they were not only treated unkindly, but many were much abused." What's more, the Mormon settlements expanded farther into the Utes' "hunting grounds in the valleys" without considering the disruption that such sprawl caused their Native neighbors, trading partners, and would-be religious brethren. "And the graves of their fathers have been torn up by the whites."[99]

According to Wakara, this was the state of Mormon-Indian relations in July 1853. Ironically, instead of helping the Indians create permanent settlements, as they had pledged to do, the ever-expanding Mormon people had forced the Utes to become refugees on their own lands, "driven," as Wakara explained to Martenas, "from place to place." Martenas added his own observations about the "present excitement" between the Utes and Mormons and fears about the coming conflagration. Not only had the invaders trampled their lands, killing fish and game and disturbing the final resting places of the Indians' fathers. The Mormons had also interfered "with the long established Spanish trade," the main source of the equestrian Utes' wealth, power, and prestige. "I greatly fear that much difficulty will grow out of this present excited condition of the Indians," Martenas concluded, "should the Mormons continue their unkind treatment."[100]

Over the next ten months, "excitement" begot violence as Wakara and his forces attempted to push back Mormon encroachment. But by May 1854, like the Delaware chief Anderson before him and like the Ute chief Black Hawk after him, Wakara made peace with the whites, only to die soon after. Though the Americans in the case of Anderson, and the Mormons in the case of Wakara and Black Hawk, saw it this way, the Indian chiefs most likely did not interpret their decision to sue for peace as submission to white supremacy. Instead, it was a recognition of a new future in which the Indians would have to live with the whites. Peace became a strategy of negotiation, though one that rarely worked, by which Wakara hoped to create a future with some dignity for his people.

Wakara is no innocent. Like his "Big Chief" counterpart Brigham Young, Wakara has blood on his hands: that of the Mormons whom he and his braves killed and that of the Paiute and Shoshone women and children whom he enslaved, abused, and murdered. But Wakara's attempt at letter writing suggests that he did not want to be reduced to a character in the Mormons' faith-promoting history, in which their own delightsome worthiness (and that of their noble Lamanites) is highlighted in contrast to the dark-skinned and dark-hearted Indian. Consciously or unconsciously, Wakara recognized that writing was how he could become a historical subject in the new, literate world that the Saints were building up around him. As much as the forts, farms, and roads that the Saints constructed on the land of his forefathers—and according to Wakara, sometimes literally digging up his forefathers' graves to do so—the written word was a keystone to the infrastructure of Zion.

Yet Wakara wrote back. On paper, he challenged the Mormon-constructed "Walker" paper Indian. The war chief did so by chronicling his Native American people's last stand (think Mormon at Cumorah [Mormon 6]). He used words to repel a violent army of colonizers (think the Lamanites) bent on seizing his Native American land and destroying his Native American way of life.

EPILOGUE

Performing Red, Black, and White American

Jane Manning James is dressed in her Sunday best. She wears a dark silk dress. It is cinched at her neck and adorned with a white collar—the preferred fashion of many late nineteenth-century Mormon women. The dress bundles at her waist, then flows down to her feet. She is seated, leaning slightly on her left arm, which is bent at a ninety-degree angle and placed on the drape-covered table next to her. Clutching a white handkerchief, her right hand is positioned in her lap. Her hair is parted in the middle and pulled back to a bun. Her ears are gilded with gold rings (fig. E.1).

James looks straight into the camera as Salt Lake City photographer, English convert to Mormonism, and captain of the tragic 1856 Martin handcart company Edward Martin takes her likeness.[1] From her choice of fashion to her stern, unsmiling face and stiff pose, Jane Manning James's image—first recorded on a plate-glass negative and then printed as a carte-de-visite sometime in the 1860s or 1870s—is the model of Mormon respectability. Peering through his lens, Martin sees a black woman who stares back to send a message. Despite her blackness, James asserts that she has successfully conformed to the standards of piety and bodily discipline that should earn her a place in the white, Mormon sacred community—a community itself forced to face down a racialized gaze from anti-Mormon Americans who viewed them as something less than white.[2]

In 1878, within months of her death, Sally Kanosh also sat either for Martin or, more likely, for Charles R. Savage, the most sought-after photographer in Utah. After he and his partner, George Ottinger, opened their studio in 1861, less than a hundred yards south of Temple Square, dignitaries including Sally's adoptive father, Brigham Young, prominent Indian chiefs like her husband, Kanosh, and hundreds of other Latter-day Saints visited Savage to have their likenesses taken.

Sally's dress, expression, and pose resemble a collodion copy of James's carte-de visite (fig. E.2). The evolution of cheaper and more reliable photographic technologies provided marginalized women in Zion like James and Sally Kanosh another way to make their mark in the Mormon archive.[3] These photographs become a visual "hidden transcript" in which they per-

Fig. E.1. Jane Manning James's carte-de-visite, ca. 1870. (Courtesy of the Church Archives, the Church of Jesus Christ of Latter-day Saints)

Fig. E.2. Sally Young Kanosh's carte-de-visite, 1878. (Photo # 14401, Utah State Historical Society, Salt Lake City)

form Mormon identities against the limitations placed on their racial identities. Ironically, the technology's limitations also helped make their case that, through their performance of acculturation to the standards of Mormon nineteenth-century piety and respectability, James and Sally Kanosh should be recognized as members of the (white) Mormon people. The black and white photography's inability to detect the various shades of these women's skin tones results in the washing out of their faces.[4]

For nonwhite Mormons, earning respectability involved such demonstrations of adherence to standards of Mormon identity. Not only did they need to show that they could dress and speak the part. For men, performing Mormon identity also included demonstrating a capacity to cultivate land or practice a trade. For women, performing Mormon identity included cultivating what, in titling a composite sketch of two dozen rosy-cheeked Mormon babies whom he had photographed, Charles Savage dubbed "Utah's Best Crop."[5] Sally Kanosh, who died childless, did not contribute to this bounty. But Jane Manning James did, raising six children in Mormon Utah. In large measure, her letter-writing campaign to gain access to the temple was the result of a parent's desire to care for the eternal souls of her offspring. James's literary performances in the 1880s and 1890s—a single type of performance that was triply Mormon, in that it called attention to her faithfulness, her literacy, and, implicitly, her persecution—was in service of her progeny. As she had wished for herself, James hoped that her children and grandchildren could learn to shed their supposed accursed identities, so that they, too, could become members of the white (raceless) Mormon people.

James tried to teach her children the key to this aspirational identity—the ability to chronicle on paper their life stories as respectable Mormons. There is evidence of the early, tentative fruits of such lessons, evidence that is literally written into a copy of the sacred Mormon archive. On a blank page in the James family's *Doctrine & Covenants*, with gestures similar to but perhaps with more success than those of Wakara from 1851, Jane Manning James's young daughter, Vilate James, put pen to paper, leaving her own mark in a leather-bound copy of some of the most treasured and important written records of early Mormon history.

Vilate, who was born in 1859 in Salt Lake, appears to be doodling (fig. E.3). It's the work of a daydreaming child, perhaps sitting quietly in a Sunday church meeting. Like many children, after she tries her hand at writing her signature on paper, she looks around to observe her surroundings. And Vilate draws a profile of a woman dressed in her Sunday best. It is hard not to read Vilate's sketch together with her mother's carte-de-visite, despite

Fig. E.3. Vilate James's drawing, ca. 1865, in Doctrines & Covenants: Revelations by God *(Liverpool: S. W. Richards, 1852). (Private collection; courtesy of Dr. Robert Van Uitert)*

what appears to be significant embellishments to her mother's modest ensemble—adding a train, a bustle, and perhaps an elaborate hairdo. One can perhaps read in these two images the attempts of Jane Manning James to have her likeness frozen on paper as the ideal of Mormon respectability and of Vilate to draw her mother on paper as the respectable but fashionable Latter-day Saint.

Although he did not photograph Jane Manning James for her carte-de-visite, Charles Savage did document James and her family's uniquely visible presence in turn-of-the-century Utah. Savage helped establish Old Folks Day, an annual recreational outing for the oldest members of the Mormon community, which he often chronicled with his camera. As a regular attendee, James was able to perform her own status as the "colored" exemplar of the 1847 Mormon pioneer class in front of her own aging cohort of pioneers and, with the help of Savage, the rest of the Mormon people. In June 1907, Savage photographed the octogenarians Jane Manning James and her brother Isaac Manning at the Old Folks gathering at the Lagoon amusement park on the shores of the Great Salt Lake. This photo of Jane and Isaac, standing upright but leaning on their canes, was featured in the *Deseret News* report of that year's Old Folks Day. Less than year a later, the same photo was reprinted with James's death announcement on the paper's front page.[6]

Vilate James was not in Utah to see her celebrated mother's photograph appear on the front page of the church's newspaper of record. To be sure, Jane Manning James tried to teach her daughter that she, too, could earn a place among the white Mormons of Zion. Like any Latter-day Saint who had known Joseph Smith, James certainly regaled Vilate with memories of the beloved and big-hearted prophet. She certainly told Vilate of her halcyon days in Nauvoo, when her race did not define her destiny. And to be sure, Vilate was, as Charles Savage might have noted, a crop of Utah. But among the Mormons, her kind was seen as less fruit and more weed. Like all of her brothers and sisters, Vilate left the church. And like most of her brothers and sisters, she also left Utah to settle in California. There she married a black Methodist minister. She spent six years in Africa as a missionary before dying in Oakland in 1897 at the age of thirty-eight.[7] Vilate felt more at home among those who, unlike her mother, did not feel the need to break from their African heritage to find a spiritual community.

Whitening the Mormon Archive

Vilate understood something that her mother's dedication to her memories of Joseph Smith blinded her to: that the church's evolving anti-black theologies meant that Vilate's and Jane Manning James's blackness was seen as a fixed, immutable identity. No matter how many letters she wrote, no matter how pious and obedient she proved herself to be—and did so before the camera—in the eyes of the gatekeepers to full acceptance in the restored church, Jane Manning James, her husband, and their children would forever be the children of Ham. As such, the doors to the temple and to the highest levels of heaven would be closed to them until the Lord who "changeth the seasons," as James's first patriarchal blessing pointed out, also changed their supposedly accursed identity.

As such, at the beginning of the twentieth century, Jane Manning James's presence in Zion presented a problem for the leading brethren who believed that black and Mormon were mutually exclusive identities. During the seven decades since the founding of the church, Mormonism's original universal covenant had contracted, circumscribing itself to exclude black people from its most intimate and sacred spaces. James's passing in April 1908 provided these church leaders with the occasion to begin to make these racialized distinctions of identity more explicit. A visible vestige from Mormonism's more racially inclusive beginnings would no longer disturb the picture of an all-white Zion when the church gathered for important meetings. Thus after eulogizing her in April 1908, in August of that same year, church president Joseph F. Smith met with the Quorum of the Twelve Apostles and voted, for the first time in church history, to formalize a policy toward the "negro race." In 1844, church patriarch Hyrum Smith told James that if she demonstrated worthiness, then the Lord would remove her from the cursed lineage into which she was born and make her one with the blood of the covenantal Mormon people. Sixty-four years later, Hyrum's son made it clear that the Lord would do no such thing for James or for any descendant of Cain and Ham. In August 1908, the quorum passed a motion that allowed "negroes or people tainted with negro blood" to be baptized in the church, but nothing else. The motion also called on the church secretary to search the church's records for "rulings of former councils on this question, also the public utterances of President [Brigham] Young and others on the same subject."[8]

Soon after James's death, the church hierarchy thus searched the archive for pronouncements from Joseph Smith's successors. And in that archive, they found plenty of pronouncements from past church prophets with which the church could justify the exclusion of black converts from the gospel principles beyond baptism.[9] At the same time, the black Mormons of the past like James, who once occupied reserved a seat at special gatherings at the Tabernacle, mostly disappeared from the official historical narratives of the church.[10] B. H. Roberts's multivolume *Comprehensive History of the Church of Jesus Christ of Latter-day Saints*, released in 1930 as part of the centennial celebration of the church's founding, includes no indication that the early church had black members. Instead, Roberts only mentions the "black race (Negro)" to explain that the curse against people of African descent originated with the "descendants of Egypt."[11]

Since the 1840s, when Orson Hyde first suggested what became known as the "pre-existence" thesis, some Mormons even placed the advent of African accursedness back before biblical times.[12] In the twentieth century, church leaders, including Joseph F. Smith's son, longtime church historian, and briefly church president and prophet Joseph Fielding Smith, made this thesis all but doctrinal. In his book *The Way to Perfection*, an extended treatise on Mormon practical divinity published in 1931 and reprinted well into the twenty-first century, Smith writes that during a premortal war between the forces of God and Satan, certain souls "were indifferent" or even "sympathized with Lucifer," while other souls proved their worthiness by siding with God. Smith explains that the "worthiest" souls enter mortality through the most favored of Israelite lineages, notably Ephraim, whereas those souls who did not stand "valiantly" with the forces of "Righteousness" enter the mortal life through the lineage of Ham.[13]

To be sure, there were prominent and public Mormon dissenters from these views and from the race-based exclusions they justified. Such dissenters included University of Utah professor Sterling McMurrin. McMurrin told the Senate committee hearing considering his nomination to become President John F. Kennedy's U.S. commissioner on education, "I do not agree with the policies of the Mormon church with respect to Negros." While running for governor of Michigan in 1962, George Romney declared his "political independence" from the church regarding civil rights and black church membership.[14] Dissenters also came from Mormon historians, including Lester Bush, Henry Wolfinger, and Newell Bringhurst, who in the late 1960s began examining the church archives related to the priesthood and temple bans. There they found written evidence of a more inclusive black Mormon past—notably the records of Jane Manning James and Elijah Abel. Mid-twentieth-century church leaders insisted that restrictions on black membership were a "direct commandment from the Lord," as the First Presidency asserted in August 17, 1949, and had been in place since "the days of its organization."[15] As such, this history of a black Mormon past had been perhaps "purposefully forgotten," to borrow from Paul Ricoeur, in order to provide continuity between the church that Joseph Fielding Smith served as historian, president, and prophet in the twentieth century and the church that his great-uncle Joseph Smith Jr. and his grandfather Hyrum Smith established a century before.[16]

Most importantly, dissenters also came from black Mormons in Utah, such as Darius Gray, Eugene Orr, and Ruffin Bridgeforth, who, with the support of the church's apostles, established in 1971 the Genesis Group. To this day, several decades after the 1978 revelation lifted priesthood and temple restrictions for black Mormons, the Genesis Group meets monthly as a social auxiliary of the church, tasked with helping black members cope with the isolation—and sometimes the stigmatization—of being black people in a predominantly white church.

The Conquest of Utah's American Indian

At least officially, Joseph Fielding Smith and his church did not forget about the less favored branches of Israel. In *The Way to Perfection*, Smith announces, "A better day is dawning for the Jew and the Lamanite." When he wrote the book in 1931, Smith saw it as providential that the British had taken control of Palestine. As the end times approached, the Lord had seen fit to remove the curse on the deicidal remnant of Judah scattered throughout Europe and Asia. Soon they, too, would be permitted to return to their homeland. Smith also foresaw the day when the Lamanite in America would again receive the attention of the white Latter-day Saints who had been called to redeem them.[17] In 1947, apostle Spencer W. Kimball spearheaded the Indian Student Placement Program. White Mormon families fostered Native American children, providing educational opportunities to which these children did not have access in their Native communities. (Following decades of accusations that it undermined Native American values and that church leaders coerced Natives to participate, in the 1990s the placement program stopped enrolling new pupils. It graduated its last student in 2000.)[18] Still, during much of the half century between Brigham Young's death in 1877 and the advent of the placement program, the church again postponed Lamanite redemption.[19] With Lamanite restoration forestalled until the last of the latter days, in the final decades of the nineteenth century, Mormons understood Native Americans as did most other white Americans: a quickly disappearing race whose conquest was met with feelings of both triumphalism and nostalgia.

Some Indian conversions did occur. And when they did, the Latter-day Saints read them as the realization of providence. In his 1881 speech in Salt Lake's Assembly Hall highlighting the triumphs and trials of the Saints' fifty years of evangelizing to the Lamanites, the long-serving missionary John Nicholson mentioned that three hundred Indians had recently been brought into the Mormon fold, an event that Nicolson understood as the fulfillment of the Book of Mormon promise that the "remnants" of the Lamanites would be restored "to a knowledge of their progenitors." Nicholson was likely referring to the mass baptisms of a band of Paiutes in the 1870s, which Charles R. Savage photographed near the Southern Indian Mission that Jacob Hamblin established three decades before.[20]

But Savage did not take most of his Indian photographs in the mission field. Instead, in his Salt Lake City studio, Savage photographed prominent Indians like Kanosh and the Shoshone chief Washakie, who was briefly a member of the church in the 1880s. He also took dozens of carefully staged photographs of unnamed Indians.

To sit for these images, Savage's anonymous female and male Indian subjects wore threadbare shirts and pants, "traditional" Indian clothing, or almost nothing at all. Indian mothers posed with their young "pappooses." And they sat on fur-skin robs, limestone rocks, or beds of grass and sticks (fig. E.4). Perhaps owing to improving photographic techniques, unlike the "white" image of Sally Kanosh, the icon of Lamanite civilized redemption, Savage managed to capture these Indians' darker skin tones. To be sure, this increased sensitivity can be attributed to improved photographic techniques. Yet even when considering technological advances, these photographs were clearly not of Lamanite Mormons. Instead they captured Indians in photographic stills and in what Savage imagined was the Indians' natural state.

Savage's Indian photographs were to be read not as biography or history but as ethnology, with the emphasis on "ethno." Like many other white American photographers at the turn of the century, Savage documented the disappearing Indian race, visually preserving the vanishing traditional Indian customs and Indian bodies.[21] As such, these photographs belong not only, nor even principally, to the archive of Mormon history. Instead, they belong to the archive of American history. Attendees at the 1893 World's Columbian Exposition in Chicago inspected Savage's award-winning exhibit in the Utah Territory's exhibition house, which included landscapes, infrastructure under construction, and portraits of Utah's Indians.[22] As John Gast's famous painting *American Progress* (1872) exemplifies, the teleological narrative of American triumphalism over the frontier required not simply wild wilderness, which plucky Americans and intrepid European immigrants tamed with farms and railroads, telegraph wires, and great cities. It also required the image of conquered Indians and their bison herds, fleeing ever westward. By the last decades of the nineteenth century, these Indians were rendered so benign that Savage could bring them into his studio, tell them what to wear, where to sit, and how to pose. They were an ahistorical people, frozen in silver-coated paper while American history fulfilled its destiny. Coincidence or not, Savage's Indian subjects were most often members of Wakara's Utes who fifty years before presented the biggest threat to Mormon expansion.

Not only did the conquered Indians become literal and metaphorical set pieces. They also became artifacts in the Mormon and American archive and were displayed as such in Mormon and American museums. In

Fig. E.4. Charles Savage's photograph of Utes, ca. 1890. (Courtesy of the Church Archives, the Church of Jesus Christ of Latter-day Saints)

1830, Andrew Jackson spoke of American progress inevitably treading "on the graves of the extinct [Indian] nations." Two decades later, Wakara bemoaned the disturbance of his forefathers' graves. Yet even Wakara, whose sacrificial horses and Paiute children were meant to serve him in the afterlife and help protect his remains from disturbance, was not immune to grave robbers-cum-ethnographers. In fact, it was precisely Wakara's elaborate burial that intrigued Henry C. Yarrow. Under the auspices of the Bureau of American Ethnology, Yarrow led the excavation of the chief's remains in the 1870s. Yarrow sent the skull of "Wah-ker, a celebrated Ute Chief, long the terror of the People of Utah, New Mexico, and California," along with the "cranial bones of a Piede or Piute Indian said to have been buried with him," to the Army Medical Museum in Washington, D.C. There scientists measured the skulls' cranial volume in order to compare them with dimensions of other "races."[23]

Forty-five years later, in 1919, the same year Peter Gottfredson published his *Indian Depredations in Utah*, the bones of the Mormons' other chief Indian enemy, Black Hawk, went on display in the church's history museum in Salt Lake City. When the exhibit opened in September, the *Deseret News* publicized the event. A front-page story was accompanied by photos of the new exhibit and of the smiling miner who unearthed the remains posing with Black Hawk's skull as he stood over the chief's emptied grave (fig. E.5). As the *Deseret News* put it, "A case on the north side of the L.D.S. Church museum is destined to become the center of interest to many a student of early-day Utah history. . . . For resting peacefully in the midst of the very white settlers whom he loved to harass is all that remains of Chief Black Hawk." The paper explained that, decades before, under Black Hawk's command, an army of Indian warriors attacked both the infrastructure and the people that made up Mormon civilization. "Women and children were tortured and carried away, homes devastated, ranchers murdered, and all sorts of Indian deviltry." But the chief had since been defanged. He had been turned from a devil into a benign, friendly ghost—captured forever under a glass case into which Mormon children could peer and dream up their own games of pioneers and Indians.[24]

Redface, Blackface, and White Faces

Mormons began recasting Mormon-Indian pioneer history as a sanitized pastime well before 1919. In 1878, the *Deseret News* reported that at a Pioneer Day celebration in Provo, thousands of residents witnessed a reenactment of the first "Indian War" of 1849. White Mormons dressed up as Indians entered Old Fort Utah on horseback, yelling "war whoops . . . firing

Bones of Black Hawk Indian Warrior. Now on Exhibition L. D. S. Museum

Benjamin Goddard Takes Precaution to Verify Discovery of Grave of Indian Chief by Affidavits Before Placing Skeleton in Institution.

A CASE on the north side of the L. D. S. Church museum is destined to become the center of interest to many a student of early-day Utah history. For resting peacefully in the midst of the very white settlers whom he loved to harass is all that remains of Chief Black Hawk who in the early sixties was dreaded and feared in many a town and settlement of Utah. What are declared to be the bones of the Indian desperado have been brought from their final resting place near Spring Lake Villa and now along with spurs, beads, sleighbells, ax, bucket, brass buttons and all such comforts which were supposed to accompany him to the Happy Hunting grounds are on display to the eyes of the White trespassers whom he so much resented.

Before placing the skeleton on exhibit Benjamin Goddard, in charge of the museum, has made every possible effort to prove their authenticity and has obtained a mass of evidence which seems to prove unquestionably that none other but the famous chief reposes in the museum. Mr. Goddard has not only secured the affidavits of the persons who exhumed the remains, but of early settlers near Spring Villa who knew the chief and saw his funeral cortege pass up the mountain a little to the east of the Utah county town. There are also a number of interesting photographs showing the place where the body was found, and of the region where Black Hawk started on his last journey.

Severely Wounded.

Utah historians and Black Hawk veterans declare that Chief Black Hawk died at Spring Lake Villa, a small settlement situated between Payson and Santaquin, Utah county, in 1870. The old chief is declared to have been severely wounded in the fight at Gravelly Ford on the Sevier river some three or four years before. He was assisting one of his wounded braves to his horse when sited by one of the settlers during a battle. The white man not being able to see the chief shot through the horse which shielded him and wounded him severely. He still seems to have taken an active part in the war on the white settlers after this mishap and actually before his death gained permission to visit every town and village from Cedar City on the south to Payson on the north to make peace with the people he had harassed. According to stories told by Indian war veterans he had caused so much misery to the settlers during his raids on the Utah towns and was so hated and feared that a number of heroes are declared to have arisen about the state who claim the honor of killing him. The old chief, however, it seems, died in his wigwam near Spring Lake Villa and was buried in the nearby foothills immediately south and east.

The story of the Black Hawk war in Utah chiefly culled from the declarations of Black Hawk war veterans is one of the pitiful last stands taken by the Red men to save the land of their fathers from the inroads of the pale face. It was also a story of the heartbreaking fight of the early day settlers to establish their small home-

Fig. E.5. *"Bones of Black Hawk Indian Warrior Now on Exhibition at L.D.S. Museum,"* Deseret News, *September 20, 1919.*

their guns and shooting arrows." Other Mormons, some of whom were veterans of the conflicts, dressed in their old Nauvoo Legion uniforms. They ceremonially rebuffed the Indian raid by firing the fort's cannon, just as the stronghold's original defenders had done three decades before. In the reenactments, and in the accompanying storytelling, the 1853–54 conflict between the Utes and the Mormons was dubbed the "Walker War." The complicated and charismatic chief who brokered and broke allegiances based on what was best for his tribe and himself was reduced to the caricature of the savage Indian aggressor.[25]

From the 1890s to the 1920s, when the last of their cohort died, veterans of the Nauvoo Legion made such reenactments at Fort Utah annual affairs. By day, the legionnaires reenacted the violence that they had endured and perpetrated. Some played the role of the Indians, adorning their faces with Indian war paint and sporting quivers full of arrows on their backs. By night, they swapped stories of anti-Mormon Indian violence. Many of their tales were reprinted in Gottfredson's *Indian Depredations in Utah.* As was the case in William Cody's Buffalo Bill shows, which debuted in 1883 at North Platte, Nebraska, along the Old Mormon Trail, in these reenactments and in their complimentary archived records, the Mormons became actors in the theater of "inverted conquest." The Euro-American conquerors of the American West retold the history so that they, and not the Indians—whose land they took often through force, deceit, and disease—were the victims of unprovoked aggression.[26]

Even Indian children adopted by white Mormons participated in these performances. Though he was a combatant on the "white" side of the original conflict in the 1860s, during the annual gatherings of the Black Hawk War veterans in the 1920s and 1930s, the Mormon-reared Indian Zenos Hill played the role of Chief Black Hawk. As a reporter from the *Spanish Fort Press* noted in 1937, Hill wore the medals and ribbons, which marked him as a veteran legionnaire, pinned to his chest. But because he was "red-skinned in the true sense that the words apply to Indians," Hill was cast as the Saints' last significant Indian adversary during the annual performances.[27]

The Mormons played redface. They also played blackface. And they did so like other Americans, as a response to national anxieties over the changes to race relations created in the aftermath of the Civil War. Many church leaders did not like the growth of Utah's black population in the late nineteenth and early twentieth centuries. Opportunities in mining, ranching, railroad construction, and service in the growing tourism industry led to a twenty-five-fold increase in the numbers of African Americans in the Salt Lake Valley, from 59 in 1860 to 1,446 by 1920.[28] Nor did the brethren appreciate the federal government placing an all-black infantry regiment at Fort Douglas, built on the hills overlooking Salt Lake City. Ostensibly, in 1896, Washington sent the troops to Utah to help monitor the Indian populations in Utah, Colorado, and Wyoming. Yet Mormon officials believed that anti-Mormon Republicans decided to station a large black military force in Salt Lake City to monitor and antagonize the church hierarchy.[29]

One block west of Charles R. Savage's studio, starting at the height of the Civil War and continuing into the early twentieth century, on the stage of the church-financed Salt Lake Theater, minstrel shows as well as farcical productions of *Uncle Tom's Cabin* and *The Octoroon* entertained packed houses of Utahns. The minstrelsy performances became such a regular feature that the theater developed its own collection of curly black wigs, "nigger coats," calico-colored "nigger shirts," and a banjo.[30] A 1905 article in the *Deseret News* explained that one minstrel troupe, whose "cast included the most prominent members of the younger set of Salt Lake Society," performed in the Salt Lake Theater to raise funds for philanthropic organizations. "In addition to burnt cork and grease paint faces of jet black, [the players] wore pure snow white hair, and big white chrysanthemums."[31] Kentucky-born Mormon pioneer, *Deseret News* editor, and amateur actor Scipio Africanus Kenner played "Sambo" in his troupe of minstrels, which regularly performed for leading members of the church hierarchy when the brethren wintered in southern "Dixie" Utah.[32] Ironically, Kenner's unusual middle name caused him trouble when he asked the parents of Isabella Park to bless his and Isabella's marriage engagement. In 1870, Kenner wrote to Brigham Young requesting that the prophet intervene on his behalf. The Parks had accused him of having "negro blood in [his] veins" and thus initially refused to support the marriage. They worried that such a union would result in an unholy mixing of white and black blood.[33]

Scipio Africanus Kenner performed blackface on stage, as did redface reenactors on the former battlefields of the Mormon-Indian conflicts. After the shows and reenactments, performers took off their "nigger wigs" and Indian headdresses. They washed off their black and red masks to reveal their whiteness, a possibility that, by the turn of the century, church leaders asserted was impossible for those black and Indian Mormons.[34] These red- and blackface performers' intended audiences were local—even as local as one's prospective in-laws—as well as national. After all, Scipio Africanus Kenner was not the only Mormon whose whiteness was in question. The increase in Washington's prosecution of "co-habiting" Mormon men during the 1870s and 1880s reenergized the anti-Mormon press, which depicted Mormon wives as "white slaves" of the lascivious sultanlike patriarchs of the Utah deserts and described the offspring of these unions as less than white "Mormon coons."[35] In his 1880 *New Overland Tourist and Pacific Coast Guide*, designed to encourage Americans to exploit the expanding rail networks and visit the wonders of the West, George A. Crofutt included two front pieces. The first was the largest mass printing of Gast's *American Progress*. The second was a reprinting of Charles Savage's *Utah's Best Crop*. Yet the painting's original celebration of Utah families' fecundity was inverted to imply that Columbia, too, would eventually conquer the onetime Indian and "hostile Mormon" foes of white American overland travelers. Crofutt wrote that the arrival of the railroad to Utah had already begun to check the accumulation of Mormon wealth and property, as "nearly all the religious denominations have secured a foot-hold [in Salt Lake City]." This better breed of Christians would soon produce a better crop of American children in Utah.[36]

The Changing Face of Mormon Universalism

In 1896, six years after church president Wilford Woodruff announced that the Latter-day Saints would abandon the practice of polygamy, thus removing the major barrier to Utah's full acceptance in the American political culture, Utah became the forty-fifth state of the United States. Yet statehood did not end the marginalization of the Mormon population in the Gentile imagination, a marginalization that continued to be cast in racialized terms. Some Saints countered this marginalization, as did some Jewish immigrants.[37] Performing blackface as well as redface allowed Jews and Saints to play against the tropes of the grotesque "African" and the savage "Indian," making themselves appear white and "American" by contrast.

As a generation of scholars have noted, over the twentieth century the Latter-day Saints succeeded, in large measure, in making Mormonism synonymous with white, and, for that matter, American, if American means patriotic, politically and socially conservative, religiously devout, and family oriented.[38] In the early twentieth century, the most visible example of the Mormon ascendency to the status of "super-Americans" was the growing popularity of the Mormon Tabernacle Choir. George Pyper, the manager of the Salt Lake Theater, which served as the longtime home to many Mormon minstrel troupes, was also manager of the choir in 1911. That year, the choir completed a six-thousand-mile tour of the eastern United States, which included performances at Madison Square Garden and the White House. Over the next several decades, through its extensive touring, weekly radio broadcasts, and later television programs celebrating national holidays like the Fourth of July and Memorial Day, as well as Christmas and Easter, the Mormon Tabernacle Choir became "America's choir," as Ronald Reagan dubbed it when the choir sang at his first inauguration. It served as a symbol of the (all but) exclusively white face of the American family, nation, and (increasingly generic) Judeo-Christian faith.[39]

Against this most well-worn of backdrops of Mormonism—Mormons as the epitome, or the stereotype, of white, conservative America—this book's central goals have been to demonstrate that the story of Mormonism and race is not simply a story of how Mormons became "super" white Americans. This holds true for the first half century of Mormon history, the period about which this book has been most concerned, as it holds true for the century that followed, even as the lines in Mormon culture between blacks and whites, and to a lesser degree Native Americans, grew increasingly rigid. Throughout the twentieth century, even as they attempted to erase the church's own black Mormon past, leading Latter-day Saints participated in national debates about race and American democracy. For example, in their public support for Booker T. Washington and his Tuskegee Institute as an instrument of black uplift, which they saw as similar to their own efforts to create prosperous, self-sufficient communities, the Mormons' participation involved more than simply arguing for the perpetuation of segregation and white supremacy.[40] What's more, throughout this period, not only did black people in Utah join the church, but so did black people in Africa and in the African diaspora. And, as did their black brethren like Jane Manning James and Elijah Abel before them, these new members petitioned for access to the priesthood and the temple, which forced the church to continually rearticulate the restrictions until it was eventually motivated to end them.[41]

Almost exactly a century after the death of Brigham Young, the church president and prophet who first articulated the ban, in 1978 another church prophet and president, Spencer W. Kimball, received a revelation to lift it. A week after the announcement of the revelation, an article in the LDS paper *Church News* claimed that Mormon prophets—from Joseph Smith and Brigham Young down to current President Kimball—had all "spoken of the day when the blessings of the priesthood would come to blacks." Conspicuously absent, however, were any universalistic statements from Joseph F. Smith or Joseph Fielding Smith. In the same edition, *Church News* printed an article describing Jane Manning James and Elijah Abel as steadfast converts and pioneers. Yet the article neglected to state that Abel was a priesthood holder. And the article did not mention that both James and Abel had waged decades' long campaigns to get access to the temple.[42]

For much of the last thirty-five years since the revelation, the church has generally held to the position articulated in 1998 by then church president Gordon B. Hinckley. On the twentieth anniversary of the 1978 revelation, in response to calls from some black Mormons that the current hierarchy disavow the racist positions of their prophetic predecessors, Hinckley declared, "[The revelation] speaks for itself."[43] In recent years, however, the church has made great efforts to place the increasingly racial and international diversity of its membership at center stage. Launched in 2011, the "I'm a Mormon" campaign—with billboards, radio, and TV spots in major American markets—is the church's own intervention into the media landscape in which outsiders often define what Mormonism is and who the Mormon people are. The most visible part of the "I'm a Mormon" campaign is a carefully curated set of video testimonials posted at mormon.org of "typical" Mormons. For example, one of the campaign's earliest stars was Mia Love, a Mormon convert, a first-generation Haitian immigrant, and, when the video was produced, the mayor of Saratoga Springs, a booming bedroom community in Utah Valley. Love, who in 2014 became the first black female Republican elected to the House of Representatives, shot to fame during her first unsuccessful run for Congress when she spoke at the 2012 Republication National Convention when Mitt Romney became the first Mormon ever to be nominated by a major political party for president.

The "I'm a Mormon" campaign mirrors the church's own bottom-up and top-down organization—a religious institution run by local lay leaders that is also overseen by a strong, centralized hierarchy. At mormon.org, all Latter-day Saints can create their own profiles in which they are encouraged to place Mormonism within the context of the rest of their lives. As such, the "I'm a Mormon" campaign has become an ever expanding, twenty-first-century Mormon archive in which Mormons and their church perform modern-day Mormonism—a faith that is increasingly nonwhite and non-American—before audiences on the worldwide web.

Though not directly a part of the "I'm a Mormon" campaign, even the world's most famous Mormon family participated in presenting this new, racially inclusive image of Mormonism. On Christmas Eve, 2013, Mitt Romney tweeted a family Christmas photo featuring the former Republican presidential candidate and his wife, Ann, surrounded by their twenty-two grandchildren. Kieren, Romney's adopted African American grandson, sat on his grandfather's right knee (fig. E.6).

This is the present face of Mormonism, or at least the face the church and many of its members hope to showcase. Yet it is a face that not everyone is ready to accept. During a December 29, 2013, segment of her MSNBC

Fig. E.6. Romney family Christmas photo, December 24, 2013.

show, Melissa Harris-Perry and her guests mocked the photo, deriding it as incongruent with Romney's (white) faith and his (white) politics.[44] Even within certain Mormon circles, this new image of a racially diverse Mormon family has not always sat well. During Romney's run for the White House, in a March 2012 *Washington Post* article about the history of race and Mormonism, Randy Bott, a popular professor at Brigham Young University, not only cited the book of Abraham curse as justification for discrimination against the supposed black descendants of Cain and Ham. He also compared allowing blacks to have the priesthood before 1978 with giving the keys to the family car to a child before the child knows how to drive.[45]

Troubling as they are, both of these reactions to the depiction of a more racially diverse modern Mormonism highlight that when it comes to race and Mormonism, the past is not history. In response, the church has turned to the Internet, where it has provided its own take on the history of race and the faith. At the end of 2013, the church added a new article, "Race and the Priesthood," to the lds.org "Gospel Topics" website, an official church resource for historical and theological issues. A group of historians working for the Church History Library wrote the new two-thousand-word history lesson, which celebrates the fact the Joseph Smith opposed slavery when he ran for president in 1844 and embraced the likes of Jane Manning James and Elijah Abel as church members. Unlike the 1978 *Church News* articles, the new history lesson acknowledges that Abel was a priesthood holder, that he and James were denied access to the temple, and that church leaders often cited the curse of Cain as justification for such exclusion. What's more, in this statement, the church officially acknowledges that the restrictions on black membership were a product not of divine design but "merely the opinion of men"—in particular, the opinions of the church's own prophets, from Brigham Young to Joseph Fielding Smith.[46] The church still offers no apology for its past exclusionary policies and theologies. However, in what is perhaps the lesson's most important passage, the church states, "Today, the Church disavows the theories advanced in the past that black skin is a sign of divine disfavor or curse, or that it reflects actions in premortal life; that mixed-race marriages are a sin; or that blacks or people of any other race or ethnicity are inferior in any way to anyone else."[47]

From Joseph Smith Jr. to his grandnephew Joseph Fielding Smith, the presidents and prophets of the church taught that black skin marked people of African descent as unworthy of full participation in the restored church, though the first Mormon prophet believed that blacks could overcome their curses and become white and delightsome members of the Mormon covenant. In 2013, for the first time, the church officially repudiated the view that black and Mormon are, or should have ever been considered, mutually exclusive identities.

However, to end where this book began—with the Book of Mormon—this modern move to decouple the "peculiar" Mormon identity with any particular racial identity started at least two decades before. In 1981, the church released an updated Book of Mormon, which included footnotes correlating Mormonism's foundational text with other texts in the Mormon canon, including the Bible. The new edition also included twenty significant revisions to the text itself.[48] Perhaps the most significant change was to 2 Nephi 30:6, in which the phrase "they shall be a white and a delightsome people"—the passage cited countless times to support the belief that Native Americans could be redeemed from their ancient curses—to "they shall be a *pure* and a delightsome people." Many critics of the church have asserted that this change was an attempt to cover up a belief in white supremacy in the faith's foundational text.[49] However, the church and Mormon apologists have argued that the change was a restoration itself. They point out that in the 1840 edition of the Book of Mormon, Joseph Smith made the same scriptural adjustment, though subsequent printings did not follow suit.[50]

Whatever the reason, in 1981 the choice to change "white" to its signifying synonym "pure" corresponds with a post-1978 church attempting to become the spiritual home to all nations, kindreds, tongues, and peoples. This universalism—be it a restoration or an innovation—has become decoupled from whiteness in the modern church. Yet in Mormon culture whiteness and purity have another synonym: unity.[51] Joseph Smith's mandate to end schisms within the human family remains central to the church's modern mission. In today's church, this manifests in the centralized authority invested in the hierarchy in Salt Lake City. The literal gathering of the church to Zion has ended. But, starting in the second half of the twentieth century, as the central tent pole in Salt Lake has attempted to correlate every stake and branch across the globe—to have Latter-day Saints in Kenya and Kentucky, Provo and Prague, literally on the same page each Sunday—the metaphorical gathering continues. This gathering occurs around a unified set of intersecting identities: upwardly mobile, (heterosexually) married with children, and socially conservative, if not also politically so.

This gathering is also virtual. Every spring and fall, Mormon communities from around the world tune in to the church's semiannual general conference, now broadcast live online. And as they look at the all but exclusively white brethren, they might remark, as one black Mormon woman, Jerri Harwell, who frequently reenacts Jane Manning James's autobiography before civic and religious gatherings throughout the Salt Lake Valley, has quipped, "Zion is still all white. All is well in Zion."[52]

This will change. More nonwhite Mormon men—Mormon authority, of course, remains patriarchal—will achieve such levels of success in their career and family life that they will be called to join the ranks of the hierarchies of seventy, twelve, three, and perhaps even of one. Yet the image of these successful men (as well as a handful of women), whose talks are projected outward from the grand conference center to the rest of the Mormon world, demonstrate that, even as whiteness slips off of the Mormon body, the Mormon identity remains aspirational, in this world and the next.[53]

To be Mormon is not to *be* but to *become* pure and delightsome.

NOTES

Abbreviations

BofM — Joseph Smith Jr., *The Book of Mormon*, 1st ed. (Palmyra, N.Y.: E. B. Grandin, 1830) (Note: when citing the first edition of the Book of Mormon, I provide the page number of that edition, followed by the related 1981 edition's book, chapter, and verse—e.g., BofM, 22 [1 Nephi 15:17])

BYP — Brigham Young Papers, CR 1234 1, Church History Library, the Church of Jesus Christ of Latter-day Saints, Salt Lake City

CHL — Church History Library, the Church of Jesus Christ of Latter-day Saints, Salt Lake City

D&C — *The Doctrine and Covenants of the Church of Jesus Christ of Latter-day Saints: Containing Revelations Given to Joseph Smith, the Prophet, with Some Additions by His Successors in the Presidency of the Church* (Salt Lake City: Church of Jesus Christ of Latter-day Saints, 1981) (Note: when citing earlier editions of *D&C*, I indicate the year of publication and section of that edition, followed by the related 1981 *D&C* section and verse—e.g., *D&C* (1835), sec. XVIII [*D&C* 57:1–4])

DHC — *History of the Church of Jesus Christ of Latter-day Saints*, edited by B. H. Roberts, vols. 1–7 (Salt Lake City: Deseret News, 1902–32)

DN — *Deseret News*, Salt Lake City, June 15, 1850–present

E&MS — *Evening and the Morning Star* (Independence, Mo.), June 1832–July 1833; (Kirtland, Ohio), December 1833–September 1834

EPB — *Early Patriarchal Blessings of the Church of Jesus Christ of Latter-day Saints*, edited by H. Michael Marquardt (Salt Lake City: Smith-Pettit Foundation, 2007)

GCM — General Church Minutes, CR 100 318, Church History Library, the Church of Jesus Christ of Latter-day Saints, Salt Lake City

JD — *Journal of Discourses by Brigham Young, His Two Counsellors, the Twelve Apostles and Others*, vols. 1–26 (Liverpool and London: various publishers, 1854–86)

JH — *Journal History of the Church*, Church History Library, the Church of Jesus Christ of Latter-day Saints, Salt Lake City

JSH1 — *The Joseph Smith Papers*, Histories, vol. 1, *Joseph Smith Histories, 1832–1844*, edited by Karen Lynn Davidson et al. (Salt Lake City: Church Historian's Press, 2012)

JSPP — Joseph Smith Papers Project, Church History Department, the Church of Jesus Christ of Latter-day Saints, http://josephsmithpapers.org

LPB	*Later Patriarchal Blessings of the Church of Jesus Christ of Latter-day Saints*, edited by H. Michael Marquardt (Salt Lake City: Smith-Pettit Foundation, 2012)
M&A	*Latter-day Saints' Messenger & Advocate* (Manchester), May 1840–March 1842; (Liverpool), April 1842–March 3, 1932; (London), March 10, 1932–December 1970
MS	*Latter-day Saints' Millennial Star* (Manchester), May 1840–March 1842; (Liverpool), April 1842–March 3, 1932; (London), March 10, 1932–December 1970
RT1	*The Joseph Smith Papers*, Revelations and Translations, vol. 1, *Manuscript Revelation Books*, edited by Robin Scott Jensen, Robert J. Woodford, and Steven C. Harper (Salt Lake City: Church Historian's Press, 2011)
RT2	*The Joseph Smith Papers*, Revelations and Translations, vol. 2, *Published Revelations*, edited by Robin Scott Jensen, Robert J. Woodford, and Steven C. Harper (Salt Lake City: Church Historian's Press, 2011)
T&S	*Times & Seasons* (Commerce/Nauvoo, Ill.), November 1839–February 1846

Prologue

1. Here I draw from the source of the first published versions of the "History of Joseph Smith," which appeared in *T&S* beginning in 1842. "History Drafts, 1838–ca. 1841," *JSH1*, 220–22. During his lifetime, Smith wrote or dictated several versions of his history. See "Series Introduction," *JSH1*, xiii–xxxiv.

2. On Joseph Smith's money digging, see Bushman, *Rough Stone Rolling*, 48–54, 232–33.

3. "History Drafts, 1838–ca. 1841," *JSH1*, 220–21.

4. Ibid., 208–15. For the evolution of the "First Vision," see Bushman, *Rough Stone Rolling*, 30–56.

5. "History Drafts, 1838–ca. 1841," *JSH1*, 222–40.

6. Kidd, *Forging of Races*, 138–40, 235.

7. On Mormon men taking "Lamanite" women as wives so "that their posterity become white, delightsome and Just," see W. W. Phelps to Brigham Young, August 12, 1861, reprinted in Hardy, *Works of Abraham*, 35–37.

8. In this book, I consider "Mormon," "Latter-day Saint," and "Saint" as synonyms. I also use "Mormon" as parts of proper names (e.g., "Book of Mormon") and as an adjective ("Mormon pioneer"). Although the "Mormon Church" has long been the most common nickname for the church, I use the church's official name, "The Church of Jesus Christ of Latter-day Saints," as the first reference in each chapter and refer to it as "the church" thereafter. See Neilson, *Exhibiting Mormonism*, 4n3.

9. Kane, *Mormons*, 72; George A. Smith, "Indian War," October 7, 1853, *JD* 1:197. There is some debate about the relationship between Wakara and Arapeen. Sondra Jones has explained that most early Mormon writers wrongly identified Arapeen and

other Ute chiefs as Wakara's brothers, failing to understand the Ute kinship system in which brothers, half-brothers, and cousins would have all been considered brothers in Ute culture. Jones, *Trial of Don Pedro Léon Luján*, 147–48n25.

10. Visions of Arapine, BYP.

11. Ibid.

12. Gates, "'Aunt Jane' James," 551.

13. James and Roundy, "Biography of Jane E. James"; Gates, "'Aunt' Jane James."

14. "History Drafts, 1838–ca. 1841," *JSH1*, 204.

15. Jane E. James to John Taylor, Salt Lake City, December 27, 1884, transcribed in Wolfinger, "Test of Faith," 148.

16. Barney, "Jane Manning James."

Introduction

1. Bloom, *American Religion*; Hatch, *Democratization of American Christianity*, 113–22; Park, "Early Mormon Patriarchy," 183–84.

2. Givens, *Viper on the Hearth*, 177.

3. Haws, *Mormon Image in the American Mind*, 5, emphasis in original.

4. Mueller, "History Lessons."

5. By adding the category of race, this book attempts to join recent studies that have demonstrated how the institutional church and the Mormon people played a critical role in defining the boundaries of religious, legal, political, and cultural American identities in the late nineteenth and early twentieth centuries. See Fluhman, *"Peculiar People"*; Gordon, *Mormon Question*; and Flake, *Politics of American Religious Identity*.

6. For the most prominent example, see Reeve, *Religion of a Different Color*, 14–51, 171–214. Jacobson, *Whiteness of a Different Color*, 40–52; Goldstein, *Price of Whiteness*; Roediger, *Working toward Whiteness*.

7. James, "Making Sense of Race and Racial Classification," 32.

8. Bloom, *American Religion*, 83.

9. Joseph Young, "Remarks on Behalf of the Indians," July 13, 1855, *JD* 9:230; Fluhman, *"Peculiar People,"* 1–18.

10. May, "Mormons," 47, 61; Shipps, "Making Saints," 71–80; Reeve, *Religion of a Different Color*, 14–51.

11. Sussman, *Myth of Race*, 11–42.

12. Caldwell, *Thoughts on the Original Unity*, 9–18, 65, 72–73, 74–81. On early modern racial science and its relation to racialized scriptural exegeses, see Kidd, *Forging of Races*, 12–167.

13. Quoted in Lepore, *Name of War*, 6.

14. Ibid., 28–29; Goetz, *Baptism of Early Virginia*, 91–95.

15. Gookin, "Historical Collections of the Indian of New England," 223, 144; Lepore, *Name of War*, 6.

16. See Rebecca Goetz's description of the English settlers' and planters' notion of Indian and African "hereditary heathenism." Goetz, *Baptism of Early Virginia*, 5–12.

17. Lepore, *Name of War*, ix–xxiii.

18. Jackson, "On Indian Removal."

19. Quoted in Goetz, *Baptism of Early Virginia*, 59.

20. Ibid., 10.

21. Quoted in Hayne's *Noah's Curse*, 129; Mather, *King Philip's War*, 46.

22. Armstrong, *Christian Doctrine of Slavery*, 133, 134.

23. In 1776, as the Continental Army fought for the colonies' freedom, Congregationalist theologian Samuel Hopkins described slavery as the nascent nation's "public sin," for which the "sons of liberty" would have to atone if they hoped to separate themselves from the British crown's tyrannical rule. In his Second Inaugural Address in 1865, Abraham Lincoln observed that the Civil War's great cost was a sign that the debt of "American slavery," on which the nation had been built, had not been repaid. Hopkins, *Dialogue Concerning the Slavery*, 11; Lincoln, *Second Inaugural Address*. In 1841, former president turned congressman John Quincy Adams described U.S. Indian policy as "among the heinous sins of this nation, for which I believe God will one day bring them to judgment." Adams, *Diaries*, June 30, 1841, 385.

24. Revelation, August 1830 [*D&C* 27:6], *RT2*, 490.

25. BofM, 104 [2 Nephi 25:16]. See also "To Man."

26. Steward, *Twenty-Two Years a Slave*, 156–57.

27. Apess, *Son of the Forest*, 20–21.

28. Kidd, *Forging of Races*, 1–53; Haynes, *Noah's Curse*, 65–104; Glaude, *Exodus!*, 3–18.

29. Noll, "Why Theology Now?"

30. Of course, the Mormons were not alone in this ambition. Centuries before Joseph Smith founded his church, Protestant and Catholic missionaries had worked to convert African and other indigenous peoples in the hopes of folding them into supposedly more civilized and Christian communities. Yet the early Mormons' insistence that conversion would lead not only to symbolic but literal change in skin color is unique. For a few of the important studies on Protestant and Catholic missions to African and Native American peoples, see Sensbach, *Rebecca's Revival*; Conklin, *Mission to Civilize*; Sandos, *Converting California*; and Sleeper-Smith, *Indian Women and French Men*.

31. BofM, 117 [2 Nephi 30:8].

32. Shipps, "Another Side of Early Mormonism," 6; Givens, *Hand of Mormon*, 4, 70; Barlow, *Mormons and the Bible*, 47–48; Underwood, "Book of Mormon Usage."

33. Givens, *Hand of Mormon*, 190–91.

34. "History of Brigham Young," May 13, 1851, quoted in Brooks, "Indian Relations," 6. See also Levi Jackman, Journal, July 28, 1847, CHL; and W. W. Phelps to Brigham Young, August 12, 1861, reprinted in Hardy, *Works of Abraham*, 37.

35. On the evolution of the church's views of people of African descent, see Bush, "Mormonism's Negro Doctrine"; Wolfinger, "Test of Faith"; Bringhurst, *Saints, Slaves, and Blacks*; Mauss, *All Abraham's Children*; and Reeve, *Religion of a Different Color*. On the evolution of the church's views of people of Native American descent, see Brooks, "Indian Relations"; Vogel, *Indian Origins*; Walker, "Seeking the 'Remnant'"; Mauss, *All Abraham's Children*; Farmer, *Zion's Mount*; and Reeve, *Religion of a Different Color*.

36. Reeve, *Religion of a Different Color*, 106–39, 171–87.

37. Following Ann Laura Stoler's approach, here I pay particular attention to the porosity of the institutional archive of the church and state, which allows for those marginalized in the official archive to write themselves into what Stoler calls the global "force field in which documents were produced." Stoler, *Along the Archival Grain*, 14. As such, I also follow Thomas Richards in rejecting Jacques Derrida's understanding of the archive as an "arkheion," a library or museum where "data" of the state are preserved and from which sections are drawn to create a narration in order to disseminate knowledge for the greater public good. Instead, I understand "the imperial archive . . . [as] a fantasy of knowledge collected and united in the service of the state and Empire." Richards, *Imperial Archive*, 6; Derrida, *Archive Fever*, 2.

38. "History Drafts, 1838–ca. 1841," *JSH1*, 222, 240. John-Charles Duffy has written, "The plates are thus a potential 'scandal' in the sense of the Greek *skandalan*: a stumbling block to conversation about Mormonism across the religious divide and hence to the mainstreaming of Mormon studies." Duffy, "Just How 'Scandalous'?"

39. Twain, *Roughing It*, 127.

40. Bloom, *American Religion*, 86. See also O'Dea, *Mormons*, 26; and Bushman, *Rough Stone Rolling*, 84–85.

41. Fish, *Is There a Text?*

42. This is also Susan Harding's conclusion about late twentieth-century Christian fundamentalists: "Christians for whom Bible prophecy is true do not inhabit the same historical landscape as nonbelievers." Harding, *Book of Jerry Falwell*, 232.

43. Hardy, *Understanding the Book of Mormon*, 27.

44. Ibid., xvi.

45. History, 1838–1856, C-1 (ID # 7513), JSPP, http://www.josephsmithpapers.org/paperSummary/history-1838-1856-volume-c-1-2-november-1838-31-july-1842?p=427&highlight=key%20stone.

46. Higginbotham, "African-American Women's History and the Metalanguage of Race," 254–55.

47. Foucault, *Order of Things*, 207–9.

48. Caldwell, *Thoughts on the Original Unity*, 81.

49. BofM, 501 [3 Nephi 21:23].

50. Ricoeur, *Memory, History, Forgetting*, 380.

51. Postcolonial theorists have been more attuned to the racial and political impli-

cations of the archive than have philosophers like Ricoeur. Said, *Orientalism*, 41–42; Hall, "West and the Rest."

52. Lepore, *Name of War*, xviii. On the importance of literacy in the construction of racial hierarchy in American history, see Gates, *Signifying Monkey*, 127–69.

53. For race and the "writerly self," see Morrison, *Playing in the Dark*, xii.

54. BofM, 109 [2 Nephi 26:33].

55. BofM, 105, 123, 518 [2 Nephi 25:22, Jacob 1:3, 4 Nephi 1:48].

56. Revelation July 20, 1831 [*D&C* 57:2], *RT1*, 159.

Chapter 1

1. For direct addresses to the Gentiles, see, among others, BofM, 524, 528 [Mormon 3:17, 5:22].

2. BofM, 29, 30, 75, 78 [1 Nephi 13:15, 13:26, 2 Nephi 6:12, 9:2]; Joseph Smith, "History Drafts, 1838–ca. 1841," *JSH1*, 328.

3. BofM, 57–58, 487–88 [1 Nephi 22:6–12, 3 Nephi 16:4–16]. See also BofM, 499–501 [3 Nephi 21:4–7, 22–24].

4. Shipps, "Prophet Puzzle," 67.

5. BofM, 29 [1 Nephi 13:10–19]; Farmer, *Zion's Mount*, 56.

6. Givens, *Hand of Mormon*, 89–116.

7. BofM, 36 [1 Nephi 15:13].

8. During the 2012 presidential campaign, biblical scholar Obery Hendricks demanded that, if he hoped to be the president of "all Americans," Mitt Romney had "to disavow the portions of your holy book that so sorely denigrate the humanity of me, my loved ones and all people of black African descent." Hendricks, "Mitt Romney and the Curse of Blackness," http://www.huffingtonpost.com/obery-m-hendricks-jr-phd/mitt-romney-curse-blackness_b_1200470.html.

9. BofM, 28, 528 [1 Nephi 12:23, Mormon 5:15].

10. Jackson, "On Indian Removal."

11. BofM, 117 [2 Nephi 30:8].

12. BofM, 529 [Mormon 6:1–6].

13. BofM, 519, 520 [Mormon 1:14, 2:3–4].

14. BofM, 518–29 [Mormon 1:5–6:1–6].

15. BofM, 5, 15 [1 Nephi 1:2, 5:14–17]. Moroni writes that the histories would have been written in Hebrew "if our plates had been sufficiently large," but Egyptian was a more compact script. BofM, 538 [Mormon 9:33].

16. BofM, 518–19, 529, 326–27 [Mormon 1:2–4, 6:6, Alma 37:1–20].

17. BofM, 531 [Mormon 7:5].

18. There are three main Nephite narrators in the Book of Mormon. Nephi, son of Lehi and founder of the Nephite people in the New World, is the narrator of the first two books of the Book of Mormon, 1 Nephi and 2 Nephi. Mormon, the last Nephite military general, is charged with abridging, editing, and narrating a millennium's

worth of Nephite history, from the Words of Mormon through Mormon 7. After Mormon's death, his son Moroni takes over the record keeping. He completes Mormon 8–9 and narrates the demise of the last Nephites. He also abridges the history of the Jaredites (the book of Ether), another Israelite people who arrived in America before Lehi and his family. Thanks to Grant Hardy for helping me shift through these complex layers of narration.

19. See, among many others, BofM, 5, 42–43 [1 Nephi, chapter introduction, 17:1–14]. On Puritan notions of the New World "wilderness" as the promised land for a people in exile, see Zakai, *Exile and Kingdom*, 156–206.

20. BofM, 6–8, 42–43 [1 Nephi 1:18–2:13, 17:7–14].

21. BofM, 71–73 [2 Nephi 5:1–24].

22. For Christ's teachings to the Nephites, see BofM, 476–510 [3 Nephi 11:1–28:12].

23. The "Lamb of God" (Christ), along with "the angel of the Lord" reveal this prophecy to the first Nephites centuries before Christ's mission in the New World. BofM, 30–31 [1 Nephi 13:23–35].

24. BofM, 509 [3 Nephi 27:23–26].

25. BofM, 31 [1 Nephi 13:35].

26. BofM, 515 [4 Nephi 1–17].

27. BofM, 517 [4 Nephi 1:35–38].

28. BofM, 526, 532, 574 [Mormon 4:21, 8:2–3, Moroni 1:2].

29. BofM, 527 [Mormon 5:5]. As Jill Lepore has written, during King Philip's War, "To many colonists . . . English possessions were, in a sense, what was at stake in the war, for these—the clothes they wore, the houses they lived in, and the things they owned—were a good part of what differentiated the English from the Indians." Lepore, *Name of War*, 79.

30. BofM, 529 [Mormon 6:6].

31. BofM, 530–32 [Mormon 7:1–Moroni 1:4].

32. BofM, 528 [Mormon 5:15].

33. BofM, 36, 528 [1 Nephi 15:17, Mormon 5:20, 14].

34. Horsman, *Race and Manifest Destiny*, 189–204.

35. BofM, 75, 57 [2 Nephi 29:14, 1 Nephi 22:6].

36. BofM, 117 [2 Nephi 30:5–6].

37. BofM, 57, 586 [1 Nephi 22:6, Moroni 10:19]. Revelation, September 1830 [*D&C* 29:31–34], *RT1*, 47–49.

38. BofM, 64–65, 536 [2 Nephi 2:19–22, Mormon 9:12], Genesis 3:6–7, Romans 5:12. However, the second article in the church's Articles of Faith, which were published in *T&S* in 1842 and canonized in 1880 as part of the Pearl of Great Price, states, "We believe that men will be punished for their own sins, and not for Adam's transgression."

39. Flournoy, *Essay on the Origin*, 5.

40. See "Extract from the Prophecy of Enoch," which reprints Smith's 1830 translation of what would become known as the book of Moses. Moses contains an elabo-

rated version of humanity's first murder, the punishment of which is a curse against Cain, which marks him off from the rest of Adam's progeny.

41. BofM, 71–72 [2 Nephi 5:3–19]. Kim, "Cain and Abel."

42. BofM, 73 [2 Nephi 5:21–23].

43. BofM, 515 [4 Nephi 1:17]. In the eighteenth century, Georges-Louis Leclerc, Comte de Buffon, along with Johann Blumenbach, proposed that the races evolved owing to their "degeneration" from a pure Caucasian origin. Degeneration could be reversed if the proper environmental and cultural conditions were established. Harris, *Rise of Anthropological Theory*, 84–85.

44. BofM, 517 [4 Nephi 1:35–39].

45. As Warren Montag has written, "One of the moments in the invention of the white race was its universalization in a movement that replaced the distinction between black and white 'races' . . . with the distinction between the human and the animal. To be white is to be human, and to be human is to be white." Montag, "Universalization of Whiteness," 285.

46. BofM, 174 [Mosiah 9:8–15].

47. There is one notable exception to this direct link between whiteness and literacy in the Book of Mormon. The descendants of Mulek are also ostensibly white. Latter-day Saints call these people Mulekites, but in the Book of Mormon, they are referred to as the "people of Zarahemla" (Helaman 8:21, Omni 1). Mulek was the only son of Zedekiah, the last king of Judah. He and his family fled to the New World after the Babylonian conquest of Jerusalem but before Lehi and his family's own arrival in the New World. By the time the Nephites discovered them and began to live among them, the Mulekites had become illiterate, "their language had become corrupted," and they had forgotten the faith of their forefathers because "they had brought no records with them" (Omni 1:17).

48. There are a few suggestions of Lamanite literacy in the Book of Mormon (e.g., Mosiah 24:5–7, Helaman 3:15, Mormon 6:2). Most explicitly, just before his people are converted to proto-Christianity, "the King of the Lamanites sent out a proclamation among all his people"—suggesting that the king was able to write—that they should not imprison, enslave, or persecute the Nephite missionaries to the Lamanites (Alma 23:1–23, 47:1). The exact contents of these proclamations are not included in the Book of Mormon.

49. BofM, 502 [3 Nephi 23:4].

50. Ibid.

51. BofM, 478, 505 [3 Nephi 11:32, 26:2].

52. BofM, 499–501 [3 Nephi 21:1, 5–6, 22–25].

53. BofM, 528, 574 [Mormon 5:15, Moroni 1:1–4].

54. Richard Bushman has written, "History is one of the spoils of war. In great conflicts, the victors almost always write the history; the losers' story is forgotten. . . . The reverse is true of the Book of Mormon. The Lamanites vanquished the Nephites and

survived; yet by virtue of a record that went into the earth with them, the Nephites' version of the story is the one we now read." Bushman, "Lamanite View," 79.

55. The concept of a "narrator's prerogative" is frequently used in literary studies but not as much in religious studies. For example, Deborah G. Plant has written, "The narrator's prerogative to withhold information is also a device to conceal anything that might upset the equilibrium she has created. It is also, perhaps, a flaunted indication of her power as narrator and as the controlling force in her world." Plant, *Every Tub Must Sit*, 27-28. Drawing from Bakhtin and Pascal, Gerald Prince describes "monologic narrative" as a "narrative characterized by a unifying voice or consciousness superior to other voices or consciousness in that narrative. . . . In monologic as opposed to dialogic narrative, the narrator's views, judgments, and knowledge constitute the ultimate authority with respect to the world presented." Prince, *Dictionary of Narratology*, 54.

56. BofM, title page, 7, 151, 527, 574 [title page, 1 Nephi 1:17, Words of Mormon 1:3, Mormon 5:9, Moroni 1:1].

57. BofM, 516 [4 Nephi 1:26].

58. BofM, 585 [Moroni 9:24].

59. BofM, 532 [Mormon 8:13-14].

60. BofM, 584-85 [Moroni 9:15, 18-19].

61. BofM, 527 [Mormon 5:9].

62. Anthony W. Marx has written that the creation of a "'family memory' of unity . . . rests upon purposeful amnesia of those deadly quarrels that tore apart the [familial or political] unit at its formation." Marx, *Faith in Nation*, 29-30.

63. German historian and theologian Peter Meinhold wrote extensively on how the Book of Mormon created for its first believers a "usable past" about America. Meinhold, "Die Anfänge des Amerikanischen Geschichtsbewusstseins," 65-86.

64. Even on what would become the Book of Mormon's title page—which Joseph Smith later described as the "last leaf" of Mormon's abridged narrative of the Nephite archive—Moroni explains that the Book of Mormon is an epistolic narrative, "written to the Lamanites" to remind them that they "are a remnant of the house of Israel." BofM, title page, 515 [title page, 1 Nephi 1:17].

65. BofM, 564, 565, title page [Ether 12:23, 40, title page].

66. BofM, 515-16, 71 [4 Nephi 1:19-21, 2 Nephi 5:1-4]; Hardy, *Understanding the Book of Mormon*, 39-44.

67. BofM, 499 [3 Nephi 21:1].

68. Lehi's wife, Sariah, is one of only three named female characters in the Book of Mormon. Even when Nephi mentions his mother (BofM, 14-15 [1 Nephi 5:1-9]), Sariah is presented as both a complaining wife as well as a witness to her husband's prophethood. Hardy, *Understanding the Book of Mormon*, 18-22, 288n3.

69. BofM, 73, 146, 228 [2 Nephi 5:24, Jarom 1:6, Alma 3:5-6].

70. BofM, 527, 526, 529 [Mormon 5:5, 4:21, 6:6].

71. Lepore, *Name of War*, 199–226.

72. Salisbury, "Red Puritans," 28; Cronon, *Changes in the Land*, 128–29.

73. Quoted in Lepore, *Name of War*, 105. Bernard Sheehan has argued that the 1622 Powhatan uprising in Virginia held the same lesson about innate Indian savagery as did King Philip's War. Sheehan, *Savagism and Civility*.

74. In September 1783, Presbyterian deacon and editor of the *Freeman's Journal* Francis Bailey cautioned his fellow countrymen not to celebrate independence too early. The "disposition of the savages," Bailey wrote, meant that America's freedom would not be secured until it was taken from the Indians by a "heavy [military] campaign" into their territories. Quoted in Silver, *Our Savage Neighbors*, 261–63.

75. Cooper, *Notions of the Americans*, 277, 281; Taylor, *William Cooper's Town*, 40.

76. Boudinot, *Address to the Whites*. This Elias Boudinot is not to be confused with the New Jersey delegate to the Continental Congress and, after the Revolution, a U.S. congressman and director of the U.S. Mint. Studies of the Book of Mormon are often more interested in this Boudinot: in 1816 he published *A Star in the West*, in which he proposed that the American Indians were the Lost Ten Tribes of Israel.

77. BofM, 56–59 [1 Nephi 22:5–31].

78. BofM, 421–22 [Helaman 5:49–52, 6:1–6].

79. Hickman, "Book of Mormon."

80. BofM, 503 [3 Nephi 23:7]. Following the custom of Book of Mormon exegesis, for clarity, I refer to Nephi whom Christ appointed as one of his New World disciples as "Nephi$_3$." Hardy, *Book of Mormon*, 701.

81. BofM, 503 [3 Nephi 23:6–13]. See Samuel's prophecy, BofM, 447 [Helaman 14:25].

82. Here the Book of Mormon is unclear whether Nephi$_3$ is the narrator of Samuel's prophecy. It is possible that Nephi$_3$ serves more as a scribe to Christ's own dictation of Samuel's testimony, which had been forgotten but never should have been. BofM, 503 [3 Nephi 23:10–14].

83. Jared Hickman describes this exchange between Christ and Nephi$_3$, and the subsequent addition of Samuel's Lamanite voice into the Nephite record, as the Book of Mormon's "archival aporia." Hickman, "Book of Mormon."

84. "Re-presenting" Samuel's prophecy in its proper historical order is of great "creative power," as Ricoeur might suggest, "opening up the past again to the future," and creating a new hermeneutic of the entire Book of Mormon racial schema. Ricoeur, *Memory, History, Forgetting*, 380. The lessons included in Samuel's prophecies are so important for the book's future readers that in the first edition of the Book of Mormon, they are given their own headnote: "THE PROPHECY OF SAMUEL, THE LAMANITE," it reads in all capital letters, "TO THE NEPHITES." BofM, 441. For the only other two instance in which the Book of Mormon addresses itself specifically to ethnically defined audiences, see headnote for Helaman 7 (BofM, 426) and BofM, title page.

85. BofM, 441 [Helaman 13:4]. Readers today, like many of the early Mormons for whom the King James Bible was the major source of literary archetypes, would likely find that Samuel's prophetic pronouncements parallel those of Amos (ca. 750 B.C.) at the walls of Samaria, the capital city of the Israelite northern kingdom, decadent and idolatrous of wealth. See Amos 6:1-9 and Jeremias, *Book of Amos*, 108-20.

86. BofM, 450, 448 [Helaman 16:7, 15:5].

87. BofM, 421-22 [Helaman 5:49-52-6:1-6].

88. BofM, 441 [Helaman 13:5].

89. BofM, 442, 472-73 [Helaman 13:7, 14, 3 Nephi 9:3, 11-13].

90. BofM, 443 [Helaman 13:21-23].

91. BofM, 444, 445 [Helaman 13:29, 14:10], emphasis added.

92. BofM, 449 [Helaman 16:1-3].

93. BofM, 448, 449, 441, 422 [Helaman, 15:4-6, 17, 13:1, 6:1-5].

94. BofM, 193 [Mosiah 18:17, 21].

95. BofM, 456 [3 Nephi 2:14-16]. As Jared Hickman has pointed out, Samuel does not belong to "the people of Ammon" who had been "converted unto the Lord" by Ammon and his brothers during their mission to the Lamanites sixty years before Jesus's birth. These (former) Lamanites lived in Zarahemla, where they had enjoyed the protection of the Nephites and became white (Alma 53:10). Hickman, "Book of Mormon," 452.

96. BofM, 472-73 [3 Nephi 9].

97. For a rare example, see the patriarchal blessing of Dana Jacobs, June 13, 1837, EPB, 165.

98. Hardy, *Understanding the Book of Mormon*, 33.

99. BofM, 121-22 [2 Nephi 33:1-4].

100. BofM, 463-64, 529 [3 Nephi 5:11, 17, Mormon 6:9].

101. BofM, 529 [Mormon 6:10]. The Mormon-raised literacy theorist Wayne C. Booth first articulated the concept of the "unreliable narrator." Booth, *Rhetoric of Fiction*, 158-59.

102. BofM, 449 [Helaman 16:1], emphasis added.

103. Hardy, *Understanding the Book of Mormon*, 105-6.

104. Thomson, "Memory and Remembering in Oral History," 79-80.

105. Of course, these records are destined to reach his "brethren" the Lamanites in the latter days. BofM, 105, 530-37 [2 Nephi 25:20-23, Mormon 7-9].

106. BofM, 154 [Mosiah 1:1-5], emphasis added. The Mulekites, who also lost the faith of their fathers as well as their ability to read and write because they did not bring records with them from Israel, serve as an important example of the connection between literacy and faith. See BofM, 149-50 [Omni 1:12-19].

107. BofM, 452, 464, 532 [3 Nephi 1:2, 5:20, Mormon 8:13].

108. Quoted in Loewenberg and Bogin, *Black Women*, 138-39.

109. As Jared Hickman has argued, "The inclusion of Samuel's voice in The Book of Mormon represents not only an aporia but an apocalypse within and of the text that completes the internal—and thus divinely approved, as it were—case for reading the Nephite narrative with a hermeneutics of suspicion." Hickman, "Book of Mormon," 454.

110. Apess, "Indian's Looking-Glass," 51.

111. Occom, *Collected Writings*, 89. Also in 1768, Occom wrote *A Short Narrative of My Life*, in which he accused white missionaries of racism after they failed to uphold their promise to recognize Indian converts as equal brothers in Christ. Elrod, *Piety and Dissent*, 33–34.

112. Boudinot, *Address to the Whites*.

113. As Joanna Brooks has argued, "English-language literate Christian converts like Occom should not be viewed primarily as intercessors with the white world but as proponents of new and powerful definitions of Indianness." Brooks, *American Lazarus*, 55.

114. Apess, "Indian's Looking-Glass," 55.

115. BofM, 445 [Helaman 14:10], emphasis added; Occom, *Collected Writings*, 58, emphasis added. In his best-known work, *A Son of the Forest*, first published in 1829, Apess goes even farther. He challenges the notion that "whiteness" is the original race of man. "It is my opinion that our [Native] nation retains the original complexion of our common father Adam." And for that reason Apess, like Boudinot, rejects the name "Indian" as a "slur upon an oppressed and scattered nation." "The proper term which ought to be applied to our nation to distinguish it from the rest of the human family is that of *Natives*." According to Apess, Anglo-Americans were the interlopers on the American continent. Apess, *Son of the Forest*, 73, 20–21.

116. See Mark 12:31. Occom, *Collected Writings*, 58; Brooks, *American Lazarus*, 61.

117. Apess, "Indian's Looking-Glass," 55.

118. Ibid.

119. BofM, 443–44, 445 [Helaman 13:26–27, 14:10]. On the "epistemic privilege" of the oppressed, see Mohanty, *Literary Theory*, 198–253.

120. BofM, 177 [2 Nephi 30:5–6].

121. BofM 109, 73 [2 Nephi 26:33, 5:21].

122. BofM, 117 [2 Nephi 30:5–6].

123. Spivak, "Can the Subaltern Speak?"

124. Apess, *Son of the Forest*, reprinted in Apess and O'Connell, *On Our Own Ground*, 60.

125. Ebersole, *Captured by Texts*, 1–4, 15–60.

126. A Church of England missionary in nineteenth-century Alaska, William Duncan records the voices of Indian converts who report that as the "Indians 'become white' . . . [they] could 'talk on paper' and 'hear paper talk' and . . . wore white folks clothes, and lived in houses with windows, and forsook the Shaman, and ate no more

dog-flesh, and no longer killed one another." Quoted in Wright, *Among the Alaskans*, 203–4.

Chapter 2

1. "Book of Mormon," *Wayne Sentinel*, March 19, 1830, emphasis added.

2. Bushman, *Rough Stone Rolling*, 80; Tucker, *Origin, Rise, and Progress*, 51–52.

3. "Book of Mormon," *Reflector*, February 14, 1831.

4. "Book of Mormon," *Wayne Sentinel*, March 26, 1830; Bushman, *Joseph Smith*, 46.

5. Quoted in Givens, *Hand of Mormon*, 60.

6. Fluhman, *"Peculiar People,"* 99–125.

7. June 19–July 1831, History, 1838–1856, vol. A-1 (ID # 7268), JSPP, http://joseph smithpapers.org/paperSummary/history-1838-1856-volume-a-1-23-december-1805 -30-august-1834?p=135.

8. The church changed its name several times in the 1830s. It finally settled on its current name, the Church of Jesus Christ of Latter-day Saints, based on an 1838 revelation. See *D&C* 115:4.

9. Revelation, October 1830 [*D&C* 33:3], *RT1*, 59.

10. Rodney Stark has called the Smiths Mormonism's "Holy Family"—akin to the family of Islam's Muhammad and Judaism's Moses—through which the news of the faith spread outward through "networks" of kin, friends, and neighbors. Stark, "Mormon Networks of Faith," 57–59.

11. "History Drafts, 1838–ca. 1841," *JSH1*, 396; Bushman, *Rough Stone Rolling*, 116–18.

12. Berkhofer, *White Man's Indian*, 134–36; Pearce, *Savagism and Civilization*, 135–68.

13. Revelation to Oliver [Cowdery], September 1830 [*D&C* 28:8], *RT1*, 53.

14. BofM 36–37, 85 [1 Nephi 15:12–17, 2 Nephi 10:18].

15. Jackson, "On Indian Removal."

16. Berkhofer, *White Man's Indian*, 134–36.

17. "The Testimony of the Three Witnesses," "And Also the Testimony of the Eight Witnesses," BofM, 589, 590 (unnumbered).

18. Bowman, "Conversion of Parley Pratt," 178–87.

19. Here I am purposefully using the original preposition "among" instead of the edited "on the borders by." This editing of the original record most likely occurred between 1833 and 1835. This change is important. It was a response to the failure of the first mission to the Lamanites as well as the Missouri "old settler" concerns over Mormon "meddling" with the Indians. Revelation, September 1830 [*D&C* 28:9], *RT1*, 53. See also Walker, "'Seeking the 'Remnant,'" 10.

20. Stein, "'Taking Up the Full Cross,'" 93–110; Lippy, "Great Awakening," 44–52.

21. Staker, Hearken, *O Ye People*, 49–65; Bushman, *Rough Stone Rolling*, 144–60.

22. Oliver Cowdery to "beloved brethren," November 12, 1830 (ID# 1613), JSPP, http:// josephsmithpapers.org/paperSummary/letter-from-oliver-cowdery-12-november -1830?p=3#!/paperSummary/letter-from-oliver-cowdery-12-november-1830&p=3.

23. At the dedication of the Kirtland Temple on March 27, 1836 (*D&C* 109:60), through revelation, Smith indirectly identified early white Mormons as "Gentiles." Yet as I show in chapter 3, by 1835 the Mormons began to change their self-perception, moving away from identifying themselves as Gentiles and toward seeing themselves as literal descendants of the Lost Tribes of Israel.

24. Out of money, while Pratt, Cowdery, and Williams visited the Delawares, Whitmer and Peterson remained in Independence to work as tailors and probably to scout the land for possible Mormon settlements. Pratt, *Autobiography*, 56.

25. It is possible that the Mormon missionaries first heard about Chief Anderson from James Poole (also spelled Pool), a blacksmith from Virginia hired by the federal government to provide translation and smithing services to the Delawares. It is also possible that they heard about the Delawares from another Indian leader, Anthony Shane, with whom the missionaries spent their first night in Indian Territory. When the Mormons met him, Shane had recently relocated with a group of Shawnees to their new lands just south of the Delawares. The Mormons' stay with Shane was brief, perhaps because the longtime Baptist missionary to the Indians Isaac McCoy was already working to establish a mission among the Shawnees. Delilah Lykins, letters to Isaac McCoy, July 29 1831, August 3, 1831, reprinted in Ella, *Isaac McCoy*, 256–57; Jennings, "First Mormon Mission to the Indians," 291–92.

26. See letters and treaties signed by Anderson, reprinted in Cranor, *Kick Tha We Nund*.

27. Richard W. Cummins to William Clark, April 2, 1831, William Clark Papers; Weslager, *Delaware Indians*, 363–69.

28. Jennings, "First Mormon Mission to the Indians," 292–93.

29. Quoted in Dowd, *War under Heaven*, 102–4; Dowd, *Spirited Resistance*, 23–46.

30. Quoted in Jortner, *Gods of Prophetstown*, 29. See also Cave, *Prophets of the Great Spirit*, 34–39.

31. Heckewelder, *Narrative of the Mission*, 409–11.

32. For a history of Chief Anderson's important role in unifying the Delawares, see Weslager, *Delaware Indians*, 329–75.

33. Ibid., 342–44, 346; Olmstead, *Blackcoats among the Delaware*, 76–77.

34. McCoy, *History of Baptist Indian Missions*, 58–59, 52–53. See also Kluge and Luckenbach, *Moravian Indian Mission*, 431, 452–54, 608, 623.

35. Olmstead, *Blackcoats among the Delaware*, 124–26.

36. Ibid., 76–77, 222, 224–25; Olmstead, *David Zeisberger*, 246.

37. Oliver Cowdery to "beloved brethren," April 8, 1831 (ID# 3878), JSPP, http://josephsmithpapers.org/paperSummary/letter-from-oliver-cowdery-8-april-1831?dm =image-and-text&zm=zoom-inner&tm=expanded&p=1&s=undefined&sm=none.

38. Isaac McCoy, Field Notes of Delaware Lands, and William Clark to Lewis Cass, September 14, 1830, William Clark Papers. Like the Mormons and many other missionaries, McCoy hoped that Indian removal would lead to the creation of a pantribal

Indian homeland, which he called an "Indian Canaan." Yet McCoy did not share the Mormons' view that whites should participate in the creation of the Indians' own country. He believed that only when they separated from white settlements and became independent of white patronage, whiskey, and exploitive land prospectors could the Indians build their own farms, civic institutions, and Christian churches. Schultz, *Indian Canaan*, 67–70.

39. Richard Cummins's letter contains the first record of the Mormons' interest in proselytizing the Indians of the Intermountain West. It also pitted the Mormons' agenda for the Indians, and not for the last time, in conflict with that of the federal government. Richard W. Cummins to Clark, February 15, 1831, reprinted in Gentry, "Light on the 'Mission to the Lamanites,'" 234.

40. Givens and Grow, *Parley P. Pratt*, 46.

41. For example, Congregationalists in Oklahoma reported to their superiors in Boston that the Osages' heathenism did not allow them "to accomplish . . . a knowledge of the art of reading." William Montgomery to the Board of Commissioners of Foreign Missions, August 27, 1832, quoted in Pearce, *Savagism and Civilization*, 62.

42. In their 2011 biography of Pratt, Terryl Givens and Matthew Grow mostly avoid Pratt's autobiography as a source for the Mormons' first mission to the Lamanites. Yet the autobiography is a valuable window into how Pratt imagined a romanticized encounter between Mormons and Delawares and the Saints' desire to fulfill Book of Mormon prophecy. Givens and Grow, *Parley P. Pratt*, 46–48.

43. Pratt, *Autobiography*, 58. For Gentile displacement and subsequent redeeming of Lamanites, see 2 Nephi 10:10, 18, 3 Nephi 20:27–28, and 1 Nephi 22:7–9.

44. Pratt, *Autobiography*, 58.

45. Ibid., 58–59, emphasis added.

46. By this I mean covenants *as contracts*, as in the legalistic term referring to a written or spoken agreement between two or more parties—in this case between a people and God—and among a community of people. For precedents to Mormon covenantal theology, see Cooper, *Promises*, 14–49; and Miller, *New England Mind*, 398–431.

47. W. W. Phelps to Brigham Young, August 12, 1861, reprinted in Hardy, *Works of Abraham*, 37.

48. Wellenreuther and Wessel, *Moravian Mission Diaries*, 48n162. See also Sleeper-Smith, *Indian Women and French Men*.

49. Gaul, *To Marry an Indian*.

50. Newell and Avery, *Mormon Enigma*, 65; Van Wagoner, *Mormon Polygamy*, 3.

51. Walker, "'Seeking the 'Remnant,'" 10; Mauss, *All Abraham's Children*, 119. See also Mormon apostate Ezra Booth's letter to Eber D. Howe: "It has been made known by revelation, that it will be pleasing to the Lord, should they [Mormon missionaries] form matrimonial alliances with the natives, and by this means the Elders, who comply with the thing so pleasing to the Lord, and for the Lord has promise to bless

those who do it abundantly, gain a residence in the Indian territory." Howe, *Mormonism Unvailed*, 220.

52. Pratt, *Autobiography*, 60.

53. Pratt (or Pratt's editors) refers to the Indian Territory just west of the Missouri state border as "Kansas," even though Kansas would not become a state until January 29, 1861. This anachronism emphasizes the retrospective nature of Pratt's account. Ibid., 43.

54. Ibid., 60.

55. Ibid. See the "Trope of the Talking Book" in Gates, *Signifying Monkey*, 127.

56. Pratt, *Autobiography*, 60–61.

57. Jennings, "First Mormon Mission," 295.

58. William Myers to Pierre Menard, August 8, 1831, William Clark Papers.

59. Cranor, *Kick Tha We Nund*, 14–15, emphasis.

60. As Ronald Walker puts it, "The history of that tiny missionary band is now a saga. En route to their destination, the missionaries preached in the Western Reserve and reaped a bounteous harvest of converts in and about Kirtland, Ohio—not of red but of white people who dramatically changed the flow of LDS history." Walker, "Seeking the 'Remnant,'" 7.

61. G. St. John Stott, "New Jerusalem Abandoned," 80–81; Campbell, *New Jerusalem*, 32–33.

62. Whitmer, *From Historian to Dissident*, 57; Howe, *Mormonism Unvailed*, 184–85.

63. Revelation, May 9, 1831 [*D&C* 50:4, 1–46], *RT1*, 137.

64. This is also true for the Moravian missions to the Delaware Indians. John Heckewelder's narrative contains lengthy dialogues between missionaries and Indians as well as speeches from Delaware chiefs, which putatively took places sometimes decades before he composed his history in the 1810s. Heckewelder, *Narrative of the Mission*, 222–25, 328–29.

65. Staker, *Hearken, O Ye People*, 44–45, 53–57. John L. Brooke has argued that early Mormon converts were particularly "prepared" to accept the Mormon message of "restoration and hermetic divinization." Brooke, *Refiner's Fire*, 62–65.

66. Connell O'Donovan's important work on the Boston Mormons—where the Book of Mormon circulated through trade guilds, most notably furniture makers—highlights a need for a thorough social history of how the text circulated through networks in other communities. O'Donovan, *Augusta Cobb Young*.

67. During his lackluster first mission, Joseph Smith's brother Samuel passed through Mendon, New York, in April 1830. There, he convinced Brigham Young's brother Phineas to purchase a copy of the Book of Mormon. Heber C. Kimball's biographer called this copy "perhaps the single most important copy of the Book of Mormon ever sold" because it led to the conversions of members of the Young and Kimball families and several other prominent early Mormons. Kimball, *Heber C. Kimball*, 14–16; Turner, *Brigham Young*, 24–28. For other prominent Book of Mormon conver-

sion stories, see W. W. Phelps, in *M&A*, September 1835; Eliza R. Snow, "Sketch of My Life"; and Beecher, *Personal Writings of Snow*, 11. See also the compilation of conversion narratives in Black, *Stories from Early Saints*.

68. Givens, *Hand of Mormon*, 235.

69. In John Whitmer's original inscription of the revelation, Smith also empowered Sidney Gilbert to "obtain a license . . . that he may send goods also unto the lamanites and thus the gospel may be preached unto them." Clearly Cowdery, Pratt, and the other missionaries to the Lamanites had informed Smith that if the Mormons hoped return to Indian Country, provide for and gather the Lamanites to New Jerusalem, then they would first need government sanction. Revelation, July 20, 1831 [*D&C* 57], *RT1*, 160–61; *D&C* (1835), sec. 18 [*D&C* 57], *RT2*, 466–67.

70. Revelation, July 20, 1831 [*D&C* 57:1–13], *RT1*, 161.

71. William Miller's Adventists were the most prolific, producing an estimated four million pieces of literature in the 1830s and 1840s. Among the most reprinted was the community's elaborate chart illustrating Miller's biblically based calculations that the world would end in 1843. See a full-size reproduction of the chart in Numbers and Butler, *Disappointed*.

72. Hatch, *Democratization of American Christianity*, 125–27.

73. Oliver Cowdery to W. W. Phelps et al., August 10, 1833 (ID # 177), JSPP, http://josephsmithpapers.org/paperSummary/letter-to-church-leaders-in-jackson-county-missouri-10-august-1833?p=1; Joseph Smith to Edward Partridge, December 5, 1833 (ID# 191), JSPP, http://www.josephsmithpapers.org/paperSummary/letter-to-edward-partridge-5-december-1833?dm=image-and-text&zm=zoom-inner&tm=expanded&p=5&s=undefined&sm=none. One surviving letter dated April 1832 from Sidney Gilbert's father, Eli, then living in Connecticut, indicates that the elder Gilbert considered gathering with the Mormons in Independence. He also mentions his plans to obtain subscribers in Connecticut for the newly established *Evening and the Morning Star*. Eli and William Gilbert to Sydney Gilbert, April 23, 1832, CHL. Samuel Bent wrote a letter to Phelps, reprinted in the April 1833 edition, requesting that a subscription of the paper be sent to Pontiac in Michigan Territory. Bent wrote that he was "a professor of the christian religion for twenty seven years, and stood among the sects," until a Mormon missionary helped him "see the error of which the different sects embrace." Like the Gilbert family, he too declared his intentions to gather "in Zion before long." *E&MS*, April 1832.

74. In July 1832, Phelps provided explicit instructions on how the paper's readership should read and study the "sacred Scriptures" in a "threefold capacity. 1. As matters of divine revelation. 2. As a rule of life. 3. As containing that covenant of grace which relations to man's eternal happiness." "Excellence of Scripture," *E&MS*, July 1832.

75. Revelation, April 10, 1830 [*D&C* 20], *RT1*, 77.

76. See side-by-side comparison of the June 1832 *E&MS* publication of the April 6

revelations in *RT2*, 202–10. Compare the April 6, 1830, revelations regarding the ordination of priests (*D&C* 20:68), baptism (*D&C* 20:73–74), and administering the sacrament (*D&C* 20:77) with BofM, 238, 478, and 575, respectively [Alma 6:1, 3 Nephi 11:23–26, Moroni 4:3].

77. BofM, 30 [1 Nephi 13:36]; *E&MS*, June 1832.

78. BofM, 36 [1 Nephi 15:13–17]. As Phelps noted in the December 1832 edition of the *Evening and the Morning Star*, Christ's commandment to the Nephites, who created and safeguarded the Nephite archive, was to "write these sayings [down]" so that they could be kept safe until the latter days, when they would be "manifested unto the Gentiles." See 3 Nephi 16:4 and Mosiah 1:1–5. What David Hall describes as the "politics of writing and reading in eighteenth-century America" carried over into the nineteenth century: "Literacy connoted cultural authority; illiteracy, cultural inferiority and exclusion." Hall, *Cultures of Print*, 153.

79. *E&MS*, December 1832; BofM, 499–500 [3 Nephi 21:4–9], emphasis added.

80. Campbell, *New Jerusalem*, 48–60. Like his expectations for Book of Mormon sales, Smith's vision for the size of New Jerusalem was nothing short of grandiose. In 1830, only sixteen American cities had populations of 10,000 to 25,000. If Smith had succeeded in gathering the number of Saints he hoped for, New Jerusalem would have been the largest city west of the Mississippi. Bushman, *Rough Stone Rolling*, 221.

81. "Prophecy Given to the Church of Christ, March 7, 1831."

82. Roberts, *Missouri Persecutions*, 72–74.

83. "Outrage in Jackson County, Missouri."

84. "Manifesto."

85. Campbell, *New Jerusalem*, 63.

86. Ibid., 26–28.

87. "Free People of Color"; "An Act Concerning Negros and Mulattoes," approved January 7, 1825, reprinted in Pettibone and Geyer, *Laws of Missouri*, 600.

88. "Manifesto"; Bush, "Mormonism's Negro Doctrine," 11–13. "Indians."

89. "Manifesto"; Jennings, "Isaac McCoy and the Mormons," 75.

90. "Extra."

91. "To His Excellency, Daniel Dunklin"; Bushman, *Rough Stone Rolling*, 222–27. The Mormons' press was not the only one destroyed by proslavery Missourians. The abolitionist Elijah Lovejoy published a series of papers until 1837, when proslavery mobs destroyed his press and killed him. Simon, *Freedom's Champion*, 61–97.

92. See "Red Men of the South" and "Red Men of the West," in Derr and Davidson, *Eliza R. Snow*, 40–41; and Derr and Davidson, "Wary Heart."

93. Pratt, *Autobiography*, 40, emphasis in original.

94. Phelps later helped craft Joseph Smith's 1844 presidential platform in which the Mormon prophet advocated for gradual abolition. Brown, "Translator and the Ghostwriter."

95. Quoted in Bringhurst, "Elijah Abel," 25.

96. Scott, *Geography*, 135–58; Collins, *Between Athens and Jerusalem*.

97. The Book of Mormon itself can be read as an antislavery text, at least against the enslavement of those who belong to the same ancient Israelite lineage. Underwood, *Millenarian World*, 102.

98. Smith claimed to have translated the Book of Mormon from the gold plates that he unearthed on Hill Cumorah. Starting in 1835, he claimed to translate the book of Abraham from ancient Egyptian papyri that he purchased from a traveling mummy exhibit. Smith did not claim to translate the book of Moses from ancient sources. Instead, Smith translated it from his inspired reading of the King James Bible. However, as Richard Bushman points out, "In the method of their creation, the three translations were alike. Joseph did not translate in the sense of learning the language and consulting dictionaries. He received words by 'revelation,' whether or not a text lay before him." Bushman, *Rough Stone Rolling*, 132.

99. "Historical Introduction," Old Testament Revision 1 (ID # 7201), JSPP, http://josephsmithpapers.org/paperSummary/old-testament-revision-1?dm=image-and-text&zm=zoom-inner&tm=expanded&p=2&s=undefined&sm=none.

100. "Extract from the Prophecy of Enoch." The book of Moses also contains an elaborated version of humanity's first murder. See Moses 5 and Genesis 4.

101. "Extract from the Prophecy of Enoch." See Moses 7.

102. "Extract from the Prophecy of Enoch"; Moses 7:62; Bushman, *Rough Stone Rolling*, 141.

103. By the late 1820s, Black Pete was probably one of a handful of free blacks in Geauga County, near Kirtland, Ohio. According to Missouri's first state census, taken in 1830, Jackson County had a population of 2,822 people, of which 193 were slaves and only 2 were free blacks. Dorsett, "Slaveholding in Jackson County." Missouri's 1825 codes were similar to those that black Mormons would face in Illinois. Not only did a "free negro or mulatto" need to provide documentation that he was "a citizen of some one of the United States" before he could settle in the state, but the legislation also empowered state officers to immediately expel any black settler who failed to produce such documentation. "Missouri's Early Slave Laws," http://www.sos.mo.gov/archives/education/aahi/earlyslavelaws/slavelaws.asp.

104. Though Ohio officially entered the Union in 1802 as a free state, its proximity to Kentucky and the gradual abolition policies of many northern states meant that slave owners often brought their slaves to Ohio without granting them freedom. According to Mark Staker, even after Pete moved with his owners to Ohio in the first decade of the 1800s, he became free only around 1820. Staker, *Hearken, O Ye People*, 29–31.

105. "Golden Bible or the Book of Mormon"; Staker, *Hearken, O Ye People*, 77, 89n50.

106. Ibid., 79.

107. Ibid., 44–58.

108. "Book of Mormon," December 7, 1830.

109. Howe, *Mormonism Unvailed*, 107.

110. Georg A. Smith, "Historical Discourses," November 15, 1864, *JD* 11:3–4.

111. It was commonplace for slaves to hide their literacy from their masters. Reading and writing slaves were always sources of anxiety in American slave communities, leading to legal restriction on slave education in many states. Cornelius, *"When I Can Read."*

112. See a side-by-side comparison of the original revelation and the version printed in the October 1832 edition of the *E&MS* in *RT2*, 237–38. For an analysis of religious enthusiasm, dissent, and prophetic authority within the early Ohio Mormon community, see Staker, *Hearken, O Ye People*, 71–174.

113. In her 1847 accounts book, the midwife Patty Sessions lists prominent Mormons who owed her money for services rendered, including "Ezra Benson," "Hosea Stout," and "P. P. Pratt." Sessions, who delivered Jane Manning James's child Silas during the Mormon trek to Utah, lists James as "Black Jane." Smart, *Mormon Midwife*, 54; Inscoe, "Carolina Slave Names."

114. *E&MS*, October 1832; Revelation, February 1831 [*D&C* 43:20–21], *RT2*, 248–49.

115. "Free People of Color," emphasis added.

116. Ibid.

117. Revelation, July 20, 1831 [*D&C* 57], *RT1*, 159–61.

118. In the original handwritten copy of this record, the references to Noah's sons are redacted with a strike-through line. However, in later official histories of the church, the references are included. June 19–July 1831, History, 1838–1856, vol. A-1 (ID # 7268), JSPP, http://josephsmithpapers.org/paperSummary/history-1838-1856 -volume-a-1-23-december-1805-30-august-1834?p=135; *DHC* 1:190–91.

Chapter 3

1. The "Manifesto" was reprinted as part of open letter "to His Excellency Daniel Dunklin, Governor of the State of Missouri."

2. "Book of Mormon," *Reflector*, February 14, 1831.

3. The Book of Mormon passage draws directly from Micah 5:8. Booth, "Mormonism No. VI."

4. Abdy, *Journal*, 55–58.

5. "Mormonites 'Hors de Combat.'"

6. "Mormons and Anti-Mormons."

7. See Revelation, December 16, 17, 1833 [*D&C* 101], *RT1*, 353; and Bushman, *Rough Stone Rolling*, 226.

8. Revelation, June 22, 1834 [*D&C* 105:5–13], *RT1*, 375.

9. Mauss, *All Abraham's Children*, 19–24; Reeve, *Religion of a Different Color*, 38–43.

10. In 1881, David Whitmer, a Book of Mormon witness, onetime church apostle, and leader of his own splinter Mormon community, told a Kansas City newspaper that many early Mormons were "northern people, who were opposed to slavery." "Mormonism," *Kansas City Journal*, June 5, 1881.

11. Klees, *Underground Railroad Tales*, 139.

12. Reeve, *Religion of a Different Color*, 150.

13. Young, "Privileges of the Sabbath," May 20, 1860, *JD* 8:58–59. Following the church leaders' discussions of slavery, Smith revealed that the "day of the Lord" would come only after "Slaves rise up against their Masters who shall be Martialed and disaplined [*sic*] for war." Revelation, December 25, 1832 [*D&C* 87:4], *RT1*, 291.

14. In a series of resolutions passed during an August 1835 church assembly in Kirtland, the Mormons acknowledged that they were called "to preach the gospel to the nations of the earth." Yet they also stated explicitly, "We do not believe it right to interfere with bond-servants, neither preach the gospel to, nor baptize them contrary to the will and wish of their masters." *D&C* (1835), sec. 103 [*D&C* 134:1, 4, 12], *RT2*, 562–64.

15. Reeve, *Religion of a Different Color*, 123.

16. *M&A*, April 1836. Kirtland's proslavery ruffians were well behaved compared to antiabolitionists in Boston—the most cosmopolitan American city—who the year before would have lynched the most famous abolitionist in America, William Lloyd Garrison, if local law enforcement had not protected him. Garrison, *William Lloyd Garrison*, 1–131.

17. *M&A*, April 1836.

18. Flournoy, *Essay on the Origin*, 5.

19. *M&A*, April 1836.

20. Roll, First Council of the Seventy, CHL; Stevenson, *Cause of Righteousness*, 10; Bringhurst, "Elijah Abel."

21. Elders License Elijah Abel Certificate, Wardle Papers. In the June 1836 issue of the *M&A*, Abel is listed along with more than a hundred other Mormon men as "Ministers of the Gospel, belonging to the church of the Latter Day Saints."

22. As Frederick Douglass explained, in the 1830s even free blacks traveling in or through slave and border states were often required to present free papers or risk enslavement. To make his own escape, Douglass borrowed the papers of a black friend, disguised himself as a sailor, and took a train north and into freedom. Douglass, *Life and Times*, 166–69.

23. Elders License Elijah Abel Certificate. Yet what the license does not mention—Abel's race—is perhaps as important as what it does. It is possible that in the missionary field Abel passed as white. In antebellum America, the "third crossing"—the progeny of a person with one black grandparent and three full-blooded white Euro-Americans—was said to "clear the blood" of any trace of black blood and thus could be accepted as white, provided that he or she did not present any typically "African" characteristics. In fact, if Abel had been such an "octoroon," as church president John Taylor later described him, he could have been considered legally white in many states. Rothman, *Notorious in the Neighborhood*, 205; Lemire, *Miscegenation*, 38. Still if Abel did pass as white, he did not follow the unwritten rules of passing, which required establishing a low-key profile so as not to draw attention to his ambiguous

racial identity. In fact, during his 1838 mission in Lawrence County, New York, just south of the Canadian border, "handbills were pasted up in every direction stating that the Mormon Elder had murdered a woman and five children and a great reward was offered for him," wrote Eunice Kinney in an 1891 letter to a friend in which she detailed the role Abel played in her conversion to Mormonism. Northern Upstate New York was experiencing its own religious revival, along with great civil unrest, as the British crown moved to squash growing independence movements in nearby Ontario. During this time of turmoil, the region's more established religious communities, including the Anglicans, Presbyterians, and Methodists, made it clear that the upstart Mormons were not welcome. Yet, at least according to Kinney, none of his persecutors raised the specter of Abel's race as a reason to be wary of him or his message. Instead, the "black elder" bravely faced down those who accused him of murder. Eunice Kinney to Wingfield Watson, My Testimony to the Latter Day Work, September 1891, CHL. On the religious revival of northern New York and southern Canada, see Ferry, "Politicization of Religious Dissent." A year later, in June 1839, word reached Kirtland that Abel was even stirring up conflict among his fellow Mormon missionaries in Upstate New York and Canada. Abel reportedly named himself the leader of the mission and "threaten[ed] to [knock] down" another Mormon who challenged his leadership. Joseph Smith, Sidney Rigdon, and Hyrum Smith were present at the council meeting when news of these incidents reached Commerce, Illinois, where the Saints were gathering after their expulsion from Missouri. The church's senior officials found nothing too remarkable in the reports to warrant punishment of Abel. And Abel's race, it seemed, was not worth remarking on either: it went unmentioned in the meeting of the church hierarchy in which the case was discussed. Bush, "Mormonism's Negro Doctrine," 52n33. More often than not, during the church's first two decades, Abel's race is absent from the archive. However, in 1853, when he arrived in Utah, Abel was turned away from the Mormon endowment house and all but stripped of the priesthood because church leaders then insisted that his African lineage rendered him innately unworthy of full membership in the sacred Mormon community. In the 1850s, Mormon leadership preceded the rest of America in adopting the "one drop" rule—that even one African ancestor, however distant in a person's genealogy, meant that he or she was "black." The one drop rule became the unofficial and later official policy in many states after Reconstruction, as well as the justification the church would use to exclude people of African descent from the priesthood and the temple for more than a century. On Mormonism and the one drop rule, see Reeve, *Religion of a Different Color*, 159–60, 192.

24. Pratt did insist that Jackson County's "neighboring tribes of Indians" acted more civilized than the "companies of ruffians," including "pretended preachers of the Gospel" like the Baptist Isaac McCoy, whom Pratt names in the paper as among those guilty of illegally forcing the Mormons out of the county. Pratt, "Extra."

25. "Public Meeting."

26. Sidney Rigdon, Joseph Smith Jr., et al. to John Thorton et al., *M&A*, August 1836.

27. Phelps, "Indians."

28. According to the editors of the JSPP, Sydney Rigdon performed the editing of the revelation in "Revelation Book 1," though it is unclear under whose direction the editing occurred. See Revelation, September 1830 [*D&C* 28:9], *RT1*, 53. See also Book of Commandments (1833), chap. 30, *RT2*, 80.

29. Oliver Cowdery to "beloved Brethren," May 7, 1831 (ID # 72), JSPP, http://josephsmithpapers.org/paperSummary/letter-from-oliver-cowdery-7-may-1831?dm=image-and-text&zm=zoom-inner&tm=expanded&p=1&s=undefined&sm=none.

30. On occasion Joseph Smith's prophecies conflate "Lamanite" and "Jew." For example, see Revelation, July 20, 1831 [*D&C* 57:4], *RT1*, 160–61. Yet more often, as did their contemporaries, the Latter-day Saints distinguished between the descendants of the two main kingdoms of ancient Israel. First were the Lost Tribes of Israel, notably the descendants of Joseph's sons, Ephraim and Manasseh, who fled the Holy Land and, according to the biblical exegetes of the 1830s, were eventually scattered throughout the world after the Assyrians destroyed the northern Kingdom of Israel in the eighth century B.C. Second were the descendants of the Kingdom of Judah (later Judea), understood to be the progenitors of the modern-day Jews. BofM, 98, 92 [2 Nephi 21:11–13, 2 Nephi 17]; Newcome and Horsley, *Literal Translation*, 79. The Book of Mormon makes clear that when Gentiles restore the Nephite archive to the "remnant of [Israel]," they would bring the Book of Mormon to those Israelites "who came out from Jerusalem" and who shared common ancestors with the "Jews" but were not Jews themselves. BofM, 117 [2 Nephi 30:4]. The Book of Mormon's title page indicates that the scripture was written to "Lamanite," "Gentile," and "Jew," also making it clear that Mormonism's foundational text differentiated between the Old and New World branches of the house of Israel.

31. Joseph Smith revealed on November 3, 1831, that at the "hour" of the Lord's return, those lost Israelites scattered "among the gentiles [shall] flee unto Zion" in America and those "of Juda[h] [shall] flee unto Jerusalem." Revelation, November 3, 1831 [*D&C* 133:12–13], *RT1*, 395. During the church's first decade, in their newspapers, the Mormons publicly pronounced their expectation for an imminent "Restoration of the Jews" as fulfillment of Book of Mormon prophecy. See "Restoration of the Jews," *E&MS*, August 1833; "Restoration of the Jews," *MS*, June 1840; Pratt, Letter.

32. On the organization of the Quorum of the Twelve Apostles, see *D&C* (1835), sec. 3 [*D&C* 107:33–100], *RT2*, 392–99.

33. See *T&S*, October 1841.

34. Hyde, *Voice from Jerusalem*, ii–iv. See also Epperson, *Mormons and Jews*, 140, 145–46.

35. 2 Nephi 10:3–6, 19:21. See Isaiah 9:21.

36. Epperson, *Mormons and Jews*, 79; Shepard, "Concept of a 'Rejected Gospel': Part 1"; Shepard, "Concept of a 'Rejected Gospel': Part 2."

37. *T&S*, October 1841; Epperson, *Mormons and Jews*, 152–53; Green, "Gathering and Election," 196.

38. Hyde, *Voice from Jerusalem*, 8–9.

39. Ibid., 20–23.

40. *DHC*, 4:455–60.

41. BofM, 66–67 [2 Nephi 3:5–15].

42. BofM, 28 [1 Nephi 13:4].

43. BofM, 67 [2 Nephi 3:15].

44. By "ethnicity," I follow Werner Sollors's description of the nineteenth- and twentieth-century phenomenon of "inventing ethnicities." "The category of 'invention' has been stressed in order to emphasize not so much originality and innovation as the importance of *language* in the social construction of reality." Sollors, *Invention of Ethnicity*, x.

45. Michael Marquardt, among others, have questioned the date, December 1833, which the church accepts as the official establishment of the Mormon patriarch. Marquardt believes it more likely that the office was actually established a year later when Joseph Smith Sr. was ordained assistant church president. *EBP*, vii–ix, 11.

46. Mauss, *All Abraham's Children*, 22. Samuel Brown has argued that naming and ordering created "a chain of belonging," linking the Saints of the latter days back to the original Israelite covenant. Brown, "Early Mormon Chain of Belonging."

47. *EBP*, 4–5, 14.

48. BofM, 213 [Mosiah 27:25]. Irving, "Law of Adoption," 3; Brown, "Early Mormon Adoption Theology"; Stapley, "Adoptive Sealing Ritual."

49. Pratt, *Voice of Warning*, 110–11; Brown, "Early Mormon Adoption Theology," 18.

50. Brown, *In Heaven*, 124–25.

51. *EPB*, 12.

52. In their blessings, William's wife Caroline and Joseph Smith Sr.'s daughters Lucy Smith and Katharine Smith Salisbury were instructed to teach members of their "sex" about "those things which the virtuous." Ibid., 17–19.

53. Ibid., 14–15, emphasis added.

54. Revelation, November 3, 1831 [*D&C* 133:34], *RT1*, 209.

55. "Extract of Letter." BofM, 133 [Jacob 5:17].

56. BofM, 488 [3 Nephi 21:6]. In March 1833, Smith revealed that it was the duty of the leaders of the church to "go forth unto the ends of the earth, unto the Gentiles first, and then behold, and lo, they shall turn unto the Jews." Revelation, March 8, 1833 [*D&C* 90:9], *RT1*, 315.

57. *EPB*, 11–19. The CHL's policy to allow only direct descendants to inspect their ancestors' patriarchal blessing means that a comprehensive study of the evolution of the ritual of patriarchal blessings has not been possible. According to the church, these blessings are too sacred to be shared with the public. However, for decades, Michael Marquardt has collected patriarchal blessings with the intent, he has writ-

ten, to "aid those who are engaged in the study of the history and doctrine of the LDS Church, and also to benefit the work of family historians and biographers." *EPB*, vii. An examination of Marquardt's recently published collection of Joseph Smith Sr.'s and Hyrum Smith's blessings suggests that the practice of naming specific lineages became commonplace for male blessing recipients by the time of Hyrum Smith's death in 1844. *LPB*, 527–58. For a systematic study of the blessings collected by Marquardt, see Shepard and Shepard, *Binding Earth and Heaven*.

58. *EPB*, 23, 99–100. If necessary, the patriarch even had the power to supersede biological family lineages. For his daughter-in-law Mary Smith, who Smith acknowledged had "left thy father's house" when she accepted the "gospel" and married Samuel Smith, Joseph Smith Sr. "united" her with his own family and thus with his own sacred and ancient family tree. Ibid., 16. Brown, *In Heaven*, 213–18.

59. *EPB*, 99. Proclaiming that Abel was "an orphan" was not unusual. In his patriarchal blessing of John Allen who like Abel was also a member of the Quorum of the Seventy, the patriarch also declared Allen an "orphan." What was unique about Abel's blessing is the absence of Smith's move to assign a lineage from the Hebraic fathers of the tribes of Israel. In contrast, as a result of the blessing, John Allen was renamed "a seed of Joseph, son of Jacob." *EPB*, 99–100.

60. *EPB*, 99. On the Book of Life, see *D&C* 88:2, 128:7.

61. See LDS Church Council Minutes, June 4, 1879, Adam S. Bennion Papers, CHL; Journal of John L. Nuttal, May, 31 1879, in Lester Bush Papers, Compilation on the Negro in Mormonism.

62. Temple theology had also evolved. By the time James received her blessing, the temple had become a site where the "Elders of Israel [would receive] their washings and anointings"—sacred endowments, as Smith declared at the April 1844 General Conference, which guaranteed their "election" to the highest levels of exaltation. *DHC*, April 8, 1844, 6:319. James was not—or not yet—a daughter of Israel. James would never receive her endowments and thus would never receive her "new name" that Saints receive when they complete their endowments. In Utah, James would be barred from the most sacred chambers of the temple because she was black and because she was a woman who was not sealed to a priesthood holding man, a matrimonial or familial covenant required for women to participate in Mormonism's most sacred ceremonies.

63. Smith, *General Smith's Views*.

64. *EPB*, 99.

65. History, 1838–1856, C-1 (ID # 7513), JSPP, http://josephsmithpapers.org/paper Summary/history-1838-1856-volume-c-1-2-november-1838-31-july-1842?p=543.

66. *EPB*, 194.

67. By the 1840s and up to the present day, the designation of lineage has been considered an essential element of a patriarchal blessing. Bates, "Patriarchal Blessings and the Routinization of Charisma."

68. The ritual of baptism for the dead, which also developed in the early 1840s, promised that even long-deceased family members need not be lost due to ill-timed births but could also join this eternal chain of belonging. Brown, *In Heaven*, 148–49, 211–18.

69. Sollors, *Invention of Ethnicity*, x.

70. On "mythic naming" to create ancient patrilineal legacies in the early Republic, see Cagidemetrio, "Plea for Fictional Histories," 31.

71. Sollors, *Invention of Ethnicity*, xi–xii.

72. Jan Shipps has written that it was the exodus trek to Utah that transformed the metaphorical concept of Israelite ethnicity into a literal one. Yet I see no reason not to take the early Mormons at their word when, in the 1830s, they declared themselves "literal" descendants of the biblical patriarchs. Shipps, "Making Saints, 71; Shipps, *Mormonism*, 59–61.

73. Allen, *Men with a Mission*, 24, 23.

74. Fielding Journal, April 10, 1838, CHL.

75. Givens and Grow, *Parley P. Pratt*, 181.

76. Stark, "Basis of Mormon Success," 211.

77. Brigham Young, "The Lords' Supper," July 11, 1869, *JD* 13:148, Stark, "Basis of Mormon Success," 213–14; Givens and Grow, *Parley P. Pratt*, 181–82.

78. Woodruff, *Wilford Woodruff*, 119. See also Allen, *Men with a Mission*, 120–30.

79. Even with the outflow of thousands of English Saints gathering first to Nauvoo and later to Utah, by 1850 there were more than 30,000 Latter-day Saints in Britain. According to the territory's first census, the "white" population of Utah in 1850 was 11,354. Stark, "Basis of Mormon Success," 211–13.

80. Wilson, *Israelitish Origin*. On British Israelism in early Mormonism, see Mauss, "In Search of Ephraim."

81. For an articulation of this British Israelism in early patriarchal blessings, see Hyrum Smith's blessings for Mary Isabella Horne, born in Rocenham, Kent, England, and the blessing Samuel Smith gave to Charles Lambert from Weatherby, England. *EPB*, 227, 263. For a late nineteenth-century articulation of "believing blood," see Whitney, "Why I Am a Mormon." Mauss, *All Abraham's Children*, 22–23, 31–34.

82. *T&S*, October 1841; Epperson, *Mormons and Jews*, 152–53.

83. Mauss, "In Search of Ephraim," 132, 149.

84. "Conference Minutes."

85. Whitney, "Why I Am a Mormon."

86. Quoted in Mauss, "In Search of Ephraim," 131.

87. *D&C* (1835), sec. 3 [*D&C* 107:40–52], *RT2*, 395–96.

88. During his time in America, Christ established the "power" of the priesthood among his Nephite disciples through the laying on of hands. BofM, 477–78, 493 [3 Nephi 11:21–27, 18:36–38].

89. "History Drafts, 1838–ca. 1841," *JSH1*, 294; Revelation, April 6, 1830 [*D&C* 20–67], *RT1*, 74–87.

90. Revelation, February 9, 1831 [*D&C* 42:11–12], *RT1*, 94–97.

91. *D&C* (1835), sec. 3 [*D&C* 107], *RT2*, 392–99. The organization and duties of the Mormon hierarchy remained in constant flux during Smith's lifetime. The modern-day priesthood took shape only after Smith's assassination when Brigham Young assumed leadership of most of Smith's followers. Quinn, *Mormon Hierarchy*, 14–38.

92. Revelation, September 22, 23, 1832 [*D&C* 84:1–26], *RT1*, 274–78; *D&C* (1835), sec. 3 [*D&C* 107:1–20], *RT2*, 392–93.

93. Brown, *In Heaven*, 148–49.

94. Revelation, September 22, 23, 1832 [*D&C* 84:34], *RT1*, 278.

95. Compare Revelation, November 11, 1831 [*D&C* 107], *RT1*, 217–219, with *D&C* (1835), sec. 3 [*D&C* 107:16, 17, 40, 69, 70, 76], *RT2*, 393–97. Green, "Gathering and Election," 198; Cooper, *Promises*, 75.

96. *EPB*, 27, 155.

97. Bushman, *Rough Stone Rolling*, 287; Brown, *In Heaven*, 139–41.

98. "Egyptian Antiquities."

99. "Translation." Although Smith translated the book of Abraham in 1835, it was not published until 1842, when *T&S* published it in serial form. For a summary of the century-long controversy over the papyri, see Ostling and Ostling, *Mormon America*, 286–90; and Ritner, "'Breathing Permit of Hor.'"

100. "Egyptian Mummies"; Bushman, *Rough Stone Rolling*, 286.

101. For the late nineteenth- and early twentieth-century use of the book of Abraham, canonized as part of the Pearl of Great Price, see Bush, "Mormonism's Negro Doctrine," 35–39.

102. The papyri also provided an authentic physical connection to the ancient world, which was particularly important owing to the conspicuous absence of the golden plates from which Smith supposedly translated the Book of Mormon. W. W. Phelps to Sally Phelps, Liberty, Mo., July 20, 1835, cited in "Introduction to Egyptian Material," JSPP, http://josephsmithpapers.org/intro/introduction-to-egyptian -material.

103. "Translation" [Abraham 1:3, 25–27].

104. Ibid. [Abraham 2: 9–11].

105. "Gospel."

106. Mauss, *All Abraham's Children*, 238.

107. Hambrick-Stowe, *Charles G. Finney*, 19.

108. As Matthew Bowman has written, "There's little sense of the radical regeneration of a depraved human soul in Mormon language about conversion; rather, Mormons emphasize process and effort. They see in conversion not metaphysical transformation but the cultivation of character." Bowman, "Conversion of Parley Pratt," 185.

109. Woodruff, *Journal*, 5:469. Reports of the "Missouri Persecutions" were frequently printed in the *MS*. See *MS*, December 1840, January 1841.

110. Kimball, "Letter to the Editor."

111. Jacobson, *Whiteness of a Different Color*, 39–90.

Chapter 4

1. As Quincy Newell has noted, the Manning party included Jane Manning; her mother, Eliza; her brothers, Isaac and Peter; her sisters, Angeline and Sarah; Sarah's husband, Anthony Stebbings; and another sister-in-law, Lucinda Manning. In the narrative, James notes that the group also included "two children, one they had to carry all the way." James's son Sylvester is likely the child whom the family carried, and Peter was the other child. This brings the Manning party to ten. It is possible that Cato Treadwell, who was James's stepfather, as well as Henry and Lucinda Tonquin, also traveled with the Mannings. Newell, "Autobiography and Interview," 263, 279n69, 290n138.

2. Gates, "'Aunt Jane' James," 551.

3. James and Roundy, "Biography of Jane E. James." In his groundbreaking study of James, Henry Wolfinger points out that although James began her autobiography in 1893, it was clearly revised and updated. For example, James implies that Joseph F. Smith was church president, a position that Smith did not assume until 1901. Wolfinger, "Test of Faith," 170n56.

4. In 1887, Roundy and Snow visited the elderly Hosea Stout, Joseph Smith's onetime bodyguard, Utah pioneer, and territorial politician, at Stout's home outside of Salt Lake City. Like James, at the end of his life, Stout, one of early Mormonism's most prolific diarists, turned to Roundy to record his memories of Smith because his health prevented him from writing them down himself. "Hosea Stout Statement." Roundy also organized a successful campaign to establish Joseph Smith's birthday, December 23, as a churchwide day of remembrance and memorialization. See "Roundy, Elizabeth Jefford Drake," in Jenson, *Latter-day Saint Biographical Encyclopedia*, 1:810–11.

5. Flake, "Re-Placing Memory."

6. "Prophet's Servant, Old Negro, Dead."

7. "Death of Jane Manning James"; "Aunt Jane Laid to Rest."

8. Bushman, *Rough Stone Rolling*, 365.

9. "Joseph Smith's Letter in Liberty Jail," March 20, 1839 [*D&C* 123:10], "History, 1838–1856, vol. C-1 (ID# 7513), JSPP, http://josephsmithpapers.org/paperSummary /history-1838-1856-volume-c-1-2-november-1838-31-july-1842?p=84; Joseph Smith et al. to the church at Quincy, Ill. [*D&C* 121:16] (ID# 430), JSPP, http://www.josephsmith papers.org/paperSummary/letter-to-the-church-and-edward-partridge-20-march -1839-a?p=9&highlight=cursed%20are%20all.

10. "Burglary! Treason! ARSON!!! MURDER!!!!" Phelps was eventually reinstated. Although Cowdery and the Whitmers were not, there is no evidence that they ever recanted their testimony to having witnessed the plates from which the Book of Mormon was translated. Givens, *Book of Mormon*, 99.

11. Ironically, in terms of white apostates earning curses, it was Phelps who drew the most explicit connection with the biblical and Book of Mormon precedents. In March 1835, Phelps wrote in the *Messenger & Advocate*, "Is or is it not apparent from reason and analogy as drawn from a careful reading of the Scriptures, that God causes the saints, or people that fall away from his church to be cursed in time, with a black skin?"

12. Smith et al. to the church at Quincy, Ill. [*D&C* 121].

13. Ibid.

14. Pratt, "Science of Anti-Mormon Suckerology"; "Warsaw and Quincy."

15. The Latter-day Saints purchased eighteen thousand acres of what were called "Half-Breed tracts"—areas that the federal government set aside for "mixed-blood" people of American Indian and European ancestry—located on or near the western bank of the Mississippi. In March 1841, Joseph Smith revealed that God called the Latter-day Saints to "build up a city unto my name" on these newly acquired lands and that this city would be named "Zarahemla" after the great Nephite capital city described in the Book of Mormon. *D&C* 125:1–4; Jensen, "Transplanted to Zion," 79.

16. August 12, 1841, "History, 1838–1856, vol. C-1, addenda" (ID# 8119), JSPP, http://josephsmithpapers.org/paperSummary/history-1838-1856-volume-c-1-addenda?p=11#!/paperSummary/history-1838-1856-volume-c-1-addenda&p=11; Coates, "Refugees Meet."

17. On Joseph Smith's 1842 "Rocky Mountain Prophecy," in which the prophet purportedly foresaw that the Saints would not find peace until they were "driven to the Rocky Mountains," see Farmer, *Zion's Mount*, 150–51. In early 1844, Apostle Lyman Wight suggested that Texas would be an ideal gathering place for "rich planters" from the southern states who had joined the church and would migrate west if they could "plant their slaves" in Texas without fear of federal interference. Wight, who in the early 1830s had been set apart as missionary to the Lamanites, also believed that a Mormon stake in Texas would allow for greater contact with Indians, including the wealthy slave-owning Cherokee and Choctaw nations who, according to Wight, were already "very desirous to have an interview with the Elders of this Church, upon the principles of the Book of Mormon." Lyman Wight et al. to Joseph Smith et al., February 15, 1844, and Wight to Smith et al., February 15, 1844, *DHC*, 6:255–60.

18. Whitney, "Scenes in Nauvoo."

19. Thanks to Laurel Thatcher Ulrich for pointing out Stout's record of the Herring brothers' activities. Stout, *Mormon Frontier*, 224, 229.

20. Thanks to Joseph Johnston for providing me with an approximation of the black population in Nauvoo.

21. Bringhurst, "Elijah Abel," 25; House Carpenters of Nauvoo, CHL.

22. On Abel's work on the temple, see Journal of John L. Nuttal, May, 31 1879, in Lester Bush Papers, Compilation on the Negro in Mormonism. Abel's time in Cincin-

nati was not without controversy. During a June 1843 regional conference, the Cincinnati branch leadership, along with a visiting delegation of church apostles including Orson Pratt and Heber C. Kimball, agreed to limit Abel's missionary outreach to the city's "coloured population." There is no indication that Abel had done anything wrong. Wanting to avoid renewed accusations that they were meddling with blacks, the church leadership wished to lower Abel's visibility. Bringhurst, "Elijah Abel," 23; Stevenson, *Cause of Righteousness*, 228–29.

23. Mace, Autobiography, CHL. The Mormons were asked to tithe one day of labor out of ten, as well as to tithe money and other supplies to the construction of the temple. Leonard, *Nauvoo*, 246.

24. LDS Church Council Minutes, June 4, 1879, Adam S. Bennion Papers.

25. September 11, 1842, Journal, December 1841–1842 (ID# 6545), JSPP, http://joseph smithpapers.org/paperSummary/journal-december-1841-december-1842?p=76.

26. Black and Black, *Annotated Record of Baptisms for the Dead*, 8–9.

27. Revelation, September 6, 1842, *D&C* (1844), sec. 105 [*D&C* 128:1–7] (ID# 7271), JSPP, http://josephsmithpapers.org/paperSummary/doctrine-and-covenants-1844?p =422#!/paperSummary/doctrine-and-covenants-1844&p=421.

28. *EPB*, 99.

29. *DHC* 4:365. Joseph Smith was eventually released on the orders of an Illinois State Supreme Court judge named Stephen Douglas. Bushman, *Rough Stone Rolling*, 425–27.

30. As Eddie Glaude has shown, the year 1843 was an important one for the "politics of respectability" in race-based American political discourse. Though not intentionally, Smith uses similar language of the "color-blind appeal of moral reform," which, according to the National Negro Convention meeting in Buffalo in 1843, would bring black Americans up to the level of white Americans. Glaude, *Exodus!*, 143–44.

31. January 2, 1843, Journal, December 1842–June 1844 (ID# 7997), JSPP, http:// josephsmithpapers.org/paperSummary/journal-december-1842-june-1844-book-1 -21-december-1842-10-march-1843?p=47#!/paperSummary/journal-december-1842 -june-1844-book-1-21-december-1842-10-march-1843&p=47.

32. James and Roundy, "Biography of Jane E. James." In her autobiography, James recalls that the family departed Connecticut in 1840. Yet an advertisement printed in the December 6, 1843, edition of the *Nauvoo Neighbor* seeking information about a trunk of James's belongings, which became separated from her during her trek, indicates that the Manning family converted sometime in 1842 or 1843. Their subsequent trek to Nauvoo happened in late 1843. Wolfinger, "Test of Faith," 162n16.

33. Jane Manning was born to Isaac and Phillis Manning. Jane Manning's mother likely changed her name to Eliza after she was freed. Jane Manning James's autobiography hints at the changing nature of her mother's name. In the original handwritten copy of the autobiography, the name Phillis is scratched out and replaced with Eliza. James and Roundy, "Biography of Jane E. James." In the patriarchal blessing Jane

Manning received in 1844, her parents are listed as "Isaac and Eliza Manning," but in her 1889 patriarchal blessing "Isaac and Phillis Manning" are listed.

34. Foster, *Witnessing Slavery*, 3; Lambert, "Representation of Reality," 63.

35. James and Roundy, "Biography of Jane E. James."

36. Scott, *Domination and the Arts of Resistance.*

37. James and Roundy, "Biography of Jane E. James."

38. In her analysis of James's autobiography, Quincy Newell argues that James's memory here is faulty. There was no Presbyterian church in Wilton in the 1840s. Instead, Brittany Chapman at the CHL has located James's membership records in the New Canaan Congregational church. Jane E. Manning is listed as having been excommunicated on February 22, 1844, from that religious community because she "without our approbation or consent wholly withdrawn and separated herself from the fellowship of this church and has since gone to a distant part of the country and thus placed herself beyond the reach of this church." New Canaan Congregational Record Book, Typescript, 27, 45–46, in the Rev. Theophilus Smith Collection; Newell, "Autobiography and Interview," 278n65.

39. Wandell and his companion Albert Merrill had been tasked with establishing branches in southern New England and eastern New York State. Merrill, History of Albert Merrill, CHL.

40. James and Roundy, "Biography of Jane E. James."

41. Ibid. In 1843, Wandell reported from Connecticut that "the brethren here are very anxious to emigrate to Illinois; so you may expect to see all of us in Zion this Fall that can possible get there." *T&S*, August 15, 1843. Wolfinger, "Test of Faith," 126–29.

42. Brigham Young famously quipped about his own conversion to Mormonism, "I reasoned on revelation." Yet in his biography of Young, John Turner asserts that Young's conversion was the result of his careful study of the Mormons' new scripture, his observations of the behavior of the Mormon people—including speaking in tongues—and his own experience with what his longtime friend and aide Heber C. Kimball described as their encounter with "the glory of God [which] shone upon us" and "caused such great joy to spring up in our bosoms, that we were hardly able to contain ourselves." Turner, *Brigham Young*, 26. See also Harper, "Infallible Proofs, Both Human and Divine."

43. Dinger, *Nauvoo City*, 480–81. In her autobiography, though she makes no mention of Wandell's trial, James does state, "During our trip I lost all my clothes, they were all gone, my trunks were sent by Canal to the care of Charles Wesley Wandel." James and Roundy, "Biography of Jane E. James."

44. Ibid.

45. See "An Act Respecting Free Negroes and Mulattoes," in *Revised Laws of Illinois*, 463–64.

46. James and Roundy, "Biography of Jane E. James."

47. Ibid.

48. "First Presidency, Report."

49. See *D&C* 124:29–30; and Baugh, "'For This Ordinance Belongeth to My House,'" 50.

50. Brown, *Nauvoo Sealings, Adoptions, and Anointings*. In her autobiography, James states that in Salt Lake, "I have had the privelige [*sic*] of going into the Temple and being baptized for some of my dead." Yet she was not permitted to partake in more sacred temple ceremonies, including sealings and endowments. See temple recommend issued to James by Angus M. Cannon on June 16, 1888, transcribed in Wolfinger, "Test of Faith," 148.

51. "An Act to Incorporate the City of Nauvoo," reprinted in *DHC*, 4:241.

52. On February 8, 1844, in the mayor's court, Joseph Smith tried "two negroes" for attempting to marry white women. For their offenses, the mayor fined one twenty-five dollars and the other five dollars. *DHC*, 6:210.

53. John Taylor, "Comment on the Negro Chism's Case."

54. Willard Richards, Journal, December 30, 1842, quoted in Bringhurst, *Saints, Slaves, and Blacks*, 56.

55. Smith, "Views on the Government and Policy of the U.S."

56. Reeve, *Religion of a Different Color*, 127.

57. On April 7, 1844, the same day Brown ordained James M. Flake into the priesthood, Brown baptized Flake's slave Green Flake, the best-documented black Mormon slave. Later that same year, Green Flake and his master moved to Nauvoo. Brown, *Autobiography*, 46. Green Flake was a member of Brigham Young's Vanguard Company, which entered the Salt Lake Valley on July 24, 1847. Before leaving Utah for the Mormons' settlement in San Bernardino, California, in 1854, James Flake's widow, Agnes Flake, tithed Green Flake to the church. According to James Flake's son, William J. Flake, Green then worked two years for Brigham Young and Heber C. Kimball before the Mormon leaders freed him. Green Flake lived in Utah in Union's small black community before settling in Idaho, where he died in 1903. In 1897, along with some 250 surviving pioneers of 1847, including Jane Manning James, Green Flake was awarded a golden badge made by Tiffany and Company in New York as part Utah's 1897 Pioneer Jubilee. Lythgoe, "Negro Slavery in Utah," 41–44; Coleman, "History of Blacks in Utah," 58–59. Throughout his journal, John Brown refers to white southern converts' slaves as "servants." Brown, *Autobiography*. In comparison, see "Slave Inhabitants in Utah County, Deseret," 1850 U.S. Census, Slave Schedules, accessed through Ancestry.com.

58. Bringhurst, "Elijah Abel," 25.

59. James and Roundy, "Biography of Jane E. James."

60. Newell, "'Is There No Blessing for Me?,'" 41–68.

61. Brigham Young organized and led the first few hundred Mormons who, between the spring of 1846 and the fall of 1847, established a viable route from Winter Quarters in Nebraska to the Salt Lake Valley and who began the farming and home-

building needed to supply and house the thousands of Mormons to follow. James was not in the famed Vanguard Company, which included three slaves—Green Flake, Hark Lay, and Oscar Crosby—who arrived on July 24, 1847, now celebrated as Utah's Pioneer Day. With the Spencer-Eldredge Company, James entered the valley on September 22, 1847. "Daniel Spencer/Ira Eldredge Company," https://history.lds.org/overlandtravel/companies/285/daniel-spencer-ira-eldredge-company. See also Arrington, *Brigham Young*, 130–53.

62. James and Roundy, "Biography of Jane E. James." I have argued that the chronological specificity James provides for her trek—spring 1846 to early fall 1847—is important for her claim to membership in Mormon pioneer history. When James was composing her autobiography, early black Mormon pioneers to Utah were being marginalized or removed altogether from the church's official pioneer narrative. Mueller, "Playing Jane," 530.

63. Patty Sessions, the great Mormon midwife credited with delivering almost four thousand babies, traveled for a time with James and her family in the pioneer company led by Daniel Spencer. On Wednesday, June 10, 1846, near Mount Pigsah, Iowa, a way station for the Saints heading to Council Bluffs, Sessions helped James deliver her second child, Silas F. James. As Sessions recorded it, "Put black Jane to bed with a son," a service for which Sessions was paid twenty-four pounds of flour. Smart, *Mormon Midwife*, 8, 24.

64. Mueller, "Playing Jane," 526.

65. Jane Manning James's brother, Isaac Lewis Manning, also lived for a time in the Mansion House, working there as a cook. "Isaac Manning Servant of Prophet Joseph Smith Dies in Salt Lake." Joseph Smith III, the son of Emma and Joseph and the first president of the Reorganized Church of Jesus Christ of Latter Day Saints (Community of Christ), describes Isaac fondly as a drummer in the Nauvoo Legion. Isaac Manning "beat [the drum] so vigorously when the Legion was on parade in Nauvoo that its reverberations could be heard, it was said, in Fort Madison, twelve miles away." Smith, *Joseph Smith III and the Restoration*, 36. In June 25, 1901, Isaac Manning, who moved to Utah sometime in the 1880s to care for his ailing sister, paraded in Salt Lake along with other veterans of the Nauvoo Legion. "Reunion of Utah Veterans." Most of the Mannings were officially accepted into the church at Nauvoo in early 1844, while others were recorded as being accepted the following year. Wolfinger, "Test of Faith," 159n10.

66. James and Roundy, "Biography of Jane E. James."

67. Brigham Young remembers the first time he participated in the sacred rituals involving such robes: "We were washed and anointed had our garments placed upon us and received our New Name. And after [Joseph] had performed these ceremonies, he gave the Key Words signs, tokens and penalties." Quoted in Buerger, "Development of Mormon Temple Endowment," 47.

68. James and Roundy, "Biography of Jane E. James."

69. Ibid.

70. October 3, 1841, "History, 1838–1856, vol. C-1, addenda" (ID # 7513), JSPP, http://josephsmithpapers.org/paperSummary/history-1838-1856-volume-c-1-2-november-1838-31-july-1842?p=401.

71. Brown, "Early Mormon Adoption Theology," 4, 28–32; Stapley, "Adoptive Sealing Ritual," 66–67.

72. In 1894, church president Wilford Woodruff transformed the temple liturgy to end the practice of Mormons adopting individuals "outside the lineage of [their] fathers." Yet in the decades before, such spiritual adoptions, especially to Joseph Smith and Brigham Young, as well as to Woodruff himself, were common. Irving, "Law of Adoption," 294, 309, 312.

73. James and Roundy, "Biography of Jane E. James."

74. Minutes, August 26, 1908, The Quorum of the Twelve Apostles, Excerpts from the Weekly Council Meetings Dealing with the Rights of Negroes in the Church, 1849–1940, George Albert Smith Papers. The racial identity of Abel (sometimes spelled Able and Ables) seems to have been fluid. The religious autobiography (1891) of one of his converts, Eunice Kinney, describes him as "a black Elder . . . ordained by Joseph, the martyred prophet." Letter from Sister Kinney, September 1891, Wingfield Watson Correspondence. Yet in the 1867 Salt Lake City directory, while the members of the James family are listed as "colored," no such label accompanies the entry for "Elijah Able." *Salt Lake City Directory*, 33, 67. Newell Bringhurst has suggested that "the Abels stood apart from the other well-known black Mormons," and his descendants, some of whom held the priesthood, may have "passed over the color line." Bringhurst, "Elijah Abel," 30.

75. See advertisement for James's lost luggage in the *Nauvoo Neighbor*, December 6, 1843. For a timeline of the presence of the Partridge and Lawrence sisters, whom James claims to have met in the Mansion House, see Newell and Avery, *Mormon Enigma*, 132–44.

76. Bassard, *Spiritual Interrogations*, 21, 87.

77. All students of early black Mormon history are indebted to the work of Henry J. Wolfinger. Yet in his article "A Test of Faith," the first scholarly examination of the archival record of Jane Manning James, Wolfinger assumes that James could not write because she used a scribe for her autobiography and perhaps for the letters she sent to leading LDS officials. Wolfinger also bases his conclusion about James's limited literacy on her having deeded her estate to her daughter Ellen M. Mclean six months before her death. In the court record involving a lawsuit that Sylvester James brought against his sister over their mother's estate, James signed her name with what appears to be an "X." Yet according to a May 21, 1909, *Salt Lake Herald* article, the court declared, "Mrs. Jane Elizabeth James . . . was mentally incompetent when she deeded her property to her daughter." "Old Woman's Deed Is Set Aside by Court." In my examination of the original letters James wrote to leading church officials, two almost

identical letters from 1890 appear to be composed in the same hand. Jane E. James to Joseph F. Smith, February 7, April 12, 1890, Joseph F. Smith Papers, CHL. A letter from 1903 does appear to be composed in a different hand. By this time, census records along with James's own testimony indicate that she was blind. James E. James to Joseph F. Smith, August 31, 1903, CHL. None of these letters indicate that they came from anyone else's hand but James's.

78. Gates, "'Aunt Jane' James."

79. James and Roundy, "Biography of Jane E. James."

80. The census records from 1870 and 1880 have separate columns in which the census taker indicated whether the individual "cannot read" and "cannot write" by marking a forward slash. In 1870 and 1880, the census taker canvasing Salt Lake City's Eighth Ward, where James lived, was recording this information, as the census taker indicated that some of James's neighbors could neither read nor write. In 1870, there is no slash in the "cannot read" column for James, but there is a slash, which is smudged and might have been erased, in the "cannot write" column. However, in the 1880 census, no slashes appear in either column for James, indicating that she could both read and write. The 1860 census is not conclusive on the question of James's literacy. In this census, only one column, which reads, "persons over 20 y'rs of age who cannot read & write," is provided to the census taker. Although this column is not marked for James's entry, the census taker did not mark the column for any of James's neighbors, suggesting perhaps that the census taker was not recording this information. The 1890 census for Utah was lost to fire. In the 1900 census, in the entry for James, the census taker wrote, "no" and "no" in the two columns dedicated to literacy, which were labeled "can read" and "can write." "Jane James," 1870 U.S. Census, Salt Lake City, Utah, p. 595B; "Jane E. James," 1880 U.S. Census, Salt Lake City, Utah, p. 39A; "Jane E[.] James," 1860 U.S. Census, Great Salt Lake, Utah Territory, p. 84; "Jane E[.] James," 1900 U.S. Census, Salt Lake City, Utah, p. 9A. All these records were accessed through Ancestry.com.

81. See David Wilson, editor's preface to Northup, *Twelve Years a Slave*, xv–xvi. For the requirement of a white reader to authenticate black writers' narratives, see Stepto, *From Behind the Veil*, 17–20.

82. The other African American listed in this volume, published by the Utah Pioneers Book Company, a group of Mormon and pro-Mormon Utahns, was Franklin Perkins, a former slave and farmer who was the father of Sylvester James's wife, Mary. See *Pioneers and Prominent Men of Utah*, 86, 1096. For a period in the 1870s, Perkins was also Sylvester James's stepfather; records show that Jane Manning James was briefly married to Perkins after she divorced Isaac James in 1870. Coleman, "'Is There No Blessing for Me?,'" 150.

83. For example, see *DN*, May 18, 1874: "Yesterday afternoon, the stable of Mr. Sylvester James, a half-breed, in the lower part of the First Ward, took fire and was soon wrapped in flames."

84. James and Roundy, "Biography of Jane E. James."

85. In their trilogy of historical novels about early black Mormons, Margaret Young and Darius Gray imagine a rape scene in the pastor's church office during which Sylvester was conceived. Young and Gray, *One More River to Cross*, 52.

86. Block, *Rape and Sexual Power*, 57–63, 171.

87. Wolfinger, "Test of Faith," 145–46, 168n73. Jane Manning James, her son, Sylvester, and her husband, Isaac James, whom she married in 1845, were the only members of the Connecticut Manning-Stebbins group who cast their lot with Brigham Young and trekked to Utah. After traveling to Winter Quarters during the winter of 1846 during the Mormon exodus from Nauvoo, most of James's family settled in Illinois or Iowa. In the 1860s and 1870s, many of this group joined the Reorganized Church of Jesus Christ of Latter Day Saints. Launius, *Invisible Saints*.

88. John Stauffer has argued that Hannah Crafts defined, in part, the difference between freedom and slavery as the ability to choose one's sexual partner, specifically one's spouse, to whom one is bound through the "holy ordinance" of marriage. Stauffer, "Problem of Freedom," 64–65.

89. As Young explained it in 1854, Cain "deprived his brother of the privilege of pursuing his journey through life, and of extending his kingdom by multiplying upon the earth; and because he did this, he is the last to share the joys of the kingdom of God." Young, "Spiritual Gifts," December 3, 1854, *JD* 2:142–43. Following Young's death, to justify the restriction, church leaders began citing passages in Joseph Smith's translations of the books of Moses and Abraham, which include references to curses against Cain and Ham. Bush, "Mormonism's Negro Doctrine," 68–86.

90. Consciously or not, in her request, James echoes Esau's plea to his father, Isaac, "Hast thou not reserved a blessing for me?" Though Esau was Isaac's eldest son, and thus his rightful heir, Jacob used deception to steal Esau's inheritance (Genesis 27). Thanks to Jonathan Sarna for pointing out this connection. Jane E. James to John Taylor, Salt Lake City, December 27, 1884, transcribed in Wolfinger, "Test of Faith," 148.

91. There is no evidence that James's own husband, whom she divorced in 1870, ever received the priesthood. Jane E. James to Joseph F. Smith, April 12, 1890, CHL; Jane E. James to Joseph F. Smith, February 7, 1890, transcribed in Wolfinger, "Test of Faith," 149. Walker Lewis, a resident of Lowell, Massachusetts, was ordained by Joseph Smith's brother, William. In May 1847, William Appleby visited Lowell and met with Lewis. Writing in his journal, Appleby noted that Lewis "appears to be a meek humble man, and an example for his more whiter brethren to follow." Yet five years before Brigham Young's first public pronouncement on the priesthood ban, Appleby also questioned the validity of Walker's ordination, writing that it was "contrary to the order of the Church or the Law of the Priesthood, as the Descendants of Ham are not entitled to that privilege." Appleby Autobiography and Journal, May 19, 1847, CHL; Stevenson, *Cause of Righteousness*, 230–31.

92. *D&C* 132:63, 19. See also Genesis 1:20–25 and Jacob 2:30. Though the July 12,

1843, entry in William Clayton's hand was most likely the first record of the revelation on plural marriage, the consensus among scholars of early Mormon polygamy is that Joseph Smith received the revelation as early as 1831. Van Wagoner, *Mormon Polygamy*, 56–60; Compton, *In Sacred Loneliness*, 4, 10, 27–28, 33; Bushman, *Rough Stone Rolling*, 323–26.

93. Clark, Messages of the First Presidency, 11. Daynes, *More Wives Than One*, 169.

94. "Varieties"; Reeve, *Religion of a Different Color*, 186.

95. "Society in the South"; Reeve, *Religion of a Different Color*, 186.

96. "Society in the South."

97. February 13, 1849, box 2, folder 8, GCM.

98. Ibid. The first pronouncement of a priesthood ban from a leading church official likely came from Parley P. Pratt during the spring 1847 confrontation at Winter Quarters with the self-professed prophet and leader of his own splinter community William McCary. A talented musician and ventriloquist, McCary claimed to be of mixed African and Native American descent. During the winter of 1846–47, he initially won acclaim from many church leaders with his musical virtuosity. He may even have been ordained a priesthood holder. Yet he lost favor with some in the church hierarchy when he began claiming prophetic authority—including to be the reborn "Adam, the ancient of days," a "Lamanite prophet," and even Jesus. When he began attracting followers, including white Mormon women, in April 1847, Pratt denounced McCary and the people who chose "to follow this Black man [McCary] who has got the blood of Ham in him in which his linege [*sic*] was cursed as regards to the Priesthood." For Pratt's pronouncement, see April 25, 1847, box 1, folder 53, GCM. On McCary's role in the advent of the race-based priesthood restriction, see Reeve, *Religion of a Different Color*, 128–36. For the most complete study of McCary's life within Mormonism and as a nationally renowned "Indian" performer, see Hudson, *Real Native Genius*.

99. Brigham Young, "The Laws of God Relative to the African Race," March 8, 1863, *JD* 10:110. In another particularly graphic example of such rhetoric, Young declared in the winter of 1852, "And if any man mingles his seed with the seed of Cane the only way he Could get rid of it or have salvation would be to Come forward & have his head Cut off & spill his Blood upon the ground. It would also take the life of his Children." Quoted in Woodruff, undated entry between January 4 and February 8, 1852, *Journal*, 4:97; Bush, "Mormonism's Negro Doctrine," 42.

100. Erastus Snow, "God's Peculiar People," May 5, 1882, *JD* 23:186–87. John Taylor, "Hostility of the World to the Gospel," February 12, 1882, *JD* 26:87–92.

101. Brown, "Early Mormon Adoption Theology," 3–5; Stapley, "Adoptive Sealing Ritual," 66–68.

102. Roundy's adoptive mother was her friend and Joseph Smith's widowed plural wife Eliza R. Snow. Church patriarch John Smith served as proxy for his uncle, and Lucy Walker Smith Kimball stood in for the ailing Eliza R. Snow. Elizabeth J. D.

Roundy, Temple Ordinance Book, CHL. Jane E. James to Joseph F. Smith, February 7, April 12, 1890.

103. Brown, "Early Mormon Adoption Theology," 38; Stapley, "Adoptive Sealing Ritual," 68–71. Thanks to Jonathan Stapley for helping me navigate this complicated and evolving theology of adoption and celestial marriage.

104. Kathryn Daynes coined the term "protopolygamy" to describe this early era of the institution. Daynes, *More Wives Than One*, 31.

105. James and Roundy, "Biography of Jane E. James." For an analysis of Joseph Smith's secret marriages to Emily Dow Partridge and Eliza Maria Partridge in March 1843 and to Sarah and Maria Lawrence in May 1843, see Newell and Avery, *Mormon Enigma*, 132–44. In his own memoir, Joseph Smith III remembers Jane Manning James's reaction to polygamy very differently. Perhaps influenced by the RLDS's views on Joseph Smith's polygamy, Joseph Smith III recalls a 1905 conversation with James, whom he misidentifies as Maria. James's brother Isaac Lewis Manning, who joined the Reorganized Church before moving to Utah, "was living in a small but comfortable house with his sister Maria who, in the old days in Nauvoo, had worked as a domestic for Mother. This aged woman made a quite characteristic statement about my mother: 'She was the best woman I ever knew.' Then she added, 'And them was all lies about the Prophet Joseph having any other wives than her!" Smith, *Memoirs*, 26.

106. Compton, *In Sacred Loneliness*, 6, 396–456, 473–85. Even before the Nauvoo period, Smith had already established a pattern of marrying servant girls who worked in his household. Fanny Alger, who was probably no older than sixteen when she lived with the Smiths in Kirtland in 1835, is likely to have been Smith's first plural wife. Daynes, *More Wives Than One*, 20–22.

107. Hall, *Abominations of Mormonism Exposed*, 58–59. In the 1840s, it was not uncommon for the church patriarch to designate a white Saint to the lineage of Manasseh. But the frequency of the Ephraim lineage designation for white Mormons became more and more the norm throughout the nineteenth century. For Gertrude Martineau, her designation of Manasseh related directly to her prophesied work for the restoration. In March 15, 1885, patriarch William McBride declared that Martineau was "of the blood of Manassah [Manasseh]." McBride foresaw that Martineau's shared bloodline with the Lamanites would allow her to "become an instrument in the hands of the Lord in doing much for the restoration of the daughters of Mannasah, in teaching them the gospel in languages that thou dost not understand, and administer ordinances unto them in the temples of the Lords that will their salvation." *LPB*, 259. Similar to Joseph Smith marrying his wards, "the Apostle to the Lamanites" Jacob Hamblin married one of his own adopted Indian children, a teenage Paiute named Eliza. Hamblin later brought her and other Indian polygamous wives on missions into Arizona, "thinking that they might be a great help in introducing something like cleanliness in cooking" to the Hopis and Navajos he was sent to convert. Compton, "Civilizing the Ragged Edge," 160.

108. See, among others, 1 Nephi 15:17, 13–14, 2 Nephi 10:18.

109. Smith, A Patriarchal Blessing of Jane Manning, CHL.

110. As recorded in the organizational meeting of the "Church of Christ" on April 6, 1830, Joseph Smith revealed, "There is a possibility that man may fall from grace and depart from the living God." *D&C* 20:32.

111. *EPB*, 226–27, emphasis added.

112. "Book of Abraham"; Smith, "Church History."

113. Quoted in Bush, "Mormonism's Negro Doctrine," 26.

114. This part of the book of Moses was initially titled "Extracts from the Prophecy of Enoch" and was published in August 1832 in *E&MS*; Moses 7:22. Reading Moses 5:32 intertextually with 2 Nephi 5:3, 19, we see that, motivated by envy, both Cain and Laman act violently against their brothers, for which they are separated from their family and marked off with dark skin.

115. Moses 5:41, 40.

116. See Daniel 2:21, "And he changeth the times and the season; he removeth kings, and setteth up kings; he giveth wisdom unto the wise, and knowledge to them that know understanding"; Smith, A Patriarchal Blessing of Jane Manning, CHL.

117. Genesis 4:7 reads: "If thou doest well, shalt thou not be accepted? And if thou doest not well, sin lieth at the door." In Moses 5:23, Joseph changes the rhetorical question found in the KJV of Genesis to a definitive period.

118. Genesis 4:8 reads: "And Cain talked with Abel his brother: and it came to pass, when they were in the field, that Cain rose up against Abel his brother, and slew him." The implications of Hyrum's use of Moses 5:23 go even deeper. In the nine verses between Moses 5:23 and 5:32, when Cain kills Abel (comprising the "plain and precious things" [1 Nephi 13] that Joseph Smith restores to the Genesis account), Smith further articulates Cain's wickedness. In fact, out of his jealousy, Cain covenants with Satan "that I may murder to get gain" (Moses 5:31).

119. Smith, A Patriarchal Blessing of Jane Manning, CHL. Again, Hyrum Smith is quoting here directly from his brother and the church's first presidency, of which he was a member. See "Report from the First Presidency." In her 1889 patriarchal blessing, Hyrum Smith's son John Smith repeats the promise that James's name "shall be handed down to posterity." James's material concerns did not abate in the forty-five years after her first patriarchal blessing. John Smith declares, "Thou shalt not lack for food raiment or shelter." Smith, Patriarchal Blessing for Jane Elizabeth James, October 10, 1889, CHL.

120. "Aunt Jane Laid to Rest."

121. As Jonathan Stapley has shown, for a brief period, "scribes recorded individuals in the temple ledgers with their adoptive parents' last name adjoined to their own. Though this naming custom was implemented only for a short time, Brigham Young preached that individuals were to use these new names publicly." Stapley, "Adoptive Sealing Ritual," 71.

122. Barney, "Jane Manning James."

123. James joined the Eighth Ward Relief Society soon after moving to the ward from Salt Lake City's First Ward after divorcing her husband in 1870. She remained a member of the Eighth Ward until her death in 1908. During her membership, James frequently bore her testimony and made "other remarks." In the form of cash and sundries, she both donated to and received support from the Relief Society's funds for the poor and sick. Yet despite her many years of membership, she was never called to any leadership or formal service position in the ward's Relief Society. Eighth Ward Relief Society Minutes and Records, CHL.

124. Lydia D. Alder, "Ladies' Semi-Monthly Meeting," *Woman's Exponent*, December 1, 1893.

125. Lydia D. Alder, "Ladies' Semi-Monthly Meeting," *Woman's Exponent*, October 31, 1896; Stapley, "Jane Manning James."

126. Zina D. H. Young to Apostle Joseph F. Smith, January 15, 1894, transcribed in Wolfinger, "Test of Faith," 150.

127. Brigham Young, "Intelligence," October 9, 1859, *JD* 7:290–91.

128. Because the Salt Lake City temple was not yet complete, in 1888 James traveled north to Logan to perform this temple work. Linda King Newell Papers.

129. Salt Lake City Temple Adoption Records, CHL. The temple record labeling James a "servitor" is unique in Mormon history. This identity of "servitor," however, might relate to the political and theological history of early Utah's experience with "white" indentured servitude and "Indian" and "African" slavery, which I discuss in chapter 6. As for why James was not permitted to participate in her own sealing, her race seems to be the most obvious reason. Yet it is also possible that because James did not have her temple endowments, which are necessary for participation in sealing rituals, she was not allowed to participate in this adoption sealing. It is also possible that James was too infirm to make the trip to the temple, though because she demonstrated such a strong desire to participate in her temple work, this seems unlikely. And James was well enough to participate in other community events, like annual "Old Folks Day" celebrations and the 1897 Jubilee. Whatever the case, Bathsheba W. Smith, who served as an ordinance worker in the Salt Lake Temple during this period, was a logical choice for a proxy for James. See "Smith, Bathsheba Wilson," in Jenson, *Latter-day Saint Biographical Encyclopedia*, 1:699–702.

130. Minutes, August 26, 1908, The Quorum of the Twelve Apostles, Excerpts from the Weekly Council Meetings Dealing with the Rights of Negroes in the Church, 1849–1940, George Albert Smith Papers.

131. Ibid.

132. Minutes, August 26, 1908, The Quorum of the Twelve Apostles, Excerpts from the Weekly Council Meetings Dealing with the Rights of Negroes in the Church, 1849–1940, George Albert Smith Papers; LDS Church Council Minutes, June 4, 1879, Adam S. Bennion Papers.

133. "LDS Church First Presidency Statement on the Question of Blacks within the Church," August 17, 1949, reprinted in Bringhurst, *Saints, Slaves, and Blacks*, 230.

134. "'Aunt Jane' Laid to Rest."

Chapter 5

1. Carvalho, *Incidents of Travel*, 188–89. See also Thomas Bullock, Minutes, May 3–11, 1854, box 2, folder 52, GCM; Woodruff, *Journal*, 4:262–74.

2. Wakara, known to the Mormons as "Walker," was the military chief of the powerful northern confederacy of Ute bands. Sowiette, whom some sources call Wakara's half-brother or uncle, was the confederacy's civil chief. Peterson, *Utah's Black Hawk War*, 60, 90.

3. Blackhawk, *Violence over the Land*, 120, 139–41.

4. Farmer, *Zion's Mount*, 19, 50; Simmons, *Ute Indians*, 13–16.

5. Quoted in Blackhawk, *Violence over the Land*, 240.

6. Gottfredson, *Indian Depredations in Utah*, 43–58. For a Gentile perspective on the "Walker War" published in the 1850s, see Heap and Beale, *Central Route to the Pacific*, 91–93. Recent scholarship has questioned how much Wakara directly orchestrated the war that bears his name. Christy, "Walker War"; Farmer, *Zion's Mount*, 131–32; Peterson, *Utah's Black Hawk War*, 63–71.

7. Nauvoo Legion Papers, CHL; Kimball, *Memoirs of Wilcox*, 34.

8. Bean to Brigham Young, May 1, 1854, BYP.

9. Carvalho, *Incidents of Travel*, 189.

10. Knack, *Boundaries Between*, 61.

11. Carvalho, *Incidents of Travel*, 193.

12. Woodruff, *Journal*, 4:272–74; Farmer, *Zion's Mount*, 87.

13. Carvalho, *Incidents of Travel*, 194.

14. Ibid., 189.

15. Bean to Brigham Young, May 1, 1854, BYP; Blackhawk, *Violence over the Land*, 241–42.

16. Martineau, Iron County Mission Historical Record, CHL. See Armand Mauss's discussion of the Mormon application of the "Doctrine of Discovery," which differentiated European colonial landownership from indigenous land occupancy. Mauss, *All Abraham's Children*, 44–66.

17. Heap and Beale, *Central Route to the Pacific*, 90–91. On the value of the labor that these Paiute children provided in the Mormons' labor-intensive settler economy, see Knack, *Boundaries Between*, 54–57.

18. Martineau, Iron County Mission Historical Record, CHL.

19. My notion of "people building" relates to the politics, policies, and ideologies of "nation building" that, as Anne Hyde has recently chronicled, took place in the two decades after the Mexican-American War brought much of the American West under the control of the United States. People building involves a conquering power that,

through systems of laws, languages, religions, and culture, imposes a set of norms—in particular, racial and citizenship norms—onto a people whom the conquering power has colonized and occupied. Hyde, *Empires, Nations, and Families*, 24, 369, 452–62. Like this American nation-building project, through the deployment of rhetoric and policies as well as through the deployment of "lawful" coercion and violence, within the incipient Mormon nation-state, such work of people building created two distinct but mutually constitutive peoples: a people whom the conquering power could incorporate into its new nation and a people whom, because this people violently resisted accepting its norms, the conquering power could justify eradicating for the peace and security of the newly formed people. I also derive my idea of "people building" from studies of more recent U.S. attempts of nation building in nations conquered and occupied as part of the War on Terror. Fukuyama, "Introduction," 3–4.

20. 2 Nephi 10:9, 1 Nephi 22:6.

21. Here I employ the tools of ethnohistory to undertake the task of reading Wakara's actions in contrast with how the Mormons wrote about them. As Daniel Richter has written, "Documentary evidence illuminates the European cast of characters, yet only imagination can put Indians in the foreground of these scenes." Richter, *Facing East*, 13. Borrowing from Raymond Fogelson's notion of "imagined events," imagination is employed here to study how the two sides of an encounter understood and thus remembered differently the same events. Fogelson, "Ethnohistory."

22. *Utah Pioneers*, 23. Not unlike the multiple versions of Joseph Smith's First Vision, the archival memory of Young's first vision of the Salt Lake Valley underwent a series of revisions, additions, and ultimately concisions. Brigham Young, "The Holy Ghost Necessary in Preaching," August 17, 1856, *JD* 4:32; Woodruff, *Journal*, 3:333–34.

23. Campbell, *Establishing Zion*, 95. On Utah's changing demography, see Perlich, "Utah Minorities."

24. Clayton, *Intimate Chronicle*, 348–53; Brooks, "Indian Relations," 3.

25. On July 21, 1847, Apostles Willard Richards and George A. Smith sent word to the Vanguard Company's advance party to bear north "toward the region of the Salt Lake" on their approach out of the Wasatch. "Young gave us his views concerning a stopping place in the Basin," wrote Richards and Smith. "He felt inclined for the present not to crowd upon the Utes until we have a chance to get acquainted with them." Quoted in Arrington, *Brigham Young*, 144.

26. Blackhawk, *Violence over the Land*, 55–145. On ethnic boundary creation as a result of Indian contact with non-Indians in the Great Basin, see Farmer, *Zion's Mount*, 30–33; and Knack, *Boundaries Between*, 4–7, 30–31, 36.

27. Parkman, *Oregon Trail*, 37.

28. Jackman Journal, July 28, 1847, CHL. On the Anglo-American tradition of establishing land ownership through "improvement," see Cronon, *Changes to the Land*, 56–63; and Banner, *How the Indians Lost Their Land*, 32–46.

29. Arrington and Bitton, *Mormon Experience*, 104; Wolfinger, "Test of Faith," 130–

32. Jane Manning James's early Utah neighbors included Eliza Partridge, whom James first met in the Smiths' Nauvoo Mansion House and who married church apostle Amasa Lyman after the death of her first husband, Joseph Smith Jr. Amasa Lyman was already married to Caroline Partridge and would eventually marry another Partridge sister, Lydia. Eliza Partridge Lyman wrote in her journal that in April 1848, with her husband in California on church business, her family was on the brink of starvation. On April 25, she noted, "Jane James, a colored woman, let me have about two pounds of flour, it being about half she had." Lyman Journal, April 25, 1848, CHL. Eliza's sister (and sister wife) Lydia composed a poem to James, which reads in part, "an angel in disguise / Came in at our door / She brought with her a precious gift / That precious gift was flour." James's act of generosity is now memorialized on a bronze plaque on her grave marker in the Salt Lake City cemetery. Thanks to Tamra Bybee for sharing the poem with me.

30. During what was dubbed the Black Hawk War (1865-72), the Ute leader Sanpitch, along with his son Antonga (Black Hawk), created a pan-Indian alliance that violently resisted the growth of Mormon settlements in southern Utah. Mormon militiamen killed Sanpitch in 1866. Peterson, *Utah's Black Hawk War*, 300.

31. In her introduction to the *U.S. Army/Marine Corp Counterinsurgency Field Manual*, Sarah Sewall writes, "The field manual directs U.S. forces to make securing the civilian, rather than destroying the enemy, their top priority. . . . The real battle is for civilian support for, or acquiescence to, the counterinsurgents and host nation government. The population waits to be convinced. Who will help them more, hurt them less, stay they longest, earn their trust." Sewall, "Introduction," xxv.

32. Jackman Journal, July 28, 1847, CHL.

33. Carvalho, *Incidents of Travel*, 191; Young, *Memoirs*, 55.

34. Warner, *Domínguez-Escalante Journal*, 32-33, 38-41, 63-72; Blackhawk, *Violence over the Land*, 94; Farmer, *Zion's Mount*, 19, 30.

35. Hoxie, *Final Promise*, 1-81.

36. Levi Jackman, Journal, July 28, 1847.

37. 1 Nephi 22:6-12; Turner, *Brigham Young*, 217.

38. Huntington to Brigham Young, May 18, April 19, 1849, BYP; Farmer, *Zion's Mount*, 64.

39. Special Order No. 2, January 31, 1850, Utah Territorial Militia Records, https:// familysearch.org/pal:/MM9.3.1/TH-1951-22024-3922-55?cc=1462415&wc=14229733; Christy, "'What Virtue,'" 303.

40. Special Order No. 2, issued by Daniel H. Wells to G. D. Grant, January 31, 1850.

41. Peterson, *Utah's Black Hawk War*, 52-57; Farmer, *Zion's Mount*, 74-75.

42. Gunnison, *Mormons*, 146-47.

43. Farmer, *Zion's Mount*, 54-140. As Anne Hyde has argued, the Mormons, like other white American settler colonialists of the West in the mid-nineteenth century, created not a nation of laws but instead "a nation of squatters who used violence to

establish rights and to dispossess other people." Hyde, *Empires, Nations, Families*, 484.

44. Gunnison also took note of the irony "that those whose *mission* [emphasis in original] it is to convert these aborigines by the sword of the spirit, should thus be obliged to destroy them." Gunnison, *Mormons*, 147.

45. February 10, 1850, box 2, folder 17, GCM; Farmer, *Zion's Mount*, 73.

46. January 31, 1850, box 2, folder 17, GCM; Howard, "'What Virtue There Is in Stone,'" 302.

47. Quoted in Farmer, *Zion's Mount*, 76.

48. Wells, "Daniel H. Wells' Narrative," 126; Farmer, *Zion's Mount*, 77.

49. Many of the Ute chiefs were Wakara's relations. Peterson, *Utah's Black Hawk War*, 60.

50. January 31, 1850, box 2, folder 17, GCM.

51. Kane, *Mormons*, 72.

52. Young to Chief Walker, November 22, 1849, BYP.

53. Big Chief Brigham Young to Pe-tete-net, Walker, Tow-ee-ette, Blackhawk, Tabbee, and other good Indian Chiefs, May 6, 1850, quoted in Coates, "History of Indian Education by the Mormons," 73–79.

54. Brigham Young to Chief Walker, November 22, 1849, BYP.

55. Huntington, Minutes of Meeting with Indians, May 14, 1849, BYP.

56. Christy, "Open Hand and Mailed Fist," 221–22.

57. Farmer, *Zion's Mount*, 65–66.

58. Lawrence Coates has described Manti as Brigham Young's "peace corps" for Chief Wakara's Indians. Coates, "Brigham Young and Mormon Indian Policies," 440. Yet because Young and other Mormon leaders were always prepared to use force to quell Indian resistance to Mormon settlement expansion, the better modern analogy might be that Manti was part of the Mormons' "counterinsurgency" efforts. Sewall, "Introduction."

59. Morley to Brigham Young, March 15, 1850, BYP; Walker, "Wakara Meets the Mormons," 226.

60. Morley to Brigham Young, April 17, 1850.

61. The Presidency to Isaac Morley and the Saints in Sanpete, March 24, 1850, quoted in Walker, "Wakara Meets the Mormons," 226.

62. Ibid.

63. Meeting with Utes, May 22, 1850, BYP.

64. Walker Statement, BYP; Bean to Brigham Young, May 1, 1854, BYP; Farmer, *Zion's Mount*, 19, 34–35, 85.

65. As Ned Blackhawk has argued, negotiated accommodation and compromise was also the practice of the Colorado Ute chief Ouray when settlers flooded into the Utes' longtime homelands in the 1860s. Blackhawk, *Violence over the Land*, 177–225.

66. In a 1777 letter to the Spanish crown, the cartographer for the Domínguez-

Escalante Expedition, Bernado de Miera, described the "Lake of the Timpanogos" (Utah Lake) region as "the most pleasant, beautiful and fertile in all of New Spain" and large and fecund enough "to support a city with as large a population as that of Mexico City." Pachecho, "Miera's Report," 114; Farmer, *Zion's Mount*, 30.

67. Meeting with Utes, May 22, 1850, BYP. See also Isaac Morley to Brigham Young, February 20, March 15, April 13, 17, 21, 1850, BYP.

68. Bean to Brigham Young, BYP. After Wakara's death, another Timpanogos chief Highforehead (Ton-om-bu-gah) repeated Wakara's rejection of the Saints' demands to buy land outright. At a July 1855 meeting with Mormon leaders in Provo, through translation Highforehead demanded, "Why shall the country be broken, why shall we divide the land? He says it has been a tradition handed down to them from their fathers and their fathers['] fathers for many generations that they must not sell their country." The Mormons were welcome to live on the land "where their fathers and mothers have died," Highforehead explained. But in exchange for this land use, the "plent[iful]" Mormons must help support "poor" Indians. Remarks by Tow-om-bw-gah or Highforehead, July 15, 1855, CHL. For a precedent of Mormon-Ute reciprocity as a way to "mitigate levels of violence," see Blackhawk, *Violence over the Land*, 56–80.

69. Knack, *Boundaries Between*, 61–62.

70. Borrowing from Linford D. Fisher's description of Native Americans' engagement with Christianity in Connecticut during the eighteenth century, baptism likely signaled Wakara's interest in "affiliating" with the Saints' religion, not converting to it "in some sort of totalizing way." Fisher, *Indian Great Awakening*, 88, 84–107. Wakara would likely never have agreed to be baptized if the Mormon ritual held the same meaning as Catholic baptisms of Native Americans, which served to disconnect these Indians from their "heathen" ancestry and assimilate them into the settler culture. In the colonial outposts in New Mexico, local officials and clergy forced baptism on recently purchased Indian slaves, who were often brought south by Ute slavers like Wakara. The Utes in New Mexico did not ask priests to baptize their own children. Blackhawk, *Violence over the Land*, 72–80.

71. George A. Smith, "The Indian War," October 7, 1853, JD 1:197; Woodruff, *Journal*, 4:272–74.

72. Wakara to George A. Smith, undated, quoted in Heap and Beale, *Central Route to the Pacific*, 92.

73. Bean to Brigham Young, May 1, 1854, BYP.

74. Young, *Governor's Message*. For a study of the decimation of Utah's Indian population following the Mormons' arrival, see Stoffle, Jones, and Dobyns, "Direct European Immigrant Transmission."

75. JH, May 16, 1851; Woodruff, *Journal*, 4:26; Reeve, *Religion of a Different Color*, 78.

76. Coates, "Brigham Young and Mormon Indian Policies," 446.

77. Daniel H. Wells to John M. Bernhisel, November 20, 1850, quoted in ibid., 450.

78. Quoted in ibid., 452. In his own recollection of the meeting with Wakara in May

1854, Brigham Young described the bodily transformation that the chief underwent before accepting peace. Wakara had been "dull and sulky," unsure "whether to turn to the side of peace or of war." Yet after Young and other Mormon leaders laid their hands on him, the chief began to feel "better . . . full of kindness, and love to God" and pledged never attack the Mormon people again. Brigham Young, "The Lamanites," December 3, 1854, JD 2:143.

79. Derr, "'Strengthen in Our Union,'" 170–71.

80. Brigham Young to Isaac Haight, August 18, 1854, quoted in Coates, "History of Indian Education," 174.

81. Ibid., 172–73.

82. See fig. 1, "Map of Brigham Young's Indian Missions," in Smallcanyon, "Contested Space," 177.

83. Brigham Young, "Practical Religion," June 7, 1857, JD 4:346.

84. Carvalho, *Incidents of Travel*, 219, 215, 213, 224.

85. The Santa Clara Mission was established in 1851 at Harmony, the first official Indian mission in Utah. Abandoned following attacks related to the Walker War, it was reestablished and renamed the Southern Indian Mission. Brooks, "Indian Relations," 9–10; Knack, *Boundaries Between*, 52, 62–63.

86. Quoted in Brooks, "Indian Relations," 12.

87. Brown, "Extracts of a letter to Governor Young." See also Peterson, "Jacob Hamblin," 26; and Knack, *Boundaries Between*, 35–36, 58–59.

88. Quoted in Brooks, "Jacob Hamblin," 323. Despite his supposed low self-appraisal, Brigham Young ordained Tutsegavit a Mormon elder in September 1857. Huntington Journal, September 10, 1857, CHL.

89. Compton, "Civilizing the Ragged Edge," 160–61, 174–82; Robinson, *Life of Hatch*, 5.

90. According to Hatch's biographer, instead of serving as an intermediary, Sarah Spaneshank (Maraboots) created tension between the missionaries and the Navajos during one missionary expedition. The Navajos attempted to abduct her and "claimed her as a member of their tribe" because her father had been a prominent Navajo leader. Robinson, *Life of Hatch*, 1, 10; Hatch, *Ira Hatch*, 64–66.

91. Beeton, "Teach Them to Till."

92. Elk Mountain Mission Journal, CHL; Law, "Mormon Indian Missions, 1855," 23–36.

93. Campbell, "Brigham Young's Outer Cordon."

94. In his autobiography, Joseph Rawlins Jr., the first senator elected to represent Utah after it gained statehood in 1896, recalled that in 1855, with his father serving as a missionary at the doomed Elk Mountain Mission, his mother, Mary, kept her children fed, ran the farm, and fended off Indian attacks. "When Indians in hideous war paint surrounded the house, dancing and making the air vibrate by terrifying noise

. . . my mother stood composed, tactful and unblanched and by sheer moral courage and force of character seemed to keep the enemy at bay." While his father was away spreading the gospel in a place where "the white man had seldom if ever penetrated," at home it was only his mother, Rawlins wrote, who kept the family on this side of civilization, or they would have been either "overrun by the Indians or degraded to their condition." Rawlins, Autobiography, J. Willard Marriot Library.

95. Young, "Governor's Message."

96. In the second half of the 1860s, Young and federal Indian agents convinced some tribal leaders to accept governmental payments and consolidate in reservations in northern Utah, agreements for which Black Hawk and his allies demonstrated their disdain by increasing their raids. Peterson, *Utah's Black Hawk War*, 7.

97. After establishing the "Cherokee Branch," mission president Henry W. Miller sent a report to Salt Lake praising the Cherokee Nation, which had a constitution that grants "all preachers . . . free access" to its people, as well as "a written language, and a Bible printed in it; they nearly all read and write." This combination of religious liberty and literacy led Miller to believe that once the missionaries "get a few native Elders to work," the Cherokee Nation could be turned into a Mormon one "in a short time." Miller, "Cherokee Nation."

98. Dennis, "Captain Dan Jones." During later expeditions, Welshman Llewellyn Harris also noted the similarities between "Zuni" Indian language and Welsh. Harris Notebook, CHL.

99. Peterson, "Hopis and Mormons," 189–90.

100. Blackhawk, *Violence over the Land*, 228–30, 258–64.

101. Peterson, "Jacob Hamblin," 28–29; Reeve, *Religion of a Different Color*, 101–3.

102. Orson Pratt, "Redemption of Zion," February 7, 1875, *JD* 17:299–300. On the myth of the Three Nephites in early Utah, see Wilson, "Three Nephites."

103. Huntington, "Correspondence."

104. Maffly-Kipp, "Assembling Bodies and Souls," 67; Aikau, *Chosen People, Promised Land*, 1–54. The written record of Cannon's revelation came decades after 1851 and thus has been questioned as apocryphal. Farmer, "Review of *Chosen People, Promised Land*," 109.

105. Law, "Mormon Indian Missions, 1855," 84–121.

106. McClintock, *Mormon Settlement in Arizona*, 159.

107. Peterson, "Hopis and Mormons," 193–94.

108. John Nicholson, "The Church of Christ Organized Anciently on This Continent," February 6, 1881, *JD* 22:21–23.

Chapter 6

1. Young, Speech by Gov. Young in Council on a Bill Relating to African Slavery, January 23, 1852, CHL. See also Young, "Governor's Message to the Council of Rep-

resentatives." For a discussion of Young's prepared speech and his extemporaneous remarks on "African slavery" recorded in Pittman shorthand by George D. Watt, see Reeve, *Religion of a Different Color*, 148–52.

2. Jones, *Forty Years among the Indians*, 49; Gutiérrez, *When Jesus Came*, 153; Blackhawk, *Violence over the Land*, 78.

3. Quoted in Brooks, "Indian Relations," 6.

4. Ibid.

5. Quoted in Jones, *Trial of Don Pedro León Luján*, 49–50.

6. Jones, *Forty Years among the Indians*, 49; Blackhawk, *Violence over the Land*, 70–80.

7. On the trial of Luján, its irregularities, and Mormon biases, see Jones, *Trial of Don Pedro León Luján*, 86–92.

8. Jones, *Forty Years among the Indians*, 54–56; Young, "Proclamation by the Governor"; Farmer, *Zion's Mount*, 84; Brigham Young, "Indian Difficulties," May 8, 1853, *JD* 1:104.

9. Jones, *Trial of Don Pedro León Luján*, 95.

10. Jones, *Forty Years among the Indians*. 52–53. In June 1853, Young wrote to the commissioner of Indian Affairs, "One of Waker's [*sic*] brothers, lately killed an Indian prisoner child, because the traders would not give him what he asked for it." Quoted in Blackhawk, *Violence over the Land*, 240.

11. Brigham Young, "Indian Difficulties," May 8, 1853, *JD* 1:106.

12. Brigham Young, "Walker and His Band," July 31, 1853, *JD* 1:161–71.

13. Quoted in Jones, *Trial of Don Pedro Léon Luján*, 48.

14. Young, "'Weary Traveler,'" 109–10. See also Turner, *Brigham Young*, 215. Over the years, the contrast between the horrors of Sally's pre-Mormon life and the love with which the Mormons embraced her only grew starker in the Mormon archive. In his memoirs, published in 1920, Brigham Young's nephew John R. Young, who would have only been ten years old at the time, vividly recalls Sally's harrowing arrival at the newly completed fort in the Salt Lake Valley. "[In the] fall of 1847 a band of Indians camped near us. Early one morning we were excited at hearing their shrill, blood-curdling war whoop, mingled with occasional sharp cries of pain. Father sent me to the Fort for help." Young explains that members of "Wanship's band" of braves had captured two girl prisoners. "One of these they had killed, and were torturing the other. To save her life Charley Decker bought her, and took her to our house to be washed and clothed. She was the saddest-looking piece of humanity I have ever seen. They had shingled her head with butcher knives and firebrands. All the fleshy parts of her body, legs, and arms had been hacked with knives, then fire brands had been stuck into the wounds." Young, *Memoirs*, 62.

15. Quoted in Turner, *Brigham Young*, 216.

16. Tait, "Young Woman's Journal."

17. Gates, "Courtship of Kanosh," 21–22.

18. According to Gates, Wakara twice attempted to capture Sally. The first instance occurred when, against the wishes of her Mormon caretakers, Sally took a nighttime stroll to splash her feet in Salt Lake's City Creek. Sally narrowly escaped reenslavement by outrunning Wakara to the safety of her mistress's home. "He bad Indian," Sally described Wakara. "All Indians bad!" Ibid., 27.

19. Kimball, "From Thrilling Experiences," in Gottfredson, *Indian Depredations in Utah*, 16–17.

20. See "Sally, Indian," in entry for "Brigham Young," 1860 U.S. Census, Great Salt Lake, Utah Territory, p. 268, accessed through Ancestry.com.

21. Marriage Certificates, CHL.

22. Turner, *Brigham Young*, 347–48; Knack, *Boundaries Between*, 61–62.

23. See table 6, "Known Costs of Trade for Native American Children in Mormon Households," in Bennion, "Captivity, Adoption, Marriage and Identity," 249.

24. *Acts, Resolutions and Memorials*, 92–94.

25. Young, "Governor's Message to the Council of Representatives."

26. *Acts, Resolutions and Memorials*, 94.

27. Blackhawk, *Violence over the Land*, 70–80.

28. Young, Speech by Gov. Young in Council on a Bill Relating to African Slavery, CHL.

29. Ibid. However, in his prepared remarks, Young declared that "slavery" or any system in which "human flesh dealt in as property, is not consistent or compatible with the true principles of government. . . . My own feelings are, that no property can or should be recognized as existing in slaves, either Indian or African." Young, "Governor's Message to the Council of Representatives of the Legislature of Utah."

30. Young, Speech by Gov. Young in Council on a Bill Relating to African Slavery, CHL.

31. Bernhisel successfully lobbied members of Congress to create the Utah Territory as part of the Compromise of 1850 in part by convincing them that there were no slaves in Utah. Ricks, "Peculiar Place," 2–3, 50–133.

32. *Acts, Resolutions and Memorials*, 80–82. For a side-by-side comparison of the early and final versions of the Utah Territory "Act in Relation to Service," see Ricks, "Peculiar Place," app. 3, 161–62. An original member of the Quorum of the Twelve Apostles as well as a territorial legislature, Orson Pratt also delivered a speech before the legislature on slavery, during which he lambasted his brethren and fellow lawmakers' move to bring slavery to Utah. For a detailed discussion of the debates surrounding the 1852 "Indian" and "African" slavery legislation, see Reeve, Rich, and Carruth, *"Enough to Cause the Angels."*

33. *M&A*, April 1836. On slavery as paternalism, see Genovese, *Roll, Jordan, Roll*, 3–112. For one of many rebuttals of Genovese, see Johnson, *Soul by Soul*, esp. 108–28.

34. Young, Speech by Gov. Young in Council on a Bill Relating to African Slavery.

35. Christopher C. Rich has argued that "An Act in Relation to Service" was de-

signed, in the short term, to protect the property interest of Mormon slaveholders by legalizing slavery and, in the longer term, to solve the problem of slavery by foreseeing a day when slaves would be freed. Rich, "True Policy for Utah." In 1859, Horace Greeley asked Brigham Young if Utah's territorial laws recognized slavery. Young replied, "Those laws are printed—you can read them for yourself. If slaves are brought here by their owners in the states, we do not favor their escape from the service of their owners." Yet Young told Greeley that he expected that when Utah was admitted to the Union, Utah "shall be a free state." For Young, however, his concern in this matter was for the welfare of the masters, not for the would-be freemen and women. "Slavery here would prove useless and unprofitable," Young continued. "I regard it generally a curse to the masters. I myself hire many laborers, and pay them fair wages; I could not afford to own them." Greeley, *Overland Journey*, 211–12.

36. Young, Address to the Utah Territorial Legislature, January 5, 1852, CHL. At least before they converted to Mormonism, if not after, too, it is likely that some Mormon slave owners procreated with the female slaves. See the slave entries for Robert M. Smith in which several young children of the slave Biddy are listed as "yellow" or "Mulatto." "Slave Inhabitants in Utah County, Deseret," 1850 U.S. Census, Slave Schedules, accessed through Ancestry.com. See also Mueller, "Hemings and Jefferson Together Forever?" http://www.slate.com/articles/life/faithbased/2012/03 /sally_hemings_mormon_and_married_to_jefferson_proxy_sealings_raise_difficult _questions_for_lds_church_.html.

37. *Acts, Resolutions and Memorials*, 81; Jones-Wilson, "Race, Realities,," 119.

38. *Acts, Resolutions and Memorials*, 82; Rich, "True Policy for Utah," 68–69.

39. Carson, "Indentured Migration: Occupational Targeting"; Carson, "Indentured Migration: Observation."

40. In January 1850, Young also told the legislature that he wanted to create an environment favorable to the migration of slaveholding Mormon converts. Conversion to Mormonism and its universalistic principles had produced confusion as to the morality of slavery. Some Mormons "commence to whisper around their views upon the subject saying, 'do you think it is right? I am afraid it is not right.'" Young directed the territorial leaders to settle the question. "I know it is right, and there should be a law made to have the slaves serve their masters." Young, Address to the Utah Territorial Legislature, CHL.

41. Christopher Rich has argued that there was little difference between how the legislature and later Utah's courts envisioned the terms of service for white servants and black slaves. Children born to slaves "could only be forced to work as long as necessary to repay any debts that were owed to their parent's master," Rich writes. Influenced by the "black codes" from the Saints' former home state of Illinois, "this reflected the old gradual emancipation laws which authorized a period of servitude to be extended over the children of slaves before they were legally free. Yet, it also specifically disallowed perpetual servitude based on heredity." Rich, "True Policy for

Utah," 68. However, as would often be the case for the postemancipation system of black sharecropping, the debt ledgers would been kept by the masters, not by the slaves, thus establishing de facto hereditary debtorship, if not slavery, in the territory until the Civil War. Blackmon, *Slavery by Another Name*, 6, 8, 63, 65, 80.

42. "Message of Governor Brigham Young, Delivered to the Legislative Assembly of Utah Territory," December 11, 1854, reprinted in Young, *Teachings*, 427.

43. Although the "Act in Relation to Service" gave the Perpetual Emigration Fund the legal authority to enforce these contracts, many migrants and immigrants settled in rural parts of Utah, where a strong justice system was lacking, making legal enforcement difficult and costly. Instead, Mormon social norms pressured many debtors to honor their contracts. Carson, "Indentured Migration in America's Great Basin: An Observation in Strategic Behavior in Cooperative Exchanges."

44. Ricks, "Peculiar Place," app. 3, 160–61.

45. Young, Address to the Utah Territorial Legislature, CHL.

46. Brigham Young's plural wife Eliza R. Snow put these distinctions into verse. In 1854, soon after the end of the Mormon-Ute conflict, Snow wrote the poem "The Day Is Dawning" to commemorate the tenth anniversary of the Saints' July 1847 arrival in the Salt Lake Basin and their first contact with Utah's Indians, whom Snow names "Joseph's children in the West." As "Glory beams on Ephraim's mountain / Beauty smiles on Ephraim's plains," Snow invited the "wand'ring sons of Lehi" to "Learn the ways the white men love." If they did so, the curse that had long "rested upon you / God will soon the curse remove." Derr and Davidson, *Eliza R. Snow*, 240. In her poem "The New Year 1852," written just a few months before the Utah legislature legalized African slavery in the territory, Snow informs the children of Ham that they can do nothing but wait on the Lord to have their curses removed. "'Japhet shall dwell within the tents of Shem," Snow writes, "And Ham shall be his servant'; . . . The curse of the Almighty rests upon / The colored race: In his time, by his / Own means, not yours, that curse will be remov'd." Ibid., 419–20.

47. The number of slaves who lived in Utah at one time or another is difficult to estimate, in part due to the Mormons' efforts to hide slaves from census counters. For example, see Utah's 1850 Slave Schedule, in which the twenty-six slaves listed are noted as "Going to California," though several remained in Utah. "Slave Inhabitants in Utah County, Deseret," 1850 U.S. Census, Slave Schedules, accessed through Ancestry. com. For an estimate of the slave population in Utah, see Bringhurst, *Saints, Slaves, and Blacks*, 66–67, 219, 214.

48. Brown, *Autobiography*, 144–45. Brown tithed "Betsy" during the so-called Mormon Reformation, which took place as the Mormons prepared to do battle with the U.S. government in 1857. Young called on his followers to recommit themselves to the church through demonstrations of religious piety, including increased numbers of plural marriages as well as the consecration of property to the church. One man even tithed his own daughter. Turner, *Brigham Young*, 248. In 1850, William Lay moved to

San Bernardino and brought his slave Hark with him, separating Hark from his wife and children, who belonged to the Bankhead brothers. William Lay did try to buy Hark's wife but lacked the funds. Crosby to Brigham Young (on behalf of William Lay), March 12, 1851, BYP. Many if not most of the slaves that Mormon masters brought into Utah remained enslaved until Congress banned slavery from the territories in 1862. Some slaves chose to stay on with their former masters, while many left the territory. How these formerly enslaved people viewed their bondage is perhaps best captured in an 1899 article published in the *Broad Ax*, a black-run paper based in Salt Lake City, describing "the joyful expressions which were upon the faces of all the slaves, when they ascertained that they had acquired their freedom through the fortunes of war." *Broad Ax*, March 25, 1899; Ricks, "Peculiar Place," 154.

49. Quoted in Brooks, "Indian Relations," 6.

50. It is likely that the race-based priesthood ban was in place before Young's January 1852 speech. In his book *Mormons*, for example, John W. Gunnison explained that the Mormon belief is that the "Negro is cursed as to the priesthood and must always be a servant wherever his lot is cast." Gunnison, *Mormons*, 51. The book was published in Philadelphia in 1852, but it was based on research Gunnison conducted during the winter of 1849–50 in Salt Lake. For the most up-to-date-discussion of the historic debate regarding the origins of the Mormon priesthood ban, see Reeve, *Religion of a Different Color*, 142–61.

51. Quoted in Bringhurst, "Elijah Abel," 28–29; Bush, "Mormonism's Negro Doctrine," 22–29. On the use of the Endowment House, see Brown, "'Temple Pro Tempore.'"

52. Brooks, "Indian Relations," 42.

53. Crane, "Funeral of a Lamanite." Mormon elites and Mormon missionaries were not the only Latter-day Saints to purchase and house Indian slaves. Hundreds if not thousands of Indian children were either bought by or given to Mormon families in the second half of the nineteenth century. Juanita Brooks found documentation for some thirty-two Indian adopted children. Brooks, "Indian Relations." Michael Kay Bennion provides a much more recent count of more than four hundred children in Mormon homes. See Bennion, "Captivity, Adoption,," app. 2, table 1, 245. See also Kitchens, "Mormon-Indian Relations."

54. Bennion, "Captivity, Adoption,," 218–19. Census records indicate that Zenos Hill was literate. 1880 U.S. Census, Fountain Green, Utah Territory, p. 381B, accessed through Ancestry.com.

55. George A. Smith, "Indian War," October 7, 1853, *JD* 1:197.

56. Hatch, *Ira Hatch*, 105.

57. Brooks, *Dudley Leavitt*, 47.

58. Ibid.; Brooks, "Indian Relations," 39, 48. See census entry for Annie, Calvin, Jane, and Heleman Leavitt, in which they are listed as white. 1870 U.S. Census, Hebron, Utah Territory, p. 374, accessed through Ancestry.com. Strangely, "Jennette"

(Janet) is also listed as white. Another of Dudley and Janet's daughters, Rozena Leavitt McNight, is listed as white in 1930, while her unmarried sister Deborah, who lived with Rozena and her husband, Wright McKnight, in Beaver Dam, Arizona, is listed as Indian. The records also indicate that Rozena could "read and write" whereas her sister could not. 1930 U.S. Census, Beaver Dam, Arizona, p. 282, accessed through Ancestry.com.

59. However, for the vast majority of Indian adoptees the archive contains no record of their existence. Many of these nameless Indian children likely succumbed to disease within months of their initial placement in Mormon homes. Others ran away and returned to their Indian families. Brooks, "Indian Relations," 33–34.

60. Brooks, "Indian Relations," 47–48.

61. See entry for Sally in the 1870 U.S. Census, Salt Lake City, Utah Territory, p. 701A, accessed through Ancestry.com; Jones, *Trial of Don Pedro Léon Luján*, 109.

62. Gates, "Courtship of Kanosh," 27–28.

63. Compton, "Civilizing the Ragged Edge," 160, 174–82.

64. As Martha Knack has described the rationales behind the Mormon participation in the slave trade, "Although crass economic motivation was never admitted, the pragmatic labor value of these Paiute children cannot be underestimated for frontier settlements then constructing labor-intensive infrastructure, nor can it be ignored in any explanation of why Mormon settlers continued to remove Paiute children from their Native communities long after Utes had been driven militarily from the area." Knack, *Boundaries Between*, 57, 50–59.

65. Gates, "Courtship of Kanosh," 27–28.

66. Ibid., 31–33.

67. Blackhawk, *Violence over the Land*, 234–35, 244.

68. Smith, "Deseret." See also Martineau, Iron County Historical Record, January 1855, CHL.

69. Gottfredson, *Indian Depredations in Utah*, 84. Though the large scale of the burial site's contents was likely due to the outsized stature of Wakara, the main elements of this burial for a leading Ute were perhaps not uncommon. In 1883, Hubert Bancroft described a Ute burial in the following way: "The property of the deceased is destroyed at his burial. His favorite horse, and in some instances his favorite wife, are killed over his grave that he may not be alone in the spirit land." Bancroft, *Wild Tribes of America*, 144. See this book's epilogue, where I further discuss the fate of Wakara's burial site.

70. Young, *Memoirs*, 63.

71. Crane, "Funeral of a Lamanite." John Young's memory of Sally's death was repeated throughout the twentieth century. See, among others, Arrington, *Brigham Young*, 210; Gates and Widtsoe, *Life Story of Brigham Young*, 136; and Jones, *Trial of Don Pedro Léon Luján*, 158n21.

72. Crane, "Funeral of a Lamanite."

73. Callister, "Fillmore City." See also Kane, *Twelve Mormon Homes*, 79–80. More recently, narratives about Chief Kanosh and his relationships with Mormon elites have separated Sally's death from Mary's. Lyman, "Chief Kanosh," 99; Van Leer, "Chief Praised by Indians."

74. Besides the *DN* reports, I have found no records of Sally's and Mary's deaths in extant church or state documents. For example, Kanosh's wife Betsykin, who is blamed in some narratives for killing Sally, was never charged for the murder. Gates and Widtsoe, *Life Story of Brigham Young*, 136; Culmsee, *Utah's Black Hawk War*, 68.

75. February 10, 1850, box 2, folder 17, GCM; Farmer, *Zion's Mount*, 73.

76. The fact that these women's stories here are conflated and redacted certainly fits with the Book of Mormon precedent. Hardy, *Understanding the Book of Mormon*, 18–22, 288n3.

77. Richter, *Facing East*, 11–15, 82–83.

78. Gottfredson, *Indian Depredations in Utah*, 3, 129, 226–28. As Jill Lepore has written regarding how the history of King Philip's War was narrated and thus remembered, "War is a contest of words as much as it is a contest of wounds. . . . One Englishman said that the war, through the wounds Indians inflicted on English bodies, was Philip's only chance to be 'found in print,' 'drawing his own reportt in blud not Ink.'" Lepore, *Name of War*, 47.

79. Mormon records two sets of plates and buries one, knowing that if the records of the Nephite history and faith were "to fall into the hands of the Lamanites," then "the Lamanites would destroy them." Mormon 6:6.

80. Woodruff, *Journal*, 4:273–74.

81. Visions of Arapine, BYP.

82. Remarks by Tow-om-bw-gah or Highforehead, July 15, 1855, CHL; Farmer, *Zion's Mount*, 94–95.

83. This was neither the first nor probably the last time Arapeen called on Mormon scribes to record his messages. See Morley to Brigham Young, on behalf of Arapeen, September 1, 1851, BYP.

84. Kane, *Mormons*, 72.

85. *JH*, June 13, 1849; Meeting with Utes, May 22, 1850, BYP.

86. I have consulted a half dozen Numic and Ute language scholars. None of them detect any Native writing system in Wakara's writing.

87. Bullock, Weight, size, etc. of Indians, August 2, 1852, BYP. Simon, "Thomas Bullock as an Early Mormon Historian."

88. Morrison, *Playing in the Dark*, xii.

89. Blackhawk, *Violence over the Land*, 120. On slave traffic between Utah and New Mexico, see "Number of Ute/Paiute Captives in New Mexico, 1730–1870," in Jones, *Trial of Don Pedro Leon Lujan*, 97.

90. Remarks by Tow-om-bw-gah or Highforehead, July 15, 1855, CHL. Because the

Mormons were responsible for killing off the fish and game on which the Utes depended, Woodruff declared that it was the Mormons' responsibility to feed and clothe the Utes; instruct them in "principles of civilization," including the art of agriculture; teach them "to read and writing the English language"; and build them a "nice schoolhouse" so that they could survive the transition to a white man's existence. Woodruff, "Preaching the Gospel to, and Helping the Lamanites," July 15, 1855, *JD* 9:227; Farmer, *Zion's Mount*, 93–94.

91. Perlich, "Utah Minorities."

92. Brigham Young, "Indian Hostilities," July 31, 1853, *JD* 1:171. Suzanne Alchon has argued that Old World disease was just one factor of European colonialism that dissimilated Native populations. Alchon, *Pest in the Land*.

93. At least during the early 1850s, the Mormon-Paiute alliance, formed to stop Ute aggression and slaving, as well as the Mormons' efforts to buy and adopt Paiute children, suggest that the Mormons also learned to differentiate between Utah's Indian tribes. Knack, *Boundaries Between*, 30–36, 54–59.

94. Ibid., 57. As Andrés Reséndez has written, despite cutting off the trade of New Mexican traffickers, "the American occupation of the West," including the Mormons, "did not reduce the enslavement of Indians. In fact, the arrival of American settlers rekindled the traffic in humans." Reséndez, *Other Slavery*, 266.

95. Jacob E. Holeman to Luke Lea, September 12, 1851, March 29, 1852, quoted in Coates, "History of Indian Education," 88.

96. Day to Luke Lea, January 2, 1851, CHL.

97. Meeting with Utes, May 22, 1850, BYP.

98. Wakara to George A. Smith, undated, quoted in Heap and Beale, *Central Route to the Pacific*, 92. What Martha C. Knack has suggested in terms of later Mormon-Paiute agreements in the southern settlements of the Sanpete Valley can be applied to Mormon-Ute agreements in the late 1840s and early 1850s. "By cooperating with local bishops or even Brigham Young himself, Paiutes need not have been acknowledging white supremacy in wisdom or power or submitting themselves to political subordination; they may have been trying to manipulate the Mormon wealth by placing the Mormons under the kind of obligations Paiutes assumed would result: to share reciprocally in exchange for natives' initial gift of very land Mormons occupied." Knack, *Boundaries Between*, 61.

99. Walker Statement, July 6, 1853, BYP.

100. Ibid.; Farmer, *Zion's Mount*, 85.

Epilogue

1. See "Martin, Edward," in Palmquist and Kailbourn, *Pioneer Photographers*, 382–83.

2. Hundreds of Mormon women had their likenesses taken during the 1860s and 1870s. For among the dozens of almost identical photographs, see Charles's Savage

portrait of Vilate Kimball (1866) in George A. Smith Collection, CHL. For a discussion of the use of photography as part of the politics of respectability for black women, see Smith, *Photography on the Color Line*, 77–112.

3. For a study of 1860s photographic techniques that Savage used, see Richards, "Charles R. Savage," 143–44.

4. In contrast, the 1857 daguerreotype of the abolitionist John Brown is underexposed, making his skin appear darker. John Stauffer has suggested that Brown's darkened likeness—the image of a man who "blurs the line between white and black"—allowed him to identify further with blacks. Stauffer, *Black Hearts of Men*, 56–58, 45–70.

5. Savage, *Utah's Best Crop*, Charles Savage Photographs, CHL.

6. Richards, "Charles R. Savage," 152; "Were Royally Entertained"; "Death of Jane Manning James."

7. "The Dead." During the early to mid-twentieth century, members of the California branch of the James family periodically returned to Utah to visit relatives. Louis Duffy, great-great-grandson of Jane Manning James, interview with author, June 17, 2010.

8. Minutes, August 26, 1908, The Quorum of the Twelve Apostles, Excerpts from the Weekly Council Meetings Dealing with the Rights of Negroes in the Church, 1849–1940, George Albert Smith Papers.

9. Such a search would have uncovered pronouncements like those from an August 18, 1900, meeting, during which George Q. Cannon reported that "President Young held to the doctrine that no man tainted with negro blood was eligible to the priesthood; that President [John] Taylor held to the same doctrine, claiming to have been taught it by Prophet Joseph Smith." There is no evidence, however, that Smith held such a position during his lifetime. However, it is possible that Cannon and others extrapolated this teaching from their readings of Smith's translations of the books of Abraham and Moses. During that same meeting, "Cannon read from the Pearl of Great Price showing that negroes were debarred from the priesthood." See August 18, 1900, Presidency Meeting, in Lester Bush Papers, Compilation on the Negro in Mormonism. For similar discussions, see Joseph F. Smith and Anthon H. Lund to Rudger Clawson, November 18, 1910, and First Presidency to Milton H. Knudson, January 13, 1913, in ibid.

10. In the 1914 edition of the *Church Chronology*, assistant church historian and Danish immigrant Andrew Jenson includes the deaths, in 1903, of Green Flake, probably the first black person to settle in the Salt Lake Valley, and, in 1908, of Jane Manning James, the first black Mormon woman to settle in Utah. Yet even though Jenson's historical precision extends far enough to point out that Flake and James were "colored," he indicates that they were "original" or "early" pioneers, failing to credit them with the status of a "pioneer of 1847," which was Jenson's convention when indicating the deaths of the white Mormons who settled the valley in 1847. Jenson, *Church Chro-*

nology (1903 ed.), 17, (1908 ed.), 19. Perhaps Jenson's notation of Green Flake as an "original" pioneer meant that he was part of Young's famed Vanguard Company. Yet John Brown, who baptized Flake and his master, James M. Flake, in Mississippi and who also was in the Vanguard Company, is listed as a "pioneer of 1847" in his death notice in the chronology. Ibid. (1897 ed.), 213. Jenson does not include James or any of her family members in any edition of his popular biographical encyclopedia. In volume 3, he includes Elijah Abel, noting that he was "the only colored man who is known to have been ordained to the Priesthood." Jenson writes that Abel's ordination was an "exception . . . with regard to the general rule of the Church in relation to colored people." Jenson, *Latter-day Saint Biographical Encyclopedia*, 3:577. In the fourth volume, Jenson includes biographies of Green Flake, Oscar Crosby, and Hark Lay, the three slaves (Jenson calls them "servants") who were part of Young's Vanguard Company. Ibid., 4:703, 697, 711.

11. Roberts, *Comprehensive History*, 2:128.

12. Bush, "Mormonism's Negro Doctrine," 27.

13. Smith, *Way to Perfection*, 43–44, 97–111. *The Way to Perfection* was available as a Kindle e-book until the church removed it from Amazon.com in the wake of racist comments from a BYU professor in March 2012, which brought unwanted attention to the church's complicated relationship with people of African descent. Mueller, "Mormon Church and Racism," http://www.slate.com/articles/life/faithbased/2012/03/mormon_church_and_racism_a_new_controversy_about_old_teachings_.html.

14. Mueller, "Pageantry and Protest," 133–37; Mueller, "Twice-Told Tale," 168.

15. "LDS Church First Presidency Statement on the Question of Blacks within the Church," August 17, 1949, reprinted in Bringhurst, *Saints, Slaves, and Blacks*, 230. By 1969, facing greater pressure to change its policies—including boycotts against BYU football games and other collegiate events—the church softened its tone a bit, explaining that "from the beginning of this dispensation, Joseph Smith and all succeeding presidents of the Church have taught that Negroes, while spirit children of a common Father, and the progeny of our earthly parents Adam and Eve, were not yet to receive the priesthood, for reasons which we believe are known to God, but which He has not made fully known to man." "1969 First Presidency Statement," December 15, 1969, reprinted in Bringhurst, *Saints, Slaves, and Blacks*, 231.

16. Mueller, "History Lessons," 145–47.

17. Smith, *Way to Perfection*, 134–35.

18. Morgan, "Educating the Lamanites."

19. Mauss, *All Abraham's Children*, 74–114.

20. John Nicholson, "Prophecy Fulfilled, Prophecy Fulfilling," February 6, 1881, *JD* 22:21–22; Savage, Baptism of Shivwits, March 19, 1875, CHL.

21. Williams, *Framing the West*, 12–26.

22. Wadsworth, *Set in Stone*, 109.

23. Fabian, *Skull Collectors*, 197–203; Otis, *List of the Specimens*, 50–51. Along with

collecting skeletal remains and other artifacts, Yarrow noted that the grave site, situated "upon the side of an almost inaccessible mountain," had been created when "a number of bowlders [*sic*] had been removed from the bed of the [rock] slide until a sufficient cavity had been obtained; this was lined with skins, the corpse placed therein, with weapons, ornaments, etc., and covered over with saplings. . . . In the immediate vicinity of the graves were scattered the osseous remains of a number of horses which had been sacrificed, no doubt, during the funeral ceremonies. In one of the graves, said to contain the body of a chief, in addition to a number of articles useful and ornamental, were found parts of the skeleton of a boy, and tradition states that the captive boy was buried alive at the place." Yarrow, "Further Contribution," 142. The disturbance of the grave did not go unnoticed. In August 1874, a group of Mormons, in the company of Kanosh and other friendly Indian leaders, visited the site. In a letter to Dimick Huntington, R. A. McBride wrote, that "of the once saceread [*sic*] but now desicratead [*sic*] Burying ground of the great Chief Walker," all that was left were "fragments." Apparently, the site had become a cemetery for other local Natives. McBride noted that the bodies of Kanosh's brother and son were also "entirely gone." "Kanosh hardly knows how to Express his indignation." McBride to D. B. Huntington, August 18, 1874, BYP.

24. "Bones of Black Hawk." The Church History Museum displayed Black Hawk's remains for the next several decades. They were eventually moved to BYU's Museum of Peoples and Cultures. There they stayed in storage until 1995 when, as part of his Eagle Scout project, Shane Armstrong tracked them down and petitioned the U.S. Forest Service to have them registered with the service under the Native American Graves Protection and Repatriation Act. In 1997, the remains were reinterred at Black Hawk's birthplace and burial site near Spring Lake, Utah. Peterson, *Utah's Black Hawk War*, 78.

25. "The 24th in the Settlements." On late nineteenth- and early twentieth-century reenactments of the early Utah "Indian wars," see Farmer, *Zion's Mount*, 130–38.

26. White, "Turner and Buffalo Bill"; Farmer, *Zion's Mount*, 137.

27. Quoted in Bennion, "Captivity, Adoption," 218–19.

28. On the increase of the black population in Utah, see Bringhurst, *Saints, Slaves, and Blacks*, 155, 228.

29. Ibid., 156.

30. The Inventory of the Theater, October 19, 1877, quoted in Hicks, "Ministering Minstrels," 53.

31. "Leaves from Old Albums"; Hicks, "Ministering Minstrels."

32. In 1904, Kenner published his own six-hundred-page tome on Utah history, *Utah as It Is*. On Kenner's unique, racially charged family drama, see Reeve, *Religion of a Different Color*, 175–80, 199.

33. Scipio Africanus Kenner to Brigham Young, November 20, 1870, BYP.

34. Fanon, *Black Skin, White Masks*.

35. See "Mormon Coon," in *Songbook* (New York: Sol Bloom, 1905), cover reprinted in Handley, *Marriage, Violence and the Nation*, 109.

36. Crofutt, *Crofutt's Guide*, 92, 174; Handley, *Marriage, Violence and the Nation*, 29. Despite his anti-Mormonism, Crofutt saw nothing wrong with availing himself of Charles Savage's iconic photographs of Utah, including those of the Echo Canyon railroad pass, the Mormon Tabernacle, and Brigham Young. Crofutt, *Crofutt's Guide*, 80–89.

37. Rogin, *Blackface, White Noise*.

38. Jan Shipps has written that particularly during the social and political upheavals of the 1960s, "It was the dramatic discrepancy between clean-cut Mormons and scruffy hippies that completed the transformation of the Mormon image from the quasi-foreign, somewhat alien likeness that it had in the nineteenth century to the more than 100 percent super-American portrait of the late sixties and early seventies." Shipps, *Sojourner in the Promised Land*, 100. See also Mauss, *Angel and Beehive*, 21–76. To "scruffy hippies," one should add the image of protesting black civil rights leaders and their allies to the list of those people whom many leading members of the Mormon hierarchy viewed as anti-American agitators, even communist puppets, as then apostle Ezra Taft Benson described them in a 1967 church general conference talk. Ezra Taft Benson, "Trust Not in the Arm of Flesh," LDS General Conference, Salt Lake City, September 29, 1967. See also Mueller, "Pageantry of Protest," 133–36.

39. Shipps, *Sojourner in the Promised Land*, 350–51; Hicks, *Mormonism and Music*, 152–72.

40. Mueller, "Twice-Told Tale."

41. On the growth of the church in Africa and in the African diaspora in the twentieth century before the priesthood and temple bans were lifted, see Stevenson, *Cause of Righteousness*, 72–104, 188–97.

42. "Prophets Tell of Promise"; "Since Early Church Days."

43. Quoted in Ostling and Ostling, *Mormon America*, 105.

44. A week later, Harris-Perry, herself the daughter of a white Mormon mother and an African American father, offered a tearful apology to the Romneys. Walsh, "Romney Accepts Apology.".

45. Horowitz, "Genesis of a Church's Stand on Race."

46. "Race and the Priesthood."

47. Ibid. However, there is evidence that not all Mormons are ready to abandon the views of past prophets on the subject of race. Although most church members support a racially inclusive church today, many Mormons have resisted the church's recent efforts to distance itself from its past explanations of race-based exclusions. Some Mormons have even refused to accept the church's own "Race and the Priesthood" historical essay as the normative position that they should hold, accept, and espouse. Stack, "Mormon Sunday School Teacher." Terryl and Fiona Givens have also written powerfully about the restoration of Joseph Smith's original universal-

ism within the twentieth-first-century church—updated, however, to move beyond Smith's assumptions about whiteness as the universalized racial category. Givens and Givens, *God Who Weeps*, 77; Givens and Givens, *Crucible of Doubt*, 91–92.

48. Hardy, *Book of Mormon*, xv.

49. 2 Nephi 30:6, emphasis added. Abanes, *One Nation under Gods*, 420; Martin and Zacharias, *Kingdom of the Cults*, 208.

50. Hardy, *Book of Mormon*, 666. See also "Book of Mormon/Textual Changes."

51. As Willard Richards put in an 1852 *DN* editorial, "Jesus said, 'if ye are not one, then ye are not mine'; and the true extended meaning of this is, *one in all things*; one in language, one in color, one in faith, and one in act." Richards, "To the Saints."

52. Mueller, "Playing Jane."

53. For a study of how televangelists create aspirational identities for their national and international audiences, see Frederick, *Colored Television*.

BIBLIOGRAPHY

Manuscript Primary Sources

Provo, Utah

    L. Tom Perry Special Collections, Harold B. Lee Library, Brigham Young
        University

        Adam S. Bennion Papers, MSS 1

        Jacob Hamblin Papers, MSS 815

Salt Lake City, Utah

    Church History Library, The Church of Jesus Christ of Latter-day Saints

        Adam S. Bennion Papers

            LDS Church Council Minutes

        Biography of Jane E. Manning James, ca. 1902, transcription by Elizabeth J. D.
            Roundy, MS 4425

        Brigham Young, Address to the Utah Territorial Legislature, January 5, 1852,
            box 9, vol. 22, CR 100 102

        Brigham Young, Speech by Gov. Young in Council on a Bill Relating to African
            Slavery, January 23, 1852, box 1, folder 14, CR 100 317

        Brigham Young Papers, CR 1234 1

            Brigham Young to Chief Walker, November 22, 1849, box 16, folder 18

            Dimick Huntington to Brigham Young, April 19, 1849, box 21, folder 16

            Dimick Huntington to Brigham Young, May 18, 1849, box 21, folder 16

            Dimick Huntington, Minutes of Meeting with Indians, May 14, 1849, box 16,
                folder 17

            George W. Bean to Brigham Young, May 1, 1854, box 23, folder 10

            Isaac Morley to Brigham Young, March 15, 1850, box 22, folder 2

            Isaac Morley to Brigham Young, April 17, 1850, box 22, folder 2

            Isaac Morley to Brigham Young, on behalf of Arapeen, September 1, 1851,
                box 22, folder 7

            Meeting with Utes, May 22, 1850, box 74, folder 42

            R. A. McBride to Dimick Huntington, August 18, 1874, box 35, folder 9

            Scipio Africanus Kenner to Brigham Young, November 20, 1870, box 33,
                folder 16

            Thomas Bullock, Walker's Writing, 1851, box 74, folder 44

            Thomas Bullock, Weight, size, etc. of Indians, August 2, 1852, box 74,
                folder 46

            Visions of Arapine, box 74, folder 49

            Walker Statement, M. S. Martenas (interpreter), July 6, 1853, box 58, folder 14

William Crosby to Brigham Young (on behalf of William Lay), March 12, 1851, box 22, folder 6

Charles Savage, Baptism of Shivwits, March 19, 1875, folder 1, PH 1401

Charles Savage Photographs, ca. 1866–1906, PH 500

Clarence Merrill, History of Albert Merrill with some information and some dates of His Ancestors, MS 1101

Dimick Huntington Journal, 1845–1859, MS 1419

Eighth Ward Relief Society Minutes and Records, 1867–1979, LR 2525 14

Eli and William Gilbert to Sydney Gilbert, April 23, 1832, MS 19650

Eliza Partridge Lyman Journal, MS 9546

Elizabeth J. D. Roundy, Temple Ordinance Book, 1876–1914, MS 16964

Elk Mountain Mission Journal May-October 1855, MS 2204

Eunice Kinney to Wingfield Watson, My Testimony to the Latter Day Work, September 1891, MS 4226

General Church Minutes, CR 100 318 [GCM]

George A. Smith Photograph Collection, box 1, folder 25, PH 5962

H. R. Day to Luke Lea, Commissioner of Indian Affairs, January 2, 1851, MS 16773

Hyrum Smith, A Patriarchal Blessing of Jane Manning, May 11, 1844

Historian's Office History of the Church, 1839–1882, CR 100 102

Historian's Office Reports of Speeches, CR 100 317

Hosea Stout Statement, September 1887, transcription by Elizabeth J. D. Roundy, MS 3096

House Carpenters of Nauvoo, Ebenezer Robinson memorandum of agreement, February 20, 1840, MS 2983

Iron County Mission Historical Record, LR 6778 25

James S. Martineau, Iron County Mission Historical Record, 1850–1859, LR 6778 25

Joseph F. Smith Papers, MS 1325

Joseph Fielding Journals, 1837–1859, MS 1567

Levi Jackman Journal, March 1847–April 1849, MS 138

Llewellyn Harris Notebook, 1881, MS 16228

Marriage Certificates, 1876–1888, CR 100 424

Nauvoo Legion Papers, July–August 1853, MS 17208

Office of Indian Affairs and Indian Agent Records, 1824–1878, MS 16773

Salt Lake City Temple Adoption Records, A, p. 26. John Nicolson (temple recorder), May 18, 1894

Remarks by Tow-om-bw-gah or Highforehead, the Indian Chief, at the Bowery at Provo, July 15, 1855, interpreted by Lyman Wood, transcribed by J. Long, CR 100 137, box 3, folder 13

Roll, First Council of the Seventy, December 27, 1836, CR 3 123

Wingfield Watson Correspondence, 1891, MS 16323

Wandle Mace Autobiography ca. 1890, MS 1189

William I. Appleby Autobiography and Journal, 1848–1856, MS 15183

J. Willard Marriot Library, Special Collections

Joseph Rawlins Jr. Autobiography, Ms189

Lester E. Bush Papers, Ms0685

Compilation on the Negro in Mormonism, box 4, folders 3–8

Linda King Newell Papers, Ms0447

James D. Wardle Papers, Ms0578

Elders License Elijah Abel Certificate, box 37, folder 6

George Albert Smith Papers, Ms0036

Excerpts from the Weekly Council Meetings of the Quorum of Apostles, Dealing with the Rights of Negroes in the Church, 1849–1940, box 78, folder 7

Joseph Smith Paper Project [JSPP]. Church History Department of the Church of Jesus Christ of Latter-day Saints. http://josephsmithpapers.org/

Utah State Archives and Records

Utah Territorial Militia Records, 1849–1877, Series 2210

New Canaan, Connecticut

New Canaan Historical Society Library

Reverend Theophilus Smith Collection

Topeka, Kansas

Kansas Historical Society

William Clark Papers

Isaac McCoy, Field Notes of Delaware Lands, September 6, 1830, MS-94

Richard W. Cummins to William Clark, April 2, 1831, MS-95

William Clark to Lewis Cass, September 14, 1830, MS-94

William Myers to Pierre Menard, August 8, 1831, MS-95

Washington, D.C.

National Archives

Records of the United States Senate, 1789–1990

Published Primary Sources

Abdy, Edward Strutt. *Journal of a Residence and Tour in the United States of North America: From April, 1833, to October, 1834*. Vol. 3. London: J. Murray, 1835.

Acts, Resolutions and Memorials Passed at the Annual Sessions of the Legislative Assembly of the Territory of Utah. Salt Lake City: Brigham H. Young, 1852.

Adams, John Quincy. *The Diaries of John Quincy Adams: A Digital Collection*. Boston: Massachusetts Historical Society, 2004, http://www.masshist.org/jqadiaries.

Alder, Lydia D. "Ladies' Semi-Monthly Meeting." *Woman's Exponent*, December 1, 1893.

Apess, William. "An Indian's Looking-Glass for the White Man." In *The Experiences of Five Christian Indians, of the Pequod Tribe*, 50–60. Boston: James B. Dow, 1833.

———. *A Son of the Forest: The Experience of William Apes, a Native of the Forest*. New York: printed by author, 1829.

Apess, William, and Barry O'Connell. *On Our Own Ground: The Complete Writings of William Apess, a Pequot*. Amherst: University of Massachusetts Press, 1992.

Armstrong, George D. *The Christian Doctrine of Slavery*. New York: Scribner, 1857.

"Aunt Jane Laid to Rest: President Joseph F. Smith Speaks at the Funeral of Aged Colored Woman." *Deseret News*, April 21, 1908.

Bancroft, Hubert Howe. *The Wild Tribes of America*. New York: Bancroft, 1883.

Barney, Dr. Elvira Stevens. "Jane Manning James." *Deseret News*, October 4, 1899.

Beecher, Maureen, ed. *Personal Writings of Eliza Roxcy Snow*. Logan: Utah State University Press, 2000.

Black, Susan Easton, ed. *Stories from the Early Saints: Converted by the Book of Mormon*. Salt Lake City: Bookcraft, 1994.

Black, Susan Easton, and Harvey Bischoff Black, eds. *Annotated Record of Baptisms for the Dead, 1840–1845*. Provo, Utah: Center for Family History and Genealogy, Brigham Young University, 2002.

"Bones of Black Hawk Indian Warrior Now on Exhibition L.D.S. Museum." *Deseret News*, September 20, 1919.

"The Book of Abraham." *Times & Seasons*, March 1, 1842.

"Book of Mormon." *Painesville Telegraph*, December 7, 1830.

"Book of Mormon." *Wayne Sentinel*, March 19, 1830.

"Book of Mormon." *Wayne Sentinel*, March 26, 1830.

"Book of Mormon." *Reflector*, February 14, 1831.

"Book of Mormon/Textual Changes/'White' Changed to 'Pure.'" Foundation for Apologetic Information and Research, http://en.fairmormon.org/Book_of _Mormon/Textual_changes/%22white%22_changed_to_%22pure%22.

Booth, Ezra. "Mormonism No. VI." *Painesville Telegraph*, November 29, 1831.

Boudinot, Elias. *An Address to the Whites*. Philadelphia: W. F. Geddes, 1826.

Brown, John. *The Autobiography of John Brown: A Member of the Original Company of Utah Pioneers of 1847*. Edited by John Zimmerman Brown. Salt Lake City: Stevens and Wallis, 1941.

Brown, Lisle G, ed. *Nauvoo Sealings, Adoptions, and Anointings: A Comprehensive Register of Persons Receiving LDS Temple Ordinances, 1841–1846*. Salt Lake City: Signature Books, 2006.

Brown, Thomas D. "Extracts of a Letter to Governor Young." *Deseret News*, July 20, 1854.

"Burglary! Treason! ARSON!!! MURDER!!!!" *Times & Seasons*, September 1840.

Caldwell, Charles. *Thoughts on the Original Unity of the Human Race*. New York: E. Bliss, 1830.

Callister, Thomas. "Fillmore City." *Deseret News*, July 35, 1869.

Carvalho, Solomon Nunes. *Incidents of Travel and Adventure in the Far West*. New York: Derby and Jackson, 1859.

Clark, James R., ed. *Messages of the First Presidency*. Vol. 3. Salt Lake City: Bookcraft, 1966.

Clayton, William. *An Intimate Chronicle: The Journals of William Clayton*. Edited by George D. Smith. Salt Lake City: Signature Books, 1995.

"Comment on the Negro Chism's Case." *Nauvoo Neighbor*, April 1, 1844.

"Conference Minutes." *Latter-day Saints' Millennial Star*, April 1841.

Cooper, James Fenimore. *Notions of the Americans*. Philadelphia: Lea and Blanchard, 1848.

Crane, George. "Funeral of a Lamanite." *Deseret News*, December 18, 1878.

Crofutt, George A. *Crofutt's New Overland Tourist and Pacific Coast Guide*. Omaha, Neb.: Overland, 1880.

"Daniel Spencer/Ira Eldredge Company." Church of Jesus Christ of Latter-day Saints, https://history.lds.org/overlandtravel/companies/285/daniel-spencer -ira-eldredge-company.

"The Dead." *Deseret News*, March 13, 1897.

"Death of Jane Manning James." *Deseret News*, April 16, 1908.

Derr, Jill Mulvay, and Karen Lynn Davidson. *Eliza R. Snow: The Complete Poetry*. Provo, Utah: Brigham Young University Press, 2009.

Dinger, John S., ed. *The Nauvoo City and High Council Minutes*. Salt Lake City: Signature Books, 2011.

Douglass, Frederick. *The Life and Times of Frederick Douglass: From 1817–1882*. London: Christian Age Office, 1882.

"Egyptian Antiquities." *Times & Seasons*, May 2, 1842.

"Egyptian Mummies." *Latter-day Saints' Messenger & Advocate*, December 1835.

"The Excellence of Scripture." *Evening and the Morning Star*, July 1832.

"Extra." *Evening and the Morning Star*, July 15, 1833.

"Extra: 'The Mormons' So Called." *Evening and the Morning Star*, February 1834.

"Extract from the Prophecy of Enoch." *Evening and the Morning Star*, August 1832.

"Extract of Letter." *Evening and the Morning Star*, May 1833.

"First Presidency, Report." *Times & Seasons*, October 1840.

Flournoy, John Jacobus. *An Essay on the Origin, Habits, &c. of the African Race: Incidental to the Propriety of Having Nothing to Do with Negroes*. New York, 1835.

"Free People of Color." *Evening and the Morning Star*, July 1833.

Gates, Susa Young. "The Courtship of Kanosh: A Pioneer Indian Love Story." In *Improvement Era*, 9:21–38. Salt Lake City: General Board, Y.M.M.I.A., 1906.

———, ed. and comp. "'Aunt Jane' James." In "Joseph Smith, the Prophet." *Young Woman's Journal* 16, no. 12 (December 1905): 551–53.

Gates, Susa Young, and Leah Eudora Dunford Widtsoe. *The Life Story of Brigham Young*. New York: Macmillan, 1930.

Gaul, Theresa Strouth, ed. *To Marry an Indian: The Marriage of Harriett Gold and Elias Boudinot in Letters*. Chapel Hill: University of North Carolina Press, 2005.

"The Golden Bible or the Book of Mormon." *Ashtabula Journal*, February 5, 1831.

Gookin, Daniel. "Historical Collections of the Indian of New England" (1792). *Special Collection Publications*. Papers 13, http://digitalcommons.uri.edu/sc _pubs/13.

"The Gospel." *Latter-day Saints' Messenger & Advocate*, February 1835.

Gottfredson, Peter. *Indian Depredations in Utah*. Salt Lake City: Skelton, 1919.

Greeley, Horace. *An Overland Journey from New York to San Francisco in the Summer of 1859*. Lincoln: University of Nebraska Press, 1999.

Gunnison, John Williams. *The Mormons*. Philadelphia: Lippincott, Grambo, 1852.

Hall, William. *The Abominations of Mormonism Exposed*. Cincinnati, Ohio: I. Hart, 1852.

Harris, Matthew L., and Newell G. Bringhurst. *The Mormon Church and Blacks: A Documentary History*. Urbana: University of Illinois Press, 2015.

Hatch, Ira. *Ira Hatch: Indian Missionary, 1835–1909, Pu-Em-Ey*. Edited by Richard Ira Elkins. Bountiful, Utah: R. I. Elkins, 1984.

Heap, Gwinn Harris, and E. F. Beale. *Central Route to the Pacific*. Philadelphia: Lippincott, Grambo, 1854.

Heckewelder, John Gottlieb Ernestus. *A Narrative of the Mission of the United Brethren among the Delaware and Mohegan Indians*. Philadelphia: M'Carty and Davis, 1820.

Hendricks, Obery. "Mitt Romney and the Curse of Blackness." *Huffington Post*, January 12, 2012, http://www.huffingtonpost.com/obery-m-hendricks-jr-phd /mitt-romney-curse-blackness_b_1200470.html.

Hopkins, Samuel. *A Dialogue Concerning the Slavery of the Africans*. New York: Judah P. Spooner, 1776.

Horowitz, Jason. "The Genesis of a Church's Stand on Race." *Washington Post*, February 28, 2012.

Howe, Eber D. *Mormonism Unvailed*. Painesville, Ohio: printed by author, 1834.

Huntington, Dimick. "Correspondence: America." *Latter-day Saints' Millennial Star*, July 5, 1875.

Hyde, Orson. *A Voice from Jerusalem*. Liverpool: P. P. Pratt, 1842.

"The Indians." *Evening and the Morning Star*, October 1832.

"Isaac Manning Servant of Prophet Joseph Smith Dies in Salt Lake." *Vernal Express*, April 21, 1911.

Jackson, Andrew. "On Indian Removal." December 6, 1830. *Records of the United States Senate, 1789–1990*. Washington, D.C.: National Archives.

Jenson, Andrew. *Church Chronology: A Record of Important Events Connected with the History of the Church of Jesus Christ of Latter-day Saints.* Salt Lake City: Church of Jesus Christ of Latter-day Saints, 1914.

————. *Latter-day Saint Biographical Encyclopedia: A Compilation of Biographical Sketches of Prominent Men and Women in the Church of Jesus Christ of Latter-day Saints.* 4 vols. Salt Lake City: Deseret News, 1901–36.

Jones, Daniel Webster. *Forty Years among the Indians.* Salt Lake City: Juvenile Instructor Office, 1890.

Journals of the House of Representatives, Council, and Joint Sessions of the First Annual and Special Sessions of the Legislative Assembly of the Territory of Utah: Held at Great Salt Lake City, 1851 and 1852. Great Salt Lake City: Brigham H. Young, 1852.

Kane, Elizabeth Wood. *Twelve Mormon Homes Visited in Succession on a Journey through Utah to Arizona.* Philadelphia, 1874.

Kane, Thomas Leiper. *The Mormons: A Discourse Delivered before the Historical Society of Pennsylvania, March 26, 1850.* Philadelphia: King and Baird, 1850.

Kenner, S. A. *Utah as It Is.* Salt Lake City: Deseret News, 1904.

Kimball, Adelia Almira Wilcox. *Memoirs of Adelia Almira Wilcox; One of the Plural Wives of Heber C. Kimball.* New York: Stanley Kimball, 1956.

Kimball, Heber C. "Letter to the Editor." *Latter-day Saints' Millennial Star,* June 1840.

Kimball, Stanley B. *Heber C. Kimball: Mormon Patriarch and Pioneer.* Urbana: University of Illinois Press, 1986.

Kluge, John Peter, and Abraham Luckenbach. *The Moravian Indian Mission on White River: Diaries and Letters, May 5, 1799, to November 12, 1806.* Edited by Lawrence Henry Gipson. Indianapolis: Indiana Historical Bureau, 1938.

"Leaves from Old Albums." *Deseret News,* December 30, 1905.

Lincoln, Abraham. *Second Inaugural Address.* Library of Congress, Washington, D.C., https://www.ourdocuments.gov/doc.php?flash=true&doc=38.

"Manifesto." *Evening and the Morning Star,* December 1833.

Mather, Increase. *The History of the King Philip's War.* Boston: Samuel Drake, 1862.

McCoy, Isaac. *History of Baptist Indian Missions: Embracing Remarks on the Former and Present Condition of the Aboriginal Tribes; Their Settlement within the Indian Territory, and Their Future Prospects.* New York: H. and S. Raynor, 1840.

Miller, Henry W. "The Cherokee Nation." *Latter-day Saints' Millennial Star,* October 6, 1855.

"Missouri's Early Slave Laws: A History of Documents." Missouri Digital Heritage, http://www.sos.mo.gov/archives/education/aahi/earlyslavelaws/slavelaws.asp.

"Mormonism." *Kansas City Journal,* June 5, 1881.

"The Mormonites 'Hors de Combat.'" *Wayne Sentinel,* August 23, 1833.

"The Mormons and Anti-Mormons." *Painesville Telegraph,* December 13, 1833.

Newcome, William, and Samuel Horsley, eds. *A Literal Translation of the Prophets, from Isaiah to Malachi: With Notes, Critical, Philological, and Explanatory.* London: Thomas Tegg and Son, 1836.

Northup, Solomon. *Twelve Years a Slave: Narrative of Solomon Northup.* Edited by David Wilson. New York: Miller, Orton and Mulligan, 1855.

Occom, Samson. *The Collected Writings of Samson Occom, Mohegan: Leadership and Literature in Eighteenth-Century North America.* Edited by Joanna Brooks. New York: Oxford University Press, 2006.

"Old Woman's Deed Is Set Aside by Court." *Salt Lake Herald*, May 21, 1909.

Otis, George A. *List of the Specimens in the Anatomical Section of the United States Army Medical Museum.* Washington, D.C.: Army Medical Museum, 1880.

"The Outrage in Jackson County, Missouri." *Evening and the Morning Star*, March 1834.

Pacheco, Bernardo de Miera y. "Miera's Report." *Utah Historical Quarterly* 11 (1943): 114–20.

Parkman, Francis. *The Oregon Trail: Sketches of Prairie and Rocky-Mountain Life.* Boston: Little, Brown, 1886.

Pettibone, Rufus, and Henry Sheffie Geyer. *Laws of the State of Missouri: Revised and Digested by Authority of the General Assembly.* Saint Louis: E. Charles, 1825.

Phelps, W. W. "The Indians." *Latter-day Saints' Messenger & Advocate*, January 1836.

Pioneers and Prominent Men of Utah. Salt Lake City: Utah Pioneer's Publishing, 1913.

Pratt, Parley Parker. *The Autobiography of Parley Parker Pratt.* New York: Russell Brothers, 1874.

———. "Extra: 'The Mormons' So Called." *Evening and the Morning Star*, February 1834.

———. Letter. *Elders' Journal*, October 1837.

———. "The Science of Anti-Mormon Suckerology." *Prophet*, May 10, 1845.

———. *A Voice of Warning, and Instruction to All People, or an Introduction to the Faith and Doctrines of the Church of Jesus Christ, of Latter Day Saints.* New York: W. Sanford, 1837.

"Prophecy Given to the Church of Christ, March 7, 1831." *Evening and the Morning Star*, June 1832.

"Prophet's Servant, Old Negro, Dead." *Salt Lake Evening Telegram*, April 13, 1911.

"Prophets Tell of Promise to All Races." *Church News*, June 17, 1978.

"Public Meeting." *Latter-day Saints' Messenger & Advocate*, August 1836.

"Race and the Priesthood." Gospel Topics, the Church of Jesus Christ of Latter-day Saints, https://www.lds.org/topics/race-and-the-priesthood?lang=eng.

"Report from the First Presidency." *Times & Seasons*, April 15, 1841.

"Restoration of the Jews." *Evening and the Morning Star*, August 1833.

"Restoration of the Jews." *Latter-day Saints' Millennial Star*, June 1840.

"Reunion of Utah Veterans: Grizzled Heroes of the Past Recall Scenes of Yore." *Deseret News*, June 25, 1901.

"Review of Current Literature." *Christian Examiner*, May 1862.

The Revised Laws of Illinois. Vandalia, Ill.: Greiner and Sherman, 1833.

Richards, Willard. "To the Saints." *Deseret News*, April 3, 1852.

Roberts, B. H., ed. *Comprehensive History of the Church of Jesus Christ of Latter-day Saints*. 6 vols. Provo, Utah: Brigham Young University Press, 1965.

———. *History of the Church of Jesus Christ of Latter-day Saints*. 7 vols. Salt Lake City: Deseret News, 1902–32.

———. *The Missouri Persecutions*. Salt Lake City: G. Q. Cannon, 1900.

Salt Lake City Directory. Salt Lake City: G. Owens, 1867.

"Since Early Church Days, Blacks Have Set an Example." *Church News*, June 17, 1978.

Smart, Donna, ed. *Mormon Midwife: The 1846–1888 Diaries of Patty Bartlett Sessions*. Logan: Utah State University Press, 1999.

Smith, George A. "Deseret: Death of Walker." *Latter-day Saints' Millennial Star*, April 28, 1855.

Smith, Joseph, Jr. "Church History" [letter to John Wentworth, editor of the *Chicago Democrat*]." *Times & Seasons*, March 1, 1842.

———. *General Smith's Views of the Powers and Policy of the Government of the United States*. Nauvoo, Ill.: John Taylor, 1844.

———. "Views on the Government and Policy of the U.S." *Times & Seasons*, May 15, 1844.

Smith, Joseph, III. *The Memoirs of President Joseph Smith III, 1832–1914: The Second Prophet of the Church*. Edited by Mary Audentia Smith Anderson. Independence, Mo.: Price, 2001.

———. *Joseph Smith III and the Restoration*. Edited by Bertha Audentia Anderson Hulmes. Independence, Mo.: Herald House, 1952.

Smith, Joseph Fielding. *The Way to Perfection, Short Discourses on Gospel Themes*. Independence, Mo.: Genealogical Society of Utah, 1931.

"Society in the South." *Deseret News*, November 18, 1885.

Special Order No. 2, issued by Daniel H. Wells to G. D. Grant, January 31, 1850, Utah Territorial Militia Records, 1849–1877, Utah State Archives and Records, Series 2210.

Steward, Austin. *Twenty-Two Years a Slave, and Forty Years a Freeman*. Rochester, N.Y.: William Alling, 1857.

Stout, Hosea. *On the Mormon Frontier: The Diary of Hosea Stout, 1844–1889*. Edited by Juanita Brooks. Salt Lake City: University of Utah Press, 2009.

"To His Excellency, Daniel Dunklin." *Evening and the Morning Star*, December 1833.

"To Man." *Evening and the Morning Star*, June 1832.

"A Translation." *Times & Seasons*, March 1, 1842.

Tucker, Pomeroy. *Origin, Rise, and Progress of Mormonism*. New York: D. Appleton, 1867.

Twain, Mark. *Roughing It*. Hartford, Conn.: American Publishing, 1872.

"The 24th in the Settlements: Provo City." *Deseret News*, July 31, 1878.

The Utah Pioneers: Celebration of the Entrance of the Pioneers in to Great Salt Lake Valley. Salt Lake City: Deseret News, 1880.

Van Leer, Twila. "Chief Praised by Indians, Whites Alike." *Deseret News*, March 12, 1996.

"Varieties." *Deseret News*, November 23, 1864.

Walsh, Michael. "Mitt Romney Accepts MSNBC's Melissa Harris-Perry Apology over Black Grandson Jokes." *New York Daily News*, January 5, 2013.

Warner, Tad, ed. *The Domínguez-Escalante Journal: Their Expedition through Colorado, Utah, Arizona, and New Mexico in 1776*. Translated by Fray Angelico Chavez. Salt Lake City: University of Utah Press, 1995.

"Warsaw and Quincy." *Nauvoo Neighbor*, April 2, 1845.

Wayne Sentinel, September 6, 1833.

Wellenreuther, Hermann, and Carola Wessel, eds. *Moravian Mission Diaries of David Zeisberger, 1772–1781*. University Park: Penn State University Press, 2010.

Wells, Daniel H. "Daniel H. Wells' Narrative." *Utah Historical Quarterly* 6 (1933): 124–33.

"Were Royally Entertained." *Deseret News*, June 26, 1907.

Whitmer, John. *From Historian to Dissident: The Book of John Whitmer*. Edited by Bruce N. Westergren. Salt Lake City: Signature Books, 1995.

Whitney, Helen Mar. "Scenes in Nauvoo, and Incidents from H. C. Kimball's Journal." *Woman's Exponent*, May 15, 1883.

Whitney, Orson. "Why I Am a Mormon." *Contributor*, January 1887.

Wilson, John. *Our Israelitish Origin: Lectures on Ancient Israel, and the Israelitish Origin of the Modern Nations of Europe*. London: J. Nisbet, 1840.

Woodruff, Wilford. *Wilford Woodruff: History of His Life and Labors as Recorded in His Daily Journals*. Edited by Matthias F. Cowley. Salt Lake City: Deseret News, 1909.

———. *Wilford Woodruff's Journal, 1833–1898: Typescript*. Edited by Scott Kenny. 6 vols. Salt Lake City: Signature Books, 1985.

Wright, Julia McNair. *Among the Alaskans*. Philadelphia: Presbyterian Board of Publications, [ca. 1883].

Yarrow, H. C. "A Further Contribution to the Study of the Mortuary Customs of the North American Indians." In *First Annual Report of the Bureau of Ethnology . . .* , by J. D. Powell, 87–203. Washington, D.C.: Smithsonian Institution, 1880.

Young, Brigham. *Governor's Message to the Senators and Representatives of the State of Deseret*. Salt Lake City, December 2, 1850.

———. "Governor's Message." *Deseret News*, December 19, 1855.

———. "Governor's Message to the Council of Representatives of the Legislature of Utah." *Deseret News*, January 10, 1852.

———. "Proclamation by the Governor." *Deseret News*, April 30, 1853.

———. *The Teachings of President Brigham Young.* Vol. 3, *1852–1854*. Edited by Fred Collier. Salt Lake City: Collier's, 1987.

Young, John R. *Memoirs of John R. Young, Utah Pioneer, 1847*. Salt Lake City: Desert News, 1920.

Young, Zina D. H. "'A Weary Traveler': The 1848–1850 Diary of Zina D. H. Young." Edited by Marilyn Higbee. *Journal of Mormon History* 19 (1993): 86–125.

Secondary Sources

Abanes, Richard. *One Nation under Gods: A History of the Mormon Church.* New York: Basic Books, 2003.

Aikau, Hokulani K. *A Chosen People, a Promised Land: Mormonism and Race in Hawai'i*. Minneapolis: University of Minnesota Press, 2012.

Alchon, Suzanne. *A Pest in the Land: New World Epidemics in a Global Perspective.* Albuquerque: University of New Mexico Press, 2003.

Allen, James B. *Men with a Mission: The Quorum of the Twelve Apostles in the British Isles, 1837–1841*. Salt Lake City: Deseret Book, 1992.

Arrington, Leonard J. *Brigham Young: American Moses.* New York: Knopf, 1985.

———. *Great Basin Kingdom: An Economic History of the Latter-day Saints, 1830–1900*. Urbana: University of Illinois Press, 2004.

Arrington, Leonard J., and Davis Bitton. *The Mormon Experience: A History of the Latter-day Saints.* Urbana: University of Illinois Press, 1992.

Banner, Stuart. *How the Indians Lost Their Land: Law and Power on the Frontier.* Cambridge, Mass.: Harvard University Press, 2009.

Barlow, Philip L. *Mormons and the Bible: The Place of the Latter-day Saints in American Religion*. New York: Oxford University Press, 2013.

Bassard, Katherine Clay. *Spiritual Interrogations: Culture, Gender, and Community in Early African American Women's Writing.* Princeton, N.J.: Princeton University Press, 1999.

Bates, Irene M. "Patriarchal Blessings and the Routinization of Charisma." *Dialogue: A Journal of Mormon Thought* 26, no. 3 (Fall 1993): 1–29.

Baugh, Alexander L. "'For This Ordinance Belongeth to My House': The Practice of Baptism for the Dead outside the Nauvoo Temple." *Mormon Historical Studies* 3, no. 1 (Spring 2002): 47–58.

Beeton, Beverly. "Teach Them to Till the Soil: An Experiment with Indian Farms, 1850–1862." *American Indian Quarterly* 3, no. 4 (1977): 299–320.

Bennion, Michael K. "Captivity, Adoption, Marriage and Identity: Native American Children in Mormon Homes, 1847–1900." M.A. thesis, University of Nevada, Las Vegas, 2012.

Berkhofer, Robert F. *The White Man's Indian: Images of the American Indian from Columbus to the Present.* New York: Vintage, 1979.

Blackhawk, Ned. *Violence over the Land: Indians and Empires in the Early American West.* Cambridge, Mass.: Harvard University Press, 2009.

Blackmon, Douglas A. *Slavery by Another Name: The Re-Enslavement of Black Americans from the Civil War to World War II.* New York: Anchor, 2009.

Block, Sharon. *Rape and Sexual Power in Early America.* Chapel Hill: University of North Carolina Press, 2006.

Bloom, Harold. *The American Religion: The Emergence of the Post-Christian Nation.* New York: Simon and Schuster, 1992.

Booth, Wayne C. *The Rhetoric of Fiction.* Chicago: University of Chicago Press, 1965.

Bowman, Matthew. "The Conversion of Parley Pratt: Investigating the Patterns of Mormon Piety." *Journal of Mormon History* 37, no. 1 (2011): 178–87.

Bringhurst, Newell G. "Elijah Abel and the Changing Status of Blacks within Mormonism." *Dialogue: A Journal of Mormon Thought* 12, no. 2 (Summer 1979): 22–36.

———. *Saints, Slaves, and Blacks: The Changing Place of Black People within Mormonism.* Westport, Conn.: Greenwood, 1981.

Brooke, John L. *The Refiner's Fire: The Making of Mormon Cosmology, 1644–1844.* New York: Cambridge University Press, 1996.

Brooks, Joanna. *American Lazarus: Religion and the Rise of African-American and Native American Literatures.* New York: Oxford University Press, 2003.

Brooks, Juanita. *Dudley Leavitt, Pioneer to Southern Utah.* N.p., 1942.

———. "Indian Relations on the Mormon Frontier." *Utah Historical Quarterly* 12, no. 1–2 (1944): 1–22.

———. "Jacob Hamblin: Apostle to the Lamanites." *Pacific Spectator* 2 (1948): 315–30.

Brown, Lisle. "'Temple Pro Tempore': The Salt Lake City Endowment House." *Journal of Mormon History* 34, no. 4 (Fall 2008): 1–68.

Brown, Samuel Morris. "Early Mormon Adoption Theology and the Mechanics of Salvation." *Journal of Mormon History* 37, no. 3 (Summer 2011): 3–52.

———. "The Early Mormon Chain of Belonging." *Dialogue: A Journal of Mormon Thought* 44, no. 1 (Spring 2011): 1–53.

———. *In Heaven as It Is on Earth: Joseph Smith and the Early Mormon Conquest of Death.* New York: Oxford University Press, 2012.

———. "The Translator and the Ghostwriter: Joseph Smith and W. W. Phelps." *Journal of Mormon History* 34, no. 1 (2008): 26–62.

Buerger, David John. "The Development of the Mormon Temple Endowment Ceremony." *Dialogue: A Journal of Mormon Thought* 20, no. 4 (1987): 33–76.

Bush, Lester E. "Mormonism's Negro Doctrine: An Historical Overview." *Dialogue: A Journal of Mormon Thought* 8, no. 1 (Spring 1973): 11–68.

Bushman, Richard Lyman. *Joseph Smith and the Beginnings of Mormonism.* Urbana: University of Illinois Press, 1987.

———. *Joseph Smith: Rough Stone Rolling.* New York: Vintage, 2007.

———. "The Lamanite View of Book of Mormon History." In *Believing History: Latter-day Saint Essays*, edited by Reid Larkin Neilson and Jed Woodworth, 79–92. New York: Columbia University Press, 2004.

Cagidemetrio, Alide. "A Plea for Fictional Histories and Old-Time 'Jewesses.'" In *The Invention of Ethnicity*, edited by Werner Sollors, 14–43. New York: Oxford University Press, 1991.

Campbell, Craig S. *Images of the New Jerusalem: Latter Day Saint Faction Interpretations of Independence, Missouri*. Knoxville: University of Tennessee Press, 2004.

Campbell, Eugene E. "Brigham Young's Outer Cordon: A Reappraisal." *Utah Historical Quarterly* 41 (1973): 220–53.

———. *Establishing Zion*. Salt Lake City: Signature Books, 1988.

Carson, Scott Alan. "Indentured Migration in America's Great Basin: An Observation in Strategic Behavior in Cooperative Exchanges." *Journal of Institutional and Theoretical Economics* 157, no. 4 (2001): 651–76.

———. "Indentured Migration in America's Great Basin: Occupational Targeting and Adverse Selection." *Journal of Interdisciplinary History* 32, no. 3 (2002): 387–404.

Cave, Alfred A. *Prophets of the Great Spirit: Native American Revitalization Movements in Eastern North America*. Lincoln: University of Nebraska Press, 2006.

Christy, Howard A. "Open Hand and Mailed Fist: Mormon-Indian Relations in Utah, 1847–52." *Utah Historical Quarterly* 46 (Summer 1978): 216–35.

———. "The Walker War: Defense and Conciliation as Strategy." *Utah Historical Quarterly* 47, no. 4 (1979): 395–420.

———. "'What Virtue There Is in Stone' and Other Pungent Talk on the Early Utah Frontier." *Utah Historical Quarterly* 59 (Summer 1991): 300–319.

Coates, Lawrence G. "Brigham Young and Mormon Indian Policies: The Formative Period, 1836–1851." *BYU Studies* 18, no. 3 (1978): 428–52.

———. "A History of Indian Education by the Mormons, 1830–1900." Ph.D. diss., Ball State University, 1969.

———. "Refugees Meet: The Mormons and Indians in Iowa." *BYU Studies* 21 (Fall 1981): 491–514.

Coleman, Ronald. "A History of Blacks in Utah, 1825–1910." PhD diss., University of Utah, 1980.

———. "'Is There No Blessing for Me?': Jane Elizabeth Manning James, a Mormon African American Woman." In *African American Women Confront the West, 1600–2000*, edited by Quintard Taylor and Shirley Ann Wilson, 144–64. Norman: University of Oklahoma Press, 2008.

Collins, John J. *Between Athens and Jerusalem: Jewish Identity in Hellenistic Diaspora*. Grand Rapids, Mich.: Wm. B. Eerdmans, 2000.

Compton, Todd M. "Civilizing the Ragged Edge: The Wives of Jacob Hamblin." *Journal of Mormon History* 33, no. 2 (Summer 2007): 155–98.

———. *In Sacred Loneliness: The Plural Wives of Joseph Smith*. Salt Lake City: Signature Books, 1997.

Conklin, Alice L. *A Mission to Civilize: The Republican Idea of Empire in France and West Africa, 1895–1930*. Stanford, Calif.: Stanford University Press, 1997.

Cooper, Rex Eugene. *Promises Made to the Fathers: Mormon Covenant Organization*. Salt Lake City: University of Utah Press, 1990.

Cornelius, Janet Duitsman. *"When I Can Read My Title Clear": Literacy, Slavery, and Religion in the Antebellum South*. Columbia: University of South Carolina Press, 1991.

Cranor, Ruby. *Kick Tha We Nund: The Delaware Chief Anderson and His Descendants*. Anderson, Ind.: printed by author, 1989.

Cronon, William. *Changes in the Land: Indians, Colonists, and the Ecology of New England*. New York: Hill and Wang, 1985.

Culmsee, Carlton Fordis. *Utah's Black Hawk War: Lore and Reminiscences of Participants*. Logan: Utah State University Press, 1973.

Daynes, Kathryn M. *More Wives Than One: Transformation of the Mormon Marriage System*. Urbana: University of Illinois Press, 2008.

Dennis, Ronald. "Captain Dan Jones and the Welch Indians." *Dialogue: A Journal of Mormon Thought* 18, no. 4 (1985): 112–19.

Derr, Jill Mulvay. "'Strengthen in Our Union': The Making of Mormon Sisterhood." In *Sisters in Spirit: Mormon Women in Historical and Cultural Perspective*, edited by Maureen Ursenbach, 153–207. Urbana: University of Illinois Press, 1992.

Derr, Jill Mulvay, and Karen Lynn Davidson. "A Wary Heart Becomes 'Fixed Unalterably': Eliza R. Snow's Conversion to Mormonism." *Journal of Mormon History* 30, no. 2 (2004): 98–128.

Derrida, Jacques. *Archive Fever: A Freudian Impression*. Translated by Eric Prenowitz. Chicago: University of Chicago Press, 1998.

Dorsett, Lyle. "Slaveholding in Jackson County, Missouri." *Missouri Historical Society Bulletin* 20, no. 1 (1963): 27–37.

Dowd, Gregory Evans. *A Spirited Resistance: The North American Indian Struggle for Unity*. Baltimore: Johns Hopkins University Press, 1993.

———. *War under Heaven: Pontiac, the Indian Nations, and the British Empire*. Baltimore: Johns Hopkins University Press, 2004.

Duffy, John-Charles. "Just How 'Scandalous' Is the Golden Plates Story?: Academic Discourses on the Origin of the Book of Mormon." *John Whitmer Historical Association Journal* 26 (2006): 142–65.

Ebersole, Gary L. *Captured by Texts: Puritan to Postmodern Images of Indian Captivity*. Charlottesville: University Press of Virginia, 1995.

Ella, George Melvyn. *Isaac McCoy: Apostle of the Western Trail*. Springfield, Mo.: Particular Baptist Press, 2002.

Elrod, Eileen Razzari. *Piety and Dissent: Race, Gender, and Biblical Rhetoric in Early American Autobiography*. Amherst: University of Massachusetts Press, 2008.

Epperson, Steven. *Mormons and Jews: Early Mormon Theologies of Israel*. Salt Lake City: Signature Books, 1993.

Fabian, Ann. *The Skull Collectors: Race, Science, and America's Unburied Dead*. Chicago: University of Chicago Press, 2010.

Fanon, Frantz. *Black Skin, White Masks*. New York: Grove Press, 2008.

Farmer, Jared. Review of *A Chosen People, A Promised Land: Mormonism and Race in Hawai'i*, by Hokulani K. Aikau. *Nova Religio: The Journal of Alternative and Emergent Religions* 17, no. 2 (2013): 108–10.

———. *On Zion's Mount: Mormons, Indians, and the American Landscape*. Cambridge, Mass.: Harvard University Press, 2008.

Ferry, Darren. "The Politicization of Religious Dissent: Mormonism in Upper Canada." *Mormon Historical Studies* 5, no. 2 (Fall 2004): 61–78.

Fish, Stanley Eugene. *Is There a Text in This Class?: The Authority of Interpretive Communities*. Cambridge, Mass.: Harvard University Press, 1980.

Fisher, Linford, D. *The Indian Great Awakening: Religion and the Shaping of Native Cultures in Early America*. New York: Oxford University Press, 2012.

Flake, Kathleen. *The Politics of American Religious Identity: The Seating of Senator Reed Smoot, Mormon Apostle*. Chapel Hill: University of North Carolina Press, 2004.

———. "Re-Placing Memory: Latter-day Saint Use of Historical Monuments and Narrative in the Early Twentieth Century." *Religion and American Culture* 13, no. 1 (2003): 69–109.

Fluhman, Spencer. *"A Peculiar People": Anti-Mormonism and the Making of Religion in Nineteenth-Century America*. Chapel Hill: University of North Carolina Press, 2012.

Fogelson, Raymond D. "The Ethnohistory of Events and Non-Events." *Ethnohistory* 36 (1989): 133–47.

Foster, Frances Smith. *Witnessing Slavery: The Development of Ante-bellum Slave Narratives*. Madison: University of Wisconsin Press, 1979.

Foucault, Michel. *The Order of Things: An Archaeology of the Human Sciences*. New York: Vintage, 1994.

Frederick, Marla F. *Colored Television: American Religion Gone Global*. Stanford, Calif.: Stanford University Press, 2016.

Fukuyama, Francis. "Introduction: Nation-Building and the Failure of Institutional Memory." In *Nation-Building: Beyond Afghanistan and Iraq*, edited by Francis Fukuyama, 1–18. Baltimore: Johns Hopkins University Press, 2006.

Garrison, Wendell Phillips. *William Lloyd Garrison, 1805–1879: The Story of His Life Told by His Children*. New York: Houghton, Mifflin, 1894.

Gates, Henry Louis, Jr. *The Signifying Monkey: A Theory of African-American Literary Criticism*. New York: Oxford University Press, 1989.

Genovese, Eugene D. *Roll, Jordan, Roll: The World the Slaves Made*. New York: Vintage Books, 1976.

Gentry, Leland H. "Light on the 'Mission to the Lamanites.'" *BYU Studies* 36, no. 2 (1996): 226–32.

Givens, Terryl L. *The Book of Mormon: A Very Short Introduction*. New York: Oxford University Press, 2009.

———. *By the Hand of Mormon: The American Scripture That Launched a New World Religion*. New York: Oxford University Press, 2002.

———. *The Viper on the Hearth: Mormons, Myths, and the Construction of Heresy*. New York: Oxford University Press, 2013.

Givens, Terryl L., and Fiona Givens. *The Crucible of Doubt: Reflections on the Quest for Faith*. Salt Lake City: Deseret Book, 2014.

———. *The God Who Weeps: How Mormonism Makes Sense of Life*. Salt Lake City: Deseret Book, 2012.

Givens, Terryl L., and Matthew J. Grow. *Parley P. Pratt: The Apostle Paul of Mormonism*. New York: Oxford University Press, 2011.

Glaude, Eddie S. *Exodus! Religion, Race, and Nation in Early Nineteenth-Century Black America*. Chicago: University of Chicago Press, 2000.

Goetz, Rebecca Anne. *The Baptism of Early Virginia: How Christianity Created Race*. Baltimore: Johns Hopkins University Press, 2012.

Goldstein, Eric L. *The Price of Whiteness: Jews, Race, and American Identity*. Princeton, N.J.: Princeton University Press, 2008.

Gordon, Sarah Barringer. *The Mormon Question: Polygamy and Constitutional Conflict in Nineteenth-Century America*. Chapel Hill: University of North Carolina Press, 2002.

Green, Arnold. "Gathering and Election: Israelite Descent and Universalism in Mormon Discourse." *Journal of Mormon History* 25, no. 1 (1999): 195–228.

Hall, David D. *Cultures of Print: Essays in the History of the Book*. Amherst: University of Massachusetts Press, 1996.

Hall, Stuart. *Stuart Hall and "Race."* Edited by Claire Alexander. New York: Routledge, 2011.

———. "The West and the Rest: Discourse and Power." In *The Formations of Modernity; Understanding Modern Societies: An Introduction, Book 1*, edited by Stuart Hall and Bram Gieben, 275–332. Cambridge: Polity, 1993.

Hambrick-Stowe, Charles E. *Charles G. Finney and the Spirit of American Evangelicalism*. Grand Rapids, Mich.: Wm. B. Eerdmans, 1996.

Handley, William R. *Marriage, Violence and the Nation in the American Literary West.* New York: Cambridge University Press, 2009.

Harding, Susan Friend. *The Book of Jerry Falwell: Fundamentalist Language and Politics.* Princeton, N.J.: Princeton University Press, 2000.

Hardy, B. Carmon. *Doing the Works of Abraham: Mormon Polygamy: Its Origin, Practice, and Demise.* Norman: University of Oklahoma Press, 2007.

Hardy, Grant. *The Book of Mormon: A Reader's Edition.* Urbana: University of Illinois Press, 2005.

———. *Understanding the Book of Mormon: A Reader's Guide.* New York: Oxford University Press, 2010.

Harper, Steven C. "Infallible Proofs, Both Human and Divine: The Persuasiveness of Mormonism for Early Converts." *Religion and American Culture* 10, no. 1 (Winter 2000): 99–118.

Harris, Marvin. *The Rise of Anthropological Theory: A History of Theories of Culture.* Walnut Creek, Calif.: Rowman Altamira, 2001.

Hatch, Nathan O. *The Democratization of American Christianity.* New Haven, Conn.: Yale University Press, 1991.

Haws, J. B. *The Mormon Image in the American Mind: Fifty Years of Public Perception.* New York: Oxford University Press, 2013.

Haynes, Stephen R. *Noah's Curse: The Biblical Justification of American Slavery.* New York: Oxford University Press, 2002.

Hickman, Jared. "The Book of Mormon as Amerindian Apocalypse." *American Literature* 86, no. 3 (2014): 429–61.

Hicks, Michael. "Ministering Minstrels: Blackface Entertainment in Pioneer Utah." *Utah Historical Quarterly* 58, no. 1 (1990): 49–63.

———. *Mormonism and Music: A History.* Urbana: University of Illinois Press, 2003.

Higginbotham, Evelyn Brooks. "African-American Women's History and the Metalanguage of Race." *Signs* 17, no. 2 (1992): 251–74.

Hobsbawm, Eric, and Terence Ranger, eds. *The Invention of Tradition.* New York: Cambridge University Press, 2012.

Horsman, Reginald. *Race and Manifest Destiny: Origins of American Racial Anglo-Saxonism.* Cambridge, Mass.: Harvard University Press, 1981.

Howe, Daniel Walker. *What Hath God Wrought: The Transformation of America, 1815–1848.* New York: Oxford University Press, 2009.

Hoxie, Frederick E. *A Final Promise: The Campaign to Assimilate the Indians, 1880–1920.* Lincoln: University of Nebraska Press, 2001.

Hudson, Angela Pulley. *Real Native Genius: How an Ex-Slave and a White Mormon Became Famous Indians.* Chapel Hill: University of North Carolina Press, 2015.

Hyde, *Empires, Nations, and Families: A New History of the North American West, 1800–1860.* New York: Ecco, 2012.

Inscoe, John C. "Carolina Slave Names: An Index to Acculturation." *Journal of Southern History* 49, no. 4 (1983): 527–54.

Irving, Gordon. "The Law of Adoption: One Phase of the Development of the Mormon Concept of Salvation, 1830–1900." *BYU Studies* 14, no. 3 (1974): 291–314.

Jacobson, Matthew Frye. *Whiteness of a Different Color: European Immigrants and the Alchemy of Race*. Cambridge, Mass.: Harvard University Press, 1999.

James, Angela. "Making Sense of Racial Classification." In *White Logic, White Methods: Racism and Methodology*, edited by Tukufu Zuberi and Eduardo Bonilla-Silva, 31–46. Lanham, Md.: Rowman and Littlefield, 2008.

Jeremias, Jorg. *The Book of Amos: A Commentary*. Louisville, Ky.: Westminster John Knox Press, 1998.

Jennings, Warren A. "The First Mormon Mission to the Indians." *Kansas Historical Quarterly* 37 (Fall 1971): 288–99.

———. "Isaac McCoy and the Mormons." *Missouri Historical Review* 61, no. 1 (1966): 62–82.

Jensen, Richard L. "Transplanted to Zion: The Impact of British Latter-day Saint Immigration upon Nauvoo." *BYU Studies* 31, no. 1 (Winter 1991): 77–87.

Johnson, Walter. *Soul by Soul: Life inside the Antebellum Slave Market*. Cambridge, Mass.: Harvard University Press, 1999.

Jones, Sondra. *Trial of Don Pedro Leon Lujan*. Salt Lake City: University of Utah Press, 1999.

Jones-Wilson, Faustine C. "Race, Realities, and American Education: Two Sides of the Coin." *Journal of Negro Education* 59, no. 2 (1990): 119–28.

Jortner, Adam. *The Gods of Prophetstown: The Battle of Tippecanoe and the Holy War for the American Frontier*. New York: Oxford University Press, 2011.

Kidd, Colin. *The Forging of Races: Race and Scripture in the Protestant Atlantic World, 1600–2000*. Cambridge: Cambridge University Press, 2006.

Kim, Angela Y. "Cain and Abel in the Light of Envy: A Study in the History of the Interpretation of Envy in Genesis 4.1–16." *Journal for the Study of the Pseudepigrapha* 12, no. 1 (2001): 65.

Kitchens, Richard D. "Mormon-Indian Relations in Deseret: Intermarriage and Indenture, 1847–1947." Ph.D. diss., Arizona State University, 2002.

Klees, Emerson. *Underground Railroad Tales: With Routes through the Finger Lakes Region*. Rochester, N.Y.: Cameo Press, 2000.

Knack, Martha C. *Boundaries Between: The Southern Paiutes, 1775–1995*. Lincoln: University of Nebraska Press, 2004.

Lambert, Neal. "The Representation of Reality in Nineteenth Century Mormon Autobiography." *Dialogue: A Journal of Mormon Thought* 11 (Summer 1978): 63–74.

Launius, Roger D. *Invisible Saints: A Study of Black Americans in the Reorganized Church*. Independence, Mo.: Herald, 1988.

———. *Joseph Smith III: Pragmatic Prophet.* Urbana: University of Illinois Press, 1988.

Law, Wesley R. "Mormon Indian Missions, 1855." M.S. thesis, Brigham Young University, 1959.

Lemire, Elise. *Miscegenation: Making Race in America.* Philadelphia: University of Pennsylvania Press, 2009.

Leonard, Glen M. *Nauvoo: A Place of Peace, a People of Promise.* Salt Lake City: Deseret Book, 2002.

Lepore, Jill. *The Name of War: King Philip's War and the Origins of American Identity.* New York: Vintage, 1999.

Lippy, Charles H. "The Great Awakening." *Ohio Journal of Religious Studies* 2, no. 1 (1974): 44–52.

Loewenberg, Bert James, and Ruth Bogin. *Black Women in Nineteenth-Century American Life: Their Words, Their Thoughts, Their Feelings.* University Park: Penn State University Press, 2010.

Lythgoe, Dennis. "Negro Slavery in Utah." *Utah Historical Quarterly* 39 (Winter 2001): 40–54.

Maffly-Kipp, Laurie F. "Assembling Bodies and Souls: Missionary Practices on the Pacific Frontier." In *Practicing Protestants: Histories of Christian Life in America, 1630–1965,* edited by Laurie F. Maffly-Kipp, Leigh Eric Schmidt, and Mark R. Valeri, 51–76. Baltimore: Johns Hopkins University Press, 2006.

Martin, Walter, and Ravi Zacharias. *Kingdom of the Cults.* Minneapolis, Minn.: Bethany House, 2003.

Marx, Anthony W. *Faith in Nation: Exclusionary Origins of Nationalism.* New York: Oxford University Press, 2003.

Mather, Increase. *The History of King Philip's War.* Edited by Samuel G. Drake. Boston: printed by editor, 1862.

Mauss, Armand L. *All Abraham's Children: Changing Mormon Conceptions of Race and Lineage.* Urbana: University of Illinois Press, 2003.

———. *The Angel and the Beehive: The Mormon Struggle with Assimilation.* Urbana: University of Illinois Press, 1994.

———. "In Search of Ephraim: Traditional Mormon Conceptions of Lineage and Race." *Journal of Mormon History* 25, no. 1 (1999): 131–73.

May, Dean. "The Mormons." In *Mormons and Mormonism: An Introduction to an American World Religion,* edited by Eric A. Eliason, 47–55. Urbana: University of Illinois, 2001.

McClintock, James H. *Mormon Settlement in Arizona.* Tucson: University of Arizona Press, 1985.

Meinhold, Peter. "Die Anfänge des Amerikanischen Geschichtsbewusstseins." *Saeculum* 5 (1954): 65–86.

Melville, Maud C. "Chief Kanosh, the Peacemaker." In *Indian Chiefs of Pioneer Days,* edited by Kate B. Carter, 16–18. Salt Lake City: Daughters of the Utah Pioneers, 1937.

Miller, Perry. *The New England Mind: The Seventeenth Century*. Cambridge, Mass.: Harvard University Press, 1982.

Mohanty, Satya. *Literary Theory and the Claims of History: Postmodernism, Objectivity, Multicultural Politics*. Ithaca, N.Y.: Cornell University Press, 1997.

Montag, Warren. "The Universalization of Whiteness." In *Whiteness: A Critical Reader*, edited by Mike Hill, 281–93. New York: New York University Press, 1997.

Morgan, Brandon. "Educating the Lamanites: A Brief History of the LDS Indian Student Placement Program." *Journal of Mormon History* 35, no. 4 (Fall 2009): 191–217.

Morrison, Toni. *Playing in the Dark*. New York: Random House, 2007.

Mueller, Max Perry. "Hemings and Jefferson Together Forever?" *Slate*, March 29, 2012, http://www.slate.com/articles/life/faithbased/2012/03/sally_hemings_mormon_and_married_to_jefferson_proxy_sealings_raise_difficult_questions_for_lds_church_.html.

———. "History Lessons: Race and the LDS Church." *Journal of Mormon History* 41, no. 1 (January 2015): 139–55.

———. "The Pageantry of Protest in Temple Square." In *Out of Obscurity: Mormonism after 1945*, edited by Patrick Mason and John Turner, 123–43. New York: Oxford University Press, 2016.

———. "Playing Jane: Re-Presenting Black Mormon Memory through Reenacting the Black Mormon Past." *Journal of Africana Religions* 1, no. 4 (2013): 513–61.

———. "Twice-Told Tale: Telling Two Histories of Mormon-Black Relations during the 2012 Presidential Election." In *Mormonism and American Politics*, ed. Randall Balmer and Jana Reiss, 155–74. New York: Columbia University Press, 2015.

Neilson, Reid. *Exhibiting Mormonism: The Latter-day Saints and the 1893 Chicago World's Fair*. New York: Oxford University Press, 2011.

Newell, Linda King, and Valeen Tippetts Avery. *Mormon Enigma: Emma Hale Smith*. Urbana: University of Illinois Press, 1994.

Newell, Quincy D. "The Autobiography and Interview of Jane Elizabeth Manning James." *Journal of Africana Religions* 1, no. 2 (2013): 251–91.

———. "'Is There No Blessing for Me?': Jane James's Construction of Space in Latter-day Saint History and Practice." In *New Perspectives in Mormon Studies: Creating and Crossing Boundaries*, edited by Eric F. Mason and Quincy D. Newell, 41–68. Norman: University of Oklahoma Press, 2013.

Noll, Mark A. "Why Theology Now?" *Modern Intellectual History* 10, no. 2 (2013): 449–61.

Numbers, Ronald L., and Jonathan M. Butler. *The Disappointed: Millerism and Millenarianism in the Nineteenth Century*. Bloomington: Indiana University Press, 1987.

O'Dea, Thomas F. *The Mormons*. Chicago: University of Chicago Press, 1957.

O'Donovan, Connell. *Augusta Cobb Young: The Lioness of the Lord*. Salt Lake City: University of Utah Press, forthcoming.

Olmstead, Earl P. *Blackcoats among the Delaware: David Zeisberger on the Ohio Frontier*. Kent, Ohio: Kent State University Press, 1991.

———. *David Zeisberger: A Life among the Indians*. Kent, Ohio: Kent State University Press, 1997.

Ostling, Richard, and Joan K. Ostling. *Mormon America: The Power and the Promise*. Rev. ed. New York: HarperCollins, 2007.

Palmquist, Peter E., and Thomas R. Kailbourn. *Pioneer Photographers of the Far West: A Biographical Dictionary, 1840–1865*. Stanford, Calif.: Stanford University Press, 2000.

Park, Benjamin E. "Early Mormon Patriarchy and the Paradoxes of Democratic Religiosity in Jacksonian America." *American Nineteenth Century History* 14, no. 2 (Summer 2013): 183–208.

Pearce, Roy Harvey. *Savagism and Civilization: A Study of the Indian and the American Mind*. Berkeley: University of California Press, 1988.

Perlich, Pamela S. "Utah Minorities: The Story Told by 150 Years of Census Data." Bureau of Economic and Business Research, David Eccles School of Business, University of Utah, Salt Lake City, 2002.

Peterson, Charles S. "Hopis and Mormons." *Utah Historical Quarterly* 39, no. 2 (Summer 1971): 179–94.

———. "Jacob Hamblin, Apostle to the Lamanites, and the Indian Mission." *Journal of Mormon History* 2 (1975): 21–34.

Peterson, John Alton. *Utah's Black Hawk War*. Salt Lake City: University of Utah Press, 1999.

Plant, Deborah G. *Every Tub Must Sit on Its Own Bottom: The Philosophy and Politics of Zora Neale Hurston*. Urbana: University of Illinois Press, 1995.

Prince, Gerald. *A Dictionary of Narratology*. Lincoln: University of Nebraska Press, 2003.

Quinn, D. Michael. *The Mormon Hierarchy: Origins of Power*. Salt Lake City: Signature Books, 1994.

Reeve, W. Paul. *Religion of a Different Color: Race and the Mormon Struggle for Whiteness*. New York: Oxford University Press, 2015.

Reeve, W. Paul, Christopher B. Rich Jr., and LaJean Purcell Carruth. *"The Angels in Heaven Will Blush": Race and the 1852 Utah Territorial Legislature*. Salt Lake City: University of Utah, 2018.

Richards, Bradley W. "Charles R. Savage, the Other Promontory Photographer." *Utah Historical Quarterly* 60, no. 2 (Spring 1992): 137–57.

———. *The Savage View: Charles Savage, Pioneer Mormon Photographer*. Nevada City, Calif.: Carl Mautz, 1995.

Richards, Thomas. *The Imperial Archive: Knowledge and the Fantasy of Empire*. New York: Verso, 1993.

Richter, Daniel K. *Facing East from Indian Country: A Native History of Early America*. Cambridge, Mass.: Harvard University Press, 2003.

Ricks, Nathaniel R. "A Peculiar Place for the Peculiar Institution: Slavery and Sovereignty in Early Territorial Utah." M.A. thesis, Brigham Young University, 2007.

Ricoeur, Paul. *Memory, History, Forgetting*. Translated by Kathleen Blamey and David Pellauer. Chicago: University of Chicago Press, 2006.

Ritner, Robert K. "The 'Breathing Permit of Hor' Thirty-Four Years Later." *Dialogue: A Journal of Mormon Thought* 33, no. 4 (200): 91–119.

Robinson, Ezra Clark. *The Life of Ira Hatch, Famous Indian Missionary and Scout*. Bountiful, Utah: N.p., 1940.

Roediger, David R. *Working toward Whiteness: How America's Immigrants Became White: The Strange Journey from Ellis Island to the Suburbs*. New York: Basic Books, 2005.

Rogin, Michael. *Blackface, White Noise: Jewish Immigrants in the Hollywood Melting Pot*. Berkeley: University of California Press, 1998.

Rothman, Joshua D. *Notorious in the Neighborhood: Sex and Families across the Color Line in Virginia, 1787–1861*. Chapel Hill: University of North Carolina Press, 2003.

Rust, Val D. *Radical Origins: Early Mormon Converts and Their Colonial Ancestors*. Urbana: University of Illinois Press, 2004.

Said, Edward W. *Orientalism*. New York: Vintage, 1979.

Salisbury, Neal. "Red Puritans: The 'Praying Indians' of Massachusetts Bay and John Eliot." *William and Mary Quarterly*, 3rd ser., 31, no. 1 (1974): 27–54.

Sandos, James A. *Converting California: Indians and Franciscans in the Missions*. New Haven, Conn.: Yale University Press, 2008.

Schultz, George A. *An Indian Canaan: Isaac McCoy and the Vision of an Indian State*. Norman: University of Oklahoma Press, 1972.

Scott, James C. *Domination and the Arts of Resistance: Hidden Transcripts*. New Haven, Conn.: Yale University Press, 1990.

Scott, James M. *Geography in Early Judaism and Christianity: The Book of Jubilees*. New York: Cambridge University Press, 2005.

Sensbach, Jon F. *Rebecca's Revival: Creating Black Christianity in the Atlantic World*. Cambridge, Mass.: Harvard University Press, 2005.

Sewall, Sarah. Introduction to *The U.S. Army/Marine Corps Counterinsurgency Field Manual*. Chicago: University of Chicago Press, 2006.

Sheehan, Bernard. *Savagism and Civility: Indians and Englishmen in Colonial Virginia*. New York: Cambridge University Press, 1980.

Shepard, Gordon, and Gary Shepard. *Binding Earth and Heaven: Patriarchal Blessings in the Prophetic Development of Early Mormonism.* University Park: Pennsylvania State Press, 2012.

Shepard, William. "The Concept of a 'Rejected Gospel' in Mormon History: Part 1." *Journal of Mormon History* 34, no. 2 (Spring 2008): 130–81.

———. "The Concept of a 'Rejected Gospel' in Mormon History: Part 2." *Journal of Mormon History* 34, no. 3 (Summer 2008): 142–86.

Shipps, Jan. "Another Side of Early Mormonism." In *The Journals of William McLellin, 1831–1836,* edited by Jan Shipps and John Woodland Welch, 3–12. Urbana: University of Illinois Press and BYU Studies, 1994.

———. "Difference and Otherness: Mormonism and the American Religious Mainstream." In *Minority Faiths and the American Protestant Mainstream,* ed. Jonathan D. Sarna, 81–98. Urbana: University of Illinois Press.

———. "Making Saints: In the Early Days and the Latter Days." In *Contemporary Mormonism: Social Science Perspectives,* edited by Marie Cornwall et al., 64–86. Urbana: University of Illinois Press, 2001.

———. *Mormonism: The Story of a New Religious Tradition.* Urbana: University of Illinois Press, 1987.

———. "The Prophet Puzzle: Suggestions Leading toward a More Comprehensive Interpretation of Joseph Smith." In *The New Mormon History,* edited by D. Michael Quinn, 53–74. Salt Lake City: Signature Books, 1992.

———. *Sojourner in the Promised Land: Forty Years among the Mormons.* Urbana: University of Illinois Press, 2000.

Silver, Peter Rhoads. *Our Savage Neighbors: How Indian War Transformed Early America.* New York: W. W. Norton, 2008.

Simmons, Virginia McConnell. *The Ute Indians of Utah, Colorado, and New Mexico.* Boulder: University of Colorado Press, 2000.

Simon, Jerald. "Thomas Bullock as an Early Mormon Historian." *BYU Studies* 30, no. 1 (1990): 71–88.

Simon, Paul. *Freedom's Champion: Elijah Lovejoy.* Carbondale: Southern Illinois University Press, 1994.

Sleeper-Smith, Susan. *Indian Women and French Men: Rethinking Cultural Encounter in the Western Great Lakes.* Amherst: University of Massachusetts Press, 2001.

Smallcanyon, Corey. "Contested Space: Navajos and Hopi in the Colonization of Tuba City." M.A. thesis, Brigham Young University, 2010.

Smith, Shawn Michelle. *Photography on the Color Line: W. E. B. Du Bois, Race, and Visual Culture.* Durham, N.C.: Duke University Press, 2004.

Sollars, Werner, ed. *The Invention of Ethnicity.* New York: Oxford University Press, 1991.

Spivak, Gayatri Chakravorty. "Can the Subaltern Speak?" In *Marxism and the Interpretation of Culture*, edited by Cary Nelson and Lawrence Grossberg, 271–316. Urbana: University of Illinois Press, 1988.

Stack, Peggy Fletcher. "This Mormon Sunday School Teacher Was Dismissed for Using Church's Own Race Essay in Lesson." *Salt Lake Tribune*, May 5, 2015.

Staker, Mark Lyman. *Hearken, O Ye People: The Historical Setting of Joseph Smith's Ohio Revelations*. Sandy, Utah: Greg Kofford Books, 2010.

Stapley, Jonathan A. "Adoptive Sealing Ritual in Mormonism." *Journal of Mormon History* 37, no. 3 (Summer 2011): 53–117.

———. "Jane Manning James in the Woman's Exponent." *By Common Consent*, http://bycommonconsent.com/2007/10/19/jane-manning-james-in-the-womans -exponent..

Stark, Rodney. "The Basis of Mormon Success: A Theoretical Application." In *Mormons and Mormonism: An Introduction to an American World Religion*, edited by Eric A. Eliason, 207–42. Urbana: University of Illinois Press, 2001.

———. "Mormon Networks of Faith." In *The Rise of Mormonism*, edited by Reid Larkin Neilson, 57–82. New York: Columbia University Press, 2005.

Stauffer, John. *The Black Hearts of Men: Radical Abolitionists and the Transformation of Race*. Cambridge, Mass.: Harvard University Press, 2004.

———. "The Problem of Freedom in the Bondwoman's Narrative." In *In Search of Hannah Crafts: Essays on the Bondwoman's Narrative*, edited by Henry Louis Gates Jr. and Hollis Robbins. New York: BasicCivitas, 2004.

Stein, Stephen J. "'Taking Up the Full Cross': The Shaker Challenge to the Western 'Christians.'" *Discipliana* 65, no. 3 (2005): 93–110.

Stepto, Robert B. *From behind the Veil: A Study of Afro-American Narrative*. Urbana: University of Illinois Press, 1991.

Stevenson, Russell W. *For the Cause of Righteousness: A Global History of Blacks and Mormonism, 1830–2013*. Salt Lake City: Greg Kofford Books, 2014.

Stoffle, Richard W., Kristine L. Jones, and Henry F. Dobyns. "Direct European Immigrant Transmission of Old World Pathogens to Numic Indians during the Nineteenth Century." *American Indian Quarterly* 19, no. 2 (Spring 1995): 181–203.

Stoler, Ann Laura. *Along the Archival Grain: Epistemic Anxieties and Colonial Common Sense*. Princeton, N.J.: Princeton University Press, 2010.

Stott, G. St. John. "New Jerusalem Abandoned: The Failure to Carry Mormonism to the Delaware." *Journal of American Studies* 21, no. 1 (1987): 71–85.

Sussman, Robert Wald. *The Myth of Race: The Troubling Persistence of an Unscientific Idea*. Cambridge, Mass.: Harvard University Press, 2014.

Tait, Lisa Olsen. "The Young Woman's Journal: Gender and Generations in a Mormon Women's Magazine." *American Periodicals: A Journal of History, Criticism, and Bibliography* 22, no. 1 (2012): 51–71.

Taylor, Alan. *William Cooper's Town: Power and Persuasion on the Frontier of the Early American Republic*. New York: Vintage, 1996.

Thomson, Alistair. "Memory and Remembering in Oral History." In *Oxford Handbook of Oral History*, edited by Donald A. Ritchie, 77–95. New York: Oxford University Press, 2011.

Turner, John G. *Brigham Young: Pioneer Prophet*. Cambridge, Mass.: Belknap Press of Harvard University Press, 2012.

Underwood, Grant. "Book of Mormon Usage in Early LDS Theology." *Dialogue: A Journal of Mormon Thought* 17, no. 3 (Autumn 1984): 35–74.

———. *The Millenarian World of Early Mormonism*. Urbana: University of Illinois Press, 1993.

Van Wagoner, Richard S. *Mormon Polygamy: A History*. Salt Lake City: Signature Books, 1989.

Vogel, Dan. *Indian Origins and the Book of Mormon: Religious Solutions from Columbus to Joseph Smith*. Salt Lake City: Signature Books, 1986.

Wadsworth, Nelson B. *Set in Stone, Fixed in Glass: The Mormons, the West, and Their Photographers*. Salt Lake City: Signature Books, 1996.

Walker, Ronald W. "Seeking the 'Remnant': The Native American during the Joseph Smith Period." *Journal of Mormon History* 19 (1993): 1–33.

———. "Wakara Meets the Mormons, 1848–52: A Case Study in Native American Accommodation." *Utah Historical Quarterly* 70 (Summer 2002): 215–37.

Walker, Ronald W., Richard E. Turley, and Glen M. Leonard. *Massacre at Mountain Meadows: An American Tragedy*. New York: Oxford University Press, 2008.

Weslager, C. A. *The Delaware Indians: A History*. New Brunswick, N.J.: Rutgers University Press, 1990.

White, Richard. "Frederick Jackson Turner and Buffalo Bill." In *The Frontier in American Culture*, edited by James R. Grossman, 7–66. Berkeley: University of California Press, 1994.

Williams, Carol J. *Framing the West: Race, Gender, and the Photographic Frontier in the Pacific Northwest*. New York: Oxford University Press, 2003.

Wilson, William A. "The Three Nephites." In *Encyclopedia of Mormonism*, edited by Daniel H. Ludlow, 1477–78. New York: Macmillan, 1992.

Wolfinger, Henry. "A Test of Faith: Jane Manning Elizabeth James and the Origins of the Utah Black Community." In *Social Accommodation in Utah*, edited by Clark Knowlton, 126–72. Salt Lake City: American West Center, University of Utah, 1975.

Young, Margaret Blair, and Darius Aidan Gray. *One More River to Cross*. Salt Lake City: Deseret Books, 2000.

Zakai, Avihu. *Exile and Kingdom: History and Apocalypse in the Puritan Migration to America*. New York: Cambridge University Press, 2002.

INDEX

Abdy, Edward Strutt, 93

Abel, Elijah, 95, 97–98, 107, 126–28, 132–33, 230, 261n22, 266n74; missionary work, 95, 97–98, 194, 254n23, 262n22; ordination to the priesthood, 95, 106, 127, 152, 190, 231, 253n21, 253n23, 289n10; patriarchal blessing, 106–8, 127, 257n59; and the priesthood and temple ban, 132, 137, 152, 194, 219, 228, 254n23; in Utah, 194, 254n23

Abolitionism, 18, 81, 84–85, 93, 95–98, 107, 132, 142, 250n91, 251n104, 253n16, 288n4. *See also* Slavery

Abrahamic covenant, 2–3, 31, 36, 79, 94, 102–4, 111, 118, 122, 136–37, 141–42. *See also* Lineage

"Act for the Relief of Indian Slaves and Prisoners, An," 189. *See also* Slavery

"Act in Relation to Service, An," 189–94, 281–82n35. *See also* Slavery

Adams, John Quincy, 236n23

Africa/Africans, 13, 15–16, 24, 34, 39, 62, 85–86, 94, 97, 183, 217–18, 228, 236n16, 236n30, 291n41. *See also* African Americans; Cain: curse of; Ham: curse of; Race

African Americans/blacks, 5–7, 8, 11–12, 25, 41, 56–59, 62, 82, 139, 217, 238n8, 240n45, 262n30, 291n44; and the curse of Cain/Ham, 2, 7, 16–18, 21, 39–42, 90, 109, 115–17, 122–24, 127, 141–51, 182, 190, 193, 218, 230–31, 240n40, 261n11, 268n89, 271n114, 118; in early Mormonism, 5–7, 10, 20,

23–24, 27–29, 70, 81–90, 92, 96–98, 107–9, 116–52, 163, 193–94, 212, 218–19, 228–32, 254n23, 257n62, 264n57, 265n62, 266n74, 268n85, 269n98; in Utah, 5–7, 29, 96, 138, 163, 181, 190–93, 225–26, 264n57, 282–83n41, 288n10; free, 10, 17, 81, 88, 92, 119, 131, 163, 193, 251nn103–104, 253n22; enslaved, 17–18, 81, 85, 92, 96, 119, 163, 181, 190–93, 264n57, 282–83n41, 288n10. *See also* Priesthood and temple ban; Race

Alger, Fanny, 270n106

Algonquian Indians, 66

Allen, John, 106, 257n59

Alvord, James Watson, 96–97

American Colonization Society, 85

American Progress (Gast), 221, 227

Anderson, William (Kikthawenund), 66–76, 210, 246n25

Anglicans, 15, 244n126, 254n23

Anti-Mormonism, 1, 61, 63, 76–78, 88, 143, 208, 212, 226, 291n36; violence, 1, 20, 78, 93, 117, 124; in Missouri, 78, 92, 98, 117, 124, 166; in print, 92, 98; and Native Americans, 177, 225

Apess, William, 18, 56–59, 244n115

Appleby, William, 268n91

Arapeen, 3–6, 11, 29, 59, 170–71, 184–85, 189, 203–4, 208, 234n9, 286n83

Arizona, 176–79, 270n107

Armstrong, George D., 16

"Articles of Faith," 147, 239n38

Augustine, 79

Bailey, Francis, 242n55

Baptism for the dead, 3, 28, 127, 132, 136, 144, 258n68, 264n50

Baptists, 1, 67–70, 73, 77, 79, 82, 246n25, 254n25

Barney, Elvira Stevens, 149

Batiste, 186

Bean, George, 156, 172, 174

Beckwourth, Jim, 155

"Believing blood," 110–12, 130, 258n81. *See also* Lineage

Benson, Ezra Taft, 291n38

Bernhisel, John, 119, 133, 144, 190, 281n31

Betsy (enslaved woman), 283n48

Bible, 237n42, 243n85; and the curse of Cain/Ham, 2, 7, 35, 39, 85–87, 97, 116–18, 127, 129, 149, 190–93, 218; in early America, 13–16, 47; and the Book of Mormon, 17, 19, 22, 35, 37, 39, 47, 79, 85–86, 101, 231; and Native Americans, 18, 47, 279n97; and slavery, 97, 190–93; Joseph Smith's translation of, 85–87, 116, 148, 251n98; and polygamy, 142

Black codes, 131, 282n41

Blackface, 223, 225–27

Black Hawk (Antonga), 166, 178, 195, 201–2, 210, 223–25, 275n30, 279n96, 290n24

Blackhawk, Ned, 189

Black Hawk War, 163, 202, 225, 275n30, 279n96

Blackness/darkness, 7, 13–16, 19, 25–27, 33–46, 50–54, 58, 84–86, 148–49, 210, 221, 231, 271n114, 261n11, 288n4; and whiteness, 7, 16, 25, 34, 42, 89, 127, 138–40, 212, 217; "scales of darkness," 39, 58. *See also* Cain: curse of; Ham: curse of; Laman: curse of; Race; Whiteness

Black Pete, 87–89, 97–98, 251n103

Blake, James, 166

Bloom, Harold, 12, 22

Blumenbach, Johann, 240n43

Boggs, Lilburn, 124, 166

Book of Abraham, 116, 128; as justification for priesthood and temple ban, 115–17, 122, 147, 230, 259n99, 268n89, 288n9; origins of, 115, 251n98, 259n99, 259n101; and the curse of Ham, 116, 147, 151

Book of Mormon, 2, 26–28, 76–79, 94, 101–5, 110, 112, 115–16, 127, 135, 139, 238n18, 241n63, 241n68, 242n76, 80, 82, 83, 243n85, 243n95, 244n109, 248nn66–67, 250n80; and race, 2, 11, 13, 17, 19–20, 23–24, 26–27, 33–36, 38–43, 46–53, 58–59, 76, 80–86, 91, 117, 123, 145, 183, 194, 231, 240n47, 242n84; publication of, 2, 18, 23, 35, 47, 60–62; translation of, 2, 22–23, 31, 35, 40–42, 65, 78, 88, 135, 139, 251n98, 259n102, 260n10; and Native Americans, 3, 10, 24, 28, 31, 38–39, 46–48, 63–75, 79–80, 92–93, 100, 125, 145, 159–60, 165, 169–74, 177–79, 183, 187, 189, 194, 196–97, 202–3, 220, 247n42, 261n17; universalism in, 17, 19–20, 26, 30, 35, 40–41, 57, 93, 104–6, 117, 231, 255n30; and Gentiles, 24, 31–33, 37–39, 43–46, 53, 60, 64, 78–80, 85–86, 101–3, 247n43, 250n78, 255n30; Christ's mission in, 26, 31–55, 79–80, 239n23; and literacy, 26, 33, 38–49, 55, 59, 69, 72, 76, 79, 187, 202, 240nn47–48, 250n78; title page of, 32, 46, 64, 102, 241n64, 255n30; and slavery, 85, 159, 251n97; and Polynesians, 179; changes to, 231

Book of Moses, 85–86, 116, 147, 251n98, 271n114, 271n118; and the curse of Cain, 86–87, 90, 117, 147–48, 239–40n40, 271n114, 271n118; as justifica-

Dana, Lewis, 125
Davies, James, 178
Day, H. R., 208
Decker, Charles, 186, 188, 280n14
Decker, Vilate, 186
Declaration of Independence, 107
Delaware Indians, 27, 82, 140, 167, 210, 248n64; Mormon mission to, 27, 59, 65–76, 79, 98, 100, 102, 125, 165, 169, 177, 180, 246nn24–25, 247n42
Deseret, proposed state of, 159–61, 174
Deseret News, 121, 142, 152, 199–200, 217, 223–24, 226
Domínguez, Francisco Atanasio, 164, 276n66
Douglas, Stephen, 262n29
Douglass, Frederick, 128, 138, 253n22
Doyle, Arthur Conan, 9
Duncan, William, 244n126

Ebersole, Gary, 59
Egyptus, 116, 218
Eliot, John, 47
Elk Mountain Mission, 177, 278n94
Endowment House, 194–95, 254n23
England, 101, 110–11, 117–18, 130, 166, 192, 258n81
Ephraim, 28, 94, 112, 118, 143–46, 179, 193, 195, 219, 255n30; and patriarchal blessings, 105, 114, 146, 270n107. *See also* Lineage; Patriarchal blessings
Escalante, Silvestre Vélez de, 164, 277n66
Ethnicity, 109–10, 231, 255n44, 258n72. *See also* Race
Europeans, 8, 11, 18, 34, 85, 95, 101–2, 131, 221, 261; converts to Mormonism, 5, 26, 29, 180, 192; colonizers and missionaries, 5, 67, 72–73, 125, 162, 164, 171–72, 273n16, 274n21, 287n92; as descendants of Japheth, 13, 16, 62; Jewish, 101–2, 111, 220

Evening and the Morning Star, 28, 77–91, 92, 96, 98, 105–6, 147, 249n73, 250n78

Fielding, James, 110
Fielding, Joseph, 110
Finney, Charles Grandison, 117
First Presidency, 113, 152, 219
Fish, Stanley, 22
Flake, Agnes, 264n57
Flake, Green, 163, 193, 264n57, 265n61, 288–89n10
Flake, James M., 264n57, 289n10
Flake, William J., 264n57
Flournoy, Jacob, 97
Fort Utah, 165–66, 170, 172, 223, 225
Foucault, Michel, 24, 62
Fox Indians, 125
Freeman's Journal, 242n74
Frémont, John C., 153–54, 176
French, 72–73
Friends of the Indians, 164, 183

Garrison, William Lloyd, 138, 253n16
Gast, John, 221, 227
Gates, Susa Young, 187–88, 196–98, 281n18
Gathering, 4–5, 17, 24, 31, 39, 45, 77, 87, 94, 99, 101–2, 109, 112, 131, 192, 231–32, 249n69, 249n73. *See also* New Jerusalem
Gelelemend (William Henry Killbuck Jr.), 67–68
Genesis Group, 219
Gentiles, 84, 92, 95, 99–100, 102–3, 250; white Europeans and Americans as, 24, 27, 31, 38–39, 41, 43–46, 53, 62–65, 70, 76–80, 85–87, 90, 105–7, 108–9, 117–18, 155, 160–63; in the Book of Mormon, 24, 31–33, 37–39, 43–46, 53, 60, 64, 78–80, 85–86, 101–3, 247n43, 250n78, 255n30; as non-Mormons,

Iowa, 125, 265n63, 268n87

Iroquois Indians, 66

Jackman, Levi, 126, 165

Jackson, Andrew, 15, 34, 38–39, 64, 74, 82, 84, 99, 223

Jackson County, Mo., 27–28, 61, 70, 77, 80–82, 90, 92–100, 103, 107, 125, 251n103, 254n24. *See also* New Jerusalem

Jacob (biblical patriarch), 14, 24, 28, 94, 102–5, 109, 112, 115, 136, 268n90

Jacobs, Harriet, 128, 138

Jacobson, Matthew Frye, 11

James, Angela, 12

James, Isaac, 119

James, Jane Manning, 5–7, 11, 25–26, 28, 59, 89, 186, 212–13, 215, 230, 232, 262n33, 263n38, 264n57, 265n61, 266–67n77, 267n79, 268nn90–91, 270n105, 272n123, 275n29, 288n10; autobiography of, 5–7, 119–23, 128–34, 137–145, 146, 149–50, 152, 260n3, 262nn32–33, 263n38, 263n43, 264n50, 264n57, 265n62, 266n77; conversion to Mormonism, 5–7, 120, 129; relationship with Joseph Smith Jr., 5–7, 121–22, 128–29, 133–37, 141, 143–45, 194–95, 217, 272n129; and the priesthood and temple ban, 7, 122–23, 129, 132–34, 136–37, 141–45, 150–52, 194–95, 217–19, 228, 230, 257n62, 272n129; patriarchal blessing(s), 107, 146–49, 190, 257n62, 271n119; children, 134, 138–41, 143, 163, 215–17, 252n13, 260n1, 265n63, 267n82, 268n87

James, Silas, 134, 163, 252n113, 265n63

James, Sylvester, 138–44, 150, 163, 260n1, 266n77, 267nn82–83, 268n85, 268n87

James, Vilate, 215–17

Japheth, 13, 16, 24–25, 40, 62, 79, 85, 91,

95, 97, 107, 116. *See also* Europeans; Lineage

Jefferson, Thomas, 82

Jerusalem, 36, 95, 101–2, 111, 240n47, 255n30

Jews/Jewish people, 11–12, 26, 36, 77–78, 95, 100–103, 112, 118, 153, 220, 227, 255n30

Jones, Daniel W., 182–85

Joseph (biblical prophet), 14, 28, 94, 104–6, 118; in the Book of Mormon, 94, 102–3, 112, 183, 188

Kane, Thomas L., 168, 204

Kanosh, 156, 172–73, 187–88, 197–201, 212, 220, 286nn73–74, 290n23

Kanosh, Betsykin, 286n74

Kanosh, Mary, 200–201, 286nn73–74

Kanosh, Sally (Kahpeputz), 186–88, 195–201, 212, 214–15, 221, 280n14, 281n18, 286nn73–74

Kennedy, John F., 219

Kenner, Scipio Africanus, 226, 290n32

Kimball, Adelia, 156, 199

Kimball, Heber C., 77, 110, 118, 125, 153, 156, 199, 248n67, 262n22, 263n42, 264n57

Kimball, Lucy Walker Smith, 269n102

Kimball, Spencer W., 220, 228

King Philip's War, 47, 239n29, 242n73, 286n78

Kinney, Eunice, 254n23, 266n74

Kirtland, Ohio, 65, 75, 80, 84, 87, 89, 92, 96–98, 100, 111, 115, 126, 248n60, 251n103, 253n16, 254n23

Laman, 34, 36, 43, 50, 53; curse of, 40–41, 44, 51, 55, 86, 117, 127, 187, 193, 197, 271n114. *See also* Lamanites

Lamanites, 2, 35–46, 49–59, 86, 89, 102–3, 105, 112–13, 140, 240n48, 241n64,

231; Americans' (and American government's) views of, 9, 20, 61, 63, 69–70, 77–78, 92–93, 98, 117, 123–24, 142, 164, 212, 226–27, 247n39, 254n23; and violence, 9, 27, 29, 93, 132, 155–56, 160–62, 166–67, 173–74, 182–85, 196, 201, 209–11, 225, 274n19; ethnic peculiarity of, 11, 13, 103, 109–10, 117, 121, 231, 258n72; and settler colonialism, 20, 27, 155–59, 162–67, 171–80, 181–86, 207–11, 273–74n19, 275n43; priesthood, 28, 78, 94–95, 113–18, 122–26, 136–37, 141–43, 146–47, 150–52, 190–91, 194, 228–30, 254n23, 259n91, 268n91, 169n98, 284n50; hierarchical organization of, 114, 229, 259n91. *See also* Anti-Mormonism; Book of Mormon; Hermeneutic of restoration; Lineage; Mormon archive; Race

Mormon archive, 23, 97, 109, 137, 160, 171, 186, 221, 229, 237n37; and race, 19–21, 25–29, 42, 46, 53–55, 58–59, 76, 87–89, 97, 107, 120–28, 137–40, 149, 160, 171, 186–88, 195–97, 201–2, 215, 217–219, 254n23, 280n14, 285n59; and the Book of Mormon, 23, 26–27, 35–37, 42, 46–50, 53–55, 58, 69, 112, 140, 241n64, 250n78, 255n30. *See also* Narrator's prerogative

Mormon Tabernacle Choir, 9, 227–28

Mormon Wars (Missouri), 124

Moroni, 1–3, 35, 38, 42–46, 55, 71, 79, 200, 238n15, 239n18, 241n64

Narrator's prerogative, 27, 42–46, 49, 53–55, 59, 137–38, 160, 197–201, 241n55. *See also* Book of Mormon; Mormon archive

Native Americans, 1, 6, 8–10, 15, 18–19, 25, 33, 48, 57, 58–59, 65, 68, 93, 125, 153, 158–167, 172, 181, 183, 189, 194, 202,
207, 210–11, 236n30, 244n115, 277n70, 290n23; as Lamanites, 2–4, 19, 27, 29, 31, 33–34, 38–39, 46–48, 56, 62, 64–65, 68–80, 87, 90–91, 94–95, 98–100, 111, 125–26, 148, 159–64, 167, 170–80, 182–89, 192–202, 209–11, 220–21, 234n7, 245n19, 249n69, 261n17, 269n98, 270n107; slavery, 3–4, 11, 20, 29, 155, 156–59, 162–64, 168, 172, 174, 176–77, 181–97, 199, 201, 204, 207–10, 272n129, 277n70, 281n18, 281n32, 284n53, 285n64, 286n89, 287nn93–94; Mormon intermarriage with, 4, 10–11, 20, 29, 72–73, 125, 145, 177, 186, 192, 195, 200, 234n7, 247n51, 270n107; Mormon adoption of, 4, 29, 176–77, 186–88, 195–97, 200, 212, 220, 225, 284n53, 285n59, 285n64, 287n93; as descendants of Shem, 62, 85, 91; Mormon missions to, 5, 19–20, 27, 41, 63–79, 81, 84, 87, 90, 94, 98, 102, 106, 145, 163, 167–68, 170, 175–80, 182, 188, 195, 201, 220, 245n19, 246n25, 247n51, 249n69, 261n17, 270n107, 278n85, 279n97, 284n53. *See also* Indian Removal Act; Lamanites; names of individual tribes

Nauvoo, Ill., 5, 28, 104, 107–8, 114, 119–35, 137, 139–40, 144–52, 193–94, 217, 258n79, 262n32, 264n57, 265n65, 270n105

Nauvoo Legion, 124, 156, 165, 167, 173, 178, 209, 225, 265

Nauvoo Neighbor, 125, 132, 262n32, 266n75

Navajo Indians, 100, 162, 179–80, 183, 201, 270n107, 278n90

Neolin, 66–67

Nephi (Book of Mormon prophet), 35–55, 69, 79, 86, 90, 103, 177, 200, 238n18, 241n68

biography of, 70, 73–76, 84, 129, 140, 247n42; announcement of the priesthood and temple ban, 269n98

Presbyterians, 1, 16, 48, 57, 79, 95, 117, 130, 242n73, 254n23, 263n38

Priesthood, 7, 28, 78, 87, 94–95, 113–18, 126, 136–37, 258n88, 259n91

Priesthood and temple ban, 7, 137, 141, 284n50; and Jane Manning James, 7, 122, 136–37, 140–52, 194–95, 228, 257n62; and Joseph Smith, 7, 122, 146, 228, 288n9; curses of Cain/Ham as justification for, 7, 143, 230, 268n89, 268n91; revelation ending, 9–10, 219, 228; and fears of interracial marriage, 7, 191; and Joseph Fielding Smith, 228, 231; book of Abraham as justification for, 117, 122, 147, 152–53, 230, 268n89, 288n9; book of Moses as justification for, 122, 147–48, 152–53, 268n89, 288n9; and white apostates and anti-Mormons, 124–25; and Joseph F. Smith, 137, 150–52, 228; and Elijah Abel, 137, 152, 194, 228, 254n23, 266n74, 289n10; and Brigham Young, 141, 143, 147, 150, 190, 194, 228, 231, 268n89, 268n91, 288n9; announcement of, 143, 147, 269n98; 1908 church statement on, 151; 1949 First Presidency statement on, 152, 289n15; and "Race and the Priesthood" essay, 230–31, 291n47; and Walker Lewis, 268n91; and William McCary, 269n98; and John Taylor, 288n9. *See also* African Americans; Book of Abraham; Book of Moses; Cain: Curse of; Ham: Curse of; Priesthood; Temple(s)

Protestants, 1, 11, 70, 113, 117, 130, 164, 236. *See also* Missionaries; names of individual denominations and churches

Provo, Utah, 156, 184, 203, 207, 223, 232, 277n68

Puritans, 36, 47, 54

Pyper, George, 227

Quorum of the Seventy, 97, 113, 127, 232, 257n59

Quorum of the Twelve Apostles, 101, 113, 151, 218, 232, 281n32

Qur'an, 22

Race, 8, 11, 15–16, 25, 47–48, 56–57, 138, 201, 244n111, 244n115, 262n30, 274n19

—and biblical curses, 7, 10, 13–14, 19, 39–41, 106, 190–93, 230

—Mormon conceptions of, 2–5, 7, 8–13, 16–21, 24, 26–30, 62–63, 92–94, 106–7, 112, 118, 127, 132, 183, 212–13, 225, 227–32, 283n46, 291n47; in the Book of Mormon, 2, 4–5, 20–24, 26–27, 33–59, 84, 196, 240n47; Native Americans, 3–5, 19–20, 25–29, 46–48, 63, 84, 98–100, 187, 196–97, 220–21; African Americans, 7, 10, 19–20, 25–29, 63, 80–91, 97–98, 106–8, 122–23, 128–29, 133–36, 141–45, 148, 151, 190–94, 217–19, 253–54n23; racialization of white Mormons, 11, 28, 212, 227–28

—and secularization, 12–13

—and slavery, 3–4, 16, 19, 97–98, 159, 190–92. *See also* Africa/Africans; African Americans; Cain: curse of; Ethnicity; Ham: curse of; Laman: curse of; Lineage; Mormon archive: and race; Mormon/Mormonism: and race; Slavery

Rawlins, Joseph, Jr., 278–79n94

Reagan, Ronald, 228

Redface, 223–27

Reeve, W. Paul, 143

Reflector, 92

146–50, 190, 218, 254n23, 257n57,
271nn118–119

Smith, John, 269n102, 271n119

Smith, Joseph, Jr., 1–3, 5–6, 7, 16–17, 30,
69, 76, 80, 84, 88, 92–93, 101–3, 105,
110, 137–41, 217–19, 236n30, 250n80,
257n58, 259n91, 270nn105–106,
274n22, 275n29; and the Book of Mormon, 1–2, 18–24, 31, 42–48, 52, 60–65,
71, 77–78, 81, 84, 103, 167, 241n64,
251n98, 271n118; revelations of, 2–3,
10, 19, 23, 63–64, 72–73, 78–80, 85,
88–90, 94–96, 99–100, 103, 105–6, 113,
115, 117, 123, 246n23, 249n69, 250n76,
251n98, 255n28, 255n31, 261n15,
269n92; racial attitudes of, 2–3, 28,
40, 72–73, 75, 85–87, 97–100, 106–8,
115–17, 119–37, 144–48, 150–52, 163,
180, 190, 228, 231, 262n30, 264n52,
288n9, 292n47; and Mormon universalism, 3, 27–28, 62, 109–10, 193,
232, 291n47; assassination of, 10, 61,
109, 124, 144; views on slavery, 10,
85–86, 95–97, 107, 191, 230, 253n13;
and the book of Moses, 85–87, 116,
148, 239n40, 268n89, 288n9; and
Mormon priesthood, 113–17; and the
book of Abraham, 115–17, 147, 259n99,
259n102, 268n89, 288n9. *See also*
James, Jane Manning: relationship
with Joseph Smith

Smith, Joseph, III, 265n65, 270n105

Smith, Joseph, Sr., 1, 94, 103–9, 113–15,
127, 256n45, 256n52, 257n58

Smith, Joseph F., 7, 121–22, 129, 133, 137,
141, 144, 150–52, 218, 228, 260n3

Smith, Joseph Fielding, 10, 218–20, 231

Smith, Lucy, 256n52

Smith, Lucy Mack, 95, 135

Smith, Mary, 257n58

Smith, Samuel, 248n67, 257n58, 258n81

Smith, Thomas "Pegleg," 155

Smith, William, 104–5, 126, 256n52,
268n91

Snow, Eliza R., 63, 77, 84, 121, 269n102,
283n46

Snow, Erastus, 143

Snow, Lorenzo, 129

Sollors, Werner, 109

South Park (TV show), 9

Sowiette, 170–71, 187, 208–9, 273n2

Spanish, 1, 154–55, 162–64, 168, 172, 178,
182, 189, 197, 204, 209–10, 276n66

Spanish Fort Press, 225

Spencer, Daniel, 265n63

Spivak, Gayarti Chakravorty, 58

Stebbings, Anthony, 260n1

Stebbings, Sarah, 260n1

Steward, Austin, 18

Stout, Hosea, 126, 128, 252n113, 260n4

Stowell, William Rufus Rogers, 146

Strong, Eliel, 105

Study in Scarlet, A (Doyle), 9

Taylor, John, 129, 132, 141, 143, 253n23,
288n9

Tecumseh, 67

Temple(s), 7, 28, 42, 46, 101; in the Book
of Mormon, 5, 36, 46; and Afri-
can Americans, 7, 10, 115–17, 122–23,
126, 133–36, 141, 143, 147, 149–52, 194,
215–17, 219, 228, 231, 254n23, 257n62,
264n50, 291n41; rituals, 7, 108–9, 115–
16, 135–36, 149, 151, 257n62, 264n50,
265n67, 266n72, 270n107, 271n121;
Independence, Mo., 77, 91; Kirtland,
115, 126, 246n23; Nauvoo, 123, 125–
26, 132, 135–36, 144, 262n23; Logan,
144, 272n128; Salt Lake City, 151, 194,
272nn128–129. *See also* Priesthood
and temple ban

Tenskwatawa, 67–68

ism, 232, 292n47. *See also* Blackness;
White universalism
White River (Anderson, Ind.), 67
White universalism, 3, 7, 20, 26, 30,
34–35, 39, 193. *See also* Whiteness
Whitmer, David, 124, 252n10, 260n10
Whitmer, John, 75, 124, 249n69, 260n10
Whitmer, Peter, Jr., 64, 246n24
Whitney, Orson F., 112
Wight, Lyman, 261n17
Wilcox, Adelia, 156
Williams, Frederick, 66, 246n24
Williams, Roger, 14
Wilson, David, 138
Wilson, John F., 111
Winthrop, John, 15
Wolfinger, Henry, 219
Woman's Exponent, 150
Woodruff, Wilford, 111–18, 126, 129, 153,
161, 203, 207, 227, 266n72, 287n90
World's Columbian Exposition of 1893,
221
Wyoming, 178, 184

Yarrow, Henry C., 223, 290n23
Young, Brigham, 3, 12, 29, 63, 65, 72, 77,
110–12, 126, 150, 212, 248n67, 259n91,
263n42, 264n61, 265n67, 266n72,
268n87, 271n121, 274n22, 283n48; and
Indian slave trade, 3–4, 11, 20, 155,
158–59; and interracial marriage, 4,
125, 143, 145, 269n99; and slavery, 10,
96, 133, 143, 155, 158–59, 181–94, 196,
208, 264n57, 280n1, 282n35, 282n40;
and priesthood and temple ban, 10,
141, 133, 143, 147, 218, 226, 228, 231,
268n89, 268n91, 284n50, 288n9; and
Mormon-Indian relations, 29, 125,
153–78, 195–96, 198, 200, 202–10, 220,
276n58, 278n78, 278n88, 279n96,
287n98
Young, John R., 199–200, 280n14
Young, Joseph, 12
Young, Phineas, 248n67
Young, Zina D. Huntington, 77, 150, 186

Zuni Indians, 176, 279n97